# Tennis

## Confidential II

**Other Books by Paul Fein**

*You Can Quote Me on That:*
*Greatest Tennis Quips, Insights, and Zingers*

*Tennis Confidential:*
*Today's Greatest Players, Matches, and Controversies*

# Tennis
## Confidential II

More of Today's Greatest Players,
Matches, and Controversies

Paul Fein

Potomac Books, Inc.
Washington, D.C.

Library of Congress Cataloging-in-Publication Data

    Fein, Paul, 1944-

      Tennis confidential II : more of today's greatest players, matches, and controversies / Paul Fein.— 1st ed.

      p. cm.

    Includes index.

    ISBN 978-1-59797-173-7

    1. Tennis players—Biography. 2. Tennis—History. I. Title: Tennis confidential 2. II. Title: Tennis confidential two. III. Title.

    GV994.A1F45 2008

    796.3420922—dc22

                  2007051204

(alk. paper)

Printed in the United States of America on acid-free paper that meets the American National Standards Institute Z39-48 Standard.

Potomac Books, Inc.
22841 Quicksilver Drive
Dulles, Virginia 20166

First Edition

10 9 8 7 6 5 4 3 2 1

To the unsung heroes in tennis:

Tennis moms and dads, racket stringers, court maintenance workers, tournament volunteers, high school coaches, community organizers, TV camera operators, association and club committee members, and all those who work so others can play.

Without them, where would we be?

# Contents

# Illustrations

# Acknowledgments

$A$lthea Gibson, the great 1950s tennis champion, once said, "No matter what accomplishments you make, somebody helps you."

Most of all, I would like to thank pro tennis players, often busy and focused on their next match or training session, for taking the time to share their fascinating stories. To our sport's great credit, they are intelligent, articulate, opinionated, earnest, and funny. Many of them are also determined to leave tennis better off than when they started on the tour.

I am grateful to all the other people in the tennis world who have challenged, questioned, cajoled, enlightened, and inspired me during my writing career. They have provided me with insights and information and often engaged in point-counterpoint debates that invariably increased my knowledge of our sport and advanced my pursuit of the truth.

I am very much indebted to current and former world-class players, distinguished coaches, and other authorities who have generously shared their considerable expertise and candid opinions for this book. They include Paul Annacone, Jonas Björkman, Wayne Bryan, Mary Carillo, Louis Cayer, Jim Courier, Nicolas Kelaidis, Chris Lewis, Gene Mayer, Paul Roetert, Alan Schwartz, Greg Sharko, and Rennae Stubbs.

I would like to thank all those hardworking and talented members of the ATP, WTA, ITF, USTA, other national tennis associations, and client managers from management companies, who provided me with indispensable information and insights and arranged interviews with players, coaches, officials, and authorities for me.

I owe thanks for the ongoing support of the members of The Internet Writing Workshop, particularly the members of the nonfiction critique list. Among the IWW members and other writing friends I would like to single out are Kate Reynolds, Gary Presley, Peggy Duffy, Judy Stock, Sarah Morgan, June Gallant, Sheri McGregor, Ruth Douillette, Carter Jefferson, Sarah Zobel, Kathy Highcove, Ross Eldridge, Mridu Khullar, Jessica Jacobson, and Ellen Dryer. However, I have found the entire group a wonderful source of intelligent, enthusiastic support. I have also benefited from the diverse and thought-provoking comments in the Workshop's Writing Discussion Group.

Donna Doherty, formerly the topnotch editor at *Tennis* magazine, improved my articles considerably with vital corrections and astute suggestions, as did leading Australian writer-editor Suzi Petkovski and Jeannette Cezanne of Customline Wordware.

Andy Erwin, my perceptive doubles partner, not only carries me on the court, but also reminds me of the importance of tennis' beautiful and dynamic team event. Our debates about strokes and strategy enliven practice sessions and sharpen my doubles knowledge. I also enjoy and benefit from discussing the great issues with Eddie Moylan, 1950s American tennis star and my brilliant tennis coach at Cornell University, longtime friend and teaching pro Bucky Adams, as well as Steve Sudarsky, T.J. Hanley, Tim Balestri, and Danny Ohradka, friends and practice partners.

Matt Suher, of Stanmore, England, helps my cause considerably by providing me with valuable tennis information, as does Bernie Bloome, another old and loyal friend from Springfield, Massachusetts. Cesar Jensen, a tireless tennis promoter in south Florida, keeps me apprised of rising stars. Yet another source of topical news and views is Samprasfanz, an Internet group with more than thousand members worldwide, most notably Joy Parker of Lake Lotawana, Missouri; Cynthia Smith of England; Philip Ip of Hong Kong; Cherry Chan of the Philippines; and Miriam Garcia-Poggi of Argentina.

My sister, Jane Cynthia Nielsen, a meticulous editor-proofreader in Los Angeles, gave me her sound judgment, clever way with words, and unwavering encouragement.

Prudent and patient, Kevin Cuddihy, my editor at Potomac Books, guided me skillfully throughout this project.

And, finally, thanks to you, the readers of my magazine articles and previous books, *Tennis Confidential* and *You Can Quote Me on That*. Many of you have contacted me. Your knowledgeable responses make my tennis life immensely fulfilling. Your appreciation makes it even more so.

# Foreword

If you've picked up this book, it is likely that you are a serious player and fan of the game. Even if you're just a casual tennis aficionado, *Tennis Confidential II* will turn you into a serious fan, as it is written by the least casual tennis writer I know. Paul Fein is one of the most clear-eyed, passionate tennis authors, coaches, and players we have, and in a perfect world this book would be required reading for the game's leaders and its followers. Pore over his essays, features, and interviews, and you will discover why.

It doesn't hurt that Paul's extensive background in tennis has given him a bedrock knowledge and understanding of every facet of the sport. He has quite literally built his deep perspective from the ground up—he's even helped rebuild courts in his hometown's public park. He has played high-level tennis, coached it, run satellite tournaments, umpired college matches, interviewed scores of professional players, been a broadcaster, and watched thousands of matches. Paul Fein cares about all aspects of tennis, at every level of the sport, because he has been involved in every level. There are far too few tennis writers who can appreciate the myriad layers, joys, and agonies of this remarkable game. Paul comes by his wisdom honestly—he's earned every bit of it.

You might guess that his credentials would make Paul Fein strictly Old School, through and through. In some ways the designation is apt—he is a deep respecter of the game's history and traditions. He is also partial to players who still use a full vocabulary of tennis gifts—touch, power, serve and volley, as well as groundstrokes, players whose skill sets translate well on any surface, under the toughest conditions. Amen to all that. But he is not locked in some tennis time warp; quite the opposite. His reasoning is nimble and fluid; forward thinking, in fact. There have been drastic changes in the sport over the years, and he has navigated through all of them with vision and clarity, acceptance as well as resistance.

What separates Paul from so many others is that it isn't enough for him to take on the biggest, trickiest, most subtly shaded issues, controversies, and debates in tennis. This he does, with balance and good humor. But Paul will then offer solutions to the problems—real answers to the game's hardest questions. Even if you don't agree with his conclusions, you will know that he has taken you on a thoughtful, comprehensive trip through the many minefields of the sport. He may not change your mind, but he will certainly challenge your mindset.

I am indebted to Paul for contributing so much intelligence, common sense, and uncommon sense to the dialogue of the sport. Where I come from—the land of television—things happen in a hurry, and an awful lot of opinions and judgments are hasty, sometimes spouted for effect and attention. Too many decisions get made, God help us all, for ratings. It's why I always look forward to the next Paul Fein article. I know there will be real heft to the writing, true thoughtfulness to the words on the page, real scholarship by one of the best tennis writers around. Enjoy.

—Mary Carillo
ESPN, CBS, and NBC tennis analyst

# Introduction

Tennis fans love to argue. Who has the best forehand? Which Grand Slam tournament is the toughest to win? Should tennis allow on-court coaching? Are changes in the scoring system helpful or harmful? Nothing gets passions flaring and voices blaring more than a debate about the greatest player ever.

When aficionados ask me who is the greatest of all time, I know a fierce argument is brewing. Whether they pick Roger Federer, Pete Sampras, Rod Laver, or Björn Borg, and Martina Navratilova, Steffi Graf, or Suzanne Lenglen, these fervent advocates have done their homework. I had better be ready. Over the years I've learned from these stimulating debates, and they've inspired me to write essays evaluating and rating the top champions.

Sports thrive on controversies, and like my first book, *Tennis Confidential: Today's Greatest Players, Matches, and Controversies*, this sequel gives you plenty of essays about raging, topical debates. Whether you agree or disagree with my analyses, I guarantee you'll think about these controversies in new ways. Perhaps you will even change some of your staunchly held positions.

For example, advocates of Player Challenges (the system used to implement the marvelous Hawk-Eye line-calling technology) should consider that thirteen factors make accurate human line-calling difficult and sometimes virtually impossible.

Are pro tennis' ranking systems—that don't count all tournament results—fair?

What's wrong with on-court coaching? Plenty! How about replacing entire deciding (third) sets with a mere tiebreaker? You cannot be serious! Recent rule change blunders, including ATP Tour round-robin formats (which caused an angry outcry and were rescinded), remind me of Thomas Carlyle's maxim: "Nothing is more terrible than activity without insight."

For those who wonder about America's current decline in international tennis, "How America Can Produce Tennis Champions Again" provides abundant analysis and proposals to ponder.

*Tennis Confidential II* features chronicle how Pete Sampras rebounded from his longest and deepest slump, probe the many intriguing sides of Andre Agassi, and describe famous feuds in tennis history. I'm sure you can guess several of them. How did Russia become a tennis superpower? What era produced not only a men's dynasty but also some of the most fun-loving characters ever? Since the majority of recreational players favor doubles, my piece, "Double the Pleasure—or Pressure?", should be especially appealing to them.

In-depth features also cover the fascinating evolution of women's tennis that finally, after years of obtuse resistance by male tennis leaders, culminated in 2007 with equal prize money at all Grand Slam events.

Readers have often told me that their favorite genre is the Q&A interview because only there do they get the true story about players unfiltered by a writer's edits. *TC II* contains twelve such interviews with compelling and candid characters, including Yannick Noah, Martina Hingis, Mats Wilander, Gene Scott, and Jim Courier.

Sprinkled throughout the interviews, essays, and features are tennis significa and trivia that will amuse and amaze you. Which player hires her hitting partners on the basis that, "If you can beat me, you can hit with me"? Who did John McEnroe call "the next John McEnroe"? And what reason did Maria Sharapova give in 2005 for not having a boyfriend? "Fascinating Facts" sidebars give you the answers.

I hope you enjoy reading *TC II* as thoroughly as I've enjoyed writing it. Feel free to e-mail me at lincjeff1@comcast.net with your comments.

PART 1

# The Great Debates

# Who is The Greatest Men's Tennis Player Ever?

# 2005

*The comparing and rating of athletes who were not contemporaries and did not encounter one another on important occasions is a trap in which no tennis reporter of experience should be caught.*

—Al Laney, distinguished sportswriter, in his acclaimed 1968 book,
*Covering The Court—A Fifty-Year Love Affair with the Game of Tennis*

Even Al Laney couldn't resist the temptation to ignore his own advice. Just three sentences later, he contends, "I do not think any player I have seen between that youthful Davis Cup experience of 1914 and the late 1960s could have beaten the best Tilden."

It is no wonder Laney couldn't help putting in his two cents. Debates about "Who's the greatest?" rage in every sport. Is it Jordan, Magic, or Bird? Could Ali whip Louis? Was Mays better than Ruth? And how about Pelé vs. Maradona, Tiger vs. Jack, and Marino vs. Montana? Passionate fans love nothing more than a good argument, and passions really flare when their favorite players get praised or pushed down the all-time list.

Laney's pick might be right for the pre-Open Era. But what about Rod Laver whose second Grand Slam in 1969 clinches his status as "the greatest ever" in the eyes of many cognoscenti? Just as fiercely will others argue that deadly efficient Björn Borg, while a less flashy shot-maker than either Tilden or Laver, earns that mythical accolade. The under-thirty generation that watches ESPN Classic matches featuring Borg, Jimmy Connors, and John McEnroe can't imagine how these medium-sized stylists could ever take a set off ferociously powerful Pete Sampras. Let's not forget three other brilliant champions: Don Budge from the 1930s, Jack Kramer from the 1940s, and Pancho Gonzalez from the 1950s.

Before our battle is joined, I have a confession. As a kid, I idolized Laver, a fellow lefty about my size, and even tried to imitate his diverse repertoire of eye-popping shots. I never witnessed earlier all-time greats in their primes, although I've seen many on film. And that leads me to the requisite ground rule for this debate: no subjectivity allowed. As 1920s New York governor Al Smith used to say, "Let's look at the record."

What are the fairest ways to analyze "the record"? I propose eight criteria and stress that no single criterion conclusively settles the debate.

## Grand Slams

"When we look back at the greatest players of all time, we look at the number of Slams they won," Sampras asserted in 1995. Not so fast and not so simple! But Grand Slams do count heavily.

Sampras indisputably reigns supreme here with fourteen Slam titles, a record that may never be broken. Not all majors are created equal, though, and "Pistol Pete" racked up a modern record seven crowns at Wimbledon, the most prestigious "Big Four" venue. Five titles, including his unforgettable first and last ones against archrival Andre Agassi, came at the U.S. Open, arguably co-No. 2 in Slam status with Roland Garros. Sampras notched two more Slams at the Australian Open. Only peerless Sampras in mid-career could, without boasting, announce, "It's not a good year unless I win two majors." The undeniably big gap in Sampras's resume is the French Open, but more about that later.

Roy Emerson, whose partying and work ethic were unrivalled—"Emmo closed more bars and practice courts than anybody I've ever met," said Arthur Ashe—ranks second to Sampras with twelve majors, including a career Grand Slam. Six of Emerson's trophies, however, were captured at the Oz Open, the least coveted Slam.

Laver and Borg tie for third place with eleven Slams. Eight of Laver's titles came in 1962 and 1969 when he won the Grand Slam of tennis, all four majors during one year, a feat Agassi rightly called "as great an achievement as you can have in any sport." Budge, in 1938, was the only other male player to accomplish the feat even once.

Borg, though not initially a serve and volleyer, improved both strokes enough to win a modern record five consecutive Wimbledon titles as well as his record six French Open victories in only eight attempts. Switching from Roland Garros clay to Wimby grass with only two weeks in between is one of tennis' most formidable challenges, yet Borg prevailed back to back there thrice, from 1978 to 1980.

"Big Bill" Tilden captured ten majors, seven at Forest Hills and three at Wimbledon, including his final *tour de force* there in 1930 at the age of thirty-seven. Connors, Fred Perry, Ken Rosewall, Ivan Lendl and still-active Agassi all gained eight Slams. The pugnacious Connors strutted and stormed to five U.S. Open titles on three surfaces—grass, clay (a somewhat faster version called Har-Tru) and hard—an amazing accomplishment and unbreakable record. Perry, Britain's last and most colorful men's champion, distinguished himself with a career Grand Slam.

*"Big Bill" Tilden captured ten majors, including three Wimbleton titles.*

## Davis Cup

The oldest and most renowned annual international team competition in sports is often, and erroneously, overlooked in "Who's the greatest?" debates. True, it's lost some of its former luster because a small minority of pro players cares more about dollars and ranking points than representing their country. "They say you have the best and worst moments of your career in Davis Cup," once said fair dinkum Aussie Patrick Rafter, and compatriot Emerson experienced ecstasy only with his perfect 15–0 record (9–0 in Challenge Rounds) in live rubbers.

Tilden, a city slicker from a prominent Philadelphia family, racked up a stellar 25–5 mark that featured thirteen straight victories in the Challenge Round. With some help from "Little Bill" Johnston, he spearheaded the United States to seven straight Cup titles (1920–1926) before France's "Four Musketeers" finally wore out his aging, thirty-four-year-old body in 1927.

Borg first displayed his nerveless mien at the age of fifteen in a phenomenal Cup debut win over New Zealand's well-regarded Onny Parun in 1972. He then carried Sweden to its first Cup title in 1975 and amassed a gaudy 37–3 career mark that included a record 33-match winning streak. Boris Becker's 38–3 Cup record—even more sensational since he had little support until Michael Stich arrived and he nearly always played doubles—deserves considerable acclaim. Laver boasts an abbreviated (due to turning pro) but strong 16–4 Cup record. Perry won every singles match in the four Challenge Rounds he played to guide his country to four straight Cups during 1933–36. His career Cup record of 34–4 ranks among the best.

Before McEnroe failed (he was fined four times in one tie for misdemeanors) and resigned as a Davis Cup captain in 2000, he better channeled his patriotic fervor as a player en route to a superb 41–8 record and five titles. Almost as impressive, Agassi notched a 30–5 record.

Sampras helped the U.S. prevail in 1992 against Switzerland and heroically propelled it to a 3–2 triumph against host Russia on clay in 1995. Who can forget seeing Pete collapse in painful cramps and exhaustion and get carried off the court after beating Andrei Chesnokov and then return to wrap up the final? But Sampras often snubbed Davis Cup just when the "Greatest Generation" (Agassi, Jim Courier, Michael Chang and himself) could have dominated it, playing only sixteen ties in the fifteen years of his pro career for a modest 15–8 record.

## Degree of Domination

Comparing champions can also be instructive when we determine how superior they were when it counted most. Here Sampras pulls away from the competition, like the Porsche he once said was his most prized possession. Sampras racked up a terrific 14–4 record in Grand Slam finals.

Compare that with Borg's 11–5, Laver's 11–6, and Tilden's 10–5 records. Lendl actually competed in nineteen Slam finals, more than any other man, but he agonizingly lost eleven of them, thus becoming the only champion with seven or more majors who lost more finals than he won. Only Emerson's 12–3 final record surpasses Sampras's (on a percentage basis) among double-digit Slam titlists. That clutch play is diminished when one considers he faced amateurs only during his prime, but more about that shortly.

The case for Sampras is furthered bolstered by his extraordinary domination in his fourteen victorious Grand Slam finals. He didn't just beat opponents; he usually whacked them. Out of a possible twenty-eight sets "Pistol Pete" could have lost, he surrendered only seven. Only once was Sampras forced to go to five sets. Rocket-serving Goran Ivanišević extended him that far in the 1998 Wimbledon final, but even then Sampras crushed the Croat 6-2 in the deciding set. (Interestingly, Steffi Graf, the most successful Open Era women's champion, was forced to go three sets in thirteen of her twenty-two Slam final triumphs.)

Sustained domination can be measured in other ways, too. Sampras eclipsed Connors's 1974–1978 record of consecutive years finishing number one when he, despite losing hair and getting ulcers, pulled off the incredible by doing it six years straight, 1993–1998. That's the Open Era record, while Tilden also ranked No. 1 for six straight years, 1920–1925 in the amateur era.

Way back then, A. Wallis Myers, an authoritative journalist, produced widely accepted rankings. Subsequently, highly regarded journalists John Oliff, Lance Tingay, and Bud Collins produced unofficial but generally accepted rankings, though various magazines worldwide also published their own. ATP computer rankings started in 1973. The considered judgments of yesteryear's journalists proved superior to the erroneous and widely denounced "Best 14" computer ranking system during the 1990s. Unbelievably, the "Best 14" threw out, on average for top 100 players, more than 40 percent of tournament results. Since Sampras, who suffered very few early-round losses, was severely penalized for averaging just eighteen tournaments a year during 1993–1998, his number one rankings become even more impressive.

What isn't controversial, though, is the criterion of tournament titles. From 1912 to 1930, when Tilden was an amateur, he won an astounding 138 of 192 tournaments and reached twenty-eight more finals. No man has come close to that long-term domination.

### Excellence on All Surfaces

Before the U.S. Open in 1978 replaced its clay courts (which had replaced its grass courts in 1975) with Deco-Turf II hard courts, the four Grand Slam tournaments were contested on grass and clay only. Highest marks go to Grand Slammers Budge and Laver, plus Perry, Emerson, and Agassi, who all claimed every major title at least once during their storied careers.

Connors and seven-Slam champion, Mats Wilander, get an asterisk for their all-surface achievements. Even though Connors won the 1976 U.S. Open on clay with an impressive four-set decision over clay king Borg, he failed to capture Roland Garros. Wilander triumphed on grass at Melbourne in 1983 and 1984, but never advanced past the quarters at Wimbledon.

Detractors knock Sampras for not winning Roland Garros. Fair enough. Even more damaging is that in thirteen tries he never even reached the final. Was Sampras really inept on clay? On the contrary, in 1996, just weeks after his coach Tim Gullikson died, he gained the French semis with five-set victories over former two-time titlists Sergi Bruguera and Courier before bowing to eventual champion Yevgeny Kafelnikov. Often overlooked is Sampras's 1994 Italian Open title, the second most prestigious clay event. At Rome, he dropped only one set en route to the final where he routed Becker 6-1, 6-2, 6-2. "He is playing tennis like they will play the game in the 21st century," marveled Becker. Furthermore, there is the surprising fact that Sampras, tennis' premier serve and volleyer, ranked seventh (minimum sixty matches played) on the ATP Tour in won-lost percentage (71.11) on clay with a 64–26 record during 1991–1999, ahead of Agassi (70.13) with a 54–23 record.

Borg failed to win the U.S. Open in nine attempts, but to his credit he reached the final on four occasions, and thrice when the event was played on hard courts. To his discredit, he entered the Australian Open only once, losing in the third round in 1974, during his relatively short nine-year Slam career.

Tilden had only three cracks at the French Championships (which didn't admit international players until 1925), all when he was past his prime; yet he made the final in 1927 and 1930. Kramer never entered Roland Garros, while Gonzalez had only two chances, in his third Slam event in 1949 and as a forty-year-old in 1968.

Still he gained the semis both times.

In sum, Sampras's *bete noire* was clay, and in late career he quipped, "It would take an act of God" to win the French. That conceded, Super Sampras conquered every other surface: seven Slams on grass, five Slams on American hard courts plus three more titles at Miami (which some consider the world's fifth most important tournament), two Slams on Australia's slower hard courts, and five indoor titles on hard courts and carpet at the prestigious, season-ending ATP Tour World Championships. After Sampras annihilated him in the 1997 Wimbledon semis, an awed Todd Woodbridge spoke for many victims, saying, "He's human, but not by much."

## Quality and Depth of Opposition

In 1995 Gonzalez compared his era forty years earlier with contemporary players, averring, "If we had ten great players in my time, they have one hundred now. The level of tennis is hard to believe because the shots are so phenomenal. They're quicker, faster, sharper mentally. And with the money, they're more competitive."

Gonzalez also didn't mince words comparing the elite players of both eras. "Pete has the most complete game of anyone I've ever seen. Andre has made a complete turn-around in the last five, six months and is on the same level as Pete. I think these two guys would beat the pants off anybody in the past."

From the 1930s, when Tilden, Ellsworth, Vines, and Perry turned pro, to 1968, when Open Tennis arrived, neither the barnstorming pros nor the often-diluted amateurs boasted all the top stars. Confining this criterion to the Open Era, I believe the 1980s were blessed with the strongest array of top players on all surfaces. Borg, McEnroe, Wilander, Lendl, Edberg, and Becker, all great champions, ruled during parts of the decade, and thus their accomplishments should be evaluated more favorably.

Conversely, the mid- and late-1970s, when Borg reigned, was the weakest period, particularly on grass. Authoritative British journalist Rex Bellamy accurately put the first four of Borg's five Wimbledons into historical perspective when he wrote, "He emerged when the great days of serve-and-volley exponents such as Rod Laver, John Newcombe, and Stan Smith were over and McEnroe had yet to happen. Pre-McEnroe the best grass court expert Borg had to beat was Roscoe Tanner, who was just short of the highest class."

From 1990 to the present, the depth of talent increased enormously by any criterion. Tennis, once a formful sport, often became downright unpredictable as stars were ambushed everywhere. Example one: Grand Slams were won by long-shots, such as 66-1 pick Michael Stich (1991 Wimbledon), 33-1 pick Sergi Bruguera (1993 French), and No. 66-ranked Gustavo Kuerten (1997 French). Example two: In 1996, thirteen different players gained sixteen Grand Slam semifinal berths, and in 1997 nine of the sixteen men's semifinalists at Grand Slam tournament were unseeded. Example three: In 1998 the top two seeds reached the singles final in only five of the seventy-nine ATP tour events. Example four: In 1998, 2001, and 2002 eight different players reached Slam finals. Contrast that extraordinary depth with 1937-38 when Budge won ninety-two straight matches, and in 1938 when three of his Slam finals astonishingly required less than an hour.

Summing up the changing times, in 2001 Goran Ivanišević said, "In tennis now, you don't have any favorites. It doesn't matter if it's clay or grass or hard court. Anybody can beat anybody."

## Then and Now

When comparing old-time champions with their modern counterparts, the edge has to go to moderns for quality and depth of competition, but each side can find plenty of support in other respects. Media pressure is far more omnipresent and invasive now, and some players resent mandatory press conferences and sensationalist tabloids. Today, hard courts, tough matches in every round, and a ten-and-a-half-month season have resulted in far more frequent and severe injuries than ever.

On the other hand, today's performers can globetrot on super-sonic jets rather than spend weeks on ocean liners, recline in comfy chairs for ninety seconds and chow down during changeovers rather than briskly switching sides, and whack balls with huge space-age rackets rather than little wooden ones. They play twelve-point tiebreakers instead of protracted sets, and get a fortnight to play seven rounds at Grand Slams instead of the eight days Ted Schroeder had to play six rounds at the 1949 U.S. Championships. Today's athletes also benefit from advances in training and nutrition. Also, the greats and near-greats reap unprecedented fortunes from tournament prize money, exhibitions, and endorsements.

## Missed Opportunity

Laver supporters are ready to pounce right about now. How many times have we heard their battle cry: "Just think how many more Grand Slam titles 'Rocket' would have copped if he hadn't missed out during his five prime years [1963–1967] because he was a pro."

The flip side of their claim is a two-part question: How many of his first six Slams, won during 1960–1962, might Laver not have won if he had to face Gonzalez, Lew Hoad and Rosewall and other barnstorming professionals? Laver, who lost nineteen of his first twenty-one matches to Rosewall and Hoad as a pro, later admitted, "I didn't find out who were the best [players] until I turned pro and had my brains beaten out for six months at the start of 1963."

Second, even though Laver emerged as the top pro in 1964, who knows how many of those potential twenty-one missed majors he would have captured? Ah, more than one can play the "What if?" game. When asked in 2000 how many Grand Slam titles Sampras would have won if three of the four majors were still played on grass, Courier replied, "He'd be on twenty-five easily, if not thirty by now."

If Laver were the victim of fate, consider the misfortunes of other champions born too soon to capitalize on Open Tennis. Rosewall turned pro in 1957 and missed eleven prime years. Equally durable Gonzalez competed in only five majors and one Davis Cup tie before turning pro in late 1949. He lost an incredible eighteen years. Kramer turned pro after winning Wimbledon, Forest Hills and the Davis Cup in 1947 at the age of twenty-six. What's more, like so many young men of his generation, he fought for his country during World War II and lost some of his best early tennis years, too.

Budge turned pro in 1939, the year cocksure Bobby Riggs bet on himself to win a rare Wimbledon triple (all three events) and won $108,000. Both sacrificed some prime years while in the military, but Budge got heavier and slower and was never the same after the war. "I put Don Budge right at the pinnacle," said Kramer. "If it weren't for the prohibition against the pros at Grand Slams and the interruption of World War II, he would have won so many major titles that you wouldn't have been able to count them."

Finally, international travel was so time consuming and costly and expense money often so low in the first half of the twentieth century that few amateurs competed at all the Grand Slams. Tilden, Henri Cochet, René Lacoste, Riggs, and Kramer never played the Australian, and Budge, Vines, and Jean Borotra did only once. Far different were the inexcusable absences Down Under of Borg, McEnroe, and others in the 1970s and '80s, who claimed the tournament had lost stature, a problem their snubs only worsened. Some also regrettably skipped Roland Garros before French administrator Philippe Chatrier revitalized it.

## The Early Pros

The post-war pro game, an amalgam of one-night stands and conventional tournaments with draws of various sizes, was loaded with most of the world's premier players. Therefore, its top guns demand the highest consideration for greatest-ever honors.

How does Gonzalez, who only had time for two U.S. titles during his brief amateur stint, stack up among the other greats? Savvy veteran Kramer disposed of Gonzalez 96–27 in his first pro tour in 1949–1950. After Kramer retired, the fiercely competitive Mexican-American—"Pancho gets fifty points on his serve and fifty points on terror," Kramer once said—beat Budge, Pancho Segura, and Frank Sedgman in a 1954 tour to become king of the pros. He reigned until 1961.

From 1951 to 1964 Gonzalez captured the U.S. Pro title a record eight times, and from 1950 to 1956 he won Wembley, considered the world pro championship, four times. At the age of forty, Gonzalez amazingly routed second-seeded Tony Roche, the Wimbledon finalist, 8-6, 6-4, 6-2 at the inaugural U.S. Open. In 1969 ageless Gonzalez defeated Newcombe, Rosewall, Smith, and Ashe (6-0, 6-2, 6-4 in the final) to win a Las Vegas tournament and climbed to No. 6 in the world rankings.

Kramer's resume, while shorter because an arthritic back led to a premature retirement, was spectacular, too. The Kramer pro dynasty began in late 1947 when he ruled his tour with Riggs, sixty-nine matches to twenty. After dominating Gonzales 96-27, Kramer overpowered shrewd and steady Pancho Segura 64-28 during their 1950-51 tour. There was no main tour in 1952, but "Big Jake" retained his World Pro title and outplayed Sedgman, an athletic Aussie star, 54-41 in their series in 1953.

Back again to our "What if?" game. In his authoritative, albeit inevitably slanted, 1979 memoir, *The Game: My 40 Years in Tennis*, Kramer speculated who would have been "the probable winners of Wimbledon and Forest Hills if they been open to pros and amateurs from 1931 to 1967." Kramer would have captured five of each, Budge would have added six more U.S. titles, while Gonzalez would have benefited the most with seven more U.S. and six more Wimbledon crowns.

More objective was a panel of tennis writers who in late 1969, after Laver pulled off his second Grand Slam, ranked their all-time greats. Their top ten were, in order: Tilden, Budge, Laver, Gonzalez, Kramer, Perry, Henri Cochet, René Lacoste, Hoad, and Vines. In late 1997 a panel of one hundred current and past players, journalists and tournament directors voted for the top twenty-five players of the past twenty-five years, and Sampras, who then had won ten majors, was selected number one.

This selector unequivocally rates Sampras the greatest ever. His sensational Grand Slam record, awesome degree of domination, excellence on several surfaces, and tough contemporary competition (especially on clay) make his shortcomings—no French title and modest Davis Cup record—pale in significance.

Subjectively, if I may break my ground rule, Sampras often played sublime tennis, particularly at crucial stages of high-stakes matches. While he relied on his explosive first and incomparable second serve, he showcased plenty of other weapons: a solid volley and athletic net game, impeccable smash, powerful running forehand, touch shots, agility and speed, courage, and smart strategy. Yes, his backhand did occasionally break down under pressure and in long rallies, but that was his only weak link.

Sampras's leading rivals—from McEnroe, Becker, and Edberg early in his career to "Greatest Generation" compatriots Agassi and Courier to rising stars Marat Safin and Andy Roddick—showered him with superlatives. Most typically, they praised Sampras as the best and most complete player they've ever faced or seen. Indeed they should. Sampras beat them more often than not and won about twice as many major titles as the best among them.

After he demolished Agassi in the 1990 U.S. Open final, Sampras self-deprecatingly called himself "a nineteen-year-old punk from California." Before his last *tour de force* at the 2002 U.S. Open, when everyone had written him off as a slump-ridden has-been, Sampras reminded everyone, "You've got to remember who I am and what I've done here."

I'll always remember who Sampras was—the greatest tennis player ever.

### My All-Time Top 10
1. Pete Sampras
2. Bill Tilden
3. Rod Laver
4. Pancho Gonzalez
5. Björn Borg
6. Jack Kramer
7. Don Budge
8. Jimmy Connors
9. Ivan Lendl
10. John McEnroe

## Paeans to the Champions
"He can hit shots the rest of us can't hit and don't even think of hitting." —Jim Courier, on Pete Sampras (1991)

"Tilden always seems to have a thousand means of putting the ball away from his opponent's reach. He seems to exercise a strange fascination over his opponent as well as the spectators. Tilden, even when beaten, always leaves an impression on the public mind that he was superior to the victor. All spectators seem to think he can win when he likes." —Rene Lacoste, on Bill Tilden, in his 1928 book, *Lacoste on Tennis*

"Rod Laver is my tennis god. He's such a humble, nice man who doesn't say anything bad about anybody, even if you try to get him to do it. He's our Babe Ruth. He was the first guy who did everything, came over the ball, served and volleyed, hit from the baseline and sliced." —John McEnroe, on Rod Laver, in *Tennis* magazine (2002)

"He is the greatest natural athlete tennis has ever known." —Tony Trabert, on Pancho Gonzalez (1955)

"They should send Borg away to another planet. We play tennis. He plays something else." —Ilie Năstase, on Björn Borg

"Kramer had an air about him, a type of aggression that is hard to define. There was nothing personal about it, but he played every point as though it was a life-and-death situation." —Adrian Quist, on Jack Kramer, from his book, *Tennis: The Greats (1920–1960)*.

"I consider him the finest player 365 days a year that ever lived." —Bill Tilden, on Don Budge, in the 1947 edition of Tilden's autobiography, *My Story.*

"Looking back from the early 1990s, with Connors still playing well, I see that he was the greatest male tennis player, bar none, in the two and a half decades since the Open era began in 1968." —Arthur Ashe, on Jimmy Connors, from his 1993 book, *Days of Grace.*

"You know what the name Lendl means to me? Dedication, hard work, over-coming everybody, although maybe he didn't have the tennis talent of a lot of guys. I admire him immensely." —Pete Sampras, on Ivan Lendl (1994)

"In terms of tennis talent, I have never seen anyone better than John." —Arthur Ashe, on John McEnroe.

## Where Does Federer Rank?

Since the article was written, Roger Federer soared toward the top of the pantheon of all-time greats. Consider these sensational statistics going into 2008:

- Federer won twelve of the last eighteen Grand Slam tournaments he contested.
- He lost only two of fourteen Grand Slam finals—to Rafael Nadal at Roland Garros in 2006–2007.
- He owns the record for winning consecutive tournament finals, twenty-four, doubling the previous mark set by Bjorn Borg and John McEnroe.
- He holds the Open Era records for most consecutive match wins on hard courts, fifty-six, and for most consecutive match wins on grass, fifty-four.
- He captured four year-end Tennis Masters Cup titles without dropping a set in the finals.
- He is the only player to reach ten consecutive Grand Slam finals in history of the sport
- He is the only man in the Open Era to capture at least ten titles in three consecutive seasons (eleven in 2004–2005, twelve in 2006)
- He ranked number one in the year-end rankings for four consecutive years, 2004–2007.

Two glaring gaps, however, mar the twenty-six-year-old Swiss's otherwise awesome resume. Federer hasn't won the French Open, although he gained the final twice. Representing his country, he owns an impressive 23-6 Davis Cup record (chiefly against weaker early-round foes), but at the Athens Olympics eighteen-year-old Tomas Berdych upset him in the round of sixteen.

On a more subjective level, I would argue that while the men's game boasts more depth from number twenty to number one hundred than ever before, Federer's competition among elite players has been relatively weak and shallow. During 2003-2007 the best he faced were an aging Agassi with a chronic back injury, mentally fragile Safin, big-serving but otherwise flawed Roddick, a middleweight counterpuncher in Hewitt, and highly talented but still-developing Djokovic.

What about three-time French Open champion Nadal who enjoys an 8-6 career record against Federer? The clay superstar never even reached a Grand Slam semifinal on hard courts and emerged as a big threat on grass only in 2007.

Furthermore, the absence of outstanding serve and volleyers (like Sampras, Becker, Edberg, Rafter, Ivaniševic, and Krajicek in the 1990s) makes Federer's five straight Wimbledon crowns much less meaningful. Most important, the paucity of multi-Slam champions contrasted strikingly with the primes of Sampras, Borg, and Laver. Federer fans counter that topnotch rivals, aside from Nadal on clay, were non-existent simply because Federer overwhelmed everyone else with his dazzling shot-making and athleticism.

My greatest-ever verdict hangs precariously because Federer shows no signs of slowing down. Back in 2006, Sampras enthused, "I'm a fan of how he plays, what he's about . . . He's a class guy on and off the court. He's fun to watch. Just his athletic ability, what he's able to do on the run. I think he can and will break every tennis record out there."

---

**FASCINATING FACT:**
- When New York Buzz owner Nitty Singh introduced Pete Sampras as "the best player of all time" during a World TeamTennis match in July 2007, Sampras corrected her and said he was only one of the greatest ever.

---

This article received 1st Place in the 2005 United States Tennis Writers' Association Writing Contest in the Feature Story division.

# 2

# Who is The Greatest Women's Tennis Player Ever?
## 2007

*When I first started playing tennis, I wanted to be No. 1. Then I wanted to be the greatest of all time. And the closer I got to being called that, the more I realized that's bullshit because you can't compare different generations. Because if I had played in Suzanne Lenglen's generation, I would have been a different player. But you can see how much players dominated their own generations.*

—Martina Navratilova

If granted one tennis wish, I'd travel in a time machine and savor a dream match between high-flying divas Lenglen and Navratilova and all the theatrics that would inevitably enliven it. Other time-travelers might choose a baseline battle between relentless heavy hitters Helen Wills and Steffi Graf, or a "Big Babe" athletic showdown featuring Margaret Court against Serena Williams.

Navratilova won't engage in inter-generational comparisons, but her fervent supporters unequivocally select her for the mythical greatest-ever title. Proponents of Lenglen and Wills, queens with near-perfect records between the two world wars, also stake their claims. And how about Court and Graf, the career leaders in Grand Slam titles?

How thoroughly and for how long the great ones dominated their generations will serve as the overriding criteria for our debate, with the quality of opposition also taken into consideration.

To truly dominate, a superstar must prevail with regularity on all surfaces, and no one did that better than Graf. Consider this: on her least productive surface, clay, the fraulein with the fearsome forehand still captured six French Open titles.

Who can forget her dramatic *tour de force* at Roland Garros in 1999? Not only did Graf become the first Open Era woman to beat the top three players in the world at the same event—Lindsay Davenport, Monica Seles, and Martina Hingis—but in a wild 4-6, 7-5, 6-2 final, her poise and professionalism contrasted sharply with the Swiss teen's unsporting antics.

Although Graf, a svelte 5'9" blonde, was not a serve and volleyer, she dethroned the ultimate grass court practitioner, Navratilova, at Wimbledon in 1988. Seemingly unstoppable with six straight Wimby titles, the ex-Czech streaked to a 7-5, 2-0 lead before equally athletic Graf whacked winners galore to take the final 5-7, 6-2, 6-1. Graf's powerful serve and vicious slice backhand complemented her booming forehand on grass as she racked up seven Wimbledon crowns, behind only Navratilova's nine and Wills' eight. Graf also amassed nine Grand Slam titles on hard courts, five at the U.S. Open and four at the Australian Open, making her the only champion, male or female, to win at least four times at every Slam venue.

As much as Navratilova yearned for the unofficial "greatest ever" accolade, in 1996 she conceded, "Steffi is the best all-around player of all time, regardless of the surface."

Recurrent back and knee ailments and assorted illnesses periodically sidelined Graf and made the Graf Era all the more remarkable. Equally injurious was her unstable father, Peter, who undermined her career in 1990 after so skillfully guiding it for years. Sensational front-page stories revealed his extra-marital affair with a call girl who, with a boxing promoter, was trying to extort $400,000 from the Grafs. After upset losses at Roland Garros and Wimbledon, Graf confided, "I could not fight as usual because of all the turmoil. Tennis is a game won with the head, and lately my head has not been on tennis." Graf was rocked by another scandal in 1995 when her Bad Dad was arrested and imprisoned for income tax evasion while managing her fortune.

Still, in 1988, this intense perfectionist pulled off an unprecedented "Golden Slam": winning all four Grand Slam titles, plus the Olympics gold medal. In no less than four other dominant years—1989, 1993, 1995, and 1996—she captured three Slam crowns each. Her total of twenty-two Grand Slams was more impressive than Court's record twenty-four, but more about that later.

To clinch the case for my nomination of Graf as the greatest ever, she ranked No. 1 eight times, No. 2 twice, and No. 3 once. During Graf's 1983–1999 career, she faced stellar opposition from superstars Chris Evert, Navratilova, and Seles, Grand Slam titlists Arantxa Sánchez Vicario, Gabriela Sabatini, Hingis, and Davenport, as well as budding stars Venus and Serena Williams.

When Graf's mother Heidi asked her why she never smiled on the court, fiercely competitive Steffi replied, "Would you rather see me smile or win?" Her grimly stoical demeanor belied Graf's enormous joy for the sport. Announcing she would continue to play the pro tour in 1999, she said, "Tennis is my life. I need the fabulous emotions playing tennis gives me."

Passion for play may explain one requisite for greatness because after winning seven titles in the 2003 season, Navratilova, then forty-seven-years-young, chirped, "I'm so excited about next year that I can't even stand it." Navratilova joined the pro tour at the age of sixteen way back in 1973 when rackets were mostly wood, balls were white, the Australian and U.S. Opens were contested on grass, and Billie Jean whipped Bobby in a "battle of the sexes" extravaganza that helped ignite America's tennis boom.

That same year the Women's Tennis Association was born, the Virginia Slims circuit was gaining momentum, and for the first time a tournament, the U.S. Open, offered equal prize money to men and women. It was an auspicious time for modern Martina to arrive on the scene. Two years later Navratilova courageously defected from Czechoslovakia to America where she knew her prodigious talent could best blossom.

By 1990 the muscular, 5' 8 ½", 145-pound lefthander had won eighteen Grand Slam titles. Navratilova might well have collected more had she not skipped the Australian and French Opens—tournaments that had declined in stature—five times each in the 1970s.

Nerves sometimes betrayed Navratilova, however, and she lost a stunning fourteen Grand Slam finals. She especially struggled at the U.S. Open, which she didn't win until her eleventh attempt, although she then captured four titles in five years, 1983–1984 and 1986–1987.

*Helen Wills won an amazong 158 sraight matches, plus every set in those matches.*

Her glittering resume also boasts three Australian and two French crowns and eight WTA Championships, along with a perfect 20–0 singles record in Fed Cup competition. All told, Navratilova grabbed 167 singles titles, an Open Era record. She ranked No. 1 seven times, and No. 2 and No. 3 thrice each.

Blessed with superb hand-eye coordination, strength, reflexes, agility, and speed, Navratilova took the exciting art of serving and volleying to new heights. She and Evert, a confirmed baseliner, thrilled crowds for sixteen years with an eighty-match rivalry (43–37 for Navratilova), which far surpasses any other in women's sports history.

Navratilova revolutionized training methods and left no stone unturned. The "Bionic Woman," as the media dubbed her, was created in the early 1980s by Nancy Lieberman's punishing conditioning program, Rick Elstein's reflex training, Mike Estep's analytical coaching, and nutritionist Robert Haas's low-fat, high-carbohydrate diet and thirty-nine different blood tests every month. Both the Associated Press and United Press International named Navratilova "Female Athlete of the Decade" for the 1980s. When asked in 2000 who is the greatest player ever, Graf replied, "For me, she [Navratilova] is the uncontested number one; she has left a mark on the sport like no one else."

Helen Wills, a Phi Beta Kappa at the University of California, aspired for something higher than being No. 1 or even dominating her generation. "I know I would hate life if I were deprived of trying, hunting, working for some objective within which there lies the beauty of perfection," she wrote in her autobiography, *Fifteen-Thirty*. Ah, elusive perfection. Yet during the zenith of her brilliant career, from 1927 to 1932, Wills not only won every match she played—158 straight—but also every set to achieve the perfection she coveted.

"Little Miss Poker Face," as she was dubbed by renowned sportswriter Grantland Rice, showed her emotions about as often as she lost. Wills captured a phenomenal nineteen of the twenty-two Grand Slam events she played—a then-record eight Wimbledons, seven U.S. Championships and four French crowns—and reached the final three other times. Had she taken the long boat journey to Australia, she undoubtedly would have amassed many more major titles.

Donning a white middy blouse, pleated skirt, and trademark white eyeshade, the classically beautiful Wills exuded class and a bit of mystery. "Helen's facial expression rarely varied and she always tended strictly to business," wrote contemporary doubles star George Lott, "but her opponents were never in doubt as to what she held: an excellent service, a powerful forehand, a strong backhand, a killer instinct, and no weaknesses. Five of a kind! Who would want to draw against that kind of hand?"

Certainly not some of her male practice partners. In a San Francisco exhibition against her friend Phil Neer in 1928, Wills beat the former NCAA champion and eighth-ranked American man in a hard-fought 6-3, 6-4 match. The Associated Press, in its 1950 rankings of the top players of the first half-century, put Wills No. 1 and Lenglen at No. 2.

While they were not archrivals because Lenglen and Wills played only once, their ballyhooed encounter at an otherwise unimportant tournament on the French Riviera in 1926 turned into a classic. "La Grande Suzanne," in her prime at twenty-six, triumphed 6-3, 8-6 over the less-experienced college girl, but not before the hundreds of reporters and cameramen and a crowd filled with distinguished guests witnessed sensational shotmaking, theatrics, and controversy.

Ferdinand Tuohy, a correspondent, wrote, "A simple game of tennis, yet a game which made continents stand still and was the most important sporting event of modern times exclusively in the hands of the fairer sex." (For years afterwards talk of a rematch circulated with the money offer peaking at $100,000 since Lenglen turned pro in 1926; but the powerful United States Lawn Tennis Association ruled it out because open tennis was "a menace to the game.")

After the Great War, Lenglen became a truly national figure, the symbol of resurgent French pride. Her fiery Gallic temperament combined with her daring mid-calf skirt and sleeveless dress, colorful bandeaux, gold bracelet, lipstick (she was the first woman to wear it on court at Wimbledon), all-court athleticism, and balletic grace made her tennis' first female superstar. Indeed, the imperious Bill Tilden, a magnetic figure of sport's "Golden Age" in the 1920s, admitted that Lenglen was the only player who was a bigger draw than he was.

From 1919 to 1926, the incomparable Lenglen captured six Wimbledons, six French titles, and astoundingly lost only twice in tournaments, defaults caused by illness. She never played the Australian, but her sole visit to the U.S. Championships in 1921 proved a disaster. Suffering from bronchitis and coughing, Lenglen lost the first set to defending champion Molla Mallory and then retired, weeping, with unsympathetic fans and reporters calling her a quitter.

Lenglen was such a phenomenal performer that the French Davis Cup committee asked permission to include her on their nation's team. While "the record" gives a razor-thin edge to Wills over Lenglen, when asked in 1941 who was better, Elizabeth Ryan, nineteen-time Wimbledon doubles champion who played and partnered them both, replied, "Suzanne, of course. She owned every kind of shot, plus a genius for knowing how and when to use them." Even Tilden, who never disguised his contempt for Lenglen, wrote in his 1948 memoir, "For sheer genius and perfect technique, Lenglen was the greatest woman star of all time."

For sheer numbers, namely her all-time record twenty-four Slam singles titles, Margaret Smith Court towers above the competition. It may be heresy to say this Down Under, but on closer inspection, her resume looks less awesome. Eleven of those titles came at the Australian Open, the least prestigious of the "Big Four" championships. Furthermore, from 1960, when "Mighty Maggie" first won it as a seventeen-year-old, to her final triumph in 1973, the fields were decidedly weak. Among the elite, Billie Jean King played there only thrice; Maria Bueno, Virginia Wade, Nancy Richey, Rosie Casals, and Ann Haydon twice; and Darlene Hard once.

Nervousness occasionally got the better of Court—King called it the "el foldo"— particularly at Wimbledon, which she won "only" three times. Court, now a lay minister in Perth, once said she would have won six Wimbledon singles titles "if I'd known then what I know today about the study of the word of God and the power of it."

Nonetheless, the 5'10 1/2", 156-pound Court blended a classic serve-and-volley game with aggressive groundstrokes to rank No. 1 seven times and No. 2 twice. She achieved the second women's Grand Slam in 1970, was unbeaten in twenty Fed Cup matches, and captured a mind-boggling 194 singles titles.

Court's important tennis legacy was to pioneer training methods for women. As a skinny fifteen-year-old, she left home to train under the guidance of early 1950s champion Frank Sedgman, physical culturist Stan Nicholes, and coach Keith Rogers in Melbourne. To gain strength and muscle, she lifted weights, a first for women tennis players. She also exercised on the bars and trampoline and did rigorous calisthenics, such as rope and kangaroo jumps and shorts sprints, to improve her speed, agility, leaping ability, and stamina. Noticing the marvelous physical specimen that Court had become, King later visited Sedgman to copy the grueling regimen. Contemporary star John Newcombe rated Court "undoubtedly the most athletic woman tennis player I've ever seen. Stronger than most men."

Extraordinary consistency at a very high level, rather than dominance, marked the nineteen-year career of Evert. Unlike Graf, Navratilova, Wills, and Court, she never won three or more Slam crowns in a given year. Evert did, however, win eighteen Grand Slam titles, highlighted by seven French and six U.S. Opens, to tie Navratilova for fourth place. She finished No. 1 five times and No. 2 seven times and notched a gaudy 40–2 Fed Cup record.

The 5'6" Floridian also parlayed her accurate, error-free ground-strokes game into three records that will likely never be broken: winning at least one Grand Slam title for thirteen straight years, reaching the semifinals or better in her first thirty-three Grand Slam events, and winning 125 consecutive matches on clay.

Chris America, our girl-next-door sweetheart, will be remembered for her compelling rivalry with Navratilova, her attractive femininity, and helping popularize (with Jimmy Connors, her former fiancé, and Bjorn Borg) the two-handed backhand. But her most lasting legacy was impeccable sportsmanship and grace under pressure. A survey by American Sports Data in 1991, two years after she retired, found she was the most recognized athlete (91.8 percent) among Americans over thirteen.

King places just behind Evert at number seven, but she transcended tennis even more. As a twelve-year-old daughter of a southern California fireman, she vowed to change a sport she found elitist, stuffy, and discriminatory. She tirelessly led the charge to create the ground-breaking Virginia Slims Circuit, championed equal prize money, founded (with her husband, Larry) and became commissioner of World Team Tennis, became the first woman to coach a pro team (the Philadelphia Freedoms) with men, and founded and was president of the Women's Tennis Association.

One wonders how she found the time, energy, and focus to win twelve Grand Slam singles titles (plus twenty-seven more in doubles), highlighted by six Wimbledon crowns. Like her good friend Navratilova, King served and volleyed brilliantly. But King handled pressure far better—Court praised her as "the greatest competitor I've ever known"—losing only six Slam finals. Despite a series of knee surgeries, King managed to rank No. 1 five times and No. 2 on four occasions. She also sparked the U.S. to seven Fed Cup titles, going 26-3 in singles.

On her inextinguishable passion for tennis, King once said, "Ask Nureyev to stop dancing, ask Sinatra to stop singing—then you can ask me to stop playing tennis." For changing and elevating her sport, the iconic King was named number five on *Sports Illustrated's* Top 40 Athletes list for the previous forty years in 1994. For founding the Women's Sports Foundation and fighting for women's rights, *Life* magazine picked her as one of the "100 Most Important Americans of the 20th Century."

King once said that Maureen Connolly might have smashed all records had not a freak horseback riding accident severely injured her leg and prematurely ended her short but sensational career in 1954. Who could argue with that?

Connolly won the U.S. title at the age of sixteen in 1951 and then remained undefeated at Slams and lost only four matches anywhere. Nicknamed "Little Mo" for her booming and unerring ground strokes—a reference to the big guns of the famous battleship "Missouri" or "Big Mo"—5'4" Connolly shot down distinguished champions, such as Doris Hart, Louise Brough, Margaret Osborne duPont, and Shirley Fry, during her meteoric reign. She grabbed nine Grand Slam titles, including three each at Wimbledon and Forest Hills, dropping only one set in those finals. Connolly joined the pantheon of tennis immortals in 1953 when she became the first woman to win the Grand Slam.

Like Lenglen, the obsessed Connolly fascinated the sporting public and was not as happy as she looked. In her 1957 autobiography, *Forehand Drive*, Connolly confided, "I have always believed greatness on a tennis court was my destiny, a dark destiny, at times, where the tennis court became my secret jungle and I, a lonely, fear-stricken hunter. I was a strange little girl armed with hate, fear, and a Golden Racket."

Nearly forty years later, another driven but happier teen queen with devastating groundies suffered a bitter tragedy in her early prime. Monica Seles, a rare double-hander on both sides, had taken over her exciting rivalry with Graf, beating her in a high-caliber Australian Open final in 1993 for her eighth Grand Slam crown. Three months later during a changeover at a Hamburg tournament, her whole world was turned upside down. A crazed German fan of Graf stabbed her in the back.

While the wound was not life threatening, the traumatized Seles did not return to competition for twenty-seven months. She battled migraine headaches until 1997 and was never the same player again, winning only one more major title, the 1996 Australian Open, over a relatively weak field. Critics contended that Seles stayed away from the pro tour far too long when she became considerably overweight and then remained so for the rest of her career. Supporters insisted that, if not for the stabbing, Seles, and not Graf, would have ruled the 1990s. We'll never know, of course, but storied rivalries often fluctuate, and the dedicated, determined Graf should never be underestimated.

Several contenders vie for the number ten spot among the all-time greats. Alice Marble carved a niche as the first female serve-and-volley champion in the late 1930s. "Alice was so special because she played like a man," recalled Don Budge. "At that time there was no woman who played anything near like a man." Marble won four U.S.

titles and a Wimbledon, but would have racked up many more had she not been dogged by injuries and illness (anemia and pleurisy) and then turned pro at the end of 1940.

Pauline Betz isn't usually mentioned on greatest-ever lists, but cognoscenti from her era knew better. Jack Kramer, in his 1979 autobiography, wrote Betz was the second best player (after Wills) he'd ever seen. From 1942 to1946, the popular Betz used her splendid backhand, speed, stamina and competitiveness to capture five Slam titles and rank No. 1 four times. After the USLTA suspended her from amateur play in 1947 for merely discussing professionalism, "Bobbie" topped the pro ranks for seven more years.

From the late 1950s to the mid-1960s, Brazil's Maria Bueno captured four U.S. and three Wimbledon titles and captivated fans with her sultry beauty and pretty dresses as much as her stylish strokes. "She had presence. She had that fantastic body and feline grace on the court and you were left with a fabulous memory," recalled Virginia Wade.

With a serene temperament and shot-making nonchalance, Evonne Goolagong enchanted spectators around the world. Hall of Fame sportswriter Bud Collins put it best: "She plays Wimbledon and the other big tournaments as though she were a kid playing in a meadow." A Wiradjuri Aborigine and daughter of an itinerant sheep shearer from Australia, Goolagong won Wimbledon twice, the Australian Open four times and Roland Garros once and reached eleven other Grand Slam finals from 1971 to 1980 to become an international star.

Adversity marked the career of Justine Henin ever since her mother passed away when she was twelve. Later she was estranged from her father and siblings for seven years and in 2007 divorced her husband, Pierre-Yves Hardenne. Yet neither these setbacks nor assorted injuries, illnesses and her lightweight 5' 5 ¾", 126-pound physique deterred the dedicated and disciplined Belgian. During 2003–2007 she captured seven majors, including four French titles, and three year-end number one rankings with a vast repertoire of shots and dazzling athleticism that reminded experts of another superstar. "She's as tough as they come. She's the female Federer," raved 1980s legend John McEnroe.

An African-American also from humble beginnings—in violent, gang-ridden Southeast Los Angeles where she and her sister Venus ducked flying bullets at the public courts—Serena Williams gets my vote for the number ten spot. At the age of twenty-six, the immensely talented and powerful Serena has already won two Wimbledons, two U.S. Opens, three Australians and a French title for a career Grand Slam. As King said, "Serena's got great body strength, she has a strong mind. There's no weakness, really. Forehand, backhand, serve. She's very fluid. She's got everything."

Women's tennis has come a long way since Englishwoman Charlotte "Lottie" Dod, one of the first Wimbledon champions, advised, "Ladies should learn to run and run their hardest, too, not merely stride." No easy task then considering the fair sex wore near-suffocating dresses and corsets. Just imagine how Dod would have relished the vast change from 19th century underhand serves to today's overhand 120-mph rockets.

Dod never played Lenglen who never played Navratilova, but, all things considered, Steffi Graf most epitomized Dod's advice in training and competing. When it counted most, at the most prestigious tournaments, against the toughest competition, and on all surfaces, the record shows Graf did it consistently better than anyone.

You want to debate that?

**My All-Time Top 10**

1. Steffi Graf
2. Martina Navratilova
3. Helen Wills
4. Suzanne Lenglen
5. Margaret Court
6. Chris Evert
7. Billie Jean King
8. Maureen Connolly
9. Monica Seles
10. Serena Williams

---

**FASCINATING FACTS:**

- In 1998, Helen Wills bequeathed $10 million to the University of California, Berkeley to fund the establishment of a Neuroscience institute. The resulting institute, the Helen Wills Neuroscience Institute, began in 1999 and is now home to more than 40 faculty researchers and 36 graduate students.  (Source: Wikipedia)

- Sixteen-year-old star Maureen Connolly stopped signing autographs following her first U.S. Championships title in 1951 because she was tricked into signing a bogus check for a con man.

- All-time great Martina Navratilova told *The Times* (UK) in 2006 that she had to stop meditating "because I got too mellow."

- After Justine Henin-Hardenne won the 2004 Pacific Life Open and told *Inside Tennis*, "I know the impossible is nothing for me now," adidas turned the quip into its worldwide "Impossible Is Nothing" campaign.

- Roger Federer says the greatest athletes of all time are Michael Jordan, Michael Schumacher and Martina Navratilova.

# 3

# Is This The Sport We Want?
# 2007

*"Sport is entertainment, of course. But it must be credible."*

—Francesco Ricci Bitti, president of the International Tennis Federation

"Hey, Roger, while you're down on the court making history, can you also call your own lines—even the ones eighty feet away?" ridiculed veteran TV analyst Mary Carillo, openly making fun of the Player Challenge system during the Federer-Gonzalez final at the 2007 Australian Open.

Patrick McEnroe, the U.S. Davis Cup captain (and also a TV analyst), disagrees completely. "Anyone who is against Player Challenges," he declared, as fans cheered the Hawk-Eye technology adjudicating close line calls on the stadium video screen, "is out of their minds!"

Who's right? And why?

## Purpose of Officiating

The *raison d'etre* of sports officiating is fairness by means of the impartial application of the rules. For tennis line calling, fairness means accuracy, getting it right. Bill Tilden, an imperious 1920s superstar, insisted that a linesperson's error often decided a match as much as a player's performance. He even worked as a linesman himself on occasion. One can easily imagine Tilden's frustration in a sport where extremely close line calls abound. He was competing for prestigious titles in an amateur era when big-time tennis relied largely on untrained volunteers.

Happily, today Hawk-Eye's ten high-resolution cameras track the trajectory of the ball and exact location of the bounce to within three millimeters. That is near-perfect 99.9 percent accuracy. Replays can be shown from any angle within two seconds and can be sent to a monitor, handheld device, or mobile phone. In theory, players

24

shouldn't have to worry about a thing. And they certainly shouldn't have to call their own lines or challenge questionable line calls made by others. Therefore, it's nothing less than a tragic irony that Player Challenges, the system used to implement marvelous Hawk-Eye technology, frequently result in bad line calls.

## The Limits of Human Vision

The thirteen factors that make accurate line-calling difficult and sometimes virtually impossible for tennis players are as follows:

1. The Parallax Factor (also called Motion parallax)—Motion parallax: The apparent relative motion of several stationary objects against a background when the observer moves gives hints about their relative distance. This effect can be seen clearly when driving in a car, when nearby things pass quickly, while far off objects appear stationary. (For an animated demonstration of motion parallax, go to: http://psych.hanover.edu/Krantz/MotionParallax/MotionParallax.html.)

2. The Angle Factor—Linespeople are positioned so that their line of vision is exactly on the line they are watching. Tennis players are seldom in this ideal position, even when they are not moving. "Another good example of parallax and angle is dramatically illustrated with rifle shooting when the near and far sights must be aligned to achieve the best aim," notes Graham B. Erickson, O.D., FAAO, FCOVD, a professor at Pacific University College of Optometry, author, and head of the Sports Vision Section of the American Optometrics Association.

3. The Distance Factor—The farther a person is away from a given object, the more difficult it is to see that object, all other things being equal.

4. The Occlusion Factor—This occurs when the net and/or a player blocks completely or partly the vision of the other player. When you stand two feet behind the baseline—the most common position during matches on the pro tours—you must look entirely (or almost entirely) through the net to see the other side of the court.

5. The Speed Factor—When serves are regularly whacked 120 or more miles per hour and forehands whiz 100 miles per hour, it becomes increasingly difficult to see the ball accurately during its flight and the split second when it hits the court.

6. The Height Factor—Linespeople typically crouch as low as possible to have an optimum look at where the ball lands. On the other hand, players see the ball—depending on how tall they are and how erect they're standing—from a much higher point. The height factor is most adverse for the chair umpire, who sees the ball from eight to ten feet above court level.

7. The Depth Perception Factor—Depth perception skills, of even the world's top athletes, vary considerably.

8.  The Light Factor—As light decreases during twilight, and even on very cloudy days, seeing the ball becomes more difficult. Conversely, the glare of an extremely bright sun also can diminish vision, unless the player or official wears sunglasses.

9.  The Shadow Factor—Tracking and seeing a ball as it emerges into shadows and then leaves shadows and/or then lands in shadowed areas is more difficult than seeing a ball on a tennis court without shadows.

10. The Weather Factor—Mist, light rain, and other forms of precipitation reduce visual acuity.

11. Color Contrast Factor—As yellow balls become darker due to dirt, clay or grass stains, they become harder to see because their color contrasts less with the darker colors of the tennis court.

12. The Focus Factor—The sole role and responsibility of linespeople is to watch the lines in order to make accurate line calls. The goal of tennis players is to play their best so that they can win. To do that, players must focus on hitting the ball as effectively as possible. To do that, they must get to the ball on time and then produce excellent footwork, swings, and timing. They must watch the ball very closely to achieve those goals. Incidentally, they also see the ball most, but not all the time, the split second when it lands on the tennis court. Their focus is not on making line calls, nor should it be. Close line calls happen approximately 50 percent of the time on each side of the court. When the close line call happens on the player's side, he often is most focused, as I have just described it, and vice versa.

13. The Interactive Factor—All these factors can generally affect the precision of a line call. Some have a more significant impact than others," asserts Dr. Erickson. "The parallax and angle factors probably have the most significance for a player attempting to 'call' his own shots, other than an outright occlusion. *Importantly, all these factors also interact substantially which can considerably diminish vision.*"

Several factors—distance, occlusion, speed, light, shadow, weather, color contrast, and interactive—also reduce the vision of linespeople. Besides these eight factors, chair umpires are additionally hampered by the height and angle factors.

## Human Error

It's not at all surprising that the fallibility of the human eye—as the above thirteen factors pointed out and which television viewers have witnessed with instant replay for years—was confirmed at the 2006 Nasdaq-100 Open. There Hawk-Eye, making its eagerly awaited debut, overturned 33 percent of the line calls (53 of 161) that were challenged by players. Since then players have been proved right—and linespersons and chair umpires wrong—at least 30 percent of the time at every pro tournament that has used Player Challenges. At the 2007 Australian Open, 49.2 percent of the men's singles challenges were correct, along with 41.7 percent of the women's singles challenges.

While the players are right about a third to a half of the time, they are wrong about half to two-thirds of the time. That's bad enough. But the fallibility of players is further demonstrated when they fail to challenge many other incorrect line calls because they don't see them well or at all or don't play the gimmicky challenge "game" well. (See sidebar with the Player Challenge Rules.)

A case in point is the outrageous robbery that took place in a 2006 Pilot Pen semifinal at New Haven. Trying to escape her sixth match point in the second set tiebreaker, Samantha Stosur belted a shot that landed—as ESPN viewers saw on Instant Replay—smack on Lindsay Davenport's baseline. It was called out. Stosur didn't challenge. End of match!

Did this gross injustice bring an outcry from the commentators? *Au contraire.* Patrick McEnroe was pleased that former world No. 1 Davenport said nothing, and he shockingly advocated that tennis players become much more like baseball, football, and basketball players and try to get away with as much as they can. Mary Joe Fernandez, a former French and Australian Open finalist, blamed the victim, calling Stosur's failure to challenge "a no-brainer." When Chris Fowler sensibly tried to interject the importance of fairness and getting the line call right, he was interrupted and ignored. Afterward Stosur, who had two challenges left, confided, "I wanted to question it. It was match point and I guess I didn't want to look like an idiot [if the call were reversed]." That's understandable. Stosur was watching a ball land eighty feet away.

Researcher Vic Braden did a study for the United States Tennis Association, shooting at 10,000 frames per second, and concluded: "As the ball is only on the court for approximately three milliseconds, the human eye is not able to see the actual landing spot."

Stosur shouldn't have to do any challenging in the first place. What then is a confused player to do in such high-pressure circumstances?

Not to worry. At the 2007 Australian Open, when Andy Murray, no shrinking violet, failed to challenge a line call that was incorrect by two inches, ESPN commentator Cliff Drysdale had a bright idea. He suggested Murray should have asked coach Brad Gilbert, who was sitting nearby, if he should challenge. When Carillo reminded him that coaching is illegal, Drysdale replied, "That's okay." Ethics be damned seems to be the credo of some ESPN commentators. What's next? Will we see coaches and friends of players bringing tiny TVs into players' boxes so they can signal players when to challenge or not challenge with 100 percent accuracy?

Keep in mind that players lose a challenge every time they incorrectly challenge. That fallibility factor inhibits players who have only one challenge left, particularly early and in the middle of a set, and completely undermines them when they run out of challenges. In the latter case, they cannot challenge incorrect line calls, no matter how well they see them or how egregious the mistakes. It apparently doesn't matter to TV sports executives that millions of viewers also witness these incorrect and unfair line calls.

Serena Williams, who was fatally victimized by egregious human errors and ultimately beaten by Jennifer Capriati in the 2004 U.S. Open quarters, was again treated unfairly, this time by Player Challenges, in the 2007 Australian Open semis. Ahead 7-6, 5-4, Serena was cheated on her fifth match point when Nicole Vaidisova pounded a backhand that bounced an inch outside Serena's singles sideline. The linesperson wrongly called it in, while Serena and Shot Spot saw it clearly out. Sadly, Serena was out of challenges and could do nothing about it. Fortunately, this time it didn't cost her the match.

During the memorable Andre Agassi-Marcos Baghdatis match at the 2006 U.S. Open, the colorful Cypriot desperately wanted a replay deep into the fifth set, but he, too, was out of challenges. As award-winning *San Francisco Chronicle* tennis writer Bruce Jenkins rightly stressed, "What's the point of innovative technology if you can't use it when it matters most?"

That potent argument, which should be self-evident, doesn't bother advocates of Player Challenges at all. "One of the greatest things about the challenge system is that it gives you peace of mind," insists Fernandez. "You don't have to dwell on it." Tell that to Stosur, Williams, Baghdatis and the many others who, knowingly and unknowingly (until they learned later), have been cheated out of points, games, sets, and even matches by incorrect calls by linespeople, umpires and, ironically, even themselves.

## Entertainment

"If we are really going to grow the sport, we will do what is best for television," averred Arlen Kantarian, USTA chief executive of professional tennis and a fervent advocate of Player Challenges, in *Street & Smith's SportsBusiness Journal*. Like the immortal saying about General Motors, Kantarian's credo could be paraphrased as "What's best for television is what's best for tennis." Since television is the greatest vehicle for entertainment in human history, his conclusion is that Player Challenges, even though they are distracting and result in inaccurate and thus unfair line calls, should win the day.

However, as Carillo rightly argues, "The powers that be at the networks don't trust that the sport is compelling enough. They'll do anything to trick it up because they don't understand and appreciate its beauty, its subtleties, its very nature. And please, no gimmickry. If you so believe in the need for electronic line calls, extend that logic and use it *all the time*."

Will Player Challenges make tennis more popular? "If tennis administrators seriously think that bringing Hawk-Eye into play on a few show courts is going to broaden their fan base in a significant way, they are as self-delusionary as an aspiring professional with a wood racket," rightly wrote the respected *New York Times* tennis writer Christopher Clarey last year. The popularity of tennis, whatever the era or country, has always been based predominantly on two factors: charismatic champions and riveting rivalries. High-caliber, close matches, exciting playing styles, supportive media, and skillful marketing of stars and tournaments also boost TV ratings and tournament attendance to some extent. But officiating is virtually irrelevant. Some spectators enjoy

Player Challenges; others believe they harm the sport's integrity and credibility. The latter understand that great shots and points won by their favorite players are something to cheer about—not line calls.

## The Human Element

The crux of Kantarian's entertainment thesis is the proverbial "human element." But what exactly does "the human element" mean? It includes anything from player banter with spectators to displays of exuberance to mild protests to emotional meltdowns to raging, profane altercations between players and officials. Some aficionados relish that conflict; others find it disgusting and distracting; while most of us like it as long as it's not too raucous and time-consuming.

The end of line-calling rhubarbs, though, won't result in the death of the human element in tennis by any means. Disputes will always arise over rule infractions, such as foot-faults, double bounces, touching and crossing over the net, illegal coaching, etc. And wherever fiercely competitive players give their all for fame, fortune, titles and pride, they'll glare, swear, and trash talk. They'll smash and throw rackets. They'll stall, fake injuries, and bend and break rules, such as when Nicolas Kiefer tossed his racket to distract Sebastien Grosjean during their contentious 2006 Australian Open quarterfinal.

The human element and the excessive attention paid to officiating in a sport with an extraordinary imbalance of thirteen officials for only two or four players was perceptively noted by the late Gene Scott, *Tennis Week* publisher and former world No. 11. "The human element should be the two players on the court, *not* the officials," Scott told FOXSports.com. "The best officials are the ones you never notice. The nature of the game made officials too noticeable a part."

Ivan Lendl, the no-nonsense 1980s champion, smartly summed up the fairness vs. entertainment issue. "I would like to see *all* [close] line calls get called automatically with no challenges," said Lendl. "I hate the fact that someone may lose the match on a bad call. Yes, there are people who say it takes the human element out of the game. To them, I would say: Let it be 5-all in the fifth set tiebreaker in the U.S. Open final, and you get bad calls and lose the match. What do you say now?"

## The Solution

Keep Hawk-Eye, instant replay, and the indispensable linespeople. Get rid of unfair and gimmicky Player Challenges. Armed with a courtside computer monitor displaying Hawk-Eye's results, the chair umpire should immediately overrule errors by linespeople, clicking a button and instantly putting Hawk-Eye's image of the correct call on the stadium video board. When a line call is correct but a player protests—in the traditional manner—the umpire also displays Hawk-Eye on the stadium video board. If tennis fans yearn for even more Hawk-Eye, tournaments should display it whenever balls land within three (or four or five) inches of the outer edge of the lines.

Used wisely as a means for accurate line calling, Hawk-Eye improves our sport. Misused alongside Player Challenges, it gives tennis a black eye.

## Player Challenge Rules

Each player receives two challenges per set to review line calls.

If the player is correct with a challenge, then the player retains the same number of challenges.

If the player is incorrect with a challenge, then one of the challenges is lost.

During a tiebreaker game in any set, each player will receive one additional challenge.

Challenges may not be carried over from one set to another.

Challenges can be made only on the last shot of a rally.

---

**FASCINATING FACTS:**

- In early 2006 Paul Hawkins, the British inventor of the revolutionary Hawk-Eye electronic line-calling technology, in *The Times* (UK) tellingly advised the ATP and WTA Tours: "You've chosen this route, now just be careful how you use it."

- On three occasions Ana Ivanovic sportingly corrected an erroneous line call to concede a point during her 6-1, 6-2 loss to Justine Henin in the 2007 French Open final.

- Sixty of the 2006 Wimbledon line judges reportedly complained that their tournament-issued trousers tore open when they were squatting down to make line calls.

- David Stern revealed he would like to be commissioner of tennis if he were not the NBA commissioner.

- In 2005, Serena Williams, who had been victimized by bad line calls at major tournaments, wore a T-shirt with the printed message: "THE BALL WAS IN!"

# 4

# Is On-Court Coaching Good for Tennis?
# 2006

*"Look to the essence of a thing, whether it be a point of doctrine, of practice, or of interpretation."*

—Marcus Aurelius

The battle for the soul of tennis rages on. Each new ATP and WTA Tour reform adds fuel to the fire of controversy. No-Ad scoring, tiebreakers in lieu of full deciding sets, round-robin formats, frequent and lengthy bathroom and trainer breaks, player challenges, best-17 rankings, and on-court coaching have all been either adopted or experimented with. Arlen Kantarian, the USTA chief executive for professional tennis, confidently predicts, "In the next three to five years, we'll see more change in tennis than in the last twenty-five."

I don't know where all these reforms—many of them radical and counter-productive—will end. But I do know what inspires most of them: television.

In their 1993 book, *A Brief History of American Sports*, Elliot J. Gorn and Warren Goldstein profoundly analyze the essence of television. "Sports entrepreneurs, including television networks, have a different approach to games from that of fans," they write. "Because television networks make money by, in effect, renting audiences to advertisers, they have considerably less interest in the internal structures, particular histories and traditions, or distinctive rhythms of a given sport—except insofar as they affect the number of viewers."

To placate television moguls and their relentless quest for ratings, the ATP and WTA are trying to transform tennis into what they claim is a more attractive television package. The most dubious WTA experiment—permitting on-court coaching (which has long been barred at ATP, WTA and Grand Slam tournaments)—merely recycles a past failure. The ATP tried limited on-court coaching at five World Series tournaments in 1998, allowing the coach on the court during the first two-minute changeovers after the first and second sets. Interestingly, the ATP estimated that about 90 percent of the players used coaches during the beginning of the trial, but by the summer events, that number dropped far below 50 percent. Fans weren't enamored with the idea either, and the ATP shelved it. This time WTA players may request their coach on court once per set during changeovers as well as during the break between sets. Coaches wear microphones so TV viewers can hear the consultations.

"Our business partners—ESPN and Eurosport networks and tour sponsor Sony Ericsson—challenged the Tour to enhance the entertainment value of the sport," explains WTA Tour president Stacey Allaster. "Tennis faces stiff competition from other sports and entertainment options. On-court coaching, by adding a new interesting 'actor' to the storyline of a match and adding an element of strategy, can make the sport even more exciting for fans."

The view here is that on-court coaching of any kind is an idea whose time will never come for the individual sport of tennis. Here are the reasons why.

## Tennis' Unique Battle of Skill and Will

Much of tennis' historical and enduring appeal comes from its fair and complete test of athleticism, skill, stamina, courage, and strategic acumen. That unique test is achieved without on-court coaching, substitutions, lengthy halftime or between-period breaks, or being saved by a game-ending clock. Put differently, self-reliance makes the individual sport of tennis singles a highly respected and entertaining battle of skill and will between two finely tuned and mentally resilient athletes.

On-court coaching unquestionably diminishes these cardinal virtues. "That's like taking an examination and your teacher giving you all the answers," argues ESPN, NBC, CBS, and HBO tennis analyst Mary Carillo, an Emmy and Peabody Award winner. "I want these players to know their craft and figure out how to win. And if they can't, they lose. One of the reasons I love tennis is because you're out there on your own." Former world top-tenner Jimmy Arias, an analyst for The Tennis Channel, agrees: "A better coach shouldn't determine who wins the match. This is an individual sport— *mano a mano*." Matches would also come down to two-versus-one in the case of players who can't afford or didn't want a coach. And when two opponents share the same coach, imagine the conflict of interest, not to mention the probable conflict.

Why exactly does on-court coaching make such a big and unfair difference?

Sarah Palfrey, a shrewd strategist who captured eighteen Grand Slam titles in singles, doubles and mixed doubles from 1930 to 1945, in her book, *Tennis for Anyone!*, explains, "In no other sport are the strategic possibilities so numerous, the ways to outwit your opponent so rich and varied within the accepted sportsmanlike bounds."

Think of what on-court coaching could do for Andy Roddick, an honors student during his school days, yet, until recently, one of the most unintelligent Top 5 players in tennis history. A savvy coach would urge the under-achieving, twenty-four-year-old American to position himself closer to the baseline; hit the vast majority of approach shots down the line instead of crosscourt; use slice backhands sparingly (rather than repetitively); and chiefly to change pace, recover position during rallies, and approach net, and run around his backhand only if he intends to whack forehands very aggressively.

That said, Roddick favors the current rule because "Tennis is unique in the fact you actually have to think for yourself. Most sports, you've got a coach talking to you or a caddie talking to you or a pit crew talking to you or something. I like the fact it's kind of one-on-one."

Andre Agassi, who occasionally tanked matches early in his career and supported on-court coaching in 1998, now staunchly opposes it. The eight-time Grand Slam champion rightly contends, "Tennis is one-on-one combat. It's a sport that forces you to solve problems by yourself. It's a vehicle for education, a great thing for somebody's life. That message needs to be sold better." Tournament tennis not only reveals character; it builds character.

Besides making players smarter strategically, on-court coaching can aid players—but, regrettably, reduce their self-reliance—in several other crucial ways. Soothing words would relax the nervous Jana Novotná, calm the vesuvian Goran Ivaniševic, and comfort the despondent Vera Zvonareva who has cried during matches.

Amélie Mauresmo, a highly talented athlete who didn't win her first Grand Slam until age twenty-six at the 2006 Australian Open, concedes nerves often had caused her downfall. Even so, Mauresmo avers, "With tactical or mental coaching, it makes a huge difference. I think the very essence of tennis historically is finding the keys and solutions oneself on the court. It's what makes the beauty of the sport."

Quick tips from a coach can improve stroke technique and footwork, too. Just think how many more first serves would go in if players were instructed to toss the ball a bit higher, or how much more quickly they would get to distant shots if they were reminded to keep bouncing on their toes between points, or how much more penetrating their volleys would be if they were told to contact the ball more out in front. Davis Cup and Fed Cup captains and college coaches give valuable tips, and they've turned many a match around. Fair enough, but only for team competitions.

Finally, simple advice, such as slowing the hyperactive player down between points, or telling the struggling player to switch to a racket with slightly looser (or tighter) strings, or reminding the absent-minded player to eat or drink during changeovers, can also improve performance considerably.

Support for the time-tested no-coaching rule even comes from an unlikely source, Maria Sharapova, who participated in the five-tournament experiment last year. It's unlikely because her notorious father, Yuri, has frequently and blatantly cheated, even though he's received only two code violations (one during the U.S. Open semis) and one fine (at Birmingham) in 2006. During Sharapova's U.S. Open final triumph, Yuri and hitting partner Michael Joyce frantically signaled her by waving a banana and holding up four fingers to remind her to eat and stay hydrated. Nonetheless, Sharapova says, "Our sport is an individual sport and you play by instinct. What makes it so good is that you're the one who has to decide what you're going to do. If you're calling your coach down, it's a little strange. It's like you're telling your opponent, 'I need some help.'" If only the Siberian siren would practice what she preaches.

Her compatriots, Svetlana Kuznetsova, Nadia Petrova, and Elena Dementieva, along with comebacking Martina Hingis are somewhat more receptive to on-court coaching, or at least experimenting with it. Interestingly, Hingis, the cleverest teenage tactician ever, who in 1998 criticized on-court coaching "as a way to help players who can't think for themselves," now blandly says, "It's nice to try something different."

However, most of the current top ten women, including Justine Henin-Hardenne, Kim Clijsters, and Nicole Vaidišová—plus former No. 1 Serena Williams—have declared their unminced opposition to on-court coaching. Top twenty players, who are televised the most and whom the WTA most wants to promote, have backed their words up by using on-court coaching the least of all.

Billie Jean King, a legend on the court and a visionary off it, opined, "If it gets the media talking and brings us exposure, that's always good." So would, of course, women playing topless, but that certainly isn't the foremost criterion. King negated her media reason and hit the essence of the issue when she tellingly added, "[But] I never cared if I even had a coach, because personally, I was brought up to think for myself."

## Spectator Appeal

On-court coaching is supposed to expose TV viewers to new personalities as well as inside strategy. "It gives commentators and producers some more color, another actor in the play, a peek behind the curtain," WTA CEO Larry Scott told *USA Today*. However, tennis coaches, just like baseball coaches and managers talking to a struggling pitcher on the mound, will frequently prevent their advice from ever being overheard. No prudent coach would reveal the advice and information he gives to his player simply because it can be used against her in that match or in future matches.

So the idea that watching a coach and a player speaking to each other during a two-minute break between sets or a ninety-second changeover is a boon to fans is dubious at best and fatuous at worst. Yet another barrier is language. Coaches on the polyglot women's circuit are permitted to talk in whatever language they're most comfortable. Keep in mind that only two of the top thirty and only thirteen of the top 100 female singles players come from countries where English is the primary language. Their older coaches and parents, as surrogate coaches, may be even less multilingual. When the language chosen does not match with a broadcaster's language, broadcasters have the option of either simultaneously translating the conversation—assuming they are capable of that—or alternatively, having a sideline reporter interview the coach right after the time-out to determine what was said.

Does that sound enticing and entertaining to you? "I can't imagine my mom running up and down the court like [Miami Heat coach] Pat Riley," weighs in Serena Williams. "What's going to be so exciting about it? If you have people that are going to speak Russian, no one's going to be able to understand that."

The often inaudible and incomprehensible chit-chat does nothing to liven up the dead time in a sport already bogged down by ninety-second changeovers, dawdling between points (although the men are the worst offenders), and frequent and lengthy bathroom breaks and trainer time-outs that ruin the rhythm and momentum of matches.

Most of all, fans want action—not matches where the ball is in play sometimes a shockingly low 15 percent of the total match time.

## Enforce the Current Rule

The "Everyone's coaching [illegally] anyway, so let's just legalize it" argument is intellectually absurd and morally wrong-headed. The ATP, WTA, and tour umpires deserve the blame for not cracking down on this frequent and often obvious rule infraction. "The cheating is out of control," veteran pro Daniela Hantuchova said during the U.S. Open. "There are signals and words instructing the players. I've complained to the umpires, wondering how they can't hear this when I can." U.S. Open semifinalist Jelena Jankovic agreed: "Hand signals and words are happening all the time." Sounding out of touch and out of ideas, Allaster told ESPN.com, "If we have a rule on our books that we can't enforce, it shouldn't be there."

Instead of unjustifiably capitulating, the WTA should quadruple its meager $250 fine for illegal coaching to $1,000 and stringently enforce the no-coaching rule without fear or favor. (Believe it or not, despite the rampant cheating, no player has been fined more than twice in 2006.) The WTA could easily do that by placing a multilingual official in the Player's Box. Now chair umpires assess a warning on the first offense, followed by a point penalty. I advocate that the third offense result in an automatic fine and the removal of the offender from the Player's Box. Those heftier penalties would sharply reduce violations and stigmatize violators. For the ultimate in deterrence, require coaches to sit beside each other. If Brad Gilbert or Jimmy Connors shouted advice to their respective charges, Andy Murray and Roddick, during a big match, all hell might break loose, but it wouldn't happen again.

## Too Soon To Panic

"If we don't add some characters to the game and do some new things, there's not going to be any major tournaments anymore," well-known coach and on-court coaching proponent Nick Bollettieri told *The New York Times*. Tennis' popularity depends chiefly on charismatic characters and their riveting rivalries, but these compelling characters always have been, and always will be, players, especially stars, not coaches. Regrettably, Bollettieri cares much less about the integrity of the game. He once confessed, "Over the years I've probably broken the [coaching] rules more than anyone else."

Allaster tried to justify on-court coaching with a questionable assertion when she told ESPN.com, "We're facing diminishing or flat [TV] ratings, and the sport couldn't be better."

NBC ratings for the Wimbledon and French women's finals fell in 2006, but declining enthusiasm can be attributed to fields weakened by injuries to elite players and the decline of charismatic, former superstars Serena and Venus Williams. On the other hand, ESPN and ESPN2 ratings for pro tennis have increased 18 percent from 2004 to 2006. The rating for the U.S. Open women's final was 3.2, a 3 percent increase over 2005 and a 28 percent increase over 2004. The national overnight rating for the

2006 U.S. Open men's final was 4.1, the second-best rating for the men's final since 2002 when Pete Sampras defeated Andre Agassi. The Agassi-Marcos Baghdatis match equaled USA Network's highest rating in four years.

It is also worth stressing that the United States doesn't and shouldn't rule the tennis world. Ratings in the 200-plus countries that televise tennis vary considerably and often fluctuate greatly depending on whether the country or continent boasts a star or rising star. Therefore, the ITF, ATP, and WTA should evaluate international TV tennis ratings, not American ratings, when considering international rule changes. One thing is for sure: on-court coaching won't materially affect ratings. What will?

"From my experience with ratings, more people watch when the match-up is compelling," asserts Carillo, a TV commentator for twenty-five years. "They don't give a damn whose coverage it is, how spectacular the teases or on-court interviews or features are, and they don't care who's in the booth. What they want to see is a good tennis match, live. Still, there are ways to enhance the coverage for the viewers, with good camera angles, telling replays, a sense of the moment, the environment, the atmosphere, and insightful commentary. And well-applied, state-of-the-art technology always enhances the viewing of a match, whether it's a terrific one or a poorly played one. But most of all, it's about who's competing on the court."

Furthermore, tennis overall is much healthier in America than Allaster suggests. The Tennis Industry Association reports that all sectors of the sport have grown, from sales of equipment to increases in the number of recreational players (up 1.1 million in 2005 to reach 24.7 million, the most total players since 1992) and fans. According to a 2006 Sporting Goods Manufacturers Association survey, tennis is the only traditional sport in America that has grown in the past five years—up 10.3 percent.

A few print and electronic media people claim that a rule change would be justified because on-court coaching would add another dimension to their stories. As a veteran tennis writer, I can assure you these fascinating and timely stories about players, events, issues, and trends already abound—even on the slowest news day. The more enterprising media seek and find them. Furthermore, for pre-match and/or post-match stories, tour coaches typically are quite cooperative, knowledgeable, and opinionated. And significantly, only a tiny minority of them, chiefly Bollettieri and Brad Gilbert, have spoken out in favor of on-court coaching.

Finally, does anyone want self-aggrandizing coaches boasting how clever their coaching strategy is after their players pull out tight matches? Or bombastic Don King types dashing up to the microphone after matches and exclaiming, "We played great today!"—as Bollettieri did early in his career? The last thing tennis needs is ego-driven, attention-seeking coaches taking the spotlight and glory away from the real stars. As the late Gene Scott wrote in *World Tennis* in 1971, "The event with the intrinsic ability to create a new star is the most important ingredient in the promotion of tennis."

## Conclusion

Allaster stresses, "Importantly, any change must be made with an eye towards respecting the important traditions in the game that have made women's tennis the leading global sport for women." Etienne de Villiers, the innovative CEO of the ATP Tour, echoed those sentiments in *Inside Tennis*: "We're not going to be disrespectful to the sport. It has too much going for it. We are going to innovate around the edges."

The only way to honor those wise pledges is to preserve the *essence* of tennis and its unique mystique. That means, above all, our sport must remain a fair test of skill, will and self-reliance; and only when that *sine qua non* test is passed, can tennis leaders strive to make it more entertaining. Chris Evert, the ultimate court thinker and competitor, superbly captured the essence of the coaching debate in 1998 when she told *The New York Times*: "When you go down in history as the world champion, you'd better have done it yourself. You can get all the coaching you want before the match."

Amen.

## FASCINATING FACTS:

- The Lawn Tennis Association's (UK) interview of coaching candidates includes "a visit to a psychologist to determine a candidate's bonding possibilities," according to *The Times* (UK).

- Serena Williams says she picks her hitting partners on the basis that "If you can beat me, you can hit with me."

- Anna Kournikova, who ranked a career-high No. 8 in singles and No. 1 in doubles, "failed," her former coach, Nick Bollettieri told *Inside Tennis*, because her mother "never truly let go of the reins to put faith in the coach.".

- Isabelle Demongeot, a former touring pro who alleges she was sexually abused by a former coach, met with new French president Nicolas Sarkozy in July 2007 to discuss the problem of manipulative and exploitative coaches in girls' sports.

- Many Hollywood actors require their tennis teacher to sign a confidentiality agreement.

# 5

# What's Wrong with the ATP's Doubles Reforms?

# 2005

*For sheer enjoyment, thrills and satisfaction, you can't beat a good game of doubles be-tween two evenly matched teams of first rank.*

— Don Budge in his 1939 book, *Budge on Tennis*

After three decades of policy blunders, the Association of Tennis Professionals stands on the brink of delivering the *coup de grace* to the great event of doubles and its talented stars. To try to entice leading singles players to enter doubles events, ATP tournaments plans to use No-Ad scoring and sets played to five games (instead of six) with a tiebreaker when games reach 4-4. This scoring system is not even approved by the International Tennis Federation, which governs the rules of tennis. These and other highly important rule changes were made without consulting the ITF and only a few present and past singles and doubles standouts whose expertise, experience, and ethics the ATP sorely needs. The reforms will go into effect after the U.S. Open unless the ATP either grudgingly accepts how misguided and damaging they are, or the ATP is pressured by the growing protest movement in the tennis world to rescind them.

Let's examine the radical ATP rule changes from various angles.

## A Difference of Opinion

A June 30 press release titled "ATP to Implement Doubles Enhancements" states that a Research & Development Doubles Project Team—which was chaired by Horst Klosterkemper, ATP President Europe and Player Relations, and included player rep-resentatives, tournament directors, and ATP staff—"evaluated data from surveys from four target groups: fans, players, media, and tournaments. One hundred players equally represented from Top 100 in doubles and singles were interviewed, and 4,837 fans responded to an ATPtennis.com survey." The fact that the ATP does not reveal this data suggests that the data may not have supported its position. What other reason is there for being secretive?

The leading doubles players and teams have the greatest stake in the planned doubles reforms, and several immediately denounced them. "We hate these rule changes," says Mike Bryan, who with his twin brother Bob won the 2003 French Open and reached the Australian, French, and Wimbledon finals this year. "All of the players Bob and I have talked to think they are going to be bad for doubles and fans. People are going to lose a lot of respect for doubles. There's not a lot we can do with this system, because the players voted against it, and the tournaments passed it, so it's a pretty corrupt system."

Money is the root of the ineptitude, according to Bob Bryan. "Doubles players have almost no voice in the ATP. Decisions are made by penny-pinching businessmen who are frustrated to pay an extra five bucks to accommodate their product. Even though doubles prize money was cut 30 percent a couple years ago—the cuts were put right into the singles prize money—tournament directors still constantly complain about the money they pay for extra hotel rooms and food tickets for doubles players. Most directors don't respect doubles and appreciate its value to the sport and their tournaments.

"They should promote doubles and doubles players rather than damage the sport with absurd rule changes," concludes Bryan. "Five-game sets with No-Ad scoring will bring an exhibition atmosphere to a professional sport we all have sweated blood working at our whole lives. Like most of the other players on the tour, we feel cheated by the ATP."

All-time doubles great Todd Woodbridge, who owns twenty-two Grand Slam doubles titles and served as president of the ATP Player Council in 2001–2002, denies he and other cognoscenti were even consulted. "The entire ATP board should resign, because they have made changes without asking what the rest of the tennis world thinks," says Woodbridge. "Their decisions during the past two-and-a-half years helped improve the positions of their own tournaments—Indian Wells (Charlie Pasarell) and Metz (Patrice Dominguez) are the biggest beneficiaries—but were clearly not in the best interest of other tournaments on the calendar. The player representatives on the Board—Bob Brett, Tomás Carbonell, and Ricardo Acioly—have defied the clear wishes of the Player Council by passing this latest doubles directive."

Mark Woodforde, who captured seventeen Grand Slam doubles crowns, including eleven with Woodbridge, is "shocked to the core" about the coming doubles changes. "Anyone who believes that shortening sets, No-Ad scoring, etc., will enhance the game of doubles is a bloody idiot," blasts Woodforde. "And there's no way these changes will allow more doubles matches to be played on center court early in the week."

Swedish veteran Jonas Björkman, ranked No. 1 in doubles, also fingered the ATP as the problem and not the solution. "They're doing a lousy job of promoting doubles. That's the problem," Björkman told the *Ft. Lauderdale Sun-Sentinel.*

## What Does the ATP Really Want?

"The ATP's doubles enhancements are not enhancements at all, just the tournament directors looking for cost savings," rightly notes Bill Oakes, former director of the ATP's tournament in Atlanta and now an analyst for the show, MatchPoint America on The Tennis Channel. "They should just admit it. I have heard many tournament directors whine about having to pay for doubles players' hotel and food and even prize money." Put differently, the badly-intentioned goal is to drive doubles standouts out and replace them in doubles draws with singles specialists.

## What Do Singles Stars Really Want?

The ATP's main rationale for its rule changes is to induce leading singles players to enter doubles events more often. But that won't happen, according to Mark Knowles, former world No. 1 in doubles and current vice president of the ATP Players Council. "I've done a lot of research. All of the ten or so singles players ranked in top twenty that I've talked to have stressed that they won't play any more doubles events throughout the year, regardless of any of these proposed rules changes," notes Knowles. "I've spoken directly with Roddick, Agassi, Henman, Cañas, Stepanek, Ljubicic, and in the case of Federer, his close friend, Yves Allegro.

"The guys in top ten earn such huge amounts of prize money and endorsements that it's not worth it for them to risk injury and exhaustion to sacrifice their singles preparation for a minimal amount of prize money and prestige in doubles," explains Knowles. "Also, some singles players aren't very good in doubles and others simply don't enjoy doubles. A couple of top singles players have told me that literally standing at the net while their partner is serving is the scariest thing in the world.

"Most tournament directors really disrespect the top doubles teams and feel that any top singles player, if he wanted to, would be at the top of the doubles rankings," says Knowles. "But I totally disagree. Doubles is a different science, a different discipline. If you look at the top ten singles players' doubles records and the top ten doubles players' doubles records, it's unbelievably one-sided."

## The Television Factor

The ATP Research & Development Doubles Project Team did not include any print or electronic media, and the ATP press release did not include any reactions from the media about the survey results or the rules. Since doubles appears rarely on TV, except for Davis Cup coverage, one wonders how this critical problem can be rectified. "As for the ATP doubles debacle, what a colossal error those knuckleheads have made this time," says Mary Carillo. "I almost couldn't believe the press release. I thought it had to be a joke. Then I approached both my bosses at ESPN and NBC during Wimbledon, and I asked them if the new format for doubles would get doubles more air time. Both network execs laughed at the notion. The ATP has dropped the ball so many times so many ways, but this could be the stupidest 'innovation' of all."

## The Flawed Premises

Leading doubles players are especially outraged by two discriminatory reforms that are extremely wrongheaded and counter-productive even by ATP standards. In

2004 the ATP adopted an entry ranking system with acceptance in doubles draws based on a player's ATP Entry Ranking either in singles or doubles, whichever is higher. Beginning in 2008, only a new combined doubles ranking will be used to determine entries in doubles, counting 50 percent of a player's singles points and 50 percent of his doubles points. Second, also in 2008, only players in the main draw singles will be allowed to enter doubles—with two exceptions. Tournaments can still award wild cards, and in 2008 and 2009, spots will be reserved for players with the best combined ranking not playing in the singles draw: two entries reserved in a sixteen-team draw, four entries in a twenty-four-team draw, and six entries for twenty-four- and thirty-two-team ATP Masters Series draws.

That the ATP would rank doubles players and teams based in part on their singles results is stupid, absurd, unethical, and unfair. The sport of tennis is composed of three different events: singles, doubles, and mixed doubles. Therefore, all ranking systems must include separate singles, doubles, and mixed doubles rankings based only on results in those different events. It should go without saying that how one fares in singles has absolutely nothing to do with how one fares in doubles, and vice versa.

Throughout tennis history some players have always been far better in doubles than in singles, and vice versa, regardless of how diligently they train, how hard they compete, and how well they are coached. Today that fact of life is even more pronounced because frequent serve and volleyers are virtually extinct among the elite singles players, and there are a dozen at most in the singles top 100.

To complete the blatant discrimination against doubles players—which the proposed ranking system almost accomplishes—the ATP will ban almost all doubles players and teams from doubles draws unless they are playing in the main singles draw.

Had the 2008–2009 reform been in effect for the first six months of 2005, the Bryan brothers, America's Davis Cup duo and one of the tour's top teams this decade, might not have played in most and perhaps not in any ATP tournaments. The top twenty-ranked doubles players would pretty much all be out of the sport too, aside from possibly No. 2 Max Miryni (No. 33 in singles) and No. 12 Fabrice Santoro (No. 50 in singles).

In exchange for these proven doubles standouts, doubles events might include a few probable excellent doubles players—but only if they chose to enter doubles—such as Roger Federer, 2000 U.S. Open doubles champion Lleyton Hewitt (with Mirnyi), and Rafael Nadal, who has already notched good wins with various partners. Keep in mind, though, that these singles stars may shine less brightly in doubles, and the great ATP hope that they would somehow revitalize doubles—assuming it needs to be revitalized this way in the first place—may never materialize. And watching singles stars fare poorly in doubles would prove more of a letdown than a treat for their diehard fans.

Based on recent past results, that's exactly what would happen. The top ten singles players (none of whom serve and volley often) in the ATP Champions Race, as of June 12, 2005, compiled a dismal 180–196 doubles record with ten titles and no Grand Slam titles during the previous two and a half years. In stunning contrast, during the same period, the top ten doubles players, as of June 12, 2005, racked up a 1,224–488 record with ninety-seven titles and fourteen Grand Slam titles. The worst-case scenario is that a whole host of singles specialists, will lose early and often and then, even worse (or better, depending on your viewpoint), abandon doubles.

Big-time tennis must be a meritocracy where the best doubles players, based on their hard earned and legitimate doubles records, fill up the doubles draws. It must not be a plutocracy where misguided tournament directors, who are hell-bent on driving doubles standouts from the sport to save money, fill up doubles draws mostly with singles players whose scant and/or weak doubles records don't merit inclusion.

Is No-Ad Fair? The ATP's desperate gamble also depends significantly on how the No-Ad scoring system works out. Klosterkemper said, "Singles players said they would *consider* (italics added) playing doubles on a more consistent basis if changes were made, citing the length of matches, which average more than ninety minutes, and scheduling difficulties as reasons for lack of participation."

Let's analyze No-Ad using various criteria.

Does the scoring system offer a fair test of superiority, a *sine qua non* of any athletic competition? Under the traditional scoring system, the odds are clearly greater that the more skillful player and team will eventually win a given game, i.e., that the cream will rise to the top. Unquestionably, the No-Ad method unfairly boosts the chances of the underdog who needs only one point to win a game from deuce, or 3-all. This is because with the score 3-all in No-Ad, the fluke shot, bad bounce, net cord, or incorrect line call assumes an undue significance.

Second, No-Ad also unfairly helps the Wild Slugger. How? At 3-all, the Wild Slugger knows that he needs only one point to win the game and thus one great shot. So he is encouraged to blast away, particularly when his opponent is serving. Hitting one winner isn't so hard, he figures. However, whacking winners to win two points in a row is another story entirely. Historically, the inconsistent Wild Slugger failed at that with the traditional scoring system, particularly against skillful, sound, and smart opponents. With a truly fair scoring system, the Skill Guy usually wins the close games and beats the Wild Slugger, and not the other way around.

"I played no-ad in high school and I'm not crazy about it because it brings in an element of luck that favors the weaker player," rightly argued Pete Sampras in Tennis magazine (U.S.). "The longer the match is, the better chance the better player will win. Sometimes the [ATP] tour and the ITF [International Tennis Federation] panic and try to fix this and that. But nothing's broken here."

Third, physical stamina and the mental qualities of courage, grit, and resourcefulness that complement it have long and rightly been considered vital elements in tennis. However, the adoption of tiebreakers (which preclude protracted sets), ninety-second breaks during changeovers, and dawdling between points have significantly reduced the importance of stamina. If the No-Ad method—where no game can exceed seven points—is universally accepted, stamina will be unfairly de-emphasized.

## The Entertainment Factor

Is the scoring system interesting and suspenseful? Sudden-death tiebreakers at 3-all are certainly climactic, but No-Ad's frequent tiebreaker (4-3) games generally lessen the overall tension because they are so short-lived. On the other hand, the fluctuating crises of ad-in and ad-out—which surround the temporary sanctuary of deuce—often bring out our best and worst and thus add a true excitement and strategical richness to tennis. There are far more "key" or big points with ad-ins and ad-outs, even though they do not represent simultaneous game points, than with No-Ad scoring.

Indeed, many of the greatest matches ever played featured epic battles at deuce. The 1995 Wimbledon final most riveted fans when Steffi Graf battled tenacious Arantxa Sánchez Vicario at 5-5 in the third set for a fluctuating game that lasted twenty minutes and thirty-two thrill-packed points. Graf finally won that crucial game on her sixth break point and took the classic encounter 4-6, 6-1, 7-5.

The same "win-by-two" points formula also made possible the excruciatingly exciting 1980 Wimbledon final (who can forget the 18-16 tiebreaker) between all-time greats Björn Borg and John McEnroe. Countless matches have proved the point throughout tennis history. Other examples in the Open Era include McEnroe's dramatic marathon Davis Cup matches against Mats Wilander in 1982 and Boris Becker in 1987 as well as the quarterfinal duel between archrivals and ultimate warriors Graf and Monica Seles at the 1998 Chase Championships.

## The Time Element

Can it meet the demands of tournament scheduling and television? The tiebreaker has eliminated marathon sets and shortened matches by providing a definite ending. This thirty-five-year-old innovation has made life easier for tournament officials and has helped increase television's coverage of tennis. Whatever compactness and precision the No-Ad way adds to scheduling just would not make an appreciable difference to tournaments in most cases.

A paradox is also worth noting. Sometimes the aforementioned inferior Wild Slugger will benefit from No-Ad to tighten up a match against the Skill Guy to extend what otherwise would not have been a close match into a tiebreaker or even a third set. So No-Ad can and sometimes does prolong matches, too.

## Your Money's Worth

Can it give the paying spectator his money's worth? Any system deemed unfair—as No-Ad clearly is—would dissatisfy customers as would one that shortens matches too much. Lopsided No-Ad matches have lasted a ridiculous twenty-five minutes.

## Understanding the Score

Is it simple and understandable enough for the spiraling millions who play and watch tennis around the world? The 1-2-3-4 point scoring in No-Ad may seem more conventional than the 15-30-40 of the traditional system; yet it is certainly less understandable in the total context. When you consider that the game and set and tiebreaker scoring totals are all recorded 1-2-3-4, it quickly becomes apparent that the point scoring totals must be different and distinguishable. Otherwise, players and fans would face the unenviable task of deciphering No-Ad scores (during matches) such as 1-1, 1-1 or

2-2, 2-2 or you name it! And while No-Ad would be used in doubles, the time-tested traditional scoring system would remain in singles, creating two different scoring systems and even more confusion.

Would players abide alternating between the two very different scoring systems in the same tournament, in singles and doubles matches sometimes only hours apart? You cannot be serious!

## The Image of Tennis

John H. Gray, of Greenwich, Conn., wrote a letter that was published in the August 1974 *World Tennis* magazine. It puts both scoring methods into sharp historical and sociological perspective:

> The entertainment now being staged by World Team Tennis has so little to do with what the nations of the world call "lawn tennis" that their use of the No-Ad scoring system does not give a dangerous boost to this method of scoring. However, the same cannot be said for the action taken by NCAA coaches in approving No-Ad for the collegiate championships.
>
> Have the coaches considered what will happen to a non-contact game such as lawn tennis if bodily condition, stamina and courage are removed as part of the requirements? It will indeed become the "sissy game" which it was falsely called in the period 1900-1914. Some other games, which required skill only, and which were once very popular, such as billiards and croquet, have practically disappeared.
>
> A round of golf requires much more stamina and energy than Margaret Court had to expend in winning a twenty-minute final using No-Ad scoring at a Virginia Slims tournament in Philadelphia last year.

By the early 1990s American college tennis had largely abandoned No-Ad. John Newcombe, who captured eighteen career Grand Slam doubles titles, stressed that No-Ad robbed tennis of one of its prime attractions. "The No-Ad rule was tried in college tennis in the States, and it made the tennis very mundane and that much quicker," he said in 1998. "It takes away one of the great things about the scoring system. If you can get into a long deuce game, you have a situation where you can wear your opponent down."

America's college experience, strangely enough, only encouraged the International Tennis Federation, which wanted to dispense with the advantage rule in Davis Cup and Fed Cup matches. That decision dismayed Newcombe and others. "The ITF met Davis Cup captains of the top sixteen nations at Wimbledon where the subject of the No-Ad rule was raised, and they were all unanimous that they didn't want anything to do with it," said Newcombe in 1998.

Not deterred by that prestigious opposition, the ITF decided to experiment with No-Ad in lower divisions of the Davis Cup and the Fed Cup and other events during 1999. In one of the summer studies of No-Ad at Satellite and Futures tournaments in

Europe, the researchers found that "No-Ad matches [were] only some four minutes shorter on average."

Tournament directors, television sports executives, and ATP decision-makers should seriously note that finding.

## Please Don't Amputate!

Several of the same compelling arguments against No-Ad scoring also apply to the ATP's reform that would amputate doubles sets so that they are played to five games rather than six, with a tiebreaker played at 4-4, instead of the traditional 6-6. Again, tennis is a sport of skill and will, and abbreviated sets not only unfairly help the less-skilled team but will sometimes backfire by prolonging, rather than shortening, matches.

How then can doubles reach its vast pro potential?

## Here are 10 suggestions.

1.   Start doubles on Wednesday to encourage first- and second-round singles losers to enter.

2.   Televise all doubles finals after the singles.

3.   Assign an ATP and WTA communications director to doubles only, and publicize leading teams with a major promotional campaign. "Now you can show up at a tournament and have no idea doubles is going on because there is nothing in the program, nothing up on the walls, no draws posted," points out Knowles.

4.   *Immediately* follow the 7:00 PM singles match with a doubles match—or start the doubles at 6:30 PM, followed by a singles at approximately 8:00 or 8:30 PM.

5.   Require matching shirts and shorts for doubles teams.

6.   Have doubles teams appear together in autograph sessions.

7.   Have doubles teams conduct "Kids Days" so that doubles is explained and showcased.

8.   Nearly double the measly 17 percent of Tennis Master Series total prize money (and 20 percent overall) that doubles receives to 30 percent.

9.   The season-ending Tennis Masters Cup in Houston—where doubles-only sessions are consistently sold out—should be studied as the "doubles model" by the tour's sixty-three other tournament directors and their staffs.

10.   Scintillating doubles points, especially spectacular net duels that elicit "Wow! Did you see that?" reactions from spectators should be regularly featured on ESPN's top highlights and other "Points of the Day" segments.

The latest rule changes are a trial of the sport in general, not just doubles," warns

Woodbridge. "If these doubles rules become permanent, it will only be a matter of time before ATP events will be trying it in singles as well. Then we will have a full-fledged World TeamTennis format. That would be disastrous for pro tennis."

"Tournament directors must look after their core fans," stresses Woodbridge. "On-site fans are tennis players who buy tickets to an event early in tournament when they can afford the prices of the tickets. The corporate people are the people we need, but they come at the end of the event when it is cool to be seen, have lunch and then watch one match and go home, regardless of who is on the court. If the ATP takes away the game tennis fans play in doubles, it will anger them off to the point that they won't come at all. This will have a domino effect where they won't watch tennis on TV on the weekend, and the ratings go down, and the game falls into a further decline. Tournaments must look after the true tennis fan."

Aussie great Newcombe once rightly said, "A good doubles match can be one of the fastest and most exciting of all sports events." In doubles, fans can see highly athletic serving and volleying, an entertaining playing style almost extinct in singles. An added bonus is rapid-fire, crowd-thrilling net duels rarely seen in singles but quite common in doubles. So let's showcase as many terrific doubles matches as possible—without ruining the scoring system, discriminating against talented doubles players, or diminishing doubles.

The top doubles players, along with some singles stars, have mobilized to preserve and improve doubles. "Doubles is too great a game to destroy," says Mike Bryan. "With the help of the players, fans, officials, media, sponsors and the rest of the tennis world this summer, we'll stop these rule changes from ever happening. We'll save doubles."

Doubles lovers of the world unite!

---

**FASCINATING FACTS:**

- In 2005 Martina Navratilova, the greatest doubles player in tennis history, called the proposed doubles reforms on the ATP Tour "disgusting" and "ridiculous."
- The late Supreme Court Chief Justice William H. Rehnquist (1986-2005) always hired three law clerks per term—instead of the permitted five—in order to maintain his regular foursome for doubles matches.
- In 2007, the women's doubles champions in Israel were Nadine Fahum, an Arab, and Yulia Glushko, a Russian Jew.

# 6

# Tennis vs. Golf: Which Sport Is Tougher?
## 2007

**W**hen Tiger Woods recently said Roger Federer "is probably the best athlete on the planet," I began to believe tennis finally got the respect it deserved—from a golfer. Tennis had been dismissed in America as a "sissy sport" for its first seventy-five years, even by golfers such as President Dwight D. Eisenhower. After tennis maven Ted Tinling, a lieutenant colonel in the Royal Army Intelligence Corps in 1943, asked permission to stage an exhibition match for the Red Cross in Algiers, Gen. Eisenhower fired back a terse memo: "No, this is a man's war and tennis is a woman's game." Never mind that tennis, unlike golf, had by then diverged from its effete, country club origins and become a grueling, dynamic sport dominated by public parks players like Ellsworth Vines, Don Budge, and Bobby Riggs.

Since that period tennis champions Pancho Gonzalez, Rod Laver, Björn Borg, John McEnroe, Pete Sampras, Martina Navratilova, Billie Jean King, Steffi Graf, Justine Henin and Serena Williams have ranked among the world's elite athletes. In France at the 1979 European Superstars competition, a medley of athletic events staged as a television program, Borg beat an Olympic medal-winning hurdler, while capturing six of the eight events. In 2002 Federer, Sweden's Thomas Johansson and several other ATP players took on a National Hockey League team during the Canadian Open in Toronto and lost only 7-5. "Their anticipation was unreal," said Nick Kypreos, the leading scorer in the game and one of the extremely impressed hockey players.

When the incomparable Michael Jordan was asked which female athlete he most admired, he tellingly replied, "Tennis is a lot like basketball in physical terms, and Chris Evert did everything with class." As for golf, Jordan, a recreational player himself, contended, "You golfers may make a lot of money, but you're a long way from being athletes."

The tennis vs. golf debate was renewed when the February 5, 2007 *Sports Illustrated* ran a point-counterpoint piece titled: "Kings of the Mountain—Roger Federer and Tiger Woods are good pals who won't argue about who's the most dominant athlete around. But Two SI writers will." The golf advocate maintained Woods amassed a superior record against much stouter competition and thus is "the best athlete of his generation." His tennis counterpart pointed out that Federer won ten of the last fifteen Grand Slam events and displays his genius in a game that demands a full range of physical skills. The tennis proponent also slipped in this zinger: "Once in a while, you'll actually hear people wonder if golf is a sport."

People should wonder. If you can't make a case that golf actually is a bona-fide sport requiring true athleticism rather than merely a competition like croquet, then there is no debate. After all, you wouldn't compare the preeminent yachtsmen or bowlers with the greatest football or baseball players. To prove this self-evident assertion, let's analyze the criteria for athleticism and find out how tennis and golf compare to each other.

## Physical Fitness

Tennis players must have exceptional cardiovascular fitness or face severe consequences when competing against opponents who do. A 1986 survey of 126 men touring pros revealed an extremely low average body-fat percentage of 6.4. That was better than the measurements of pro basketball players (8.9 percent), pro baseball players (12.6 percent), and pro football linemen (15.6 percent). With both shot and foot speed faster today, there is every reason to believe men tennis players are even fitter. And the women, especially the supremely dedicated Russians, appear leaner and better conditioned than ever.

What about golfers? Veteran golf pro Bob Goalby once conceded, "Golfers aren't athletes. A golfer doesn't have to be in shape to do anything but hit a golf ball. I think an athlete should be able to run. The pro golfer is not generally in great physical shape."

Jack Nicklaus, whose eighteen major titles make him arguably the greatest golfer in history, looked as much as twenty-five pounds overweight during his prime. John Daly, the 1991 PGA and 1995 British Open champion, is obese as was Craig "The Walrus" Stadler, who at 5'10" and 250 pounds, still earned more than ten million dollars. Chris Patton, even fatter at 6'1" and 300 pounds, captured the 1989 U.S. Amateur title. Billy Casper and Lee Trevino also lost the battle of the bulge but won major titles. At the 2007 U.S. Open Championship, Ángel Cabrera, a beer-bellied, cigarette-smoking Argentine, triumphed. Massive Meg Mallon, who notched eighteen career victories, including two U.S. Women's Open titles, and ranks No. 5 on the career money list, proves that a lean and sleek body isn't required to walk, stroke and win in golf. If these hefty hitters ever tried to play pro tennis, they'd become exhausted, ill or injured after a few games.

## Hand-Eye and Foot-Eye Coordination

World-class tennis requires superb hand-eye coordination to hit a moving ball with varying amounts of oncoming speed and spin that is further affected by other variables such as the wind and at times unpredictable bounces on grass and clay courts. Returning a bullet serve of more than 120 miles per hour is nearly as challenging as hitting a Major League baseball pitch—often called the most difficult thing to do in sports—and most tennis shots are hit on the run or the dead run. Arthur Ashe, in his 1981 book, *Off the Court*, stressed, "Foot-and-eye coordination is more important in tennis than hand-eye coordination . . . It's the great feet that win Grand Slam titles." Contrast these great demands with pro golf, where a stationary person only has to swing at a stationary object about seventy times over five hours.

### Acceleration and Speed

If you can't get to the ball, you can't hit it. Every tennis champion—except for Lindsay Davenport, a phenomenal striker of the ball—has displayed excellent court coverage. "The first two steps taken toward a tennis ball usually determine whether or not the ball will be reached, and therefore instantaneous speed, or explosiveness, is much more important in tennis than either aerobic or anaerobic power," pointed out Dr. Robert Arnot and Charles Gaines in their 1984 book, *SportSelection*. Borg, Michael Chang, Lleyton Hewitt, Rafael Nadal, Federer, Graf, Navratilova and Henin possess not only extraordinary speed and acceleration but also the related movement skills of agility, recovery and leaping. None of these intrinsic athletic abilities are needed in golf. David Duval, the world's No. 1 golfer in 1999, admitted, "I would like to think of myself as an athlete first, but I don't want to do a disservice to the real ones."

In 1996 former NBA standout John Lucas, a college tennis All-American and later a World TeamTennis player, told *Tennis* magazine that Chang could have been "an unbelievable defensive guard in basketball." Lucas rated Jordan, David Thompson, Dennis Rodman, McEnroe and Jimmy Connors as the top five athletes he ever saw, coached, or competed against, saying, "They all are absolutely in the same class."

### Reflexes and Touch

Lightning-fast hand reflexes are required for skillful volleying, especially in net duels involving all four players in doubles. "A good doubles match can be one of the fastest and most exciting of all sports events," all-time doubles great John Newcombe told *World Tennis* magazine in 1977. Hand speed, split-second reactions, and the concomitant quick decision-making of any kind are never needed in golf.

Subtle touch is another valuable athletic ability involving hands, and gifted players produce dazzling drop shots, drop volleys and lob volleys. Touch does play a key role in golf when putting and hitting irons to the greens, but, importantly, it's never achieved against a fast-moving ball and on the run.

### Strength and Stamina

Physical strength counts for a lot on every shot in tennis, especially serves and smashes, except for lobs and finesse shots. Many players pump iron to gain the necessary strength to generate power and handle opponents' power. While super-strong Andy Roddick holds the fastest-serve record with an incredible 155-mph rocket, women also have embraced strength as never before. In 2004, 151 women whacked serves of 100 mph or more, and fifty-eight blasted serves of 110 mph or more. The sheer power of tennis today impresses even casual followers. When an aide introduced Federer to Pope Benedict XVI last year, the pontiff said, "Tennis is a powerful sport."

Andre Agassi, who packed 174 pounds on his muscular 5'11" frame, was renowned for a brutal training regimen devised by conditioning coach Gil Reyes. Agassi could bench press an amazing 315 pounds. Some golfers, such as Tiger Woods, at least appear in tip-top shape, and the driving distance on the pro golf tours has steadily increased to the point where some players regularly drive more than 300 yards.

However, imagine sprinting for and pounding balls for three, four, or even five hours and broiling under a ninety-degree sun without any substitutes or halftimes, and you get some sense of how much stamina tennis requires. That tennis occasionally becomes a "survival of the fittest" test (a record eight men retired due to illness and injury at the 2006 French Open) recently prompted the ATP Tour to try to abolish best-of-five-set finals at Masters Series tournaments.

Whether "golf is a good walk spoiled," as Mark Twain quipped, is debatable. What's not debatable is that walking eighteen holes with prolonged rest breaks over five hours is minimal exercise. Consider this: a golf swing takes 1 to 1.5 seconds, and the actual motion in an *entire round* totals 1.5 minutes. No wonder the *Journal of New England Medicine* magazine in 2001 reported that golf has "the exercise co-efficient of gardening." Ironically, spectators who follow a particular foursome for a round wind up with as much exercise as their favorite players.

## Mastering Technique

Nicklaus, a tennis lover who has three grass courts and a clay court at his North Palm Beach, Florida, estate, once acknowledged that golf is easier because you have basically only one swing, aside from putting. In sharp contrast, tennis ranks as one of the most difficult sports to learn and master because of its many different swings.

A typical young player today has a semi-Western topspin forehand and changes his grip and swing for a two-handed backhand and changes it again to a Continental grip to hit serves and volleys, which require completely different technique. Supplementary shots such as smashes, lobs, and drop shots entail more muscle memory. Several variations on all these shots, such as service returns, passing shots, kick serves, approach shots, drop volleys, etc., are required for a complete, all-court game. Correct stroke technique still won't guarantee topnotch shots. "By far the greatest majority of errors originate through incorrect footwork," wrote Joy and Tony Mottram in *Modern Lawn Tennis*.

Golf pros, though, must master technique for fourteen different clubs with tiny "sweet spots" to control small balls on an endlessly diverse array of challenging fairways, fiendish roughs, unforgiving sand traps, and tricky greens in changing weather conditions. "A tennis ball is on the strings for four milliseconds. A golf ball is on the club face for one half of a millisecond," pointed out Vic Braden, a noted sports science researcher and author of several tennis books, in *Inside Tennis* magazine in 1987. "We brought some of the best golfers to our center, like Jack Nicklaus and Tom Watson, and shot them at 22,000 frames per second. We found that the slightest, barely visible turn of the club face would have dramatic effects on the golf ball. In tennis, you have about a nineteen-degree range in which you can hit a ball and at least keep it in the court. But in golf, less than one degree of error means that you're in the trees."

## The Mental Game

Golfers may concede tennis is more athletic and physical, but they'll passionately maintain that nothing in sports is more terrifying than standing over a three-foot putt with $100,000, or even a twenty-dollar hacker's bet, on the line. But is golf a tough sport mentally? Is it tougher than tennis?

Let's start with the various arguments about tournament rules and formats. Golfers aver that they have no chance for redemption following a disastrous shot into a pond, while tennis players repeatedly take second serve "mulligans," no matter how atrocious their first serves. Imagine the almost unbearable pressure, they insist, if you know that just one errant shot can turn what looked like an easy par-5 hole into a nightmarish quadruple bogie 9 that ruins your round and perhaps even your entire tournament. Tennis aficionados reply that, except for a first serve fault, every other bad shot during a vital game or on a big point—especially match point, set point, or game point—can prove extremely costly. And tennis' clever scoring system, featuring deuce, ad-in and ad-out, ensures plenty of high-pressure, high-stakes points throughout the match.

Although golfers must make the cut, which the elite do almost all the time, a mediocre round allows them to muddle on. However, mediocrity often spells defeat and thus elimination in any round on the extremely talent-deep ATP and WTA Tours where upsets abound. If players don't bring their A games, they could easily lose in an hour or two. When that happens, tennis players often do something relaxing, like golf.

Ah, but golfers counter that nothing could be more treacherous than trying to conquer not only a devilish course, but also *one hundred* players. Under that absurd numbers criterion, the Boston Marathon with 20,000 runners (albeit all but a few are distant finishers) would top the "toughest competition" category. Sure, Tiger and Phil and Annika and Karrie must score better than all the other golfers, but they rarely face them directly.

"I may go out and shoot a sixty-six. But, it doesn't prevent you from going out and shooting a sixty-five," rightly asserts Charlie Pasarell, the Indian Wells tournament director and No. 1-ranked American in 1967, in the *Los Angeles Times*. "In fact, you may not even know that I've shot a sixty-six. You never have that real, direct head-on competition. However, in tennis, if I've hit a good tennis shot against you, I've probably put you in a defensive mode, and chances are, you will not hit a good shot but will probably hit a weaker shot."

"Hogan never really beats Snead, Nicklaus doesn't beat Palmer," argues Pasarell. "But, in tennis, Lendl beats McEnroe. Laver beats the world."

Agreeing with that analysis, Fuzzy Zoeller, the 1979 Masters and 1984 U.S. Open champion, said, "To me, tennis is the most impressive sport. In golf, you hit your best shot and you can brag about it. In tennis, you hit your best shot and some little [expletive deleted] is on the other side hitting it back to you."

Other golfers fire back that on occasion their game also showcases head-to-head competition: match play. But there's something embarrassing worth mentioning about that. When the going gets tough, their "Tiger" performs more like a pussycat. At the PGA's Match-Play Championships—where sixty-four leading players compete in a single-elimination draw—Tiger has won only twice in eight tries and hasn't even reached the quarterfinals during the last three years. Although Tiger can brag about his 10–1 PGA Tour record in tournament playoffs, he owns a dismal 10–13–2 career match play record in the prestigious Ryder Cup.

In contrast, The Great Ones in tennis shrug off and even thrive on *mano-a-mano* pressure. Federer has won nine of his first ten Grand Slam finals, while Sampras captured fourteen of eighteen major finals during his incomparable career. The Swiss superstar also boasts an astounding, and probably unbreakable, record of twenty-four straight victories in tournaments finals, doubling the previous record of twelve shared by Borg and McEnroe. Handling the terrific pressure from hyper-patriotic Germans, Boris Becker racked up a sensational 38–3 singles record in Davis Cup, while Navratilova was a perfect 15–0 and Evert 40–2 in Fed Cup singles. When it matters most, tennis champions often show poise, grit and courage to prevail against their toughest rivals.

Finally, Dr. James E. Loehr, the author of fourteen books including *Mental Toughness Training for Sports*, surveyed forty-three sports in 1989, to measure their physical/mental/emotional demand factors. Loehr used twenty-five criteria, such as aerobic demands, real physical opponent, no coaching, multiple competitors in a single day, no clock, one-on-one competition, opportunities for trash talking and gamesmanship, ranking system (local, regional, national), no time-outs/no substitutions, and fierce personal rivalries. Tennis placed an impressive No. 2 with 101 points, considerably ahead of golf, which had eighty-five points.

## Sports Switchers

No world-class golfer has ever taken up tennis and developed into a world-class player. Nor come even close to that. Of course, since leading golfers can often play their leisurely pastime at a relatively high level into their forties or even fifties (Nicklaus finished an amazing sixth at the 1998 Masters at age fifty-eight), they have little incentive to try more demanding sports. Still, it's noteworthy that a few former tennis stars and lesser lights have excelled, and usually rather quickly, at golf.

Ellsworth Vines, the most successful tennis/golfer, won the 1931 and 1932 U.S. Championships and 1932 Wimbledon and retired from competitive tennis in 1939 and became a golf pro. Vines twice finished in the top ten in annual money earnings during the era of Byron Nelson, Ben Hogan, and Sam Snead. The lanky Southern Californian reached the semifinals of the 1951 PGA Championship and once beat the legendary Hogan in a playoff.

Mary K. Browne, a Californian who collected thirteen Grand Slam titles from 1912 to 1926 and ranked No. 3 in the world in 1921, also transferred her athletic talent to golf. In one of the most remarkable feats in women's sports history, Browne lost in the 1924 U.S. semifinal to Helen Wills in three sets, and three weeks later she upset the renowned Glenna Collett Vare to make the U.S. Women's Golf Championships final.

Althea Gibson, who broke the color barrier in tennis and won two Wimbledons, two U.S. and a French crown in the late 1950s, belatedly turned to golf in her thirties and became the first black woman on the LPGA tour. She played in 171 tournaments from 1963 to 1977 without winning a title, though she did set a course-record sixty-eight in 1966 at Pleasant Valley in Sutton, Massachusetts.

"Time ran out on her," Kathy Whitworth, the grande dame of women's golf champions, told the *Boston Sunday Globe* in 2001. "There's no question she would have been one of the greats otherwise. Absolutely no question."

Scott Draper, a gifted Australian serve and volleyer with wins over Agassi, Jim Courier, Becker (on grass) and Patrick Rafter (on grass), retired from pro tennis in 2005. In February of 2007, Draper shot a final-round 7-under-par 65 to capture the New South Wales PGA Championship by one stroke for his first pro golf victory. It moves past the improbable to near the impossible to believe that a thirty-two-year-old, former top fifty-ranked golf pro could trade his clubs for a racket and *two years later* win an equivalent event on the pro tennis tour.

Could Fred Couples beat Sampras? Get a set or even a couple games off him? It's inconceivable. The modest Sampras likes to downplay his golf prowess, but he won a driving contest at a pro-celebrity tournament in 1997 with a 332-yard monster drive. When tour standout Couples golfed with "Pistol Pete," an 8-handicap golfer in 1999, the tennis guy won. "He played better than I did," confided Couples.

Golf is obviously not on an athletic par with tennis. But, that settled, why should it even matter to golf and tennis lovers? As the famous Latin maxim advises: "De gustibus non est disputandum"—"There is no disputing about tastes."

### Tennis

| Physical/Mental/Emotional Demand Factors | Pressure/Demand Rating |
|---|---|
| 1. One-on-one competition (individual vs team) | 4 |
| 2. No time outs/no substitutions | 5 |
| 3. No coaching | 5 |
| 4. No clock | 5 |
| 5. Multiple competitors in single day | 5 |
| 6. Ranking system (local, regional, national) | 4 |
| 7. Financial burden on parents | 4 |
| 8. Opportunity to influence outcome by cheating | 4 |
| 9. Real physical opponent | 5 |
| 10. No off season | 4 |
| 11. Fine motor skills | 4 |
| 12. Gross motor skills | 4 |
| 13. Non-continuous vs continuous play | 4 |
| 14. Younger competitors can compete with older | 4 |
| 15. Aerobic demands | 4 |
| 16. Anaerobic demands | 4 |
| 17. Fear of getting hurt (injury) | 1 |
| 18. Moment to moment concentration requirements | 4 |
| 19. Influence of variable climate/weather conditions | 4 |
| 20. Variability of playing surfaces eg. fast, slow | 3 |
| 21. Impact of equipment on outcome | 3 |
| 22. Opportunities for trash talking and gamesmanship | 4 |
| 23. Fierce personal rivalries | 5 |
| 24. Scoring system contributes to pressure dynamics | 4 |
| 25. Travel requirements involved in high level competition | 4 |
| **Total** | **101** |

| Scoring System | | | | |
|---|---|---|---|---|
| 1 | 2 | 3 | 4 | 5 |
| Not a Demand Factor | | | | Signficant Demand Factor |

**Pressure/Demand Ranking by Sport**

| | |
|---|---|
| 1. Figure Skating | 103 |
| 2. Tennis | 101 |
| 3. Boxing | 99 |
| 4. Gymnastics | 98 |
| 5. Hockey | 94 |

---

| | |
|---|---|
| Golf | 85 |
| Soccer | 69 |

## Golf (not Matchplay)

| Physical/Mental/Emotional Demand Factors | Pressure/Demand Rating |
|---|:---:|
| 1. One-on-one competition (individual vs team) | 2 |
| 2. No time outs/no substitutions | 5 |
| 3. No coaching | 2 |
| 4. No clock | 4 |
| 5. Multiple competitors in single day | 3 |
| 6. Ranking system (local, regional, national) | 3 |
| 7. Financial burden on parents | 5 |
| 8. Opportunity to influence outcome by cheating | 4 |
| 9. Real physical opponent | 2 |
| 10. No off season | 4 |
| 11. Fine motor skills | 4 |
| 12. Gross motor skills | 2 |
| 13. Non-continuous vs continuous play | 5 |
| 14. Younger competitors can compete with older | 5 |
| 15. Aerobic demands | 2 |
| 16. Anaerobic demands | 1 |
| 17. Fear of getting hurt (injury) | 1 |
| 18. Moment to moment concentration requirements | 5 |
| 19. Influence of variable climate/weather conditions | 4 |
| 20. Variability of playing surfaces eg. fast, slow | 4 |
| 21. Impact of equipment on outcome | 4 |
| 22. Opportunities for trash talking and gamesmanship | 2 |
| 23. Fierce personal rivalries | 4 |
| 24. Scoring system contributes to pressure dynamics | 4 |
| 25. Travel requirements involved in high level competition | 4 |

| | |
|---|:---:|
| **Total** | **85** |

| Scoring System | | | | |
|:---:|:---:|:---:|:---:|:---:|
| 1 | 2 | 3 | 4 | 5 |
| Not a Demand Factor | | | | Signficant Demand Factor |

© LGE Performance Systems/dba Human Performance Institute

# 7

# Should Tiebreakers Replace Deciding Sets?

# 2001

*O! many a shaft, at random sent,*
*Finds mark the archer little meant!*

—Sir Walter Scott

**A** radical scoring change is spreading across the tennis world. Tiebreakers replaced the entire traditional third sets in the mixed doubles events at the 2001 Australian and U.S. Opens. Will this highly controversial reform become the norm in singles and doubles events at all professional tournaments? Is it a brilliant innovation whose time has come, or a well-intentioned but bad idea destined to damage or even ruin tennis?

From the same land Down Under come two diametrically opposed viewpoints. "It's tragic to see where doubles is headed," says Paul McNamee, director of the Australian Open and a former doubles champion. "We want to get doubles back in front of full houses where fans can appreciate it, and we can make stars out of doubles players. We want to do it in a way that adds value to tournaments and does not hurt the integrity of doubles. It seems that two sets and a super tiebreaker is achieving all of those things."

Equally concerned about our sport's future, Todd Woodbridge, doubles great and president of the ATP Players Council, predicts, "If we start implementing a tiebreaker [instead of a third set] in mixed doubles, eventually it's going to go to men's doubles and women's doubles, and in the long term, singles as well. And then tennis is no longer a true test of skill, and nothing like we've known it. We have a successful scoring system, and we're changing that. What they're doing to mixed doubles now is the beginning of the downfall of the whole game."

The question of whether tennis should adopt a tiebreaker in lieu of a third and deciding set—a revolutionary rule change by any standard—has unfortunately engendered little public debate so far. Let's examine it from several vantage points, using the most important criteria, and determine which position holds up better under rigorous analysis.

## The Sine Qua Non Test

Professional tennis must always be a fair test of skill and will. If a scoring system does not pass that "fair test" criterion, then nothing else matters. But what constitutes a "fair test"?

The match must be long enough to determine whom the better player or doubles team is. Historically, the only debate had focused on best three-of-five set versus best two-of-three-set matches. In 1902 when the leading women players at the United States Championships were told they would no longer be allowed to play best-of-five-set singles battles like the men, they protested vehemently, but to no avail. From 1984 to 1998 the women played best-of-five singles finals in the season-ending Chase Championships to mixed reviews.

At the four Grand Slam tournaments, men's singles matches have always adhered to the best-of-five format. The rationale is that a longer test—within reason, of course, and the arrival of tiebreakers ended unreasonable marathon sets —ensures that the cream eventually rises to the top. Many champions, most notably Björn Borg, used their skill, never-say-die spirit, strategy, and stamina to overcome the loss of two early sets and prevail in the end. And memorable five-set duels, such as Ivan Lendl's 1984 French Open final turnaround against John McEnroe and Mats Wilander's comeback win over Pat Cash in the 1988 Australian Open final, rank among the most thrilling matches in tennis history. They could never have happened had mere tiebreakers replaced the deciding sets.

Ambivalence has marked the men's doubles event at the Slams. For example, fourteen of the sixteen Australian Opens from 1969 to 1983 used best-two-of-three sets, and since then the final featured best-three-of-five sets (in 2002 the final will revert to best two of three); the French and U.S. Opens switched to the shorter format in 1990 and 1993, respectively; and Wimbledon has always used the longer format. In six years from 1894 to 1900, women's doubles at the United States Championships played best-of-five sets.

Since its Grand Slam inception at the 1887 United States Championships, mixed doubles has remained a best-two-of-three-sets affair except for eleven times there from 1888 to 1901 when the longer format was in effect.

However, the shocking amputation of the deciding set in a match completely fails the fair test criterion. After Woodbridge combined with Rennae Stubbs to win the treasured 2001 U.S. Open mixed doubles crown, both derided the gimmick as a "chook raffle." That's a slang reference from Australia's less cosmopolitan past when football, lawn bowls clubs, and pubs conducted fundraising chook raffles, or lotteries, with the prize being a frozen chook (chicken).

"If you're playing at the U.S. Open, the pinnacle of U.S. tournaments and a Grand Slam event, you should play it in the toughest circumstances that you can," argues Woodbridge. "And that doesn't mean playing a shortened version of the game.

You should be playing [with a scoring system] where the strongest, the fittest, and the best win."

Indeed, playing a mere ten-point super tiebreaker after splitting two sets would be the equivalent of the NBA playing a five-minute overtime period after only three quarters of play. Or soccer playing an overtime after sixty minutes, rather than after ninety minutes of regulation.

"The third-set super tiebreaker is not a true test, and the best player or team doesn't always win," asserts Pat Cash, the 1987 Wimbledon singles champion and 1984 Wimbledon doubles finalist with McNamee. "It is usually the player or team with momentum at the time that wins.

"I know from more experience than almost anyone that the third-set super tiebreaker evens the players out," says Cash. "This [shortened] format was introduced on the seniors [Champions] tour so the older players like Connors and McEnroe could win over the younger, fitter players. But two sets and a tiebreaker for the Australian Open or a U.S. Open title and hundreds of thousands of dollars? As one of my old friends used to say, 'You cannot be serious!'"

When asked if what McNamee calls the "best of two sets"—an oxymoronic and blatantly stupid expression—is fair, McNamee fires back, "Absolutely. Of course, it is. Is the third-set tiebreaker a fair test of skill?"

Of course, it is—even if three of the four majors choose not to use a twelve-point tiebreaker in the deciding set. That's because the tiebreaker was created to shorten and enliven sets, which thirty years ago had too often become protracted, and not replace them. It should be quite obvious that a player must get to 6-all in games in order to earn the right to play a tiebreaker, regardless of which set it is.

McNamee doesn't agree with that, either. "It's where you draw the line," he claims. "To get to one-set-all, you've had two sets played. Is three sets fairer than five sets?"

But isn't best-of-three sets the minimum length required to achieve fairness? McNamee dismissively says, "the historical minimum is three sets. You're being arbitrary."

Arbitrary? On the contrary, tennis' clever and nuanced scoring system was thoroughly debated and created with wisdom and vision during the 1870s. It has indisputably passed the test of time. Unlike soccer and ice hockey, which suffer from too little scoring, and basketball, which stockpiles points at an incredible rate, tennis points count more or less depending on the situation and score. Hence, the exciting, big-point expressions, such as "break point," "game point," "set point," and "match point."

Because of that a tennis player can win fewer total points and even fewer total games and still win a match, but he still must win more sets. So winning those sets must fairly and fully test competitors athletically, physically, and mentally. And unduly shortened sets clearly preclude that.

"Doubles isn't a fair test of stamina anyway," scoffs McNamee. Doubles does generally require much less stamina than singles. But traditional-scoring doubles definitely tests a player's endurance on hot, humid days, during long, grueling matches, and whenever he is still involved in other events.

"I can tell you that a super tiebreaker would be tougher mentally than a set," insists McNamee. That's certainly not true when a super tiebreaker is compared to a final set where opposing teams battle to 6-games-all and *then* have to play a tiebreaker—which is the only valid comparison here.

Does luck—a net cord, horrendous bounce, vicious gust of wind resulting in a fluke shot, or an incorrect line call, etc.—become too big a factor when a super tiebreaker alone decides the final set, the match and sometimes a Grand Slam championship?

Compared to a regular tiebreaker (where the first player to win seven points by a margin of at least two points prevails), the super tiebreaker (where the first player to win ten points by a margin of at least two points prevails) "is a good compromise because the players feel luck is less of a factor," contends McNamee. "The super tiebreaker is like half a set of tennis." Ah, but the correct comparison is not between two different kinds of tiebreakers to replace an entire set, but between traditional scoring and the super tiebreaker for the entire deciding set.

Woodbridge rejects McNamee's so-called compromise and points to his U.S. Open mixed doubles final, his second experience with the super tiebreaker. He and Stubbs comfortably won the first set 6-4 against Leander Paes and Lisa Raymond. "We slipped a little at 6-5 in the second set, they got some momentum, and all of a sudden, we're down match point in the tiebreaker," recalls Woodbridge. "And we had to regroup quickly. Had we gone to a normal set, we thought we would have won comfortably.

"So, no, the super tiebreaker is not a test of skill because it came down to a little bit of luck," argues Woodbridge. "We actually got lucky at the end of the [11-9] tiebreaker. The tiebreaker took away an element so important in our [traditional] scoring system. That element is that you always have a chance to get back into a match, even if you're down 5-love in the final set."

McNamee regards that championship match as "very interesting. There was a lot of media commentary against it. But it actually had 20,000 people watching it and worldwide TV. The U.S. Open mixed doubles final was probably the most-watched doubles match in the last 20 years in tennis. You have to be fair and look at the positives."

More important, Mac, you have to look at the big picture. The mixed doubles final received unprecedented exposure only because it served as the warm-up act for the eagerly awaited quarterfinal showdown between fiery, rising stars Lleyton Hewitt and Andy Roddick. "Since the mixed doubles final was televised in prime time [7:30 PM EDT], I suppose one could claim it was the most-watched doubles match ever. But that's damning it with faint praise," says Lawrence Jeziak, the respected *Tennis Week* TV columnist. "I don't recall another doubles match being televised in prime time."

Did 20,000 fired-up fans really flock to see a match featuring a dynamic new scoring system, as McNamee implies? "I don't think 20,000 people watched it live," says Jeziak. "More accurately, it was played in front of 20,000 seats. Based on my TV viewing perspective, most of those seats were empty."

What McNamee does acknowledge, however, is that "generally, players have been opposed to it. Doubles players would prefer to play the maximum-length match. They obviously feel it diminishes their court time"—almost suggesting that everything would be fine if these stubborn doubles players just wouldn't be such court hogs. But everyone can see that's not why players are objecting.

## The Rationale for Reform

In January 2001, ATP Tour officers and staff, tournament directors and players' representatives met in Melbourne to discuss the future of doubles. Since nearly all of tennis' marquee men's players [viz. singles stars] have abandoned doubles and mixed doubles, the ATP decided it would reciprocate.

The bottom-line-minded ATP concluded that low-profile doubles standouts (Jonas Björkman, Don Johnson, Woodbridge, Jared Palmer and David Rikl top the doubles rankings) generate little interest and ticket, sponsor and TV revenue, and thus they didn't justify all the prize money, accommodation expenses, and court time they were receiving. Henceforth, despite the protests of numerous players, the ATP abolished tour-qualifying events for doubles.

The amputation of doubles court time particularly baffles Woodbridge. "The problem we're facing is that tournament directors want less matches on the courts. I thought the more matches you have on court the better for people to watch," maintains Woodbridge. "Keeping the qualies and playing three full sets are vital for another reason: the development of players' games. If young players can play doubles early in their careers on the ATP Tour, they develop into much-better, well-rounded singles players, too. You need doubles. That's why every player in Australia has always played doubles."

Far more important than merely reducing expenses and perhaps inducing a few wavering singles players to enter doubles events, the real rationale for reform was resuscitating doubles by making it more fan-friendly, according to McNamee.

"The problem is, in some of the doubles finals, including our own, the stadium is a third full, less than a third full," says McNamee. "What are you going to do about that?"

The McNamee solution is the "best-of-two-sets" format that he'd like to establish at all levels of the game. "We feel that format has a lot of benefits for tournaments and for the future. And that goes all the way from Grand Slam to grass-roots tennis," says McNamee. "So we were very keen to introduce it in the [Australian Open] mixed doubles event.

"From the tournament perspective, we could schedule better . . . we could value out for the spectators and get more matches on Centre Court," says McNamee. "There are three matches in the day, and then the evening session starts at seven PM. Sometimes the day session would end at four fifteen PM. Instead of just saying to everybody, 'See you later, folks, tonight's session starts at seven PM we would bring in a mixed doubles match that was originally scheduled on an outside court and put it on Centre Court, so the public would get an extra match. And then the evening session would still start on time.

"If you put a [traditional] three-set match on, there's no guarantee the evening session would still start on time," explains McNamee. "We've been caught with this [problem] before. It gives you enormous flexibility in scheduling, which three-set matches don't give you because you don't know how long they're going to last. The great advantage of best-of-two sets is it, effectively, can go only two hours maximum."

That claim doesn't ring true, though. A couple of 7-5 or 7-6 sets, especially with a lot of long games, plus a 12-10 or 16-14 tiebreaker, could easily take two-and-a-half hours, perhaps even longer. Also, couldn't the afternoon session start a bit earlier to accommodate four Centre Court matches more often?

As it turned out, only eight of the thirty-one mixed doubles matches at the 2001 Australian went three sets and used "best-of-two sets" scoring. And only two of those during the Oz Open fortnight became the Centre Court scheduling panacea McNamee fervently touts.

Those facts don't seem to dissuade or deter the bigwigs at Tennis Australia one iota. "It's basically got unanimous support within Tennis Australia," crows McNamee. "It was a recommendation from the Brand Tennis Committee, which has all the directors of the divisions in Tennis Australia represented. We all should be trying to improve tennis, the brand, because we've got to compete with other brands out there, which are other sports, other franchises, other forms of entertainment."

"The 'best-of-two' actually has a lot of momentum," continues McNamee. "It's being introduced throughout the country. It's being used in national junior doubles competitions and in league competitions in Victoria and Western Australia." (In the U.S. this format has also steadily spread in the amateur game; and college tennis has relegated doubles matches to disgracefully mutilated 8-game "pro sets.")

Geoff Pollard, the president of Tennis Australia, unequivocally supports the scoring reform. "Tennis is probably the only sport where the approximate length of the match is unknown, and the huge variation has many repercussions in scheduling and other factors for the players involved, spectators and TV," Pollard asserts. "The 'best-of-two' is the only scoring method that effectively tackles the length of a tennis match."

The power of television can never be underrated. "They [TV sports producers] love it," assures McNamee. "The Seven Network does the Australian Open. The advantages are obvious for television."

What's also obvious is that what's best for television—or what television *thinks* is best—isn't always what's best for tennis, either in the short or long run. As noted Australian tennis writer Suzi Petkovski puts it, "Since when is TV a barometer of good taste or ethics?"

Woodbridge warns, "If television producers see this scoring change for mixed doubles and doubles creates a two-hour time frame similar to a basketball game, then it's eventually going to be the same [format] for singles. And *then* you're not going to have the true champions of the game. You're going to have a lot of good players winning matches and tournaments who wouldn't be winning [as often] if you had the proper system."

## The Entertainment Quotient

Petkovski perceptively points out: "The tiebreaker-as-third set is like a punch line without the joke. Tiebreakers are dramatic when preceded by a tense, hard-fought set, not on their own."

"I disagree with that because a super tiebreaker is preceded by two hard-fought sets," says McNamee. "It's arbitrary where you draw the line in the sand."

But sometimes both preceding sets aren't close and tense, and other times the second set isn't close. In those cases there's no immediate suspense that a tiebreaker-as-third set would climax. At the other extreme of the suspense spectrum would be the confusing and anti-climactic spectacle of two tiebreakers in a row—a traditional tiebreaker to end the second set immediately followed by a super tiebreaker to end the match. Just as tennis loses credibility when defective and ill-conceived best-14 and best-17 ranking systems result in undeserving players (most recently Martina Hingis) ranking No. 1, flawed scoring systems self-destruct by such absurd and confusing anomalies.

Woodbridge got plenty of feedback after the 2001 U.S. Open when he did a charity event at his hometown club in Sydney. He recalls, "A lot of club members watched the mixed doubles final and said to me: 'What's this? I hated it. You're playing, and all of a sudden you're finished. I didn't know what was going on. I couldn't follow it. Why do you guys need to play that format?' At least twenty people told me they didn't like it. We need that feedback from the tennis fan. Woodbridge says, "At the U.S. Open I felt it wasn't well accepted by the people watching either. Some fans I talked to there felt like they were ripped off."

On the contrary, contends McNamee, who cites "best-of-two" trials in the doubles finals of ATP Tour events this year in Bucharest and Tashkent (which, it's fair to note, are hardly the most established and knowledgeable tennis venues). "Both teams were informed during the whole process, there were no expressed concerns . . . and both finals were successful and entertaining," according to a report issued by Richard Ings, ATP Executive Vice President Rules and Competition.

Gerry Armstrong, an ATP Officiating Supervisor at Tashkent, gave an even more upbeat assessment. "We allowed two hours for the match and prize giving which proved to be spot on, which was very important with the imminent arrival of the president and the consequential security issues. The tiebreaker went to 13-11. It was full of very tense and exciting tennis, definitely the highlight of the match. It was clearly enjoyed by the large crowd, and I'm sure, the players. Even the losers said it was fun. Why not play the entire [doubles] draw in this way?"

McNamee denies reports in Australian and British newspapers that he advocated extending the "best-of-two" scoring reform to men's and women's doubles at the 2002 Australian Open. "You've got to try it at tour events before you would institute it at a Grand Slam. It has to be accepted on the tour level first," explains McNamee.

"If it is greatly enhancing and promoting doubles, then there's no reason it can't be used at every level, including the Grand Slams. Philosophically, yes, I am in favor of it," admits McNamee.

Whether better fields would also enhance and promote doubles is another question. Advocates of the super tiebreaker in the mixed doubles at the U.S. Open hoped the time-saving format would attract leading singles players. As it turned out, No. 34 Wayne Ferreira was the highest-ranked men's singles player in the mixed, and Jennifer Capriati, no threat to go far with her brother Steven, was the only women's top-ten player to enter.

"The time issue is a red herring," says Petkovski. "If we regularly had the likes of Serena and Venus Williams, Anna Kournikova, Lleyton Hewitt and Andy Roddick in mixed finals, would officials be so keen to shorten matches? More likely, fans would feel ripped off at not seeing a full, three-set extravaganza."

Wouldn't more fans also fill the seats if big-name players competed in doubles?

"No. No. I can tell you right now [that] promoting doubles matches with marquee singles players is not going to get bums on seats," insists McNamee. "Putting it in a time frame that's friendly to what the spectators' viewing habits are makes far more difference than who's actually playing the match. People buy tickets to watch the marquee players play singles. They're not going to buy tickets to go watch them play doubles."

But wouldn't it make a difference if Pete Sampras, Andre Agassi, and Pat Rafter played doubles and mixed doubles?

"No, I don't think it would," maintains McNamee. McNamee, whose four major titles came in doubles and mixed doubles, says, "I love doubles, and I hate to see what's happened to it. There have been mixed doubles finals on the tour and in the Grand Slams where there have been less than one thousand people watching the match. That is not acceptable. But this trial is not going to rise or fall on what happens in the mixed doubles. What happens with the trials at men's doubles events is going to be the key to this." That prospect is just what Woodbridge and many in the tennis world dread. To supposedly save doubles, we would have to destroy the scoring system. "Doubles is the scapegoat for the problems in tennis," concludes Woodbridge. "A few people see that as the area to attack to look like they're doing something about the game. But you have to start with the singles game if you want to improve television rights and everything else that goes with improving a profile in sponsors' markets. To change the whole scoring of our game for no particular reason is a funny way of thinking about the problem."

Woodbridge is right in stressing that the focus should be shifted to how tennis is faring in those sponsors' markets.

Last year *Street & Smith's SportsBusiness Journal* surveyed what sponsors said about sports governing bodies and concluded, "The ATP has not ingratiated itself with the U.S. sponsor community. It did not achieve a 40 percent rating in a single category and came in at 15 percent or below in two key measures—how well it markets itself and the value it offers for the money.

"The ratings were no better on the women's side of the court. Again, there was not one score above 40 percent affirmative in any of the twenty categories, and the WTA came in below 20 percent in some of the most important ones. Areas in which sponsors say the WTA is in dire need of improvement include how well it markets the sport, the value it offers for the money and its responsiveness to customers."

## A Sensible Solution

Tennis leaders can both shorten total court time in doubles and increase the ratio of action time to total court time by cutting changeover time in half from ninety seconds to forty-five seconds. Doubles players clearly don't need ninety seconds of rest, and spectators don't want to see them lingering on chairs after only two non-grueling games.

Tennis fans crave action. What annoys them most is the excessive dead time between points, games, and sets. In some men's singles matches, particularly on faster surfaces, action time—when the ball is in play—amounts to less than 10 percent of the total match time. Compare that to more action-intensive sports such as basketball, soccer, ice hockey, and football, where action time is a far more entertaining 35 to 50 percent of the total game time.

If there are twelve changeovers in the average best two-of-three-sets doubles match, forty-five-second changeovers would save nine minutes. In protracted three-set doubles matches that reformers are complaining about, this solution would save about fifteen minutes. That's substantial and should go a long way toward satisfying those who seek to amputate deciding sets with tiebreakers.

All things considered, if you believe the traditional scoring system of tennis is integral to its success, or even more important, one of its crowning glories, then this battle is for the integrity and perhaps even the survival of tennis.

Where do you stand?

---

## FASCINATING FACTS:

- Fifty Swedish heart patients reportedly died of heart failure in their hospital rooms watching their hero, Bjorn Borg, win his excruciatingly tense 1980 Wimbledon final against John McEnroe.

- Gladys Heldman, the admired, former publisher of *World Tennis* magazine, in 1989 wrote that the three biggest problems in men's tennis were appearance money, exhibitions, and tanking.

- Justine Henin-Hardenne, who says she gets so nervous she can't sleep well during Grand Slam events, took her first parachute jump the day after winning her third French Open title.

- Jimmy Connors once leaped into the stands to go after a boisterous fan.

# 8

# Where Have All the Serve and Volleyers Gone? 2005

*The great beauty of tennis is the inexhaustible variety of playing methods to which one may make recourse.*

—Don Budge in his 1939 book, *Budge on Tennis*

Imagine American football without the forward pass or boxing without body punching or basketball without inside shooting. Those sports would be greatly diminished. So would tennis if serving and volleying becomes extinct.

Just such a dire fate stares tennis in the face now. Only ten players in the men's top 100 frequently serve and volley: Tim Henman (age thirty), Mario Ancic (age twenty-one), Radek Štìpánek (age twenty-six), Taylor Dent (age tenty-four), Max Mirnyi (age twenty-seven), Greg Rusedski (age thirty-one), Michaël Llodra (age twenty-five), Ivo Karlovic (age twenty-six), Wayne Arthurs (age thirty-four), and Jonas Björkman (age thirty-three). Only Henman and Ancic rank among the top 20. Another seven sometimes serve and volley: No. 1 Roger Federer (age twenty-three), Joachim Johansson (age twenty-two), Paradorn Srichaphan (age twenty-five), Feliciano López (age twenty-three), Mark Philippoussis (age twenty-eight), Nicolas Escudé (age twenty-nine), and Tommy Haas (age twenty-seven).

The women's game appears even bleaker. Only thirty-one-year-old Lisa Ray-mond and twenty-four-year-old Alicia Molik remain occasional practitioners of this dying art.

Serving and volleying has steadily decreased during the Open Era. In 1973, when three of the four Grand Slams were staged on grass, six of the top ten players nearly always served and volleyed on that surface: Ilie Nãstase , John Newcombe, Tom Okker, Stan Smith, Rod Laver, and Arthur Ashe. Three more, Jimmy Connors, ageless Ken Rosewall, and clay-bred Jan Kodeš , came in often, too.

Ten years later, with Wimbledon and the Australian Open contested on grass (the U.S. Open dropped grass in 1975), just three among the top ten served and volleyed: John McEnroe, Yannick Noah, and Kevin Curren. Many hybrid, all-court stylists, except for Connors, had disappeared, with the remaining players, such as Ivan Lendl, Mats Wilander, Jimmy Arias and José Luis Clerc, confirmed baseliners.

With Wimbledon the last Grand Slam bastion of grass in 1993 (the Australian Open went to hard courts in 1988), the trend was temporarily halted, at least among top ten competitors. Pete Sampras, Michael Stich and Stefan Edberg, all exceptionally talented and graceful serve and volleyers, were joined by Goran Ivanišević and Cédric Pioline.

Serving and volleying declined even more dramatically on the women's side. In 1975, the first year of the WTA rankings, seven of the top ten women served and volleyed frequently, at least on grass: Virginia Wade, Martina Navratilova, Billie Jean King, Evonne Goolagong, Margaret Court, Olga Morozova, and Françoise Durr. Ten years later, there were still six: Navratilova, Hana Mandlikova, Pam Shriver, Claudia Kohde-Kilsch, Zina Garrison, and Helena Suková. But by 1995, when Jana Novotna temporarily dropped out of the elite, not a single woman streaked to the net behind her serve.

Why did serve and volleying go onto the endangered species list? Several changes doomed this exciting style of play but none more than the abandonment of grass at the U.S. and Australian Opens and the subsequent death of the summer grass court circuits in America and Down Under. Today the sweet smell of grass remains only at Wimbledon, tune-up tourneys two weeks before it, and the anti-climactic Newport event after it.

"It happened because of the surfaces we grow up on," says Pete Sampras, the greatest serve-and-volleyer in history. "Laver and the Aussies of the 1950s and 1960s grew up playing on grass. Even Connors grew up on some grass. As time went on, grass became a surface we just saw once a year at Wimbledon. Kids today are playing on hard courts and clay. So they just naturally start playing from the backcourt. And that's how they are breaking through on the men's and women's Challenger Circuits. At age twenty, you end up playing like you did when you were thirteen."

## A Prescient Coach

True enough, unless you happen to be Sampras and have Pete Fischer as your coach. Until he was fourteen, Sampras counter-punched with a two-handed backhand— "I played like Andre then"—and rarely ventured to the net. Then the prescient Fischer changed his backhand to a one-hander and created a serve-and-volley game that enabled Sampras to capitalize on his supreme natural talent and capture a record seven Wimbledon titles, plus five United States and two Australian Opens.

Fischer recognized that no premier men serve and volleyers, except for Connors, had double-fisted backhands, and his goal was to see his protégé win Wimbledon. "It was risky, and I didn't want to do it," recalls Sampras. "I lost a lot of matches. I still wanted to go back to the two-handed backhand. At sixteen or seventeen, it finally clicked and I got more confidence. I stuck with it and my serving and volleying. Why? I don't know."

Sampras foresees even less serving and volleying in the future unless the ATP and ITF take his advice. "If they want to bring serve and volleyers back in five or six years, we have to have more of a grass court season," he says. "It's got to be much more than adding another week or two of grass court events between the French and Wimbledon. I don't have the answers as to where and when. But they should create Satellite and Challenger grass court circuits. Just as you have guys breaking through on clay, they would have the same opportunity on grass. The basic concept is to start kids playing on grass or a fast indoor court when they're ten or twelve and give them grass tournaments when they're sixteen, seventeen and eighteen, and then they're forced to play a certain way."

Jack Kramer refined the modern serve-and-volley game in the 1940s (Oliver Campbell served and volleyed continually when he won the U.S. singles title in 1890-1892) and popularized the term "The Big Game." He relentlessly charged net off both serves and laments the near-death of that entertaining style as well as the grass on which it flourished. "Now there's almost no grass to clean up on, only Wimbledon," says Kramer. "That's one God-damn tournament."

Kramer credits the punishing two-handed backhand for the reign of powerful baseliners today. "Instead of coming in on an approach shot as soon as you could, the pressure tactic that I found so effective, two-handed players in these last eleven, twelve years feel more comfortable banging five shots and then getting a winning placement on the sixth shot," says Kramer.

Not only do double-handers shun serving and volleying, with Ancic and Björkman the notable exceptions, but they make life miserable for those who do. "All these kids with two-handed backhands and semi-Western forehands, Agassi types, are dynamic against the serve and volleyer," says Kramer.

"In the serve-and-volley era, we weren't facing these two-handed backhands when we came in," he recalls. "Most people, except for [Don] Budge and Frank Kovacs, would produce some form of a weaker, slice backhand on service returns, if you had a high kicker second serve."

Kramer contends that the "Big Game" of yesteryear must live on because "Who in hell wants to see two backcourt players hit fifteen to twenty groundstrokes on every point? If you have only one style, there's nothing! Fans want to see two different styles of the game and which is best on the day. The best match worth watching was a good-conditioned Sampras playing a good-conditioned Agassi."

But how can tennis produce more Samprases?

"If I had a chance to advise a real good athlete, I would say, 'Don't even think about playing tennis until you're eleven or twelve.' If he starts late enough, he won't have a lot of grip problems to overcome," says Kramer, who played baseball, basketball, and football before switching to tennis. "Sampras was smart enough to overcome a grip problem and get rid of his two-handed backhand, or he wouldn't be the player he became."

That game plan is easier said than done. In this "gotta get good quick" era, many kids with future glory in mind start playing at five, six, or seven, and their grips and swings are pretty much locked in by the time they are twelve or thirteen.

Kramer recommends, "You have to find a coach who says to himself, 'Here is a real athlete, and I want to sell him and his parents that he has a chance to be a Sampras. He's going to lose in the twelves and fourteens and lose until he gets to be seventeen or eighteen when he gains full strength and ability. And when he loses, he'll get discouraged. But he's going to have to be an individual and not join the baseline chorus, and then he is going to be damn good playing the aggressive, serve-and-volley game.' It takes a special player and a special coach to pull this off."

Tony Pickard, another elder statesman of the game, guided Edberg for thirteen years to six Grand Slam titles and the No. 1 ranking. Pickard believes serve-and-volleyers are disappearing because "there aren't a lot of coaches out there who can teach it to the boys and say, 'Listen, if you put this dimension into your game, there will be a time in a match when you can use it.' The coaches coming into the game now are people who have grown up with tennis as it is today, which is basically played from the back of the court."

Pickard believes American star Andy Roddick has a perfect game to incorporate some serving and volleying. "He has a 135 miles-per-hour first serve and a great kick second serve. If he was taught to go forward off that serve, he would have so many easy shots to play, even if he weren't a great volleyer," asserts Pickard. "It wouldn't take that long to teach him how to volley really well. If Roddick did that, he could cause opponents enormous problems on *any* surface."

Pam Shriver, a Hall of Famer with twenty-two Grand Slam doubles titles, defends coaches because "if they see a certain style of play is apt to be more successful, then they are going to coach it." They are also products of their environments.

"If you come from Europe and you're used to playing on slow clay, then you're going to teach a less aggressive style. If you come from Southern California where there are mostly fast hard courts, you'll see a different style of coach," says Shriver. "Robert Lansdorp, who has been out there forever, teaches a hard, flat groundstroke, a more aggressive, penetrating shot because it's a high-percentage play there."

Because no coach knows it all, Shriver advocates specialty coaching. "Some coaches may not have a serve-and-volley background, but they can get some help from specialists," says Shriver. "People go to Lansdorp for certain specialty items, and people might go to a serve-and-volley coach. A couple hours with Roy Emerson or Tony Pickard are beautiful for the serve and volley."

Rod Laver, tennis' only double Grand Slammer (in 1962 and 1969), agrees that serving and volleying is rarely taught nowadays. "I think juniors should be learning to volley more, but not just serve and volley," he contends. "They should learn approach and volley and return of serve and volley."

Even so, Laver philosophizes, "That's just the way it is. Young players are learning to play from the baseline with big serves, like Andy Roddick. The game of tennis is fine." No one I talked with shares Laver's satisfaction about the state of the on-court game, but some, like Shriver, think playing styles go in cycles. "Did people ten or fifteen years ago, when Becker and Edberg played in Wimbledon finals and then

*Rod Laver volleying, a lost art today.* Courtesy of the International Tennis Hall of Fame & Museum, Newport, Rhode Island

Becker-Stich and Sampras-Ivanišević, ever think we would have Lleyton Hewitt winning Wimbledon and being No. 1 in the world for two years? They thought the game had passed by that style of champion, and it was always going to be power, power, huge serves, short rallies. And they were wrong!"

The fact that some playing styles—such as the Lawford chop, and Continental forehands—have disappeared forever, doesn't phase Shriver. "The game of tennis has too much variety for things not to be cyclical, and for champions to come around with different styles," she insists. "There's no reason why in the women and men's games, you won't have a serve-and-volley champion again."

Could Ancic or Dent, the youngest serve and volleyers, also be remembered in 2010 or 2015 as tennis' last one? "It's a definite possibility," concedes Dent, whom Shriver last year asserted, "has the potential to equal serve and volleying greats, such as Sampras, Edberg, Becker and McEnroe."

Dent says, "But I believe some kids growing up are going to say, 'I want to play like Sampras' or 'I want to play like Rafter.' Or if I get good enough, they'll say, 'I want to play like Taylor Dent.' Other serve and volleyers will come along, but they're going to be rare."

## Role Model Theory

One has to question that role model or idol theory since very few juniors seemingly patterned their games after the ultimate serve and volleyers, Sampras and Navratilova, during the past twenty years.

The twenty-seventh-ranked Dent, who has dropped twenty pounds to become quicker and more agile at net, offers two reasons why few can make a dent at net these days. "Guys return so well and pass so well that it's tough to be efficient serving and volleying," he says. "You don't get the free points guys got thirty years ago when it was tough to generate a lot of power and topspin with wood rackets"—when his Australian father Phil was a world-class player.

The more relevant comparison, however, is with fifteen to twenty years ago. Then relatively large graphite rackets were prevalent, yet serve and volleyers *still* flourished. "If you think back to 1985–1986, when you had Prince rackets, Wilson midsize, Head mid-size, technology had progressed dramatically by then," says Pickard. "You had people who used large racket heads that returned serves unbelievably well. But even during that time, people like Edberg and Becker succeeded over them." Sampras, of course, then ruled the 1990s, with Rafter, Stich, Krajicek, and Ivaniševic also winning major titles.

Navratilova disagrees and advocates that the ITF legislate to reduce racket head size to lessen the dominance of groundstrokes. "The modern rackets have helped ground strokes a huge amount—exponentially," she told British journalist Richard Eaton. "They are so much more powerful that now if you have to hit two or three volleys, you will probably lose the point. Smaller racket heads would change all the shots. There would be less topspin and pace. It wouldn't be possible just to play from fifteen feet behind the baseline, and it will require more skill."

Rod Cross, who with Dr. Howard Brody and Crawford Lindsay, wrote the acclaimed book, *The Physics and Technology of Tennis*, agrees with Navratilova, about topspin anyway, and proposes a reasonable, workable compromise. "The extra one inch available in the modern ten-inch wide frame—that the vast majority of world-class pros use—allows the player to get as much topspin as he or she needs," explains Cross, Associate Professor of Physics at the University of Sydney, Australia. "Consequently, a solution to what some consider boring and excessive baseline topspin is to reduce racquet width from the current ten inches to about 9 or 9.5 inches."

In July 2003 former Wimbledon champions McEnroe, Navratilova, Becker, Smith, Pat Cash, Neale Fraser, and more than thirty other former players petitioned the ITF for smaller racket heads to curb the excessive topspin and devastating power of baseliners. British TV analyst and former Davis Cupper John Barrett, who spearheaded the crusade, argues that to restore the balance between serve and volleyers and baseliners pro tennis must restrict rackets to nine inches in width. He rightly points out, "You can still hit topspin, but the difference is you need perfect timing."

"Rackets don't explain the problem," says Mary Carillo. "I agree with Pickard, even though the rackets have helped the baseliners, the returners of serve, a lot more than the serve and volleyers. It's become a dying art because of a whole set of changes. For example, a lot of players today have bigger backhands than forehands. So where the hell do you serve?

"Unless tennis changes surfaces, I don't see serve and volleying coming back," argues Carillo. "I wish they had a longer grass court season and a better-spaced grass court season from the clay court season. Other sports do a much better job of changing rules to improve their sports than tennis."

Carillo is right. Other sports monitor playing styles and regularly re-evaluate the rules to:

A) maintain a good balance between offense and defense

B) insure overall fairness

C) maintain a diversity of playing styles

D) keep the sport entertaining for fans.

Basketball, in particular, enacted major rule changes—such as the twenty-four-second clock and goaltending—during the past fifty years to accommodate the increasingly athletic style and physical size of NBA players.

Ironically, the ITF and ATP have tweaked the balls and courts only to produce some unintended consequences. "In the mid-1990s after some complaints by the media and fans, they thought that if you slow up the ball, we'd have guys serving less aces," says Björkman, a genial Swede who starred in doubles with Todd Woodbridge before teaming with Mirnyi this year. "But the heavier ball only took away from the serve and volley. And guys are still producing a lot of aces."

Björkman, the ATP Player Council president in 2000–2001, advocates that pro tournaments speed up their indoor and hard courts to keep the serve and volley alive there. "Look who is winning indoors these days," says Björkman. "They don't have to play any serve and volley at all. Nicolás Lapentti won Lyon, for instance. Albert Costa hadn't won very many matches on hard courts before. Even if he's improved a lot now, with the courts and balls slower, he reached the semis at Key Biscayne. I would rather play on high-altitude clay, than play Indian Wells. Some of the slowest hard courts are in America in the spring."

Björkman and rocket-serving Greg Rusedski also criticized Wimbledon for slowing its grass and thus handicapping serve and volleyers even more. Wimbledon kept its grass the same height (5/16") at The Championships in 2002, but the introduction of rye-grass along with a relatively dry spring produced slightly higher and slower bounces. "They were prepared the same way as ever," Eddie Seward, the chief grounds man, told the *International Herald Tribune* in 2003. Seward also noted that the ball bounced 85 percent as high as a hardcourt—compared to its normal 80 percent—due to the dry weather in the first week.

Contrarily, Sampras and Raymond detected no change in Wimbledon's lawns in recent years. "To win Wimbledon today, a serve and volleyer has to have the weather on her side," says Raymond. "If it's damp and cool, a serve and volleyer, by keeping the ball low, has a much better chance. If it's a hot fortnight and the courts are playing firm and hard, the returner has a good crack at the serve."

The bad bounces that once drew criticism from players now, ironically, are yearned for by serve and volleyers. "The bounces are so true now because there are so few serve and volleyers to chew up the court inside the baseline anymore," points out Dent. "It's a vicious circle because the serve and volleyer has always helped his own cause by chewing up the court. It's not starting to favor the baseliner, but it's equaling out a lot more."

No one I interviewed begrudged the fact that two baseliners, Hewitt and unheralded David Nalbandian, competed in the 2002 Wimbledon final, which was so boring that the women's doubles final gained higher TV ratings in America. Both earned it fair and square, whipping some net-rushers along the way. Even so, Dent confides, "I said to myself, 'I can't believe there were two baseliners in the Wimbledon final. I want a piece of these guys.'"

## Federer's Formula

Serve and volleyers Federer and Philippoussis somewhat reversed the trend, temporarily at least, when they contested the 2003 Wimbledon final. The more athletic and versatile Federer outclassed the hulking Aussie, but even he believes pure serve and volleyers are relics of the past. "It's tough. It's tough," acknowledged Federer who rarely served and volleyed en route to his last three Slam titles. "That player almost has to have a serve like Roddick and have the volleys of Henman. That's tough to get."

If men serve and volleyers rarely have enough game to win Wimbledon, heaven help the women. "It's a losing percentage game if you are going to go in with a serve anything shy of Serena's," explains Shriver. "You're going to be punished by the returns. In the twenty-five years I've been involved, the serve returns have improved more than the serve."

"Tennis has evolved into such a power game," agrees 5'5" Raymond. "The girls are a lot stronger and fitter, and because of that they are hitting their groundstrokes and service returns a lot harder. It's become much more difficult to cover the net. If you could take Serena as a mold, she would definitely be a candidate as someone who could evolve into a serve and volleyer. She is amazingly athletic and so strong and fast."

Many years ago "Big Bill" Tilden opined, "In any match between the perfect baseline player and the perfect net rusher, I would take the baseliner every time."

Shriver sees future champions emerging not from two separate schools—baseline versus serve and volley—but rather as a hybrid of styles. "Roger Federer has amazing all-court skills and can serve and volley if he chooses. Champions of the future will be able to play several different styles with equal comfort."

The desertion of top-flight singles players from doubles in the past twenty-five years has paralleled the decline of serving and volleying in singles and may have accelerated the trend. None of the top twenty-five in the ATP doubles rankings includes a player ranked in the singles top twenty-five, which means the top singles men play doubles either too infrequently or not especially well. Either way, unless these baseliners do both, they'll lack the serve and volley skills and confidence to try it even occasionally in singles.

Some pros see that critical connection and are trying to remedy the problem. "Very few of the Swedes, except for Edberg and me, served and volleyed," says Björkman. "Enqvist, [Thomas] Johansson, Norman rarely played doubles before. Now they do, and it's because they want to improve their volley."

In sharp contrast, eleven of the top thirty women in singles are also ranked in the top thirty in the WTA's individual doubles rankings. What's shocking is that so few, only about 25 percent, according to No. 10 Raymond, actually serve and volley in doubles. "The girls don't serve and volley anymore. Only about three or four teams serve and volley all the time, and the rest do it about three times a game. When Lindsay Davenport plays doubles with me, it helps her volley in singles." Tell that to outstanding baseliner Paola Suárez, No. 1 in doubles with Virginia Ruano Pascual. Suarez confides without regret that she has never served and volleyed in her entire pro doubles career.

Certainly all playing styles have their more and less attractive expressions. Most would agree, however, that endless baseline rallies test the patience of Job, while a profusion of aces and service winners are equally tiresome to watch. On the other hand, 2001 U.S. Open spectators loved the rip-roaring baseline battle between Hewitt and Andy Roddick, just as they relished the dazzling shotmaking, including rapid-fire net duels, in Sampras-Rafter and Becker-Edberg matches.

Serving and volleying, therefore, presents something of a paradox. The serve, while graceful and awesome at its best, requires the least athleticism of any tennis shot. Volleying, or more precisely, net-rushing showcases the most athleticism. Not only are lunging, reflex and touch volleys—not to mention the sprints back to whack leaping overheads—spectacularly entertaining for fans, they are also thrilling for players themselves.

"It's so much fun when you're serving and volleying well and you pretty much dominate the match," enthuses Dent. "It's very exciting," agrees Sampras. "You come out there with a lot of power and aggression. And if you're doing it well, you feel like you're unbeatable."

The extroverted Björkman enjoys it for other reasons, too. "I like to show my athletic ability and my personality, especially at the U.S. Open. Americans, especially New Yorkers, always seem to support you," says Björkman. "Often spectacular shots at net get the biggest reaction from fans. And if you get pumped up and they scream at you and you look at them, that makes them want to watch you again because that's exciting. And you get more fans on your side."

If that ego gratification does not motivate aspiring juniors to give serving and volleying a try, perhaps these encouraging words from two former Wimbledon champions will. "Guys who come to net will beat a backcourt player," contends seven-time Grand Slam titlist McEnroe. Cash, the 1987 winner, predicts, "I believe the next truly great player is going to be a serve-volleyer because as a tactic, it's a massive advantage."

What if Sampras and Navratilova, who at forty-eight is still winning doubles tournaments the old-fashioned way at net, make history in a way they never intended, as the last serve-and-volley singles champions?

"It would be a tragedy because stylistically to lose serving-and-volleying would be awful for the sport," concludes Carillo, who teamed with McEnroe to win the 1977 French Open mixed doubles crown. "I loved those Sampras-Rafter match-ups when you had two highly athletic serve and volleyers. They were astounding, great stuff.

"We had those great rivalries, McEnroe-Börg, Chrissie-Martina, Sampras-Agassi," says Carillo. The fun part was that they were so stylistically different; they had such different ways of winning points.

"If tennis lost that, it would be greatly diminished," stresses Carillo. "I'd miss it like hell. Some great baseline matches still intrigue me, *maybe* as much as serve- and-volley matches. But in the end, I want to see styles clash. I want to see strategies clash. The best matches I've ever seen have all of that going for them."

## What They Are Saying

"It's bullshit. It's not good to have a bunch of old guys sitting around and complaining when we have so many other more important issues affecting the game." —Brad Gilbert, former world No. 4 and now Andy Roddick's coach, denouncing the ITF petition to change the rules for racket width.

"In the '70s there were so many contrasting styles with serve and volleyers, baseliners and lots of flair. Now, with the technology, we just don't have that. We have guys who just bang it all day. Tennis has become pretty boring and we need to address that." —James Blake, former Harvard student and U.S. Davis Cupper.

"To me, it's almost a philosophical thing. Staying back says you take no risks, you're satisfied, you're okay with that rut. Attacking tennis is to take chances, to move forward in life. It almost inherently makes a person more interesting." —Mary Carillo, in the *San Francisco Chronicle*.

"Variety is the spice of life. Diversity is what makes tennis such a wonderful sport. The baseliner against the serve and volleyer . . . that is what people want to see. But these days what I see is a rather monotonous sport with rallying from the baseline. Something must be done if we are going to restore balance." —John Barrett.

"I personally would like to see the game played with rackets that would require more skill from the players. It's so forgiving you don't have to hit the ball on the sweet spot anymore." —Former world top tenner and baseliner José Higueras, a coach who has worked with Jim Courier, Todd Martin, Pete Sampras, and Carlos Moyá, in the *New York Times*. Higueras signed the open letter to the ITF.

"When I hear from people that men's tennis is boring, it's clear to me that they cannot be talking about the tennis. The quality of what we're seeing out there is tremendous. Men's tennis has become a power game . . . but it has not become a one-dimensional game." —Patrick McEnroe, U.S. Davis Cup captain and ESPN analyst, in the *New York Times*.

"I don't see why the argument wasn't big back in the days when Pete [Sampras] and Goran [Ivaniševic] and Michael Stich and Becker were big and powerful and dominating tennis. You really don't see a lot of guys that were retrievers whose serve wasn't their best shot and they were in the top. I really don't see the point of all the talk." —Andy Roddick.

"We have longer points, but players are staying at the baseline and hitting as hard as they can without much thought or inspiration." —Tennis Hall of Famer Bud Collins, NBC tennis commentator, who believes racket-head size should have been limited long ago to bring finesse back to the sport.

"I always enjoyed the spectacular tennis of the serve and volley rather than sitting on the baseline. There's a lot of grace in it." —All-time great Margaret Court, in *Tennis* magazine in 1980.

---

**FASCINATING FACTS:**

- Roger Federer said he served and volleyed 100 percent of the time on his first serve and more than 50 percent of the time on his second serve when he upset Pete Sampras at the 2001 Wimbledon Championships.

- Roger Federer served and volleyed only five times during his 6-0, 7-6, 6-7, 6-3 victory over Rafael Nadal in the 2006 Wimbledon final.

- In 2002 Great Britain's Prime Minister Tony Blair asked British tennis star Tim Henman: "So, how do you handle the pressure?"

- The Townsville Bulletin, an Australian newspaper, reported that a local woman inadvertently threw away her false teeth because she was so excited watching Roger Federer, her favorite player, win the 2006 Wimbledon.

- Early in Maria Sharapova's pro career, her father, Yuri, used to give her $100 every time she served and volleyed in a tournament match.

# 9

# Ten Ways to Fire Up Tennis 2005

*Sports is the only entertainment where no matter how many times you go back, you never know the ending.*

—Neil Simon, American playwright and writer

**E**nthralling rivalries and charismatic characters make tennis boom, but the sport doesn't have to plummet in popularity when they are in short supply. Here are ten surefire ways to fire up tennis.

1. **Bring back serving and volleying.** Shockingly, the most exciting and athletic playing style— exemplified by McEnroe, Becker, Sampras, Gonzalez and Navratilova and decades of Australian stars from Sedgman to Court to Rafter—is almost extinct. Imagine football without the forward pass or boxing without body punching and you get the bleak picture. Tim Henman, now thirty years old and never a champion, is the only top ten serve-volleyer, and less than a dozen top 100 players frequently do it. Among the women, only Aussie Alicia Molik and American Lisa Raymond, serve and volley even occasionally. What's the remedy? Gradually reduce the allowable overall width of the racket head from the current 12 ½" (31.75 cm) to 10" (25.4 cm). That will significantly decrease the tremendous power and vicious spin that today's high-tech rackets generate and help redress the imbalance now favoring baseliners. Increase the importance of grass-court play—where serving and volleying is most effective—by scheduling Wimbledon a week later to add another week of grass tournaments. And create some new grass-court events during the year. Get rid of slow, abrasive hard courts, such as Rebound Ace at the Oz Open, that unduly favor groundstrokers. Encourage talented youngsters to improve their volleying skills so they can develop their serving and volleying as juniors. Contrasting styles create sensational match-ups, such as McEnroe-Borg, Sampras-Agassi and Navratilova-Evert, that feature diving volleys, leaping smashes, scintillating pass-

ing shots and cunning lobs. Otherwise, tennis fans suffer baseline blahs from a menu limited almost completely to forehands and backhands whacked by incomplete players.

2. **Create informative and clear standings**. For the past thirty years newspapers have published a confusing array of tennis rankings and lists that turn off, rather than enlighten, sports fans. Want to know who's No. 1 and who's in the Top 10? It's no easy task! The men's game, for example, gives us the ATP Champions Race, which often conflicts with the ATP Entry Rankings (viz. the "real" rankings), which are different from the U.S. Open Series rankings during the summer. We also are barraged with not one but two doubles rankings: team and individual. To bewilder us further, we get weekly prize money lists, which are meaningless because they combine singles, doubles and mixed doubles earnings. Then, of course, the ITF crowns its own annual men's and women's champions—such as third-ranked Anastasia Myskina in 2004—which don't always coincide with the year-end ATP and WTA No. 1 players. Enough already! Team sports, such as the NBA, NFL, NHL, and MLB, clearly and simply tell us who are the best teams and the order of the rest with standings. No conflicts, debates, or confusion. Tennis, both an individual and team sport, can and must create easy-tounderstand and informative "standings," too. These groundbreaking, weekly Top 10 singles standings would include the player's last name, country, point average, most recent results (viz. round reached in last tournament), and next scheduled tournament. Doubles standings would include the Top 5-ranked teams with a similar format. These Monday morning standings would provide aficionados with all they need to know.

3. **Identify the players**. Big-time tennis is blessed with so much depth that unknowns and lesser lights test and upset favorites regularly. Hardly anyone outside their countries, though, had heard of Tomas Berdych, an eighteen-year-old Czech ranked No. 135, who shocked world No. 1 Roger Federer at the Athens Olympics, and No. 447 Chris Guccione, an eighteen-year-old Aussie who ambushed No. 3 Juan Carlos Ferrero at the 2004 Sydney International. Who are these guys, and where do they come from? Inquiring fans want to know. Starting in 2005, doubles players, generally much less known by spectators, should be required to wear their full names and countries on the back of their shirts, dresses, and warm-up suits. Singles players would follow suit in 2006. Then there'd be no more "Come on, whatshisname!" cries from the crowd.

4. **Rev up tournament finals.** Tennis is often compared with boxing, another *mano a mano* fiercely competitive individual sport. Dramatic entrances and colorful announcements magnify the already ear-shattering noise and exciting anticipation at title fights. Renowned ring announcer Michael Buffer's famous "Let's get ready to rumble!" climaxes his engaging introductions of the boxers and whips fans into a frenzy. Boxing great Sugar Ray Leonard once said, "When I heard [those five words], it made me want to fight. I couldn't wait to get it on." Tennis should copy that format or create other dynamic pre-final formats at non-Grand Slam tournaments.

Playing the national anthems of both finalists would heighten patriotic fervor and also rev up partisan onlookers.

5. **Connect players and fans.** Sports like NASCAR are way ahead of the game because devotees feel they know the stars of their sport. Fans chat with Jeff Gordon, Dale Earnhardt Jr., and other drivers minutes before they risk their lives at breakneck speeds. "We all know you follow someone's career more intently if you know them," points out former doubles champion Pam Shriver, now a TV analyst. "Tennis stars need to be accessible on game day before competition as well as after." To strengthen the player-fan connection, tennis should copy golf and conduct Pro-Am events benefiting charities before Tennis Masters Series and International Series tournaments. On the last weekend players could also stage adult and junior camps and seminars when the courts have opened up.

6. **Nickname players**. Whatever happened to the colorful and fun nicknames of yesteryear? I remember when players got tagged with memorable monikers such as "Muscles" (Ken Rosewall), "Snake" (Ross Case), "Rocket" (Rod Laver), "Nails" (Bob Carmichael), "Gentleman Jack" (Crawford), "Hacker" (Fred Stolle), "The Wizard" (Norman Brookes), "Sexy Rexy" (Rex Hartwig) and "Killer" (Darren Cahill). And those are only Australian men, for starters. Catchy sobriquets are rare today with the best being "The Beast" (Max Mirnyi), "The Mosquito" (Ferrero) and "Scud" (Mark Philippoussis). No one asked me, but how about "The Mad Russian" for Marat Safin and "Pocket Rocket" for Justine Henin-Hardenne?

7. **Dress like champs, not chumps**. Sex sells and not just for tennis babes whose outfits range from attractively classy to seductively skimpy. For the past ten years, however, men's attire has gone downhill fast with baggy shorts that look more like crumpled underwear and shirts with sleeves down to the elbow. Some dorks even wear baseball caps when playing indoors. What are they trying to hide, anyway? A 1980s survey revealed men tour players boasted an awesome 6.4 body fat percent average. The best sartorial innovation this century is the sleeveless shirt worn by German Tommy Haas, Spaniards Rafael Nadal and Carlos Moyá, and American James Blake. Hey, guys, show those muscles. Chicks dig them!

8. **Stop the stalling**. Sports fans crave action. But the disturbing truth is that men's singles matches, in particular, provide much too little action time. Typically, the ball is in play only 10 to 15 percent of the total match time, compared to a far more entertaining 30 to 50 percent in other leading sports, such as football, basketball, and soccer. To reduce the dead time, tennis should put a twenty-second clock on court, like the shot clock in basketball, and when the buzzer goes off, the player loses that point if he hasn't served. The WTA Tour should get rid of the ridiculous two "bathroom breaks" rule and limit on-court visits by trainers—that typically last three to five minutes—to once in best-of-three set matches and twice in best-of-five set matches. And neither tour should adopt a rule allowing players to challenge

line calls. It's yet another boring and unnecessary time-waster.

9. **Resuscitate doubles.** Back in 1991 former doubles star Frew McMillan rightly observed: "The way tournaments treat doubles reminds me of a grocer who has a good product but won't put it out on the shelf. The people would buy the product if they saw it, but most of them aren't even aware it's available because of the way it's hidden from view." Doubles is the event that recreational players favor, and as Aussie great John Newcombe once said, "A good doubles match can be one of the fastest and most exciting of all sports events."

10. **Fix the schedule**. To help reverse the epidemic of injuries, exhaustion and burn-out, shorten the grueling season so that it ends in October with the Davis Cup and Fed Cup finals. Reduce the Davis Cup World Group from sixteen to eight teams and from four to three rounds and play the first round in April so that the previous year's champion will reign for at least six months. This ten-week off-season—still small compared to other sports—will benefit fans, too. We'll actually start to miss the sport and will eagerly look forward to its January return in Australia.

# 10

# How America Can Produce Tennis Champions Again
# 2007

*It takes five years to make a tennis player, and ten years to make a champion.*

—Bill Tilden

In 1935 an article titled "What's wrong with American tennis?" appeared in *Collier's* magazine. Helen Wills Moody was then nearing the end of her magnificent reign, Ellsworth Vines had turned professional, and talented Don Budge had not yet emerged as a superstar. The United States, along with Australia, Great Britain, and ascendant France, had dominated the first third of twentieth-century tennis, and the importance of being No. 1 was already deeply entrenched in American sports.

Fifty years later, Arthur Ashe, noting that Jimmy Connors and John McEnroe were no longer world-beaters, and without any potential champions on the horizon, famously predicted: "In about three years, the bottom is going to fall out at the top of American men's professional tennis."

In both cases, it was too soon to panic. Budge, Riggs, Kramer, Gonzalez, Trabert, Connors and McEnroe, plus an equally distinguished and long list of female champions, kept America at or very near the top throughout the mid- and late-1900s. Happily, Ashe lived to see his prophecy err in the early 1990s with the arrival of the "Greatest Generation"—Sampras, Agassi, Courier, and Chang, who together amassed twenty-seven Grand Slam singles titles.

Whenever American tennis fortunes plunge, experts point out reassuringly that its tennis supremacy has always been cyclical and that a new champion will arrive sooner or later to help restore our hegemony. Such cavalier optimism no longer seems justified, because globalization has spread the sport so worldwide that more countries belong to the International Tennis Federation than the United Nations.

The New Tennis World Order finds tiny nations, such as Belgium and Switzerland, producing multiple Grand Slam title-holders, Croatia winning the Davis Cup, and the Slovak Republic capturing the Fed Cup. Indeed, Serbia, war-ravaged during the 1990s and with a miniscule tennis tradition and very few indoor courts, boasts (as of November 19, 2007) more top four-ranked players (Djokovic, Jankoviè, and Ivanoviè) than any other nation!

It gets worse. No American man has won a major title since Andy Roddick took the 2003 U.S. Open. Roddick and James Blake seem unlikely to end that drought—although Donald Young, a superb athlete from Atlanta, could in a few years. And aside from No. 5-ranked Serena Williams, age twenty-six, and her sister, No. 8-ranked Venus, age twenty-seven, the only other American women in the top ninety are No. 48 Meilen Tu, and No. 77 Lilia Osterloh, both twenty-nine years old.

Here is the multi-faceted strategy the American tennis establishment, coaches, and their families should adopt to develop champions as well as large numbers of top 100 players.

## Technique

One-handed backhands often look elegant, especially those stroked by Roger Federer and Justine Henin. But, tellingly, both superstars rate their forehands better shots. At all levels, the best two-handed backhands are much superior to the best one-handed backhands, especially on service returns and passing shots. Why? Two-handed shots both handle power and generate power far more effectively. And because two hands stay on the racket, the strokes are more grooved, consistent, and controlled. The rare exceptions have been tall, strong athletes, often serve and volleyers, with superb one-handed backhand technique.

Second, abbreviated service motions are desirable only for injured players. This technique not only results in a loss of rhythm and power, but because the timing changes—the racket arrives at the contact point sooner—it also often causes a low toss. A low toss causes three problems: It decreases the first-serve percentage, makes it more difficult to hit a kick serve, and produces a loss of forward momentum that is so essential to serving and volleying.

Third, women players throughout the world seldom have effective and reliable kick serves that bound high and fast, force errors or weak returns, and reduce doublefaults. Australians Alicia Molik, Rennae Stubbs, and Samantha Stosur, Russian Svetlana Kuznetsova, and Serena are notable exceptions. The next generation of American girls must master kick second serves by the time they are sixteen.

Fourth, the virtual extinction of serving and volleying among women players makes the approach shot more important than ever. Yet outstanding approach shots are not as common as they should be. Why? In the October 2007 *Florida Tennis* magazine, noted researcher Vic Braden wrote, "The open stance players generate a wrap-around swing with the center of gravity pulling to the side, rather than forward. In most of our studies, the approach shot hit while moving forward places the volleyer approximately *nine feet* farther into the net than the open stance player."

If Braden is correct, that poses a dilemma for coaches. The semi-Western forehand

and the two-handed backhand are taught with wraparound swings with long follow-throughs by historical standards. These two strokes, however, have become explosive weapons for most world-class competitors and create baseline slugfests. High-powered rallies eventually produce weak shots that call for either hitting winners or approach shots. But hitting open-stance or semi-open stance semi-Western style forehands leaves this player—as opposed to Eastern stylists—much farther away from the net to start the approach. Since tennis is, like many sports, a game of inches, giving away *feet* is often disastrous.

And whatever happened to the slightly closed stance slice backhand approach shot that bounces low and fast, making it difficult for opponents to hit passing shots? Too few Americans hit it well and some don't hit it at all, instead preferring to stroke flat or topspin balls that bounce hip high and are easy prey for passing shots and lobs.

Finally, for many decades students were taught the geometry of a tennis court and the "center of possible returns." That meant that approach shots were stroked down the line and deep into the corner—unless a player could hit a winner or near-winner crosscourt—and the attacker moved slightly laterally toward the same side of the net to intercept passing shots. Oddly enough, Martina Navratilova, the most devastating female volleyer in history, was the first leading pro to violate this time-tested tenet of high-percentage tennis. As a result, Navratilova was frequently burned by crosscourt passing shots into the wide-open court. Roddick is the most flagrant perpetrator of this tactical blunder, especially against Federer and Nadal, who exploit it routinely.

## Footwork

Ditch the flawed, open-stance, two-handed backhand that Venus and Serena use regularly. Use it only in emergencies. Instead, study and emulate the semi-closed stances that enabled Evert, Davenport, Pierce, Capriati, Agassi, Safin, and Connors to hit virtually perfect backhands. They struck the ball more solidly and consistently than the Williams sisters, whose strength and athleticism allow them to get away with inferior footwork (causing insufficient hip and shoulder rotation and no weight transfer)—but only to some extent and some of the time.

Second, learn to slide on clay. According to Brad Gilbert, former coach of Agassi and Roddick and current coach of Andy Murray, Henin dominates the WTA Tour on clay because, "She slides into her shots and recovers, like a guy." Gilbert rightly suggests the United States Tennis Association improve the woeful clay-court results of American players by hiring a coach to teach young players how to slide on clay.

## Surfaces

No American man has captured the French Open since Agassi in 1999, and the U.S. hit rock bottom in 2007 when, astonishingly, no male player won even a singles match. Roddick, who has captured just one clay title (St. Polten) outside the U.S., has won a mere four career Roland Garros matches in seven appearances and Blake just five matches in five years.

How can this embarrassing failure be reversed? To improve their stroke, positional and tactical shortcomings, young American prospects should learn the sport on clay and grass courts, the specialty surfaces, so they can develop into players who are clever, skillful, durable, tenacious, and versatile. Therefore, I recommend they train and compete half the time on clay and a third of the time on grass, with hard courts (and indoor carpet) allotted the least time. If they can master clay and grass, proficiency on hard courts—with its true bounce and medium speed—will come easily. But it doesn't work the other way around. We know that from analyzing the results of Blake and other leading Americans, such as Robby Ginepri, Mardy Fish, and Taylor Dent. Less play on hard courts, an unforgiving surface that punishes the body, will also decrease injuries.

Let's hope the recent arrival of the renowned Sanchez-Casal Tennis Academy in Naples, Florida, with its thirty-seven clay courts and proven track record in Spain, will impart much-needed clay court expertise to eager Americans. In 2007 the USTA moved its national training center from its facility at Key Biscayne, which has eight clay courts, to the Evert Tennis Academy in Boca Raton, with fourteen clay courts, where the leading American fourteen- to eighteen-year-olds will live and train year-round.

Finally, the 1998 venue change of the prestigious Orange Bowl World Junior Championships from the clay courts at Flamingo Park in Miami Beach to the hard courts at Crandon Park on Key Biscayne was a terrible mistake because it further de-emphasized clay play. We need more, not fewer, major junior clay court tournaments in the U.S. Now that the USTA's High Performance headquarters is located at the Evert Tennis Academy, the Orange Bowl should be staged on its well-maintained clay courts or another appropriate venue in South Florida with an adequate number of clay courts. Until then, ambitious players should compete as much as possible on foreign clay at Satellite, Challenger, Futures, or ITF junior events in Europe and South America.

## Speed

"Speed is the biggest need for our players," asserts former speedster and world No. 5 Jimmy Arias, now a respected analyst for Tennis Channel. "The fastest and best athletes in America are lured to more glamorous sports—football, basketball and baseball. Our top juniors are big servers, but they will not catapult us to dominance because they don't have the speed to stay two feet behind the baseline and take the ball early."

With rare exceptions, such as Lindsay Davenport, tennis champions are very fast. And those not blessed with terrific speed, such as Helen Wills, Chris Evert, Martina Hingis, and Agassi, anticipate and position themselves extremely well. Since today's shots whiz by faster than ever, players must run faster, too. So it's not surprising that rising Scottish star Andy Murray is improving his speed, strength, and stamina under the guidance of track superstar Michael Johnson, the world record-holder in the 200 and 400 meters. The hugely successful Russian tennis program emphasizes improving speed from the start, for their seven- to ten-year-old players.

E. Paul Roetert, Ph.D., USTA Managing Director of Player Development, reports that its program also focuses very early on speed as well as agility because tennis requires movement in all different directions. Many of the USTA conditioning drills are conducted with racket in hand and the proper work/rest ratio in mind. The USTA has worked with a number of experts, including Don Chu, Mark Grabow, and Gary Brittenham, over the years, and more recently has hired its own conditioning experts.

The 1998 book, *Biology of Sport* (written by A. Viru, J. Loko, A. Volver, L. Laaneots, K. Karlesom and M. Viru), identified two windows of trainability as potential periods for accelerated adaptations to speed training. They are six to eight years of age and eleven to thirteen years of age for males and seven to nine years of age and thirteen to sixteen years of age for females. The USTA High Performance program follows those age guidelines. Currently, the fastest kids at the national training center in Boca Raton are Frank Carleton III, Raymond Sarmiento, and Victoria Duvall.

The key to training for speed, advises Dr. Roetert, is to make it as tennis-specific as possible. Coaches should focus on making this part of the day-to-day training involving patterns that are multi-directional and drills that include the racket as much as possible.

## Position

Andy Roddick wasted several key years in his up-and-down career by positioning himself five to ten feet behind the baseline during rallies. That poor positioning has cost Roddick dearly against opponents, especially opportunistic Federer, who has won their last ten matches. If Roddick were to stand two feet behind the baseline, he would play better offensively. He would give Federer less time to react to his shots, his own shots would land deeper, he would arrive closer to net following approach shots, and he would be able to create sharper angles on his crosscourt shots. Defensively, the 195-pound Roddick, not among the tour's best movers, would be better positioned to prevent Federer from doing those same offensive things to him. He would also be better able to reach drop shots and drop volleys and would run far less during the course of a match.

Now twenty-year-old Californian Sam Querrey is inexplicably making the same mistake, albeit to a lesser degree, as Roddick. Contrast those Americans with the well-positioned Federer who hugs the baseline, hits balls on the rise like Agassi, and pounces like a panther on short, weak shots and whacks them with his terrific forehand.

## Concentration

"If I were asked to name one aspect of tennis that is the biggest weakness of players at all levels, I would probably say concentration," wrote eight-time Grand Slam champion Ken Rosewall in his 1975 book, *Play Tennis with Rosewall: The Little Master and his Method.* "However good your shots, however fast your movement and reflexes, all is lost if the mind is not controlling every move."

Rosewall's advice is as vital as ever. Serving and volleying typically entails two to six shots per point. However, today's baseline slugging or maneuvering, depending on the players and surface, often requires ten or more shots to win a point. These longer points take considerably more concentration. Second, serve-and-volley games typically were shorter because the server often won games four points to two, one or at love. Today deuce games are more common, and longer, fluctuating games, with ad-ins and ad-outs, also demand more sustained concentration. Again, that mental toughness is best developed by grueling practice matches and demanding drills, particularly on clay.

## Doubles

Starting at an early age, Americans should practice and compete in doubles as much as possible. Doubles will improve their volleys, half-volleys, overheads, reflexes, forward-backward speed, agility, kick serves, and service returns. Doubles-only tournaments are vital because players seldom have the time and energy to play both singles and doubles at the same tournament today. Navratilova, the greatest doubles player in history, talked about creating her own tennis academy to teach the dying art of serving and volleying. The ability to skillfully serve and volley in singles, even only occasionally, can prove quite valuable against certain opponents and particularly on faster surfaces. Young players can first and best learn serving and volleying in doubles where they have less court to cover and a partner to help them.

## Fitness

All fifteen Russian women in the top 100, perhaps aside from Nadia Petrova and sturdily built Svetlana Kuznetsova, carry a lean physique. That contrasts sharply with several Americans, especially overweight Serena Williams, who undoubtedly would have won more major titles had she stayed in tip-top condition. Mardy Fish and injury-plagued Taylor Dent are also too heavy. Had Fish been leaner, faster and fitter, he would almost certainly have beaten the fitter, faster and more durable Nicolas Massu in their marathon final at the Athens Olympics.

In the two months following the 2005 U.S. Open, Dent lowered his body fat from 18 percent to 11 percent with grueling training sessions. But Dent, then twenty-four and a five-year tour veteran, shouldn't have been so beefy in the first place.

Sure, some players are genetically blessed with better physiques than others. However, naturally husky players—with rare exceptions, such as muscular 6'1", 188-pound Rafael Nadal—lack the speed, agility and stamina to compete effectively in today's fast-paced game. If players don't do wind sprints, weightlifting, plyometrics and other essential off-court training to get in and stay in superb shape—a sine qua non for pro sports success—they're much more apt to lose long, exhausting matches, especially five-setters at Grand Slam events, and especially on hot days, to better-conditioned opponents. So it's no accident that the best-conditioned athletes, such as Laver, Borg, Graf and Federer (who trains in off-weeks in brutally hot Dubai), are often also the best competitors because they know they can always go the distance at virtually full speed.

## Hunger

In an October 19, 2007 SI.com column titled "Trouble on the home front—Where are all the young American women prospects?", veteran doubles star Lisa

Raymond blames America's affluence and sybaritic lifestyle. "The idea of having to work extremely hard for something, to fight tooth-and-nail, to know the difference between winning and losing could mean your family having food on the table that night—that is a foreign concept to most," argues Raymond. "Americans come from the land of excess, where you super-size this or Big Gulp that. More means everything. There are so many options, so many opportunities, and so many distractions.

"Junior players in Russia or Serbia are willing to sacrifice everything in order to taste success, to get out and find a better life for themselves and their families. They don't know any differently," writes Raymond. "American juniors lose a match or have a bad practice and they can jump into their BMWs and head home to finish playing Halo 3 on their brand new Bbox 360."

Raymond contends that hunger and desire cannot be taught. Maybe so. But whatever the complicated interplay between environment and genetics, not all poor kids are hungry or all rich kids lazy. Take John McEnroe. Although this tempestuous son of a Wall Street lawyer was notoriously unenthusiastic about practicing and training, he always competed fiercely during tournaments and Davis Cup, which he cherished.

What if you don't have the prodigious talent of McEnroe? The 6'6" Querrey, ranked No. 62, is so laid-back that he reportedly limits many of his practice sessions to only thirty to forty-five minutes. For a player who has a 7–14 record in three-set matches during 2006–2007, that's a recipe for mediocrity. Contrast that with Californians Bob and Mike Bryan, the doubles team ranked No. 1 for the past three years, who do fifty different drills during their rigorous and well-planned practices.

## Inspiration

"We have a lot of great former champions that can help make a difference," rightly points out Billie Jean King. "I know that when I hung out with Alice Marble for three months of my life, only on weekends, she was a former No. 1 player, and it spilled over on to me when I was fifteen years old. It changed my life."

Jimmy Connors was similarly inspired by hanging out with fiery Pancho Gonzalez and shrewd Pancho Segura during his formative years. Sampras got plenty of inspiration plus perspiration when he visited 1980s champion Ivan Lendl. The callow teenager was promptly subjected to a brutal daily training regimen that sent a message about dedication and fitness that he never forgot. Years later, superstar Sampras confided, "If only people knew how hard I worked to make it [look] that easy."

## Spin

Topspin is essential to win today. After Anna Chakvetadze, a 5'7" Russian ranked No. 5, beat Shahar Pe'er to gain the 2007 U.S. Open semis, she explained her pro success: "I never played like this when I was a junior. I was hitting really flat balls, and after that I just couldn't win a match. That's why I change it." When Chakvetadze was fifteen, she received coaching from Olof Aspelin and learned the high-percentage Swedish game that took Borg, Edberg, and Mats Wilander to the top.

Venus Williams won her fourth Wimbledon title in 2007 largely because she added topspin to her forehand and hit it safely crosscourt about 80 percent of the time. In the past she piled up unforced errors by recklessly whacking forehands hard, flat, down-the-line, and often either beyond the baseline or into the net. The reason she didn't make this obvious and fundamental change until age twenty-seven is that she is coached ineptly by her parents whose knowledge of tennis is modest, at best. It may be too late for James Blake, a twenty-seven-year-old, self-described "shotmaker" whose high-powered but mostly flat shots skim the top of the net and sometimes misfire, as well as for middle-echelon pros Fish and Ginepri, to upgrade their impressive but sometimes erratic games with more topspin.

### Ideal Player

The Next Great American Player will boast topspin groundstrokes, super athleticism and blazing speed, an aggressive all-court game, a powerful serve, hyper-competitiveness, finesse, and preferably be left-handed. Donald Young, a fast-improving eighteen-year-old, has all those attributes. Young barely lost, 6-2, 4-6, 7-5, to world No. 4 Nicolay Davydenko at the 2007 Pilot Pen Tennis tourney. Afterward, Davydenko called him—not Roddick or Blake—"the most dangerous American," adding, "This guy makes good winners from both sides."

---

**FASCINATING FACTS**

- According to Serena Williams, there aren't more up-and-coming American girls on the pro tour because "everyone's interested in becoming a pop star."

- According to the "2003 U.S. Tennis Participation Study," conducted by the United States Tennis Association and the Tennis Industry Association, more than 72 million Americans have tried tennis and then quit "mostly due to a poor introductory experience."

- Andrew Melkin, Panasonic vice president of television, predicted in 2006 that high-definition television "will cause a big explosion in tennis."

- In 2005 John McEnroe called 15-year-old junior phenom Donald Young, a left-handed American, "the next John McEnroe."

# PART 2

# People and Trends That Changed the Sport

# 11

# You've Come a Long Way, Ladies

# 2006

*The history of the past is but one long struggle upward to equality.*

—Elizabeth Cady Stanton, a 19th century U.S. suffragist, social reformer and author

Five hundred years before Billie Jean King whipped male chauvinist Bobby Riggs in their 1973 "Battle of the Sexes," men—and only the men—engaged in the sport of tennis. In medieval days, competition among male French bourgeoisie intensified at *jeu de la paume*, court or royal tennis, the precursor to modern tennis.

Way back in 1427, twenty-eight-year-old Margot of Hainaut stepped onto the court and fearlessly challenged the status quo. She was extraordinary, too. After she arrived in Paris, she beat all but the most powerful men at their favorite game. It's not clear whether Margot was provoked (as King was by Riggs, who blustered that "a woman's place is in the bedroom and in the kitchen") but something magnificent inspired her. Sadly, Margot's victories did not spawn an equal rights movement in sports.

Equality, or rather near-equality, would arrive centuries later, when tennis would reflect and inspire epochal societal changes. Lawn tennis, patented by British Major Walter Clopton Wingfield in 1874, experienced phenomenal growth throughout the British Empire and Europe because it attracted both sexes and provided healthful exercise and exciting competition. It quickly replaced croquet as the "in" sport at genteel garden parties in England, and it became a popular pastime among the upper class in America. Calls of "tennis, anyone?" signaled the start of wholesome amusement and often another kind of courting.

Although Mary Ewing Outerbridge introduced lawn tennis to the United States in 1874 when she brought a tennis net, rackets, and balls back from Bermuda, women were not allowed to compete in the first U.S. Championships at the glitzy Newport Casino in 1881. Women were finally accepted in 1887 when Ellen Hansell, serving underhanded, won the inaugural national women's event at the Philadelphia Cricket Club.

Those in favor of equal rights will be pleased to know that Ireland's Mabel Cahill outlasted Elizabeth Moore 5-7, 6-3, 6-4, 4-6, 6-2 in the 1891 U.S. final. Women played best of five sets, like the men, in the all-comers finals and challenge rounds for eight of the next nine years, until the all-male officers of the United States National Lawn Tennis Association—contending such lengthy matches were too strenuous for the "weaker sex"—discontinued them. The leading players, who were never consulted, protested vehemently but futilely.

Likewise, in the U.S. mixed doubles events, parity of the sexes did not exist for either Cahill in 1892 or Ellen Roosevelt in 1893, both of whom triumphed when partnered with Clarence Hobart. The poor women, you see, were not allowed to keep track of the score because it was believed to be too much of a strain.

What actually was a strain, if not a crushing burden, was the prescribed costume of the era. The fashionable female tennis player wore ankle-length skirts with starched petticoats underneath and tightly laced corsets, all supported by a girdle. If all of that weren't suffocating enough, her outfit included a stiff whalebone collar, a necktie or scarf, long sleeves, a broad-brimmed hat awkwardly attached with a pin, stockings, and a sturdy heeled boot. Often the attire was stained in blood after play. No wonder Charlotte "Lottie" Dod, in her 1903 book *Lawn Tennis*, wrote, "Ladies' dress, too, is a matter of grave consideration; for how can they ever hope to play a sound game when their dresses impede the free movement of every limb?"

Luckily, Lottie was not thus impeded, because the fifteen-year-old English school-girl was allowed to wear a white dress that ended just below the knee. The first tennis prodigy still remains the youngest player to win Wimbledon where she reigned un-beaten over five years, from 1887 to 1888 and 1891 to 1893. Defying the Victorian conventions of her time about femininity, Lottie, who relished smashing and volleying, exhorted her sisters: "Ladies should learn to run, and run their hardest, too, not merely stride."

The twentieth century's first teen tennis queen, May Godfray Sutton, also be-lieved long dresses spoiled a lady's play, and play spoiled long dresses. The athletic and boundlessly enthusiastic Californian shocked the staid Brits with her mildly eman-cipated costumes: shorter skirts, fewer petticoats, and sleeves audaciously rolled up to bare her elbows.

When eighteen-year-old Sutton, pounding vicious topspin forehands, became the first overseas player and first American to win Wimbledon in 1905, *The Leicester Chronicle* glowingly reported, "Magnificently muscular, she appears to care nothing for the minor graces, nor even the little tricks and dodges in which her male compatriots indulge. She is all for the rigor of the game." Her fame was such that three years later Wright & Ditson introduced The Sutton Star Racket with her approval. Could mon-etary compensation be far away?

While tennis was still amateur and primarily social, Dorothea "Dolly" Katherine Douglass Lambert Chambers, the daughter of an Anglican vicar, viewed it as a highly serious professional sport. A tenacious competitor, Chambers imposed herself on opponents with her intense concentration and well-conceived strategy. She captured seven Wimbledon titles from 1903 to 1914 when she was thirty-five years old.

All business off the court, too, Chambers spoke out against the discrimination seen by women who were relegated to inferior courts and indecent changing rooms. Especially vexed with the prevailing attitude that women were frail, she countered, "Is the essential feature of a woman her weakness, just as the essential feature of a man is his strength, not merely physical but mental and moral strength? I do not think so. Woman is the second edition of man, if you will; therefore, like most second editions, an improvement on the first."

The next champion, Anna Margarethe "Molla" Bjurstedt Mallory, a Norwegian who immigrated to America in 1914, did not share this opinion. This hard-hitting baseliner won five U.S. Championships from 1915–1918 and in 1920. Nicknamed "the fighting Norsewoman," she wrote, "I think a girl ought to have as much pluck and fighting spirit as a man," but stressed, "a woman has physical limitations—she is not so strong or so enduring as a man and she must acknowledge these limitations when playing tennis."

Next came Suzanne Lenglen, a woman who would neither acknowledge any limitations nor adhere to any traditions. Indeed, the uninhibited Frenchwoman, as much an actress as an athlete, embodied the post-war hedonism of the Roaring Twenties when women smoked, drank, danced, wore make-up, and exercised their franchise.

Like Bill Tilden, Babe Ruth, Red Grange, Bobby Jones, and other larger-than-life figures in the Golden Age of sports, the incomparable Lenglen fascinated the public with her *je ne sais quoi* as much as her total domination from 1919 to 1926. Lenglen was the first woman to wear lipstick on the court at ultra-conservative Wimbledon, and the first world-class player to train regularly with men. It was not uncommon for one of her breasts to pop out of her dress during matches, agitating women and titillating wealthy Riviera men—who named them Jane and Mary and inquired about them at breakfast. At times risqué, she enjoyed giving press conferences in a bathtub.

Lenglen's appeal "lay precisely in the way she fused athletic ability with heterosexual allure," explains Susan K. Cahn in her 1994 book, *Coming on Strong: Gender and Sexuality in Twentieth Century Women's Sport.* "With her unusual dress and dancelike movement, she pioneered an ideal of the female body as physical and actively erotic."

Though not pretty, *la grande* Suzanne radiated a joy and confidence that made her charismatic to both sexes. She delivered women from the tyranny of corsets and inspired a revolution in tennis fashion by wearing sleeveless cardigans, pleated knee-length skirts, colorful sashes, and her trademark wide tulle headband. That outfit completed the sartorial tennis emancipation of women, and Lenglen reveled in the freedom to hit every shot in the book and provide an exclamation point with balletic leaps. Monica Seles idolizes her, and Martina Navratilova confided, "I would have given anything to have watched her play."

With as near-perfect a record as Lenglen, the beautiful Helen Wills ruled the

*Suzanne Lenglen dominated tennis from 1919 to 1926.*

tennis world during 1927–33, 1935, and 1938 and epitomized the well-educated, upper-crust amateur of yesteryear—unlike Lenglen who joined the first pro tour in 1926. "Tennis is a diversion, not a career," wrote Wills in her insightful 1937 autobiography, *Fifteen-Thirty*. She also represented the classic baseliner who rarely ventured to net. The conventional wisdom was that serving and volleying couldn't be done by a woman. "I have yet to know a first-class volleyer among women who has consistently won from a hard-hitting baseline player," insisted Mallory.

Alice Marble proved the skeptics wrong and changed women's tennis for the better. A superb natural athlete, Marble "played like a man," the ultimate compliment then, and still kept her feminine appeal. The blonde and shapely Californian served powerfully and with an American twist, volleyed and smashed brilliantly, drop shotted cleverly, and covered the court swiftly. Men loved watching her—she wore the briefest shorts ever seen in her 1937 Wimbledon debut—as well as playing doubles with her. Despite a tragic private life (losing her father at age six and being raped at fifteen) and suffering from anemia and pleurisy, the sport's first serve-volley champion racked up twelve U.S. and five Wimbledon singles and doubles titles before turning pro in late 1940.

While Marble's game was bold and crowd-pleasing, her off-court adventures courted danger. Near the end of World War II she worked as a spy for U.S. Army Intelligence. She discovered valuable information from her former lover, a Swiss banker, about Nazi loot smuggled out of Germany, only to be shot, though not fatally, in the back by a double agent.

Five years later Marble summoned another kind of courage to help another pioneer overcome the odds and change the course of tennis history. By 1950 Althea Gibson, perennial champion of the predominantly black American Tennis Association, had emerged as a formidable player, reaching the quarterfinals of the Eastern Indoors and National Indoors events. But would she be allowed to play in the USLTA's summer grass-court tourneys in order to qualify for the Nationals at Forest Hills?

Marble, who had heroically fought Nazi racism, challenged the wavering USLTA to allow Gibson to participate. In a rousing letter published in the July 1950 *American Lawn Tennis* magazine, she wrote:

> I think it's time we faced a few facts. If tennis is a game for ladies and gentlemen, it's also time we acted a little more like gentle people and less like sanctimonious hypocrites. If there is anything left of sportsmanship, it's more than time to display what it means to us. If Althea Gibson represents a challenge to the present crop of women players, it's only fair that they should meet that challenge on the courts, where tennis is played. But if she is refused a chance to succeed or to fail, then there is an uneradical (sic) mark against a game to which I have devoted most of my life, and I would be bitterly ashamed. The entrance of Negroes into national tennis is as inevitable as it has proven to be in baseball, in football, or in boxing; there is no denying so much talent. I've never met Miss Gibson but, to me, she is a fellow human being to whom equal privileges ought to be extended.

Marble's eloquent rebuttal of the USTA's discriminatory policies resulted in Gibson's being accepted at the Orange Lawn Tennis Club in South Orange, New Jersey, the National Clay Courts in Chicago and the Nationals, where she nearly upset three-time Wimbledon champion Louise Brough in a thrilling 6-1, 3-6, 9-7 second-round battle.

Like Marble, Gibson had once been a tomboy (from the mean streets of Harlem where she often played hooky from school) and played serve-volley tennis. And like baseball pioneer Jackie Robinson, breaking the color barrier brought Gibson heartbreak as well as greatness. Nearly all the white girls, except for Angela Buxton, a Jew from England, shunned her. Hostile crowds heckled her—sometimes calling her "nigger"—or ignored her spectacular shots. Prying newspapermen pestered her, and to make matters worse, the Negro press beat her brains out because she was "not militant enough" as a civil rights crusader. Rather than admit her, some tournaments run by bigots simply went out of business.

Gibson reigned as the undisputed queen of tennis in 1957 and 1958 by capturing both the Wimbledon and U.S. championships. After winning her first Wimbledon, she received heaps of telegrams from fans and luminaries such as President Dwight D. Eisenhower, Averell Harriman, and boxing champion Sugar Ray Robinson. When she returned to New York, she was honored with a rare ticker-tape parade up Broadway to City Hall, where Mayor Robert Wagner gave her the medallion of the city.

In her 1958 autobiography, *I Always Wanted to Be Somebody*, Gibson recalled her long hard road to glory: "If I've made it, it's half because I was game to take a wicked amount of punishment along the way, and half because there were an awful lot of people who cared enough to help me. It has been a bewildering, challenging, exhausting experience, often more painful than pleasurable, more sad than happy. But I wouldn't have missed it for the world."

Neither would have Billie Jean Moffitt King, who was not a reluctant pioneer like Gibson, but a rebel with a cause. She fell in love with tennis when she was eleven, took free lessons every weekday at a different public site in Long Beach, California, and soon told her mother, "I am going to be No. 1 in the world." When the bubbly twelve-year-old was banned from a team photo at the Los Angeles Tennis Club because she wore shorts her mother made instead of the required white tennis dress or skirt, she vowed to change the sport. And how she did!

For the next fifty years King battled country club elitism and snobbery, the reactionary tennis establishment, "shamateurism," racism, homophobia, and sexism. Open Tennis arrived in 1968 enabling all the top players at last to compete in the most prestigious tournaments and earn an honest living (instead of hypocritically taking under-the-table payments as "amateurs"), but that only highlighted the across-the-board discrimination against women who felt betrayed.

Anger reached a critical mass when the 1970 Pacific Southwest tournament offered $12,500 to the men singles champion and only $1,500 to the women's titlist. Gladys Heldman, the brainy publisher of *World Tennis* magazine persuaded Joseph Cullman III, the chairman of the board of Philip Morris, to sponsor the Virginia Slims circuit with King its charismatic superstar and tireless promoter.

While the new tour steadily grew, what ignited a tennis boom and the broad acceptance of women's pro tennis in America was a riveting, almost farcical exhibition at the Houston Astrodome on September 20, 1973. It pitted a man against a woman, age against youth, and, above all, outdated sexism against enlightened equality. King's resounding 6-4, 6-3, 6-3 triumph over Riggs, performed before a record 30,492 spectators and an estimated sixty million worldwide television viewers, made a powerful statement that has endured.

"People come up to me every single day of my life since that match," said King, referring to how her victory in the celebrated "Battle of the Sexes" changed attitudes. "I have people say, 'I saw that match. You changed my life. I started to believe in myself. I went to my boss and asked for a raise. I started getting better grades in school. I started thinking of myself differently.'"

In the past thirty-five years, teen queens Chris Evert, Tracy Austin, Steffi Graf,

Seles, Martina Hingis, and Maria Sharapova, African-American stars Venus and Serena Williams, sex symbol Anna Kournikova and legendary champion Navratilova have taken tennis to almost undreamed-of heights of playing prowess, popularity, media coverage, prize money, and endorsements. Their rivalries, feuds, scandals, and love affairs have added drama and fueled controversy that turned tennis stars into glamorous international celebrities. Is there another sport where the heroines are known by their first names?

A survey by American Sports Data Inc. in 1991 revealed that 91.8 percent of Americans over thirteen recognized the retired but still enormously popular Evert, which was more than recognized male sports superstars Magic Johnson (89.0 percent) and Joe Montana (88.8 percent). In 2000 Kournikova, a contender rather than a champion, ranked No. 1 among the most-searched-for athletes in the world, according to leading Internet search engines Lycos 50 and Yahoo! Sania Mirza finished second—behind only Bollywood star Shah Rukh Khan—in a 2005 poll when Indians voted for the country's youth icon.

Tennis today boasts not only the most notable sportswomen but also by far the most quotable. Teenaged Kournikova bragged, "I have a lot of boyfriends. Every country I visit, I have a different boyfriend. And I kiss them all." Sharapova, then sixteen, asserted, "You can't compare us. People seem to forget that Anna isn't in the picture anymore. It's Maria time now." And who else but Serena, when asked if she had any tips on being a tennis superstar, would fire back, "I'm not a tennis superstar, I'm a superstar."

As tennis spread to the far corners of the earth—more countries belong to the International Tennis Federation than the United Nations—the balance of power shifted dramatically. In the year-end 2006 women's rankings, none of the top twenty singles players came from a nation where English is the primary language! Four Russians ranked in the singles top ten, and a Chinese team captured two Grand Slam doubles titles.

During her 2006 U.S. Open victory speech, Sharapova—born in Siberia, trained in Florida, and now racking up a staggering thirty million dollars a year in endorsements—said, "First and foremost, I would like to thank Billie Jean King for being such an amazing woman. Without her we would not be standing here today. What she's done for our sport and what she's done for women is absolutely incredible, and I've looked up to her since I was a little girl."

Margot, Lottie, Suzanne, and the other courageous pioneers would marvel at how far lady tennis players have come toward reaching their vast potential as athletes and entertainers. And they would urge their sisters to continue their noble battle for equality.

## TIMELINE

**1876**   The first two tournaments (albeit with tiny draws) for women were played. Miss W. Casey wins the Irish Championships in Dublin, and Mary G. Gray captures a Bermuda tournament.

**1879**    May Langrishe, only fourteen, wins what historians recognize as the first important tournament (because of the size of the draw) at the Irish Championships; Women's events are included on the first program of the newly instituted Oxford University Tennis Championship.

**1884**    Wimbledon, where men had been competing since 1877, stages a ladies singles event for the first time with Britain's nineteen-year-old Maud Watson beating her older sister Lilian in the final and receiving a silver flower basket valued at twenty guineas; Blanche Williams scores another first when she impressively umpires an important championship match that the London sports periodical *Pastime* notes is a "daring experiment by the referee."

**1886**    The Chestnut Hill (Massachusetts) Tennis Club Ladies Open takes place.

**1887**    The first U.S. Championships for women is staged at the Philadelphia Cricket Club with singles, doubles, and mixed doubles titles decided.

**1889**    On February 9, the United States National Lawn Tennis Association carried a motion that "its protection be extended to the Lady Lawn Tennis players of the country."

**1891**    In 1891 the women start playing best three-of-five set matches in the singles final (except for 1893) until 1902 when the women's singles reverts to best two-of-three sets for all matches.

**1900**    The Olympic Games in Paris includes women's tennis and women's golf—despite the fact that Pierre de Coubertin, the celebrated founder of the modern Olympics, fights against the admission of women. Two years later, he pronounced, "Women have but one task, that of crowning the winner with garlands."

**1913**    Wimbledon, after fierce resistance and continual controversy, decides to stage women's doubles and mixed doubles, thirty-six years after its first championships.

**1922**    Although men compete in the inaugural Australian Championships (then Australasian) in 1905, the women have to wait seventeen years before they are included.

**1926**    Suzanne Lenglen and Mary K. Browne become the first female players to turn pro when they join an exhibition tour with Vincent Richards, Howard Kinsey, Paul Feret, and Harvey Snodgrass.

**1928**    In a San Francisco exhibition, Helen Wills beats Phil Neer, the former NCAA champion and then the No. 8-ranked American male player, 6-3, 6-4.

**1932**    Helen Jacobs creates a sensation by wearing Bermuda shorts in her matches at Wimbledon.

**1947**    Pauline Betz Addie, the 1946 Wimbledon and U.S. champion, is suspended by the United States Lawn Tennis Association merely for her public support of a women's professional tennis tour.

**1949**   Famous couturier Teddy Tinling launches a line of sexy lingerie for American Gussy Moran; when "Gorgeous Gussie" wears her lace panties at Wimbledon, it causes a furor.

**1950**   Althea Gibson breaks the color barrier in tennis as the first black player to compete in the U.S. Championships; Ali Teslof of New York becomes the first woman umpire at the U.S. Championships.

**1953**   Teen queen Maureen Connolly, eighteen, achieves the first female Grand Slam by winning the Australian, French, Wimbledon and U.S. Championships.

**1960**   Maria Bueno, a stylish serve-volleyer, wins Wimbledon and receives a voucher of only 15 British pounds; Margaret Smith, the first female player to train with weights, captures the Australian Open at age seventeen.

**1963**   The Federation Cup (now called the Fed Cup), the premier team competition in women's tennis, is launched to celebrate the 50th anniversary of the International Tennis Federation. Sixteen nations enter the inaugural event won by the U.S.

**1967**   Billie Jean King becomes the first player to win a Grand Slam title, the U.S. Championships, with a metal racket, the Wilson T2000.

**1970**   Billie Jean King earns $600 for winning the Italian Open, while men's titlist Ilie Năstase is paid $3,500; women's professional tennis is launched when nine players sign $1 contracts with *World Tennis* magazine publisher Gladys Heldman to compete on a new women's tour; Margaret Smith Court collects $9,500 total prize money when she wins a "triple" (singles, doubles, and mixed doubles) at the U.S. Open, where she completes a singles Grand Slam.

**1971**   The Virginia Slims Circuit debuts with nineteen tournaments with a total purse of $309,100 on offer in the United States; Billie Jean King becomes the first sportswoman to earn $100,000 in a year.

**1972**   The passage of Title IX of the Education Act of 1972—which makes discrimination on the basis of gender illegal in all institutions receiving federal support—increases participation in women's interscholastic and intercollegiate sports.

**1973**   Billie Jean King founds the Women's Tennis Association, uniting all of women's professional tennis in one tour; the U.S. Open becomes the first Grand Slam tournament to offer equal prize money to men and women; Billie Jean King whips male chauvinist and former champion Bobby Riggs in the ballyhooed "Battle of the Sexes" match before 30,492 spectators, the largest live crowd ever to see a tennis match, and an estimated sixty million TV viewers in thirty-seven countries.

**1974**   The WTA signs the first television broadcast contract in the history of the association (with CBS).

**1975**     Declaring "I wanted my freedom," eighteen-year-old Czech Martina Navratilova makes worldwide headlines when she defects during the U.S. Open and receives political asylum in the U.S. "I will just play the tour, whenever I want and wherever I want."

**1976**     Chris Evert becomes the first female athlete to surpass $1 million in career earnings.

**1977**     After witnessing her first Wimbledon, Queen Elizabeth II of England comments, "I had no idea tennis girls could look so pretty."

**1979**     Tracy Austin becomes the youngest U.S. women's singles champion ever at the age of sixteen years, eight months, and twenty-eight days.

**1980**     More than 250 women are playing professionally all over the world in a tour consisting of forty-seven tournaments, offering a total $7.2 million in prize money.

**1981**     Catherine MacTavish becomes the first woman to umpire a Centre Court match in Wimbledon's 104-year history.

**1984**     The Australian Open joins the U.S. Open in offering the women's event equal prize money (although it temporarily does not between 1996-2000); only six years before that the men's prize money at the Australian Open is 8.6 times greater than the women's prize money. The Virginia Slims Champions plays a best-of-5-sets singles final, a format that the season-ending event discontinues in 1989.

**1985**     In "The Greatest American Woman Athlete of the Last 25 Years" national poll, Chris Evert, Martina Navratilova, and Billie Jean King finish 1-2-3.

**1986**     Fifteen-year-old Julia Englefield becomes the first ballgirl to work a match on Centre Court at Wimbledon.

**1988**     Steffi Graf captures the third Grand Slam in women's tennis history and makes it a "Golden Slam" by winning a gold medal at the Seoul Olympics.

**1990**     Jennifer Capriati, only thirteen, reaches the final of her first pro tournament, and *Newsweek's* "The 8th Grade Wonder" heralds her seemingly certain greatness. The WTA Tour concludes the season at Madison Square Garden in New York with the first $1 million tournament in women's sports history.

**1991**     According to a 1991 survey by American Sports Data Inc., 91.8 percent of Americans over thirteen recognize Chris Evert—more than recognize male superstars Magic Johnson (89.0 percent) and Joe Montana (88.8 percent).

**1992**     Monica Seles, at eighteen, becomes the highest-paid female athlete in the world and betters men's leader Stefan Edberg for the second year in a row.

**1993**     Monica Seles is stabbed in the back during a changeover at a Hamburg tournament by a crazed Steffi Graf fan and does not return to competition for twenty-seven months.

**1995**   To prevent mental and physical burnout among young players—most notably, Jennifer Capriati, Tracy Austin and Andrea Jaeger—the WTA Tour introduces age-eligibility rules that bars fourteen-year-olds from WTA tournaments and allows players, fifteen, sixteen, and seventeen to play more often and in more important events as they get older.

**1999**   Julia A. Levering becomes the first female president of the United States Tennis Association; Billie Jean King is named one of *LIFE* magazine's "100 Most Important Americans of the 20th Century."

**2000**   The five highest-paid female athletes in the world are tennis stars—Martina Hingis, Anna Kournikova, Venus Williams, Serena Williams, and Lindsay Davenport; at the U.S. Open more women's matches are played on the Stadium Court than men's matches for the first time in the tournament's history; Venus Williams signs a $40 million Reebok endorsement contract, the largest in women's sports history; Kournikova ranks No. 1 among the most-searched-for athletes in the world, according to leading Internet search engines Lycos 50 and Yahoo!

**2001**   Venus and Serena Williams play in the U.S. Open final, the first meeting between African-Americans in a Grand Slam final.

**2002**   Selima Sfar, a twenty-four-year-old Tunisian, becomes the first Arab woman to make it on the pro tennis circuit.

**2003**   The WTA Tour's marketing campaign uses catchy slogans reflecting the way women's tennis has redefined femininity, such as "Get in touch with your feminine side," "Some things need a woman's touch," "Serves that travel faster than gossip," and "Hell hath no fury like a woman scored on."

**2004**   A "Russian Revolution" hits women's tennis as Anastasia Myskina wins Russia's first women's Grand Slam singles title at the French Open, seventeen-year-old Maria Sharapova takes Wimbledon, and Svetlana Kuznetsova cops the U.S. Open.

In a *Sports Illustrated* magazine poll, 85 percent of respondents nominated tennis players as the sexiest female athletes during the past 50 years.

**2005**   Sony Ericsson Mobile Communications becomes the Tour's worldwide title sponsor in a landmark $88-million, six-year deal, the largest and most comprehensive sponsorship in the history of tennis and women's professional sport. As winner of the U.S. Open series, Kim Clijsters earns double prize money for winning the U.S. Open—her $2.2 million prize money is the single biggest payday in women's sports and in any official tennis event, men's or women's.

**2006**   World No. 1 Justine Henin-Hardenne, playing only thirteen tournaments, earns $4,204,810 in prize money. Brenda Schultz-McCarthy breaks Venus Williams's record of 127 mph for the fastest serve by firing a 130-mph rocket in a qualifying event. Maria Sharapova, a teenage beauty who wins the U.S. Open, rakes in more than thirty million dollars from endorsements.

**2007**  The WTA Tour pays out a record $62.4 million in prize money at sixty-two events in thirty-five countries. The All England Club announces on February 22 that it will offer equal prize money to men and women at Wimbledon, ending a 123-year tradition of inequality. On March 16, the French Tennis Federation announces that starting this year, Roland Garros will award equal prize money through all seven rounds (not only for the finalists) to both men and women—thus ending the long struggle for equal prize money at all four Grand Slam tournaments.

---

## FASCINATING FACTS:

- The highest TV rating by far for a tennis match on ESPN2 was the Serena Williams-Maria Sharapova final at the 2007 Australian Open.

- In 1989, two women hit serves that were measured at 100 miles per hour or more. In 2004, 151 women who hit serves measured at 100 miles per hour or more.

- Sania Mirza was the most searched-for personality on Google India in 2005 " ahead of film star Aishwarya Rai and cricket great Sachin Tendulkar.

- During its extensive coverage of the 2004 French Open, the new Al Jazeera Sports Channel showed its Muslim viewers Serena Williams in her revealing pink hot pants.

- Tennis (27), followed by golf (23), and track and field (10), has had the most Associated Press Female Athlete of the Year winners of any sport from 1931 to 2006.

- "The most dynamic duo" in sports, according to a 2004 reader poll in *Sports Illustrated for Kids* were Venus and Serena (47%), who left in their wake Shaq and Kobe (18%).

# 12

# Famous Feuds in Tennis History

# 2005

Ever since Caravaggio, the tormented Renaissance painter, murdered his opponent over a disputed score during a match in 1606, tennis players have fumed, feuded, and occasionally fought. Roger Taylor, a former boxer, was so incensed at Bob Hewitt's bickering and badgering during and after a 1969 pro match in Berlin that he decked Hewitt with a vicious left hook.

Fortunately, players have mostly punched volleys instead of opponents as gentlemanly behavior—inculcated by the British founders of modern lawn tennis during late 1800s—somehow survived into the Open Era. But sparks inevitably fly when hypercompetitive athletes clash in a *mano a mano* sport filled with high pressure and even higher stakes.

Brad Gilbert once recalled sitting in a 1980s locker room with intense champions John McEnroe, Jimmy Connors, Ivan Lendl, and Boris Becker. "I couldn't believe the electricity in that room. These four guys wouldn't even look at each other and wouldn't talk to each other."

Let's look at the greatest feuds and what fueled them.

### The Bad Boy vs. The Brat

It was hate at first sight when Connors, who had reigned with Björn Borg during most of the 1970s, confronted McEnroe, an equally fiery Irish-American. Proud and pugnacious Connors resented the outrageously talented punk who would take attention, money, and titles from him. Mac resented the lack of respect Connors gave him. In the 1979 Grand Prix Masters, Connors dismissively predicted, "Remember he's still a young boy. McEnroe will be good practice for me" before McEnroe upset him, 7-5, 3-0, retired, to signal the changing of the guard. "That fuckface McEnroe" was how Connors described his archrival.

The younger (by six years) McEnroe came out on top, 20–13, in their often controversial matches, although Connors led 8–7 in Grand Slam singles titles. Their verbal volleys were even, though, and always entertaining. When McEnroe hectored officials during their 1980 Wimbledon semifinal, Connors blasted, "My son is better behaved than you. I'll bring him to play you." McEnroe confided, "There were times on court when I wanted to beat Connors so bad, I felt I could easily strangle him."

By 1984 aging Connors had somewhat mellowed, winning over crowds with quips instead of alienating them with vulgarity, while irascible McEnroe was the bad actor that fans loved to hate. "I don't know that I changed all that much. They just found somebody worse," was Connors' memorable zinger. But Mac wasn't buying the nice-guy image Connors cultivated late in his career, and fired back: "I don't think I could ever be that phony."

Their rivalry resumed briefly on the senior tour, and their paths almost crossed again this century. Connors and McEnroe expressed interest in coaching promising junior players in England. Mac's involvement was short-lived, and Connors changed his mind. Then, in what would have been the shocker of 2005, the longtime antagonists agreed to share the BBC broadcasting for Wimbledon. Would that little booth be big enough for these two combustible characters—who could never stand each other eighty feet apart on a court—for a fortnight? You cannot be serious! It never happened.

## The Mouth vs. The Sisters

Hell hath no fury like a teen queen scorned, even if the queen dished the dissing better than anyone. In 1997 Martina Hingis became the youngest player (sixteen years, three months, twenty-six days) in the twentieth century to win a Grand Slam singles title, the Australian Open, with clever shot-making that belied her tender age. The Swiss Miss, who came within a match of winning a rare Grand Slam that year, saved her most potent shots, though, for razor-sharp barbs against her rivals.

Hingis, fast-rising African-American sisters Venus and Serena Williams, and Russian sex symbol Anna Kournikova, as brash as they were beautiful, were labeled "The Spice Girls." Sometimes "The Spite Girls" or "The Spat Girls" seemed more accurate. "In Hingis, Venus and Kournikova, we have the three musketeers," former teen queen and then TV tennis analyst Chris Evert said in 1998. "You couldn't find characters with as different personalities as these from any corner of the earth. To me, the off-the-court war of words is the most interesting thing. They all think they're going to be the greatest ever. They're so confident it amuses me. That's as entertaining as going out to watch them physically play against each other."

Whether the topic was their rivalry, boyfriends, fashion, education or race, Hingis and the Williamses trash talked with relish. Venus and Serena, both supremely athletic and boastful, had been told by their parents since childhood that they were destined for greatness, while precocious Hingis amazingly captured the French Open junior event when she was only twelve. Hingis would not surrender her throne without a fight—or fighting words. Venus and their bombastic father Richard frequently told the media that when Venus became No. 1, Serena would definitely be her toughest opponent. Fed up with that, Hingis in 1998 snidely countered, "Well, so far she's not [No. 1]. I mean, one day probably if I'm not playing anymore."

During the 2000 Wimbledon Serena announced that romantic entanglements could mess up a player's focus, saying, "Next thing you know, your game goes down, all kinds of things happen." To which, Martina Hingis, quite experienced after romancing tour players Julian Alonso, Justin Gimelstob, Ivo Heuberger, and Magnus Norman, replied, "I don't know if she had any experiences, so how can she talk about that? I'm doing pretty good. I'm happy with my relationship."

Venus, a fashion student who once brought seven different tennis dresses to Wimbledon because she presumed (wrongly) she'd reach the final, in 2001 panned Hingis's one-sleeved shirt: "That style was out last year. It was something that was popular from the designers right down to the popular price level." Ouch!

When Hingis claimed that the Williamses got more endorsement deals because of their race, Serena retorted, "I get endorsements because I win, and I work hard. I go out there and have a good attitude and I smile." Hingis didn't attend the 2000 Indian Wells final, but that didn't stop her from discounting Richard Williams' allegations that the booing and taunting by spectators was racially motivated. "I think it's total nonsense. I don't feel like there is any racism on the tour. It's a very international sport, and I even would say because they are black, they have a lot of advantages . . . They can always say it's racism."

Martina Navratilova best explained the sound and fury between Hingis and the best sisters in sports history when in 2001 she told *The New York Times*, "Everybody wants to be a big star, Jennifer, the Williams sisters, Martina. They're not happy that somebody else is getting as much attention. They all say, 'What about me?' It's human nature."

## The Egotist vs. The Underdog

If 1970s champion Guillermo Vilas is a god in Argentina, Guillermo Coria is the current people's choice. He's so beloved in his homeland that when he appears in restaurants he gets standing ovations. Ironically, he's far less popular with other players, including his fellow countrymen whom he nearly always (23–5 record) beats. Coria has been known to mock his opponents after he wins and seldom, until recently, gives them credit when he loses.

Like oil and water, Coria and Gaston Gaudio will never mix. They are too different. They come from different family backgrounds, and they have different approaches to tennis and life. Like Andre Agassi, Coria was pressured since he was born to be the greatest tennis player of his generation. His dad, a tennis coach, named him after Vilas; the cake for one of his first birthdays was racquet-shaped; and he has played tournaments since he was too young to remember. Gaudio enjoyed soccer and rugby in his childhood, and only picked up tennis because his older brother was playing it at the time. He discovered he liked it and was good at it. Gaudio decided to turn pro only after his father had a heart attack and the family experienced money problems: He thought tennis could be an excellent way of making money to help his family.

Like Connors, Coria needs and feeds on the rivalries, the feuds to fuel his competitiveness. His anger pushes him. He looks for other players to beat. Only some-one with a superiority complex would rent a hotel for the anticipated victory celebra-tions before the 2004 French Open final, as Coria did. Lo and behold, he lost to heavy underdog, No. 44-ranked Gaudio, who was so shocked that he confided, "I don't know how I win. I can't believe it yet. This is like a movie for me. And I don't even know it, but I'm the star."

In complete contrast, conflict-avoiding Gaudio has problems competing against many players on the tour (Mariano Zabaleta, Juan Ignacio Chela, Carlos Moyá, and others; he's even a good friend of Lleyton Hewitt) because they are his amigos and he cares about them. He also has stated many times that he's his own worst enemy be-cause he's too much of a perfectionist, and he'd rather play well than win.

The bad blood between these two 5'9" opposites started in the 2001 Viña del Mar final which Coria captured. They celebrated points by glaring at each other. A week later the simmering feud heated up when they collided in the Buenos Aires Open quarterfinals. In low voices they exchanged nasty remarks. After Gaudio won, he un-furled an Independiente flag (the soccer team he passionately supports) and jogged toward Esteban Cambiasso, the team's star who was celebrating Gaudio's triumph. Coria swears that, while Gaudio was going toward Cambiasso, he "hit" him in the face with part of the flag.

Their most bitter confrontation happened after Coria prevailed in the 2003 Ham-burg semifinal. Coria asked for the trainer when Gaudio was gaining momentum going into the second-set tiebreaker. After the short treatment Gaudio took the tiebreaker, but Coria, without showing any signs of cramping or any other injury, won the deciding set 6-0. When Coria limped to the net to shake hands, a provoked Gaudio insulted him by saying, "You are a ghost." One rumor had it that the two gauchos wanted to slug it out in the locker room and had to be separated, while another was that Gaudio's brother was the most angry man and the instigator there.

Since then the two have managed a *détente* of sorts—perhaps due to the calming influence of Coria's wife, Carla—although Gaudio admitted that he initially thought Coria was again faking cramps in the Roland Garros final. Their animosity resurfaced at the 2005 World Team Cup when Coria withdrew from his round-robin singles match against the two-time defending champion Chileans, claiming his shoulder was injured. "I'm fed up, one has to tell the truth," fumed Gaudio. "This isn't a team because there's someone who makes decisions choosing what's best for him. Coria and I were the best team, but if we were a real team this wouldn't have happened."

A well-known Argentine journalist reveals that "Gaudio told me off the record he hates when Coria gives excuses prior to a big match. He thinks he's always lying. And Gaudio thinks before some Davis Cup ties Coria faked injuries because he doesn't have the courage to represent his country.

"Coria is selfish because he's extremely competitive. Gaudio is too sincere, he will say what he thinks, and he is justifiably envious that the Argentine media and the National Tennis Association treat Coria better," he explains. "I predict the feud will remain the same. They won't talk to each other, but they will badmouth each other."

## The Legend vs. The Comer

No one's perfect—not even an Australian icon. John Newcombe, a handsome and articulate 1960s–1970s champion and later a successful Davis Cup captain, made very few mistakes during a distinguished career in which he amassed twenty-five Grand Slam singles and doubles titles. But one misstep caused a feud that festered for years.

Newcombe wrote a syndicated weekly column in the *Sunday Daily Telegraph.* The column was ghosted by a John Thirsk, a sportswriter who idolized Newcombe, but who occasionally got him in trouble. On the eve of the 1983 Australia-Sweden Davis Cup final before sold-out crowds at Kooyong Stadium in Melbourne, one infamous line in the column read, "Comparing Pat Cash to Mats Wilander is likening a crack in the wall to the Grand Canyon."

As it turned out, Cash, a temperamental eighteen year old, lost a close four-setter in the opening match to Wilander, who had upset John McEnroe and Ivan Lendl to capture the Australian Open on the same grass court a few weeks earlier. Cash, playing his first year in the competition, then became a hero by routing Joakim Nystrom to clinch the Cup title. Seven months later Cash whipped Wilander at Wimbledon and then again at the U.S. Open to avenge the defeat and refute Newcombe.

Alan Trengove, Australia's leading tennis writer and co-author of the new book, *Todd Woodbridge: The Remarkable Story of the World's Greatest Doubles Player*, recalls, "Newcombe never saw Thirsk's copy before it was published. Thirsk had made up the comment himself. And Newk was often careless in letting stuff be printed under his name that he hadn't vetted. His underlying philosophy was that all publicity was good publicity, and he wanted to keep his name before the public. I believe he regretted the gratuitous insult to Cash, who became the first Australian to win Wimbledon [in 1987] since Newcombe himself achieved his third Wimbledon title [in 1971]."

Indeed, Newcombe regretted it, as he reflected in his 2002 autobiography, *NEWK*, "I take total responsibility for the hurt it caused Pat because I had been too busy to okay the [ghost] writer's copy before it went to the printer." Newcombe didn't apologize then, and the feud was reinvigorated in January 1999 when Cash appeared on a TV current affairs show and told the viewers that Mark Philippoussis despised Newcombe and that Newcombe wasn't really the nice bloke the public thought he was.

"The day after the current affairs show aired on TV, I ran into Pat in the dressing room," Newcombe related in his book. "He said, 'Newk, I need to talk with you for a minute.' I ignored him. He kept on: 'Look, that story on TV last night, I feel really bad about it. I didn't know they were going to make such a big deal out of what I said. I'm sorry it happened.'

"I was sorry, too, for all the bad vibes that had come between us," related Newcombe. "I looked Cash in the eye, shook his hand, and said, 'Pat, it's fine.' That, for me at least, was the end of the matter."

That was hardly the end of the matter for Cash, though. In his 2002 autobiography, *Uncovered*, an unforgiving Cash, who had idolized Newk as a teenager, lashed back: "Newcombe never once had a good word to say about me . . . He was forever criticizing my behavior on court . . . He never once cared to praise me for winning the country two Davis Cups, or following him as the first Aussie to win Wimbledon for sixteen years."

## The Coach vs. The Rebel

Many incarnations ago, long before his current iconic phase as tennis' foremost philanthropist, tour elder statesman, and crowd-pleaser blowing kisses after victories, Andre Agassi was a sexy teen rebel without a cause or a pause. Besides being known for "a [mullet] haircut and a forehand," as Ivan Lendl once remarked, Andre wore lipstick, changed his hair color regularly, smoked marijuana, drank liquor often, and disdainfully wore jeans and high tops while beating opponents. About Agassi's hell-raising and rule-flouting at his tennis academy, Nick Bollettieri recalled, "When I had Andre for six and one-half years, my main job was to keep him out of jail."

Viewing the academy more as a boot camp than a tennis camp, Agassi fired back that "the only thing that took away my love of the game for a few years was being at Nick Bollettieri's academy in Florida." Agassi also took a more balanced view by commenting, "It's something I'm glad I went through, but I wouldn't wish it on my worst enemy."

When Bollettieri, who resented not sharing fairly in the fortune Agassi earned in tennis, "fired" Agassi in a two-page letter in 1993, the divorce stunned the tennis world and traumatized Agassi. How could these seeming lifers—whose friendship, mutual admiration, and loyalty withstood so much adversity en route to Agassi's 1992 Wimbledon title—break up?

Whether the odd couple, thirty-nine years apart in age, enjoyed a father-son relationship or endured a love-hate relationship or both, only they know for sure. But at the 1994 Lipton Championships, Agassi ripped his former coach and confidante, calling him "insignificant" and his knowledge of tennis "limited." Agassi added, "Nick hurt me. When things like that happen, it can make you lose hope in people. It can suck the life right out of you."

The ugly public war of words continued when a bristling Bollettieri retorted, "If I had limited knowledge, how did I get him to where he is? He has earned thirty-five million or forty-five million dollars. He's got the best Davis Cup record in the country. He's been to three Grand Slam finals and won Wimbledon, and he has spent ten years with me as his coach. If I was so limited, what the hell did he stay with me for?"

The moral of this complicated relationship seemed to be: You always hurt the ones you love—because Andre, not much later, confirmed that he missed Nick "incredibly, as a friend and father." Time and change have healed the deep wounds. Bollettieri mellowed and acknowledged his mistakes with Andre and other protégées, such as Boris Becker and Jim Courier, in his 1996 memoir, *My Aces, My Faults*. Agassi has grown into a man that Lendl recently praised as "a great role model for kids."

That feud is over. I would be remiss if I did not mention other memorable feuds.

**The Queen vs. The Beauty** — After the older and more advanced Martina Hingis embarrassed Anna Kournikova 6-0, 6-0 at the 1994 Junior U.S. Open, the acid-tongued

Russian reportedly told her: "You won, but I'm prettier and more marketable than you." But Hingis was surely right when in 1998 she crowed, "I'm sure she would like to change places with me, if she could, and have four Grand Slam titles." In November 2000 the two vixens staged a raucous locker room catfight (they reportedly threw trophies and bouquets at each other) at an exhibition in Santiago, Chile, that caused Hingis to dump her as a doubles partner. "Martina asked if I thought I was the queen—because the real queen was her," Kournikova told the media. Later, in the clubhouse, Kournikova threw a crystal vase at Hingis that smashed on the floor. "It was so bad I thought they were going to beat each other," former pro Jaime Fillol told the *New York Post*. The talented twosome happily settled their differences and reunited as a doubles team in 2001 and captured their second Grand Slam crown together at the 2002 Australian Open.

**The Almost-Champion vs. The Media** — "Henman-mania" proved almost as much a curse as a blessing to Tim Henman, a proper Englishman. The Brits pinned their hopes every year on Henman to become its first men's Wimbledon champion since Fred Perry way back in 1936. Not quite talented enough, he still made four semifinals and four quarters finals there. Late in his career, as hopes faded, the tabloids became merciless with headlines such as "No Pressure Timbo, But Choke Now, and We'll Never Forgive You" and reporters' questions less tolerable. Henman, who had held his fire for many years, finally lost his patience and perhaps prudence. He charged, "Most journalists don't know what they're talking about. A lot of people agree with me." Revealing what galled him most, Henman this year rightly charged, "I'm the fourth best player on this planet—and you're going to say I'm a failure?"

**The Rivals vs. The Starlet** — After comely seventeen-year-old Maria Sharapova pulled her 2004 Wimbledon stunner, Navratilova praised her as "the best thing that could have happened" to women's tennis. Far less enamored with her, though, are Sharapova's leading rivals from Russia. "It seems like everywhere you go, you're asked about Sharapova. All you read is about how elegant and graceful she is and how great her Wimbledon victory was for Russia. Quite frankly, I've had enough of that," groused Svetlana Kuznetsova. "If someone wants to make a fashion statement, they should go on stage and not on a tennis court." Was Kuznetsova, who had no major endorsements then, jealous of the charismatic Sharapova, who would soon earn more than $20 million a year? Elena Dementieva claimed Florida-based Sharapova "was not really Russian" because she rarely visits her native land and hadn't ever played a major tournament there (until the 2005 Kremlin Cup). And Anastasia Myskina, after losing for the first time to Sharapova at the 2004 WTA Championships, was furious at her father Yuri's abrasive antics and illegal coaching, and she refused to play Fed Cup if Sharapova did. This feud won't go away soon.

**The Intimidator vs. The Jerk** — Ivan Lendl once called Horst Skoff "the biggest jerk in tennis." Skoff earned his reputation by always finding an excuse whenever he lost, insulting linespeople, and even heading the ball back on match point against Stefan Edberg at the 1988 Seoul Olympics. Equally offensive, Thomas Muster got his kicks by trying to maim players with vicious body shots. Once when Félix Mantilla was eating a banana during a changeover, Muster walked by, grabbed it, and ate it himself. In a 1996 match at Queen's, Muster kept yelling "faggot" at Mark Woodforde whose girlfriend was watching courtside. "I'm not Mr. Nice Guy. I'm a tough cookie," bragged Muster.

Familiarity bred contempt ever since the two abrasive Austrians were juniors. Skoff took a lot of flak for being the smallest kid in training camp, and one day Muster and his pals put him into a box and taped it shut. Their hatred later became public when Muster criticized Skoff's training habits in the Austrian press. Skoff fired back by telling reporters he didn't like Muster's demands to be paid for playing Davis Cup. For years they wouldn't talk to each other. Muster upped the ante by not dressing in the same locker room as Skoff, and in 1993 he refused to play Davis Cup if Skoff were on the team.  To his credit, Skoff gradually matured, but the scowling Muster, who won the 1995 French Open and briefly gained the No. 1 ranking, never mellowed.

Ubaldo Scanagatta, Italy's leading tennis writer, recalled an irate Muster after whipping Skoff in a contentious Florence final. "In the locker room—and nobody else was there but his masseur—Thomas told me, 'I'd like one day to find myself within four walls alone with Horst and finally have a chance to hit him with a lot of punches until I knock him down.'"

**The Role Model vs. The Outsider** — "I swear, every time I passed Connors in the locker room, it took all my will power not to punch him in the mouth. It's sickening. He and Riordan could be such a good part of tennis, but will they only be satisfied when they have wrecked the whole game?" wrote Arthur Ashe, a stalwart of the ATP players' union, wrote in his diary in his 1975 book, *Arthur Ashe: Portrait in Motion*, about Bill Riordan and Connors who had sued Donald Dell and Jack Kramer, the lawyer for and director of the ATP. Before their unforgettable 1975 Wimbledon final, Connors filed a $5 million lawsuit against Ashe for calling Connors "unpatriotic" for his refusal to join the U.S. Davis Cup team. When Connors played under captain Ashe in the 1984 Cup finals in Stockholm, a miscommunication left Connors waiting in the freezing cold for a hour outside the locked practice facility. When he got inside, the infuriated Connors scrawled "Fuck you, Artie" in huge letters on the soft clay and left. Bad blood between these two opposites—the admired leader and the brash rebel—persisted throughout their careers. When journalist Peter Bodo asked Ashe, "Is Jimmy Connors really just an asshole?" Ashe replied, "Yeah, but he's my *favorite* asshole."

If you wondering why Roger Federer isn't feuding with anyone, the stylish Swiss explained it to tennis' most frequent feuder, McEnroe, in a 2005 USA Network interview. "Once I became No. 1, I started to relax. I had more people I didn't like before I became No. 1 because I looked at the game differently. I had been too anxious to win. I thought every guy I couldn't beat is an idiot," he confided. "Then I started to understand: it's not about how they play, it's about how they are as a person."

How boring! Even hyper-competitive Andy Roddick, who has lost to Federer ten out of eleven times, is confounded. "I have loads of respect for him, as a person as well. I've told him, 'I'd love to hate you, but you're really nice.' "

---

**FASCINATING FACTS:**

- John McEnroe describes his relationship with archrival Jimmy Connors during their playing days as "a love-hate relationship, mostly hate."

- In a 2003 interview, Justine Henin-Hardenne, said leaving her father was like "leaving prison." (She reconciled with her father and siblings in 2007.)

- In 2006 Australian Lleyton Hewitt was voted No. 5 in a *La Nacion* newspaper poll listing the most hated sporting figures in Argentina.

- Arthur Ashe, the 1960s–70s tennis champion and human rights activist, corresponded with six U.S. presidents.

- Six-time Grand Slam champion Boris Becker reveals in his 2003 autobiography, *Stay a Moment Longer*, that he once asked his wife to shoot him.

- A Sunni Arab tennis coach and his two Shiite players were shot to death in Baghdad on May 27, 2006, because they were wearing shorts.

- Tim Henman, fed up with mindless criticism in 2003, bluntly told some British journalists, "Why on earth would I be interested in what you are saying about my game?"

- When Art Larsen, the eccentric 1950 U.S. champion, was barred from a tournament because of an entry blank technicality, he hired a plane to seed a cloud bank over the courts in an effort to force a rain-out.

# 13

# From Russia with Love
# 2005

After hearing for years "The Russians are coming," they're finally here! Not with tanks rumbling across Europe or via intercontinental ballistic missiles. These beautiful Soviette invaders wield rackets that conquered the tennis world last year.

"There are like fifty players from Russia in the top ten. Every week you have to play an 'ova,'" Serena Williams quipped before being shocked 6-1, 6-4 by seventeen-year-old Maria Sharapova in the 2004 Wimbledon final. Just four weeks earlier, compatriot Anastasia Myskina made history as the first Russian to win a Grand Slam title at Roland Garros, and two months later nineteen-year-old Svetlana Kuznetsova, pulled yet another surprise by capturing the U.S. Open.

From only one woman ranked in the top thirty in 2002, Russia boasted four in the top six—three Slam champions and two-time finalist Elena Dementieva—plus their first Fed Cup title in 2004. How did Russia, where the average annual income is only $1,400 and where the brutal winter lasts nearly eight months, emerge as a women's tennis powerhouse so suddenly?

Rich Russian landlords played the game way back in the late 1870s, as later did luminaries Leo Tolstoy, Tsar Nicolas II, and Vladimir Lenin. Anna Dmitrieva, who had won some minor tournaments behind the Iron Curtain, made headlines in 1956 as the first player allowed outside the Soviet Union to compete on the international circuit (see sidebar). She vividly recalled her dramatic appearance at Queen's and Wimbledon. "In the newspapers, they wrote that 'just as there can't be a black bear in Africa, so there can't be good tennis players from Russia,' " Dmitrieva said in the enlightening DVD, "Anna's Army: Behind the Rise of Russian Women's Tennis." But tennis wouldn't become a popular sport for the masses until the 1990s after its young stars, its first world-class tournament, and a colorful politician galvanized interest.

Events unfolded quickly in 1989. Andrei Chesnokov issued an ultimatum to the

Soviet Sports Ministry to keep all his prize money—rather than the $750-a-year pittance allowed Russian players—or else he'd leave the organization. The Sports Committee, fearing an embarrassing emigration, gave in. About the same time Natalia Zvereva publicly challenged the tennis federation to allow her to keep her entire $24,000 prize winnings during the televised awards presentation at the Family Circle Magazine Cup. She, too, succeeded and that further broke the exploitative Russian system during the brave new world of *glasnost* and *perestroika* initiated by president Mikhail Gorbachev.

Another sea change in official policy accompanied the arrival of president Boris Yeltsin: the freedom of average Russians to travel abroad. Tournament players could now enter more than the handful of foreign events they were previously restricted to. They also could train, and even reside for long periods, elsewhere.

Enter Anna Kournikova, whose gorgeous face and nubile body would launch a thousand billboards (most memorably, for her no-bounce bra), scores of adoring websites, and several seven-figure endorsements. Like moths attracted to fire, the media could never get enough of the hottest flame in years. "The Russian Lolita" showed girls and their ambitious parents that they too could become successful, rich, and famous, especially by leaving the Motherland. Sponsored by mega-sports agency IMG, the cute-as-a-button and extremely assertive, ten-year-old prodigy arrived to train at the Bollettieri Tennis Academy in Florida in 1992. Other rising stars, such as Marat Safin, his sister Dinara Safina, and Kuznetsova, later developed their games in Spain, while Sharapova and No. 11 Vera Zvonareva trained in America and No. 12 Nadia Petrova in Egypt.

The serendipitous intersection of the resoundingly successful Kremlin Cup, the first pro tournament staged in Russia in 1990, President Boris Yeltsin, its honorary organizer and a tennis fanatic with a working class background, and Prime Minister Ivan Silaev, another tennis lover and aggressive player, captured the imagination of an increasingly prosperous and leisure-minded people. Formerly shunned by the Communists as a decadent, bourgeois pastime, tennis quickly became the "in" sport for politicians, business people, artists, and the emerging middle-class. Through his drinking buddy, tennis federation president Shamil Tarpishev, Yeltsin became friends with the leading players, and now he and Yevgeny Kafelnikov provide $10,000–$15,000 scholarships to promising junior players. A tenfold increase in courts during the past fifteen years has further fueled the tennis boom there.

Whether Yeltsin or Kournikova deserves the bulk of the credit for the Russian Revolution is debatable. "Women's tennis, in Russia and around the world, is popular because of Kournikova," says Safina. "A lot of players want to be like her." Indeed, what's not to like about her endorsement income (more than fifteen million a year at her peak) and her notoriety (she was the Internet's No. 1 most-searched-for athlete in 2004, according to Lycos, despite not playing a tournament since May 2003)—even if she never won a singles title and was more envied than liked by tour players.

"Anna's personality and her success [she ranked No. 1 in doubles and No. 8 in singles and beat five No. 1 players] and her glamour mean a lot," acknowledges Olga

Morozova, the much-respected 1974 French and Wimbledon finalist who now coaches Dementieva. "Anna did a lot, but [French and Australian titlist Yevgeny] Kafelnikov and Safin and Chesnokov earlier did even more."

Kournikova, whose ego usually is boundless—I could snap my fingers and have any man I wanted," she crows—downplays "the Kournikova Effect" and credits the renowned Spartak Club in Moscow and her primary coach there, Larissa Preobrazhenskaya. Several factors made Spartak's tennis school, which has fifteen clay courts and only two indoor courts that haven't been resurfaced in decades (but access to another three courts elsewhere) the mecca for budding talent.

"I think the success of the Russian girls is determined by the women coaches," Andrei Myskin, father of Anastasia Myskina, told *The Globe and Mail*. "Nowhere in the world are there so many female coaches. Yes, the [Spartak] tennis school doesn't have any money . . . but the school has a unique atmosphere of family house, warmth, and good technical training."

The more famous coaches also included Rauza Islanova, the mother of 2000 U.S. and 2005 Australian champion Safin and Safina, Tatiana Naumko, Chesnokov's mentor, and Nina Teplyakova, who taught Morozova. Another key to Russian success is that students start tennis very early, usually at five, six, or seven, and typically stay with the same coach for eight to ten years. That bonding enables children to benefit from a more nurturing relationship as well as a single, unambiguous teaching philosophy.

The fiercely competitive atmosphere at Spartak also brought out the best in players, especially keen rivals Kournikova, Myskina, and Dementieva, all born within four months of each other in 1981. The latter two used to play for a piece of pizza at the club, but the pride of winning tournament matches meant far more. "I was complaining that she was cheating because we played without a chair umpire, and she was complaining that I was cheating. It was kind of interesting," recalls Myskina about her sometimes heated junior rivalry with Dementieva. "[Now] we do everything together, and we're pretty good friends," adds Myskina.

Coaches encouraged the winning-is-everything mentality. For example, No. 15 Elena Bovina's coach made her bury all her second- and third-place trophies. "Sports are as big in Russia as in the United States," points out former world No. 7 Morozova. "Here you want to have only winners. It's the same thing in our country. If you finish second or third, it's not very important. In every American family, the mother and father are looking to produce a champion. But I have to say the Russian girls are working harder." Their strong, lean physiques and rigorous work ethics—Kuznetsova practiced for an hour after her first six matches en route to the 2004 U.S. Open final—attest to that.

Many of the current crop are also blessed with superb athletic genes. Petrova's father was a top hammer thrower, her mother an Olympic bronze medalist in the 400-meter relay. Sturdily built Kuznetsova's inherited her muscular thighs from her mother, a six-time world champion cyclist, and her father, a cycling coach of six Olympic champions. The father of 6'2 ½" Bovina played on the Russian national water polo team. Islanova ranked among the top ten Soviet Union tennis players.

Morozova describes the predominant Russian style of play as "steady and aggressive. We have clay for only four months and hard courts the rest of the time. You have to have an aggressive game indoors, and on clay heavy topspin is not a huge advantage anymore. That's why the Russians play a flatter shot on the rise. That's the secret of their present and future success."

Sharapova, the youngest yet most self-possessed of the Soviette baseline babes, overcame the greatest odds. She was only seven when she and her father Yuri arrived in Florida with only $700 and no relatives or friends, speaking almost no English, but dreaming of future stardom. Nick Bollettieri saw her ferocious, Seles-like determination and considerable talent and so gave her a scholarship. She regularly visits highly regarded California coach Robert Lansdorp (who taught Grand Slam champions Pete Sampras, Lindsay Davenport, Tracy Austin, and Myskina) to hone her near-perfect groundstrokes, powerful serve and improving net game. Disdaining the "tennis babe" slot Kournikova reveled in—although she signed a modeling contract with IMG Models—the lithe, 6' Sharapova dismisses comparisons with the ultimate blonde bombshell. "You can't compare us. People seem to forget that Anna isn't in the picture anymore. It's Maria time now."

Even so, Russian fans picked the outgoing Myskina, not the more comely Sharapova, as their favorite tennis player last year. The slender brunette sensationally captured the French Open—losing only fourteen games in the last three rounds—won all three matches in Russia's 3-2 Fed Cup title thriller over France, and lost a semifinal heartbreaker to Justine Henin-Hardenne at the Athens Games. A clever strategist, Myskina needs to beef up her serve and groundies to win more majors.

Kuznetsova, who also excels in doubles where she learned a lot from Martina Navratilova when they teamed up in 2003, can hit all the shots, including a formidable kick serve. If she improves her shot selection and consistency, she'll be a force for years.

Dementieva is "an incredible fighter and athlete with good groundstrokes," says Morozova. But her dismal performances in the 2004 French and U.S. finals had to scar her psyche. "It's all about my serve. I really need to have a better serve to win a Grand Slam," rightly acknowledges Dementieva, who had a shocking fifty-two double faults and only two aces at Flushing Meadows.

Nadia Petrova, who routed Serena Williams and Henin-Hardenne last year, is the most gifted athlete but worst match player among the elite Russians—she's reached only one Slam semifinal in five years. She boasts a terrific serve, solid volley, and tremendous overall power. This super-jock, who wants to "try every sport there is," needs to be more creative on the forehand and play more poised, smarter tennis, or else she'll never fulfill her vast potential.

Yuri Sharapov, while not quite the scourge of the women's tour that banned Bad Dads Jim Pierce and Damir Dokic were, has often antagonized his daughter's opponents during matches. Mr. Sharapov swears at them in Russian and makes obnoxious noises to disturb them. During her first career loss to Sharapova at the WTA Championships last November, Myskina was furious at his abrasive antics from the players' box. "He was just yelling and screaming instructions to her. I thought he might just jump onto the court at one point." Mr. Sharapov was twice warned for illegal coaching.

Despite owning one of the best records, Sharapova wasn't picked for the Athens Olympics and was snubbed from the winning Fed Cup final team last November. Myskina has threatened to skip the Cup squad this year if Sharapova joins the squad. One wonders if Sharapova will ever represent her country in Fed Cup competition. "I just don't see how her father could co-exist with the other girls' parents and team officials," said national team coach Larisa Savchenko-Neiland in Moscow. "Every time Maria was playing a Russian, his behavior was simply outrageous, nasty and out of control."

A little controversy will only give the comely Siberian capitalist more publicity. "Within a few years the name 'Maria Sharapova' will be a brand as universally recognized as Calvin Klein, BMW and Rolex," predicts Max Eisenbud, her IMG manager.

What would Comrade Lenin have said about *this* Russian Revolution?

## The Turning Point

When Soviet Communist Party leader Nikita Khrushchev pugnaciously proclaimed, "Whether you like it or not, history is on our side. We will bury you!" in a speech at a Kremlin reception in 1956, he was obviously referring to the U.S. capitalist system—not tennis. In fact, this uncouth provincial, who was born and raised in the village of Kalinovka and worked as a pipe fitter in various mines, was barely aware of the sport.

Ironically, Khrushchev helped thaw the Cold War a bit with some inadvertent "tennis diplomacy" in 1957. "The story goes that he was in London visiting as a visiting Communist Party official, and somebody asked him why no Soviet players appeared at Wimbledon," Anna Dmitrieva, now a TV tennis commentator, told the *Boston Globe's* Bud Collins. " 'What's Wimbledon?' he said, embarrassed when he found out. So [Andreyev] Potanen and I were on our way."

So was Russian tennis, even though it encountered stoppages and detours along the way. Dmitrieva, a lefty serve-volleyer, gained the girls' final in 1958 and achieved her best results in 1960 when she made the fourth round in singles, taking a set off second-seeded Darlene Hard. Olga Morozova softened the stern image of Soviets with her bubby personality as she surpassed the pioneering Dmitrieva by reaching the French and Wimbledon finals in 1974.

When the USSR boycotted South Africa in Davis Cup play to protest its apartheid policy, the International Tennis Federation banned it from tournaments from 1976 to 1984. Once the Olympic Games re-instituted tennis (as an exhibition event first) in 1984, the USSR revitalized its tennis program and allowed its elite players limited travel overseas (of course, with the KGB watching their every move). The collapse of the Soviet Union and arrival of glasnost and perestroika in 1989 finally unleashed the immense Russian talent and drive that we now witness.

# 14

# The Comeback That Proved Them All Wrong

# 2002

It happens to all the great ones. An aging, slow motion Muhammad Ali was urged to retire before he got his brains punched out. They told once-ethereal Michael Jordan to quit with six championship rings rather than embarrass himself at age thirty-nine with a mediocre team.

Proud Pete Sampras was also relentlessly bombarded with such exhortations for the first eight months of 2002. Friends and admirers of Pete worried that their hero would spiral downward until they could no longer recognize his panache. Mean-spirited critics, who had lambasted him as "boring" during his prime, now trashed him publicly for ineptness.

They cited abysmal losses to nonentity George Bastl at Wimbledon and clay-court specialist Álex Corretja in Davis Cup, also on grass, supposedly Pete's last bastion of supremacy, as indisputable proof he was washed up. One statistic didn't lie: "Pistol Pete" had fired blanks for thirty-three straight tournaments—no titles since his record 13th Grand Slam at the 2000 Wimbledon.

Often the "get out of town" crowd is right. Who could not be saddened watching Larry Holmes mercilessly pummel the hapless Ali for eleven rounds? Or baseball giant Willie Mays, in his 40s, drop routine fly balls? Or Arnold Palmer trying to break ninety at the Masters? Or Dennis Lillee, the great Australian cricketer, turn into a ghost of his former self in his ill-advised 1987–1988 comeback?

Even if the over-the-hill superstar doesn't tarnish his records and legacy or get badly hurt, he performs like a grotesque shadow of his bygone brilliance. Björn Borg became little more than a pathetic curiosity, losing all eleven first-round matches in his doomed 1991–93 comeback.

Of course, the rare great comeback, such as ice hockey legend Mario Lemieux's and cyclist Lance Armstrong's following cancer, can inspire and enrapture. And the unforgettable last hurrah, while not ending in ultimate victory, can capture our imaginations for a fortnight. Jimmy Connors calls his enthralling surge to the 1991 U.S. Open semifinals at the age of thirty-nine "the best eleven days of my career."

Unfortunately, no such happy scenario appeared in the cards for slump-ridden Sampras as the 2002 U.S. Open approached. True, he had managed to reach the previous two Flushing Meadows finals. But the harsher truth was that a more powerful shotmaker (Marat Safin) and younger legs (Lleyton Hewitt) trumped, even trounced, his fading skills and experience in those showdowns.

As the 2002 season progressed, Sampras looked more and more like another former champion who didn't know when to quit. His stunning loss to Corretja prompted controversial Russian Yevgeny Kafelnikov to say what some other players were thinking. "I think he should start thinking about quitting tennis when he is beaten by Corretja, especially on grass. That loss should tell him something, and it's a disrespect to himself to keep playing."

Predictable first-round losses on the slow clay courts at Rome, Hamburg, and Paris only deepened the slump and further eroded Sampras's confidence. If Sampras could defy Father Time anywhere, many analysts figured it would happen at Wimbledon, where his masterly serve-and-volley game thrived on the fast grass. The British had grown to appreciate Sampras, and Derek Wyatt, Labour MP for Sittingbourne and Sheppey, lobbyied to bestow an honorary knighthood on him because his seven Wimbledon titles "is an extraordinary achievement and should be recognized." Shockingly, the seven-time king played more like a commoner than a knight.

Reading supportive notes from his pregnant wife, Bridgette, on the changeovers couldn't save him as he was dumped by Bastl, a Swiss journeyman ranked No. 149, whose only other Wimbledon victory came in the previous round. A devastated Sampras called the loss "the ultimate low point of my career."

Sampras was also enraged by insinuations that his marriage to beautiful actress Bridgette Wilson—whom he called "the woman of my dreams"—caused his decline. John McEnroe had predicted it was "probably going to ruin Pete's tennis." In fact, Sampras credited his wife for keeping up his spirits when he considered hanging up his sneakers. "Don't blame my wife or my marriage," he fired back in August. "Blame me for not playing well. I didn't appreciate [the criticism] for her sake. It bothered her."

Early-round hard court losses to Tommy Haas at Toronto, Wayne Arthurs at Cincinnati, and Paul-Henri Mathieu on Long Island gave Sampras little match play and even less hope going into Flushing Meadows. Respected TV tennis analyst Mary Carillo expressed the conventional wisdom when she predicted, "Pete will never win the U.S. Open again because of the one day turnaround between the semifinal and final."

Not everyone had completely written off the four-time champion, though. When asked just before the U.S. Open if Sampras was washed up, Safin reverentially replied, "He's the greatest one. He's the best player of all times. Six years No. 1 in the world, thirteen Grand Slams. I cannot even talk about him, it's like talking about God."

Could Sampras, a fallible human at a tennis-old thirty-one, actually have another Grand Slam in him, as he had long maintained? Fed up with all the negativism, Sampras reminded everyone, "You've got to remember who I am and what I've done here."

Soon enough, he'd back up those confident words.

What drives sporting legends, such as Bill Russell (who used to vomit from the pressure before big games), Jessie Owens, Jim Brown, Wayne Gretzky, Pelé , Jordan, Ali, and Sampras, to produce extraordinary performances in difficult circumstances?

"The secret of great athletes is converting the pressure and their own insecurities into a powerful force and harnessing the electricity, the stress of the moment," says Brooks Johnson, former college and U.S. Olympic track coach in the sports science book, *Competitive Fire.*

Sampras would summon the courage, determination, single-minded focus, and athletic brilliance that made him the near-invincible champion he was in the 1990s. "When he played well, he was *easily* the best player I've ever seen," recently praised Mats Wilander, the defending champion when Sampras, then an eighteen-year prodigy, upset him at the 1989 U.S. Open.

Put simply, Sampras often played superbly when it mattered most. Consider his degree of domination. In the thirteen Grand Slams he had won in seventeen finals, Sampras surrendered only six sets to his victims, played only one five-setter, and even there took the deciding set 6-2.

The clinical precision of those decisive triumphs, as much as his reserved personality, explained why Sampras never attained the crowd-pleasing popularity of glitzy Andre Agassi or combative Connors. "You can't blame Pete Sampras for not being intense because how could he be with his game? He makes it all look so easy because he's such a great natural athlete," said Wilander.

Sampras rehired coach Paul Annacone, the ultimate chip-and-charge exponent in the 1980s, and decided on a relentless, go-for-broke strategy that had the added benefit of keeping the points short at Flushing Meadows. After blitzing eighty-something-ranked opponents Albert Portas and Kristian Pless in the opening rounds, Sampras needed five sets to overcome rocket-serving Greg Rusedski, the 1997 finalist.

Afterwards, the bitterly disappointed loser said all the wrong things. "I lost the match. He didn't win it . . . I'd be surprised if he wins his next match against Haas . . . He's a step-and-a-half slower coming to the net . . . He's a great player *from the past .* . . It's not the same player."

The quick-witted Sampras didn't dignify the Rusedski rubbish other than to quip, "Against him, I don't really need to be a step-and-a-half quicker" and "His issues have issues." But the demeaning remarks fueled his already intense determination. A much-sharper Sampras then easily took out No. 8-ranked Haas, No. 9 Andy Roddick, and No. 30 Sjeng Schalken. Roddick, purportedly the Next Great American Player, grew up idolizing Sampras and confided that during the 6-3, 6-2, 6-4 rout he marveled at Sampras's stylish all-court shotmaking. And he stressed, "I've never said he's washed up, you guys [the media] did. None of the players doubt he's capable of great tennis."

Certainly not archrival Agassi. They had dueled thirty-three times (Sampras led 19–14) in the past thirteen years, and in their first Grand Slam final, nineteen-year-old Sampras, a 66–1 pre-tournament longshot, ambushed the favored Agassi at Flushing

Meadows. The humbled loser called it "a good, old-fashioned street mugging out there." In 1995 Sampras pulled out a tough four-set U.S. Open final to clinch the No. 1 ranking. And for sustained sensational shot-making, their 2001 quarterfinal, won 6-7, 7-6, 7-6, 7-6 by Sampras, ranks as a classic.

Before the 2002 U.S. Open final, which likely was their last duel for a Slam crown, Sampras declared, "All athletes want to end it on a big bang. And that's what I want to do." Ageless Agassi, thirty-two, was just as fired up after whipping world No. 1 Lleyton Hewitt in a fierce semifinal baseline battle. "This is New York, baby," he enthused. "We're both here again, and it's going to be a blast."

Sampras blasted thirty-three aces and his relentless aggression spelled the difference in his engrossing 6-3, 6-4, 5-7, 6-4 triumph. Agassi, buoyed by a partisan, raucous throng of 23,157 in Arthur Ashe Stadium, picked it up a notch in third set but still needed sixteen points for a service break that clinched it. If Sampras looked weary at times, his nerves never faltered as he held serve on game points with three volley winners and two aces in the final set. Just as Sampras so often said, Agassi brought out the best in him. Fittingly, the two warriors walked off the court with their arms around each other.

An ecstatic Sampras, the oldest U.S. Open champion since thirty-five-year-old Ken Rosewall in 1970, admitted, "This might be my biggest achievement. This one might take the cake." He called his *tour de force* "awesome" and "pretty sweet," and we could add amazing, romantic, important, and unforgettable.

"The king is not dead," tennis Hall of Famer Tony Trabert announced to the thoroughly entertained crowd afterwards. Whether the king will abdicate the throne remains his most difficult decision and the intriguing question for the coming year. The couple's first child, Christian Charles, was born in November. Besides the joys of fatherhood, Sampras could retire with his storybook ending as the greatest tennis champion in history and look forward to starting his tennis academy and working for The Tennis Channel.

On the other hand, the thrill of competition may prove too seductive for Sampras to resist. As he once said, "The feeling of playing a great match is unbelievably exciting. Everyone knows how hard it is to find such an intense feeling in real life. It's like an addiction."

## Paeans to Pete Sampras

"Nothing in my career compares to playing against Pete. Pete's the best I've ever played against, and that forces you to get that little special rush of blood that makes you do that thing that's special." —Andre Agassi, paying tribute to archrival and fellow superstar Pete Sampras.

"He can hit the sort of shots which the rest of us can't hit and don't even think of hitting." —Jim Courier, on Pete Sampras. (1991)

"Sampras was convicted of being a vanilla scoop of serenity when he should've been celebrated for refusing to join the riotous band of village idiots headlined by Connors and McEnroe." —*USA Today* columnist Ian O'Connor.

"If there's one role model in tennis, it's Pete Sampras. He's behaving perfectly on the court, he's a nice fellow off the court, and he's playing great tennis altogether. I think he's extremely good for the game of tennis." —Boris Becker, on Pete Sampras. (1995)

"Pete has the most complete game of anyone I've ever seen." —All-time great Pancho Gonzalez. (1995)

"Pete, he's the best. He will be the best for the rest of the future of tennis. I think nobody can win thirteen Grand Slam titles. It's no chance." —Marat Safin, when asked if he could imagine anybody staying No. 1 as long—six straight years—as Pete Sampras did in the 1990s. (2001)

---

### Fascinating Facts:

- Legendary NFL coach Bill Walsh, in guiding the San Francisco 49ers to three Super Bowl titles, often pointed to Pete Sampras when coaching as a model athlete who plays his best when it matters most.

- After Andre Agassi routed 18-year-old Pete Sampras at the 1989 Italian Open, Agassi predicted "I just don't see a good future for him."

- In 2001 Pete Sampras said retirement is the most difficult decision for many athletes because "the feeling of playing a great match is unbelievably exciting."

- Some spectators in front-row seats used baseball gloves to protect themselves and catch bullet serves when 35-year-old Pete Sampras, who came out of retirement five months earlier, beat Andy Roddick 5-3, 5-3 in their "Smash Hits" exhibition match in September 2006 to benefit AIDS research.

- In 1996 Senator Robert Dole (R-Kansas) offered the position of chairperson of the Republican National Youth Convention to Pete Sampras.

# 15

# Double the Pleasure—or Pressure?

# 2004

*You either go to bed with someone or you play tennis with them. But don't do both.*

—Humorist Art Buchwald, on mixed doubles

**O**nly an hour before the sign-in at the 2002 U.S. Open, doubles star Leander Paes worriedly found himself without a mixed doubles partner. "As I walked out of the locker room," he recalls, "there was Martina standing there, saying, 'You are playing with me.' After watching her play for so many years and having so much respect for her, it was a foregone conclusion I'd accept." The serendipitous tennis marriage worked beautifully because the following year Navratilova and Paes won the Australian and Wimbledon mixed titles.

Doubles teams come to be in all sorts of ways, from the improbable to the ironic.

In June 1980 a teenaged Pam Shriver asked her coach, Don Candy, to ask Navratilova if it would be okay for Pam to ask Navratilova if she had a partner for the Australian circuit. It took Shriver two days to work up the nerve to ask Navratilova to play only to have Navratilova reply, "Oh, well, if Billie Jean [King] doesn't play, I'll probably play with Rosie [Casals]." Wrote Shriver in her book, *Passing Shots*, "I stood there with egg on my face feeling about two feet tall."

Four months later Shriver was hanging out in a tournament trailer in Florida, and she received a phone call. It was the great Martina asking *her* if she could play Australia with her. "It was certainly one of the best phone calls I've ever received in my life," recalls Shriver, then standing all 6'1" tall. "That phone call was the single biggest break in my nineteen years of playing professional tennis. And then our ten year partnership. We had a mutually respectful, fun relationship." Not to mention the greatest one in doubles history! The super-athletic native of Czechoslovakia and the well-connected American amassed twenty major titles and a 109–match winning streak, both records, and a doubles Grand Slam.

Seldom has an itinerary mistake turned out as propitiously as it did for Daniel Nestor in 1994. Without his knowledge, Nestor's father entered him in a tournament in Bogota. When Mark Knowles asked Nestor to play doubles there, Nestor replied, "Listen, I'm not going to Bogota. I don't know what you're talking about." Knowles insisted, "Your name is on the list." Because of the family miscommunication, Nestor had to honor his commitment. "We ended up playing and we won the tournament, beating the Jensen brothers in the final. We couldn't have gotten off to a better start," remembers Nestor, still together with Knowles and ranked No. 1 in doubles.

Paola Suárez never served and volleyed in her entire career, so it's not surprising that she prefers singles. In fact, Suárez admits, "In the beginning I didn't enjoy playing doubles very much." That changed when the Argentine hooked up with another confirmed baseliner, Spain's Virginia Ruano Pascual, eight years ago. Getting better with age, the world's No. 1 duo won the Australian, French, and U.S. Opens this year and amazingly reached ten finals—winning six—in the last eleven Grand Slam tournaments.

Ever wonder how a pro team competing for big bucks and big titles can smile and laugh throughout a two-hour match? "Virginia is my best friend on the tour, and on the court we enjoy," explains Suarez. "We never try to put pressure on each other. We talk about boyfriends, what we want to do tonight, where we want to eat. We can laugh and enjoy. But only on the changeovers. Between points we only talk about strategy because unless we think a lot, we cannot win." Suarez confides that they've clashed only once, at Amelia Island two years ago. "She said some things I didn't like and talked to me in an angry way," relates Suárez. "And I told her I don't like it when you talk to me that way. That tournament we didn't feel so good about each other. But at the next tournament everything was perfect again."

Of course, not all partnerships bring such success and harmony. Sparks flew from the first doubles match played at a Victorian garden party around 1875. Since then, doubles players have bantered and bickered, soothed and savaged, and enjoyed and endured. As Navratilova said in her autobiography, *Martina*, "Playing doubles with somebody sets up a strange relationship, in which you are friend, teammate and competitor."

Navratilova and Shriver played about thirty-five of their forty career singles matches during their partnership, and despite Navratilova's domination (37–3), quite a few were tense three-setters that tested their friendship. "Playing against Martina [in singles] was different because she was the best player in the world and the best athlete I ever faced across the net," says Shriver. "It was also different because we were doubles partners and really good friends.

"There were a couple of times when we did exchange [antagonistic] words on the court in the singles because we are both emotional and occasionally that happens," says Shriver. "But we were fortunate enough to be able to get by that and talk about it afterwards. Doubles is like any relationship. You have to be able to communicate. And you have to do it often."

In his 1975 book, *Lobbing Into The Sun*, legendary Australian Davis Cup captain Harry Hopman advised, "If you remember only one thing, remember that doubles is a little like marriage: nothing destroys the partnership faster than a lack of communication."

Even the best communication won't save a team, though, if its members are not compatible. Veteran Aussie Rennae Stubbs, who has won forty-eight career doubles titles with nine different partners, knows her powerful personality comes across as energizing to some but overbearing to others. "Most of my partners would say the secret of getting along with me is listening to me and trying to do what I'm advising," garrulous Stubbsy says with a laugh. "And not taking me too seriously because I've been told I can be difficult to play with. It's hard for some people not to hear it as personal criticism, rather than constructive criticism on how to win the match."

Highly talented Lisa Raymond, a quiet foil to the magisterial Stubbs, proved best at absorbing and executing strategy. During their 1996–2002 partnership, they won Wimbledon, the Australian and U.S. Opens, Rome, Miami, and the season-ending WTA Championships and an impressive fifteen titles over their last two years.

An extraordinary match at the 2002 Australian Open may have done more to sour the relationship than anything else. Anna Kournikova told the media that she and Martina Hingis, seeded third, deserved the top seeding because, though they played less frequently than Stubbs-Raymond, they beat them more often than not. The impolitic remark provoked Stubbs. Mad as a cut snake on the court, she blatantly tried to take off Anna's head rather than win points. The exasperated Raymond had to stay on her constantly to get her to simmer down and abandon her personal agenda, but the big semifinal slipped away 6-7, 6-1, 6-0.

After playing with several partners and winning only three events in 2003, Stubbs united with Cara Black this year and rebounded by capturing Wimbledon and five other titles. Like Raymond, the reserved Black complemented her rambunctious spirit. "I need my partner to be a little calmer and positive because I can be really hard on myself," says self-critical Stubbs. "I don't need somebody who is a 'rah-rah' type because that's my personality. There has to be a balance."

Whether a team is composed of a leader and a follower or comparative equals can also make or break teams. "Some people would say equality is good, but the great doubles teams usually have a personality on the court that controls the tempo," maintains Stubbs. "[John] McEnroe was the emotional leader with [Peter] Fleming. There is no question with the Woodies that Todd [Woodbridge] was the leader, the one who was up and down and was very good tactically, while Mark [Woodforde] was a lot calmer."

Sometimes the degree of domination is less marked. "Gigi [Fernandez] was probably the leader when she played with Natasha [Zvereva]," says Stubbs. "Both of them loved the limelight and loved performing in front of a crowd. That, in itself, meant there wasn't a really dominant personality, but I would probably say, [it was] more Gigi."

After playing with seventy-six partners during his pro career, the mild-mannered Paes has a more nuanced perspective on leadership. "Every team needs a leader," believes Paes. "The leader is a stronger personality, but that instinct comes out very naturally. The leader doesn't have to call all the shots, and both players have to give input into the team. When the solid player is playing well, the leader sits back and naturally lets the solid player take over. On another day, say for the final at the U.S. Open or Wimbledon, when it's a big match on a big stage, that's when the leader takes over."

Nestor, a self-confessed shy guy, disagrees even though he acknowledges that longtime friend Knowles is more outspoken during competition. "You can't have a situation where you depend on only one guy to step up and always come through and hold the team together," says Nestor. "Everyone has bad days. So equality is better."

Whatever the formula, unless you're a rare combination like fair dinkum Aussies John Newcombe and Tony Roche who never once argued in forty years, even the best of partnerships divorce, or at least separate, eventually.

In a 1985 interview with me, Ted Tinling, the longtime impresario of the WTA Tour, explained why. "They've had little kitty-catty quarrels, silly little vendettas and have broken up," said Tinling, of the leading teams on the tour. "Just three years ago there were eight top teams . . . Hobbs-Durie, Kiyomura and Barker, Casals and Turnbull, Kilsch and Pfaff, Acker and Paula Smith. Martina and Pam are the only survivors from that lot. In years before, top teams like Kerry Reid and Turnbull, Reid and Kerry Harris, and Rosie and Billie Jean broke up over personality clashes. Casals can't get a partner now. The women are too emotional and not practical. Most men submerge their differences. If you're a pro, you're out to win money. If you're a tennis player, you're out to win. Whatever the reasons for these breakups, they weren't good enough reasons. It's very sad."

Stubbs could not agree more. "That's just the way it is. Nothing has changed in twenty, thirty years. Women are still women. They get emotional. They show their emotions," says Stubbs. "Unfortunately, they also have coaches or boyfriends or husbands around them that think they are better than their partner. So they get influenced by them instead of seeing the bottom line that they are doing well."

Fernandez-Zvereva, the most outstanding tandem since Navratilova-Shriver and winners of fourteen major titles, were a classic example. "At the end of 1996 her then boyfriend convinced Natasha that she was too good for me and that I was getting old," recalls Fernandez." So after winning *only* one Grand Slam that year, they split up. The two explosive personalities couldn't live together, but they found out they couldn't live without each other either. So after Arantxa Sánchez Vicario dumped Fernandez for Hingis and Zvereva broke up with Davenport, "I asked Natasha to finish out my career together." They finished with a bang, taking the French—where they gained sweet revenge by beating Sánchez Vicario and Hingis in the semis—and Wimbledon and making the U.S. final.

"I wanted to keep playing, but she was obsessed with Lindsay and wanted to play with her," says Fernandez. "I retired. Natasha never won another Grand Slam."

Besides their riveting shot-making, the fun-loving entertainers are remembered as the original "jog bra" girls. Before Brandi Chastain's famous soccer field display at the 1999 World Cup, the better-endowed Fernandez and Zvereva celebrated their 1993 U.S. Open triumph and sixth Slam in a row by removing their shirts.

Breaking up is hard to do, and even more so after a great season. Jana Novotná, who owned a remarkable career record of twelve doubles and four mixed Grand Slam crowns, found that out. Novotná, the last female serve-volley singles champion, had paired with teen queen Martina Hingis to capture Roland Garros, Wimbledon, and Flushing Meadows in 1998 and Miami in 1999. Just before Roland Garros, however, Hingis broke her commitment to play 1999 Grand Slam events with Novotná and teamed up with Anna Kournikova.

"She told me, 'I don't want to play doubles with you anymore because you are getting old and slow,'" Novotná related at the time. "I told Martina, 'You're too young and stupid.'" Novotna also told the press: "I really can't wait to show Martina how old and slow I am when we next play doubles." Novotná now says, "We all know that [teaming with sex symbol Kournikova] may have helped Martina's image but not her doubles record." The tempestuous twosome (Martina once threw a trophy at Anna in a locker room spat in Chile and told her "I am the queen!") did manage to win a couple of Aussie Opens. Novotná retired at the end of 1999 but has no hard feelings now, saying "I enjoyed playing the most with Martina because she was so talented and fun and carefree on the court."

Even relatively stable, long-term relationships can falter. Shriver looks back at the summer of 1989 as a trying time for her partnership with Navratilova because both were struggling in singles. Navratilova felt Shriver had fallen too far out of shape, even for doubles, and decided to split up. "It was a *very, very* difficult time for me," confides Shriver, who still managed to finish the year ranked No. 1 in the individual bonus pool for most cumulative doubles points.

The plot thickened when the spurned Shriver and inexperienced Mary Joe Fernández faced Navratilova and Hana Mandlikova in the '89 U.S. Open final. The two "ovas" prevailed, but only by 6-4 in the third set, which made Shriver feel a vindication of sorts.

"Even out of shape and with seven to ten extra pounds, I was certainly a lot better at doubles than Hana Mandlikova ever was," says Shriver. "We proved that. We came within two or three points of winning the match."

Six weeks after the biggest divorce in doubles history, the former partners found themselves at the Fed Cup in Tokyo. "I'll tell you another thing that hurt me most," recalls Shriver. "Martina told the coach that if it got down to the doubles, like 1-all in matches, she didn't want to play doubles with me. She wanted to play with Zina [Garrison]. *That* was the low point of the break-up."

Happily, they reunited a month later to win their ninth season-ending Championships, and they resumed playing together again in 1991 and 1992. When Navratilova decided to defend her U.S. Open title with Fernández in 1991 despite playing with Shriver in regular tour events, Shriver paired with Zvereva to win the title, beating Novotná and Larisa Savchenko. "That was kind of sweet, too," says Shriver. Navratilova cheered for her longtime friend, which Shriver said, "was very special."

Billie Jean King offers a kinder, gentler explanation than Tinling about the "musical chairs" doubles scene. "The better teams stay together as long as they can," says King. "But sometimes one or both players are looking over their shoulders to see if there is someone better to team with. The Bryan brothers work well because they aren't looking for other partners. They make their partnership work—whatever it takes. Being a strong doubles team is like being in a rock band. When you're hot, you're hot. But, you almost always reach a point where the players want to do different things. That's not bad, it's just reality."

Maybe so, but when Leander Paes broke up with Mahesh Bhupathi in 1999, it seemed unreal. The Indian champions had just become the first men's team in forty-seven years to reach all four Slam finals in one season—they won Wimbledon and Roland Garros—and the divorce rocked a country that sorely lacked international sports heroes.

The soft-spoken, diplomatic Paes, one of the tour's most popular players, then blamed Enrico Piperno, Bhupathi's coach, for "creating an environment of mistrust between us." Bhupathi insisted the Piperno factor had been blown out of proportion and that "there are several other core issues to be settled with Leander."

How the gifted duo could have their best year on the court and one of their worst years off it still mystifies the tennis world. Paes rejects the contention of legendary Indian player Ramanathan Krishnan that "egoism could be the only root for such a split." He won't elaborate except to say, "a lot of what happened between Mahesh and myself was fabricated in the press . . . and instead of communicating with each other, we pretty much let the fabrications ride and ride. At the end of the day, the truth is known [only] between Mahesh and myself. We are basically at peace with it, and life goes on. We're back on track with different partners, and we play together, when required to, for our country."

Actually, they played together surprisingly often since their so-called break-up. In 2000 they combined for five events besides the Sydney Olympics; they played throughout 2001 and won four titles; in 2002 they captured two more titles; and this year they paired for four tournaments besides Davis Cup and the Athens Olympics.

Unlike Novotná who views doubles as a business relationship—"You go to work, win tournaments, make money, but at night go home to your family and friends"— Paes considers his off-court relationship with partners even more important than the one on the court.

"Each athlete, especially in an individual sport, has a very idiosyncratic personality on the court. But once you get away from the competitive arena, what's important is what rhythms that person then has," Paes explains. "You spend four hours a day on the court. But the rest of the day, you're either going for meals together, or hanging out in the locker room, or in the lounge playing chess or backgammon, or keeping each other relaxed during a long day session.

That bond off the court, that mutual understanding and respect actually transcends onto the court, not the other way around, so that it's not about my way or my partner's way," says Paes. "It's about what's best for both of us. There are bound to be unpleasant times; what matters is how those two individuals handle those unpleasant times—whether they are gentle or aggressive about it and whether they look at it from the other person's point of view. I'd much rather be gentle and understanding and then find a happy medium."

There was no love lost between fierce German rivals Boris Becker and Michael Stich. Yet they somehow put aside their running feud for Davis Cup and Olympic gold in Barcelona. As Becker writes in his autobiography, *The Player*, "You couldn't get the gold in such high-pressure circumstances unless you all got along really well. Michael and I made it: we got the medal." Their solidarity was short-lived, though, because instead of celebrating with the gregarious Becker and the rest of the team, Stich quickly returned to Germany. "This at the end of two weeks of joint effort and struggle, in temperatures of up to 50-degrees C (122-degrees F) in the shade!" says Becker.

Time heals many wounds, and Becker and Stich, who both suffered the anguish of divorce and the death of a parent, have become closer. "Now that we are no longer rivals, we can talk," says Becker. "No more need for masks to hide behind. The player Stich has become my friend Michael."

Do spouses that play together stay together? Both "Gentleman Jack" Crawford and Harry "The Fox" Hopman added to their marital bliss by pairing with their wives, Marjorie and Nell, to win three Australian mixed titles each during the 1930s. Another famous Aussie couple, John and Angie Newcombe, also didn't heed Art Buchwald's timeless advice. Newk, who racked up eighteen Grand Slam doubles titles, tells what happened and what may sound familiar to many husband-wife teams in their instructional, *The Family Tennis Book*.

"Playing mixed doubles with my wife in club tournaments is the most difficult thing I have ever tried . . . I wanted to win badly for Angie's sake, and quite often would try so hard that my game deteriorated. This made me mad and I would start cursing and throwing my racket. Angie would then abuse me because she said I was not enjoying playing with her. The next time we played together, I decided to give it the 'casual' treatment, hoping I would play better and not get so mad. She would abuse me once again, for not caring if we won or lost. After one year of this, I said, 'That's the last time we are playing mixed doubles in a tournament together.'"

Newk noted, however, that they still love to play social tennis together for the fun of it, but humbly asked readers, "If any of you have a solution to this, I wish you'd drop me a note and tell me about it."

Doubles can be the ultimate unifier rather than the divider. In 2002 Amir Hadad, an Israeli Jew, and Aisam-ul-Haq Qureshi, a Muslim from Pakistan, turned into a symbol of international *détente* as a doubles team at Wimbledon. The Pakistani tennis federation threatened to ban Qureshi from Davis Cup play if he continued playing with Hadad, but Qureshi defiantly refused to give in. After the International Tennis Federation said it would ban Pakistan from the Davis Cup if it followed through on its threat, Pakistani officials apologized to Qureshi and extended a Davis Cup invitation to its No. 1 player. Newspapers in both countries hailed the unique partnership.

"Our game is nothing about politics or religion," said Hadad. "I hope people will see that two people who are supposed to be enemies can get along. We play well together and we both think we have a good chance."

After one of their victories, Qureshi's mother kissed Hadad on the cheek.

# 16

# Tennis for the Bloody Fun of It
# 2006

*We loved what we were doing. We loved the travel. We loved the parties. We loved the attention. We loved being on stage and in the fishbowl.*

—Fred Stolle, on the 1950s–'60s amateur tour, from his memoirs, *Tennis Down Under*

**W**hen tennis aficionados study the record books a century from now, they'll wonder how a sparsely populated and remotely located country could rule an international sport for two decades. Tales of Australia's rollicking heroes, though, will fascinate fans as much as their on-court exploits.

From 1950 to 1967, Australia captured the Davis Cup fifteen times with a never-ending assembly line of champions: Frank Sedgman, Ken Rosewall, Lew Hoad, Rod Laver, Roy Emerson, and John Newcombe. They, along with other stars, such as Ken McGregor, Mervyn Rose, Ashley Cooper, Mal Anderson, Neale Fraser, Fred Stolle, and Tony Roche, amassed an astounding fifty-three Grand Slam singles and sixty-one doubles titles from 1950 to 1969.

These fiercely competitive yet genial Aussies didn't only lead the world in championships. They trained harder, partied heartier, and laughed more than other players. And no bloke more epitomized the good-natured optimism of postwar Australia than Emerson.

"Roy was the best celebrator in the history of the human race," recalls Stolle, his sidekick and frequent doubles partner during the 1960s. "Roy was a clown, a cut-up, somebody who liked to be loud, funny, the life of the party. He liked to horse around and wrestle in the locker rooms. He liked to be the last one out of the bar and the first one on the court. He was a complete original in everything he said and did."

Emmo called everyone "Blue" because he often forgot their names—and, win or lose, sang enthusiastically in the showers with his shorts on. For one of his favorite hits of the week, he crooned:

Many a tear has to falllll
But it's alllll
In a game
All in that wonderful game.

Happily, he shed very few tears. Roy served and volleyed to an all-time record twenty-eight Grand Slam titles (twelve in singles and sixteen in doubles) and married a woman fittingly named Joy. Emmo was admired as much as he was liked by fellow players. His sterling character never shined more brightly than in a 1966 Wimbledon quarterfinal match against compatriot Owen Davidson. Emmo, shooting for his third straight Big W title, romped through the opening set in fourteen minutes. Early in the second set, he scrambled to get a drop volley, crashed into the umpire's chair and tore the shoulder ligaments. Even though he was in considerable pain and couldn't serve, he bravely fought on. He lost in four sets.

"Emmo never grimaced, never grabbed his shoulder. It was obvious to all of us that he had problems," recalls Newcombe. "It was the only time he ever lost to Davo. He came off the court and he never offered that as an excuse. He said that Davo played too good on the day."

Setting a precedent, the august *New York Times* wrote an editorial extolling the valiant Australian for not quitting. "The true worth of a champion often emerges more in defeat than in victory. Roy Emerson won't win Wimbledon this year, but he is still a champion."

A big part of the Australian mystique of yesteryear was their famous but unwritten code instilled by legendary Davis Cup captain Harry Hopman. Emerson, who was embarrassed when others talked about his injuries and disgusted when others talked about their injuries, explained it best: "If you go onto the court, you are fit and there are no excuses if you lose. If you are not fit, don't go onto the court."

No matter how heartbreaking the loss or grueling the match, Aussies, to the envy of some players, left those feelings on the court. "In those days we were one big happy family," Stolle fondly remembers. "You came off the court and you had a drink and went off to dinner. When I lost in my first Wimbledon final to Roy, we went out to dinner and celebrated with about twenty people. Of course, I was disappointed, but I was happy for him."

Stars today who insist they can't be friendly with their archrivals, let alone be best friends, would be shocked to learn that world No. 1 Emerson and No. 2 Stolle shared a flat together and even cooked breakfast for each other before their 1964 and 1965 Wimbledon finals. Fred laughed when I asked if he ever thought of spiking Emmo's orange juice to win a coveted Wimbledon that always eluded him.

The Australian concept of mateship goes way back. "To develop this vast but lightly populated country, it was extremely important to have mates with you," explains Newcombe. "You just never let your mate down. You were there for your mate through thick and thin. It was almost like The Three Musketeers of 'all for one and one for all.'"

That almost genetic camaraderie was reinforced in three ways. In the days of amateur tennis when players weren't making a lot of money, Australian teams and players used to leave Australia in March and didn't come home again for seven months. What's more, travel from London to Sydney took about thirty-three hours. "Dependent on one another, the other players, more or less, became your family while you were overseas," says Newcombe. Playing Davis Cup, which was the ultimate Australian tennis honor, also created a strong patriotic bond with your teammates, as did doubles in which Aussies fared spectacularly well.

In 1950 Sedgman, handsome, athletic, and sporting, ignited the Australian dynasty by winning his second straight Aussie singles title and helping his mates wrest the Davis Cup from the U.S. "He was the man who came through and who we all idolized," says Stolle. "I can remember as a kid walking around pigeon-toed because everyone thought you have to walk pigeon-toed, and you'd nearly fall over half the time. We thought the reason he was so great was that he was pigeon-toed."

Dubbed the "Tennis Twins," Lew Hoad and Ken Rosewall were born only three weeks apart, and these whiz kids, opposite in many ways, captivated the tennis world. In 1953 charismatic Hoad and reserved Rosewall won the Davis Cup and captured three-fourths of a doubles Grand Slam with Rosewall, only eighteen, grabbing the Australian and French titles.

When Rosewall was fifteen, George Worthington, an Aussie tour player, saw the scrawny youngster alongside muscular Hoad in the shower, laughed, and gave him the ironic nickname, "Muscles." The 5'7", 140-pound Rosewall used his pinpoint accuracy, consistency and strategic savvy to outlast all his contemporaries.

After being barred from the greatest amateur tournaments for being a pro during his prime for eleven years until Open Tennis arrived, he amazingly captured the French again in 1968, easily beating Laver, and the Australian again in 1972 at the age of thirty-eight. "Ken may have been the best player of all-time," says Newcombe.

Hoad, a blond Adonis who was outgoing and immensely popular, owned every shot in the book and nonchalantly smacked them with devastating power. "When he was supremely fit, he was the best tennis player who ever lived," insists Stolle. When Hoadie shook your hand, he almost broke it. His favorite party trick was lifting himself off a chair on two thumbs. An incident in France in the late 1950s demonstrated both Hoad's strength and loyalty. When Hoad and Ashley Cooper saw a couple of Frenchmen trying to start their car, they gave it a push. The Frenchmen didn't like it, and one decked Cooper with a punch to the stomach. By the time Cooper staggered up from the roadway, Hoad had knocked both of them out.

Like Rosewall, Laver let his racket do the talking. And like Hoad, his idol, he was a dazzling shotmaker. If winning one Grand Slam—all four majors in a calendar year—is a stupendous achievement, how about the seemingly impossible, two Grand Slams? Laver, a 5'9" super-athletic lefty with wicked topspin and power off both wings, pulled it off in 1962 as an amateur and in 1969 as a pro. "Rod was and is the most unassuming champion we've ever had in any sport who is still recognized anywhere he goes," says Stolle. "You can talk to him today about [Roger] Federer, and he'll tell you

*Ken Rosewall, clutching two of his many trophies.* Courtesy of the International Tennis Hall of Fame & Museum, Newport, Rhode Island

Federer is great. And I'll say, 'What about you? You won two Grand Slams.' He's very modest about that."

Pride of performance was another Laver trademark. And in 1973, after not being allowed to play Davis Cup for five years since tennis went open in 1968, Australia was back and facing the U.S. in a dramatic Cup final in Cleveland. The redoubtable Aussies, led by Laver and Newcombe, quickly clinched the title 3–0 and that night drank a bit too much at the team dinner.

Laver wasn't conditioned to big nights like that and wasn't feeling well. Then thirty-five and well past his prime, he had to play Stan Smith, world No. 1 the year before and winner of their two previous matches, in a dead rubber. Newk recalls, "I said, 'Rocket, you don't look too good.' He said, 'No, I feel terrible.' I said, 'That's a pity because I hear that Stan says there's no way you can beat him.' That was the end of that. His eyes got intense, he stood right up, and he went out and gave Stan a whipping."

Newcombe and Roche, the last of the Golden Era champions, continued the Down Under doubles domination of John Bromwich-Adrian Quist, Sedgman-McGregor, Hoad-Rosewall, and Emerson-Stolle. They combined for twelve major titles, a record for a team, including five at Wimbledon. Newk, the son of a dentist, came from Sydney, while Rochey grew up in Tarcutta, a country hamlet of 300 people where his dad was the local butcher. "Tony's a loyal person. If you are his friend, you're his friend. Basically, Tony is a typical country bloke. Our personalities are opposite of one another, too, and that makes for a good combination," says the extroverted Newcombe. "It's been a unique friendship and one I'm really proud of. It's one of the great friendships in sports history." In forty years as doubles partners, running the Davis Cup for seven years, and doing Australian summer camps for twelve years, they never had an argument.

They did enjoy plenty of roughhousing, though. Newk used to watch a lot of wrestling on TV and loved all the grips they had. When they went abroad with the team in 1963 and played some matches in Saigon, Laos, and Malaysia, Newk would say to ruggedly built Rochcy, "I'll give you twenty seconds to get me in a grip and then we'll start fighting. I'd usually come out on top because I knew most of the grips and how to get out of them. But this time he started off and got me in a wrist lock, and as I was trying to get out of it, my wrist tendon snapped." So, injured Newk, not playing, traveled with the team for the next ten weeks, before it healed. "That wasn't a lot of fun, but it finished off as a very good year because in August I met my future wife, Angie. And I played Davis Cup at the end of the year for the first time."

No story about these fun-loving, fair-dinkum Aussies would be complete without Hopman, their strict disciplinarian Davis Cup captain. A 1930s doubles standout and former sportswriter, Hop, a genius for spotting and developing talent, was also renowned for his grueling training methods and character-building rules. For example, if you disobeyed his instructions on the court, you could count on taking a two-mile run around the track or 100 extra double knee-jumps. If you used the wrong spoon, dressed improperly, or missed curfew, you'd get fined a small sum.

"The Old Fox," as some called Hopman, cleverly used rewards to convey lessons, particularly during Davis Cup weeks. "During the final in Sweden, Emmo and Fred were allowed to go off to the night club for an hour or so. We had to be home in bed with lights out by ten o'clock," relates Newcombe. "So, the three of us [Newk, Roche and Davidson] were sleeping in this one big room. And we'd lie awake there for hours planning how we could kill him. The message given to us was: you guys are nineteen, twenty years of age, and when you guys have achieved what these guys have achieved, you can have a glass of beer and you can go out to a night club for an hour."

"We had a love-hate relationship with Mr. Hopman," agrees Stolle. "I cherished every moment of practice and every little exchange with the boys and with Hop. But in those days if he didn't like you and you hit a ball out of the stadium, like Bob Hewitt did, he was kicked off the Davis Cup team," recalls Stolle. "You weren't supposed to have outbursts on the court. Hopman molded all our personalities. The reason we're all friends today is because he taught you to be courteous, to do the right thing."

In *The New Yorker* magazine in 1983, Herbert Warren Wind best summed up the Australians of yesteryear, writing, "They played tennis the way it should be played, and they imparted both meaning and glamour to it."

---

This article received 1st Place in the 2007 CNW/FFWA Florida State Writing Competition in the Previously Published Nonfiction Article division.

# 17

# Andre Agassi: Rebel with a Cause
# 2003

In a half-buttoned white shirt, a smiling Andre Agassi exudes confidence in his Aramis ads. "Life. It's A Great Game," the catchy fragrance slogan, perfectly captures the latest incarnation of the most evolved tennis champion the game has ever known. Steffi Graf, whom he adores, gave birth to their second child, daughter Jaz Elle, on October 3, and life could hardly be more idyllic for him.

A man in full now, Agassi once confided that his "Image Is Everything" Canon camera commercial "brought him a lot more grief than anything else." Way back then, America's Next Great Player had dismally lost his first three Grand Slam finals. Under-achieving and angst-ridden, he lamented how his teenage years at the Bollettieri Tennis Academy "took away my love for the game" and told the *New York Times*, "I played this game for a lot of reasons, and none of them have ever quite been mine."

Being Andre Agassi has never been easy. Relentlessly pressured to be a champion since he was a toddler—his father, Mike, estimated Andre hit a million tennis balls a year between the ages of five and thirteen—he sometimes hoped rain would save him from another grueling training session.

What an unpredictable roller-coaster ride the Las Vegas showman has taken us on. He joined the tour at sixteen wearing garish neon outfits, earrings, painted nails, and bleached blond, rock-star hair. He loaded up on junk food, admitted he drank liquor, and took drugs, and practiced when the mood hit him. "When I had Andre for six and a half years, my main job was to keep him out of jail," once cracked Bollettieri, about his teenaged phenom.

Agassi dissed Wimbledon with a three-year absence, and he skipped the Australian Open (a tournament he would later win four times) for eight years. No matter. Nike signed the charismatic prodigy to a reported $100 million dollar contract.

"My accomplishments do not live up to my tennis game, Agassi told *Sports Illustrated* in May 1992. "Most people have to work really hard and win some big matches, and then they get money and popularity. For me it has been the reverse of everybody else. The exact opposite."

Agassi dismissed the esteemed ITF president, Philippe Chatrier, as a "bozo." He occasionally demeaned opponents, such as Jimmy Connors and Martin Jaite. Worst of all, when the going got tough, he tanked matches. He acrimoniously broke up with Bollettieri, his longtime coach, married and divorced actress Brooke Shields, hooked up with coach Brad Gilbert, and even managed to win three major titles before crashing in a mid-career crisis.

As Agassi tellingly put it then, "I enjoy tennis when I'm intense about it. I enjoy my life when it's intense. And you can't have both." He even considered retiring from competitive tennis.

Then something fateful happened. "For fourteen years Andre and I have taken on pretty much everything life can dish out — problems, disappointments, triumphs, coming up short, sadness, adversity and joy," relates Gil Reyes, a burly former University of Nevada-Las Vegas strength coach who became Agassi's trainer and confidante. "In 1996 Andre was going through a horrendous summer [low-lighted by a second round loss at Roland Garros and a first round loss at Wimbledon], and he was disappointed and sad," recalls Reyes. "But he looked me in the eye with a little bit of fear and a lot of hope and guts and said, 'Let's get to work. I don't know if I can do this, Gil. I'm going to need you. But I *need* to win that [Olympics] gold medal.'"

Reyes views that as the turning point in Agassi's life and career because the next morning he was running sprints up notorious Magic Mountain and then again in the searing 115-degree afternoon heat. The new and inspired Agassi went on to win his cherished Olympic gold medal in Atlanta, albeit over a weak field. Dark times again hit Agassi in 1997–98 when his ill-fated marriage to career-minded Shields was falling apart. The former No. 1 played in only one Slam tournament in 1997.

"Andre was hurting," remembers Reyes. "A lot was going on, and he went head first into life. He had no regrets about that. Tennis has never been his only world. Now he tries to give everything he can to tennis without taking from his family."

After nose diving to a humiliating No. 141 ranking and being forced to enter Challenger events, Agassi pulled off an Open Era comeback second only to Jennifer Capriati's. He rallied from two sets down to beat Andrei Medvedev for the 1999 French Open title. It resurrected his career and gave him a rare career Grand Slam. More importantly, it gave him and others hope.

Agassi talked about that emotional connection in September just before winning a second U.S. Open title, which crowned his dramatic comeback. "What turns me on more than anything is just making a difference in peoples' lives," said Agassi. "That's one thing I've taken with me and I'll keep. Probably even more so than the accomplishment itself at the French Open is the fact that somewhere along the line it gave hope to people."

Mary Carillo, the perceptive TV tennis analyst, drew a close parallel between the inspiring comebacks of Agassi and Capriati. "Jennifer felt the same thing when her long dry spell was broken by her first Australian Open win," says Carillo. "Both of them knew they'd struck a chord with so many people, even outside of tennis. It's not just a sports accomplishment; it's a triumph of the human spirit. Andre understands that well."

Agassi's brief girlfriend, actress-singer Barbra Streisand, once presciently declared, "he's very evolved, more than in his linear years." Today more than ever, he understands the importance of caring and sharing.

"He treasures his fans," says Reyes. "He understands that when things haven't gone well for him, they've been there for him. And therefore he shares it more with them when things go well and the triumphs come. "He's the same way with his friends off the court," says Reyes, whom Agassi's son, Jaden Gil, is named after. "Whenever you need him, Andre is always there with you. And if he can't be there with you, for sure he's there for you."

Reyes recalls Agassi's compassion and friendship when Reyes's mother was very sick several years ago and they were returning from Europe. "Andre was exhausted. But I said, 'I need to go see my mother, you guys go ahead and go home.' Andre's response was, 'No, I need to go see her, too.' That simple. That showed me so much, and I'll never forget that. But there are a thousand more examples of his kindness."

Agassi's "thousand points of light" radiate most brilliantly from the Andre Agassi Charitable Foundation (AACF). Agassi gets another "A"—for altruism—for creating it in 1995 with two million dollars of his own money to provide recreational and educational opportunities for at-risk children in Las Vegas.

Eight annual Grand Slam for Children concert and dinner benefits have raised an astounding thirty-five million for the Agassi foundation. On the day after Jaz was born, the celebrity-studded event raked in $12.6 million, making it the most lucrative non-political fund-raiser in Vegas history. Its concert featured Sheryl Crow, Billy Joel, and Sir Elton John, comics Dennis Miller and Robin Williams performed, and auctions involved chances to meet with Lance Armstrong, Shaquille O'Neal, and Bill Clinton. *Sports Illustrated* said the extravaganza treating a crowd of 12,000 at the MGM Grand Garden Arena "made the Emmys look like a ninth-grade talent show."

Remarkably, the ever-growing AACF boasts eleven beneficiaries: the Andre Agassi College Preparatory Academy, Andre Agassi Boys & Girls Clubs of Las Vegas, Child Haven (a shelter for abused, neglected and abandoned children), I Have A Dream Foundation (providing college scholarships), Cynthia Bunker Memorial Scholarship Fund, Inner-City Games Las Vegas, Las Vegas Sun Summer Camp, Assistance League of Las Vegas' Operation School Bell, Boys Hope/Girls Hope of Nevada, Class! Publications, and Youth Concert Series.

Carillo visited the Agassi Preparatory Academy and can't say enough about it. "Every single penny goes to the kids. It should be a template for every athlete involved in charity."

Agassi, a hands-on philanthropist, spends plenty of time at the preparatory academy, which he says "is more rewarding than tennis." During a World TeamTennis match in Avon, Connecticut, I asked him why. "This is an opportunity for children, insuring their future. So that's different from just winning a title for yourself. They're kids that deserve opportunities and hope in their lives. It's incredible to watch them grow."

Darren "Killer" Cahill, Agassi's coach for the past two years, is "amazed" at his life outside of tennis. "Anyone that gets a chance should see what Andre does for under-privileged children here in Vegas," says Cahill. "At times it can bring a tear to your eyes because of the way he goes about it and the way he gives so many kids an opportunity for an education or to get on a basketball court or a tennis court. That is really a big part of Andre's life."

Carillo ranks Agassi behind only Billie Jean King and Arthur Ashe as the tennis players who have contributed most to society. "What Andre did, what Arthur and Billie Jean did—what most athletes don't do—is that they decided to give back at the very height of their powers," points out Carillo. "They knew that while they were at their most famous, they would have the most impact on their world. Although IMG was adamantly opposed to Andre starting up his charity in the middle of his career, Perry Rogers [his manager] and Andre knew it was the time to begin. That is very impressive."

What's equally impressive, according to Cahill, is Agassi's commitment to his game. "Andre has an incredible desire to improve," says Cahill. "That desire stood out more than anything from the first day I worked with him two years ago." Cahill, who abruptly parted ways with Lleyton Hewitt after guiding the young Australian to the No. 1 ranking, says he prefers coaching Agassi and calls it "the best job in the game without question." Cahill downplays his role, saying his challenge was "not to make any dramatic changes, but slowly and surely implement small things into his game that could make him a better player."

How then has Agassi managed to average a Slam title a year for the past five years and rank No. 1 at a record "oldest" age thirty-three, for fourteen weeks in 2003?

"Gil Reyes. Without a doubt, Gil is the best in the business at what he does, the best I've ever seen," says Cahill, "and I come from a country where [legendary Davis Cup captain] Harry Hopman always stressed training and fitness. That's why Andre is as strong as ever, maybe stronger, moves as well as ever, has as much stamina as anyone on the tour, rarely gets serious injuries, and stays sharp and focused."

Agassi wouldn't argue with that. Two years ago he maintained that he, at age twenty, "would be doing good to get three games a set" from him at age thirty.

"Andre has always been a great tennis player, but he's a better athlete now," agrees Reyes, who says the 174-pound Agassi boasts a body fat percent ranging from 6 to 9 percentage and recently bench-pressed a personal record 315 pounds. "That's awfully strong. But we put in 70 percent of his training on his legs. They aren't in any way breaking down or slipping."

Last summer Agassi started what Reyes calls "a two-year plan" and stresses that "we're stepping it up rather than winding it down." So when Jaz was born, the dedicated veteran took only two days off before resuming rigorous workouts in the gym and on the courts.

Just as eighteen-year-old Pete Sampras was once exhausted and awed by the grueling training methods of fitness fanatic Ivan Lendl, No. 1-ranked Andy Roddick plans to copy Agassi's regimen to improve his December conditioning for the Australian Open. "I think [Agassi] is a great model for it," Roddick recently said.

Agassi's titles at the last three Oz Opens he's played no doubt result from the hard work he puts in late in the year. "Andre is almost on a different timeline from the other players, who understandably take the weeks before the Australian to holiday and relax," says Carillo. "Andre spends Christmas day training, knowing how physical the challenge of Oz is, willing to pay the price to win the thing. It's a great pity Andre elected not to play ten of the Australian Opens." One can only wonder how many more Slam titles he might have captured and how high that would have lifted Agassi on the all-time great list.

Agassi insists that "I have no regrets" although he does acknowledge that being the last survivor of America's "Greatest Generation"—Sampras, Jim Courier, Michael Chang, and himself—"is certainly sad, as you see your peers, especially Pete, retiring. Because of those rivalries. You expect to leave the dance with the one you came with."

If his newer rivals "don't have the same sort of personal connection," they still fire Agassi up. The season-ending Masters Cup in Houston in November proved that in spades. After not competing at a Tour event since the U.S. Open, Agassi played four straight thrilling, high-caliber three-set matches—beating French Open champ Juan Carlos Ferrero, David Nalbandian, and Rainer Schuettler, while losing a 6-7, 6-3, 7-6 heartbreaker (after having two match points) to Wimbledon champ Roger Federer—before Federer overwhelmed him in the final.

Happily retired Sampras believes Agassi "has as good a shot as anyone" to win the Australian, "but now there are a lot more guys that have a shot." As for 2004, the amazing Agassi's 18th season, Sampras predicts his longtime archrival "will win one Slam, maybe two, if things really go right. I'm rooting for him. Hey, I'm a fan now."

However Agassi fares next year, he'll be content as the ultimate family man. When asked in August what he would do if he had the whole day free of business and sports commitments, he smiled and replied, "Take a nap with my son."

---

**FASCINATING FACTS:**

* Andy Murray said that "50 or 60 percent" of the people in the men's locker room at the 2006 U.S. Open "were in tears or holding it back" when Andre Agassi, following his final pro match, received a standing ovation from the players.

---

This article received 1st Place in the 2004 CNW/FFWA Florida State Writing Competition in the Previously Published Nonfiction Article division.

# 18

# Sharapova Fires Latest Shots in Russian Revolution
# 2003

"Ova here, Ova there, the Russians are everywhere" should be the new theme song in women's tennis. No, they haven't kicked the Serena and Venus Show off the stage quite yet. But just give them a little more time because the Russkies have the numbers.

Russian talent runs so deep that five standouts reached the Wimbledon round of sixteen and Anna Kournikova plunged to No. 11 among them. Title-less Anna, who still ranks No. 1 in endorsements (about fifteen million a year), website hits, and former boyfriend superstars, withdrew from Wimbledon because of a recurring back injury.

Without the alluring woman who launched a thousand bra ad billboards, the tabloid paparazzi focused on a bona-fide Anna facsimile: beautiful Maria Sharapova. They better watch out, though, because Maria doesn't crave attention or have an ego the size of Moscow á la Anna. Maria not only finds the tabloids' leering silly but also isn't enamored with the newspaper that measured her loud grunts with a decibel counter at the DFS Classic in Birmingham.

"In a few years, hopefully, the stories won't be about my grunting or my looks, but about me being a great tennis player," Sharapova says.

Aware of past burnout victims, such as Tracy Austin, Andrea Jaeger, and Jennifer Capriati, single-minded Sharapova won't be derailed from her goal. "No one is going to push me around," she says. "I know what I want and how to achieve it. I want to be No. 1."

Six years after 16-year-old Kournikova stormed to the Wimbledon semis, tennis' newest "sweet sixteen" phenom had a June coming out party on the lush lawns of England. At Birmingham, Sharapova qualified and then ousted No. 24 Nathalie Dechy, No. 34 Marie-Gaianeh Mikaelian and No. 15 compatriot Elena Dementieva to reach her first Tour semifinal.

At Wimbledon, where reputations are built and the pressure is greatest, eighty-eighth-ranked wild card Sharapova really seized the fortnight. Walloping 100 mph-plus serves and down-the line backhands for winners, she drubbed another fast-rising teen-ager, American Ashley Harkleroad, 6-2, 6-1 in what the media had dubbed the "Battle of the Blonde Babes." Then she impressively upset twenty-first-seeded Russian Elena Bovina 6-3, 6-1 and eleventh-seeded Jelena Dokic 6-4, 6-4, slamming eight aces, be-fore yet another young Russian, Svetlana Kuznetsova, outlasted her 6-1, 2-6, 7-5.

What makes Sharapova, willowy-thin at 6' and 125 pounds, so appealing is her intense competitiveness and sheer joy of life. She clenches her fist, screams as she whacks balls, and smiles broadly after terrific shots. Like Jimmy Connors, this drama queen doesn't merely play, she performs. After knocking off Dokic, she raised her hands to the sky and blew kisses to the enthused Court 1 spectators. "I just feel I owe fans a big thank you," she says. "They are important because they root for you and you play a good match for them. If you leave the court without showing respect for them, they might not come back next time."

There's little chance that will happen, according to legendary coach Robert Lansdorp, because Sharapova is destined for greatness. "Maria can go all the way. Potentially, she has the ability to be the best," says Lansdorp, who taught Tracy Austin, Lindsay Davenport, and Pete Sampras their championship strokes and has coached Sharapova for the past five years. "Tracy was the toughest mentally of anyone I've ever had," says Lansdorp. "But shot-making goes to Maria. What I like about Maria is her attitude, her desire, the pleasure she has when she makes good shots. The desire to become great shows more with Maria. I love to work with her."

Sharapova, then eleven, both amazed and confounded Lansdorp in the begin-ning. "She was like a nightmare because of all her shots," he recalls. "She could hit a serve right-handed and left-handed. She could hit a forehand either way. It looked like she could do whatever she wanted to do. But she understood the court well. And she had this fight in her to work for every point, which is very important."

Allied with that determination is a fearlessness that Lansdorp believes will take her to the top. Only thirteen and competing in her first pro tournament in Florida, Lansdorp remembers a revealing match pitting Sharapova against veteran Dawn Buth. After Sharapova won a first-set tiebreaker and led 4-0 in the second set, Buth rallied to win the set and was on the verge of winning the match.

"Maria saved several match points. She was hitting the ball even harder, even better," says Lansdorp proudly. "There was never any sign she was getting nervous. Right there, I had the feeling Maria was playing like some of my other [top] players, like Tracy. They would never get nervous when the chips were down. They would just fight. Champions have that quality."

If Sharapova reflects the hungry attitude of the new wave of Russian standouts, her improbable saga explains why. The Sharapova story began in the little town of Nyagan in remote Siberia, where Maria was born the daughter of Yuri an engineer, and Yelena. The family moved to Soichi when she was two, to escape the radioactivity caused by the Chernobyl nuclear disaster. Sharapova was discovered at age six by the greatest tennis "ova" ever, Martina Navratilova, then playing an exhibition in Moscow. Navratilova told her parents that Maria's tremendous talent could best develop where hers did nearly thirty years ago, in America, the proverbial "land of opportunity."

So Yuri and little Maria left Yelena behind and used the $900 he had saved up to fly to Miami to pursue their dream. "We had no money in our pocket," Yuri told The Maria Sharapova Page website. "I knew no words of English except 'to eat' and 'to sleep.'"

They journeyed to Bradenton where Yuri looked for a job, they shared a bicycle, and Maria quickly adjusted to their new environment. Highly intelligent, she recalled, "I learned English in one month. I told myself I should listen. In the next month I could talk to everyone. I was so happy I could do one thing . . . I could talk."

Even better, the prodigy could play so well that after coming to Nick Bollettieri's Academy uninvited, she was enrolled there at age eight. Because of visa problems, Yelena had to wait back home in Sochi for more than two years before they could be reunited. "It was very hard on Maria to be without her mother for so long," Yuri said.

Although Maria has resided and practiced at Bollettieri's ever since, she frequently travels across the continent for weeks of two-hour daily coaching sessions with Lansdorp at the South Bay Tennis Center in Torrance, California.

Former president Boris Yeltsin, a tennis lover, helped popularize the sport in Russia after it had been shunned for years by the Communist party as a decadent, bourgeois pastime. The success of Yevgeny Kafelnikov, who gave four-year-old Sharapova a tennis racket she still treasures, and Kournikova further accelerated the Russian Tennis Revolution during the 1990s.

Ironically, Kournikova, who peaked at No. 8 in singles and No. 1 in doubles, and Sharapova, immigrated to the U.S. while other promising Russians left for greener pastures in Europe. Kuznetsova and Marat Safin moved to Barcelona, Spain, to nurture their talent as teenagers.

Kuznetsova, born in St. Petersburg, encountered a common obstacle for Russian players: lack of financial support. "My father, all his life, pays for everything for me," Kuznetsova, now Navratilova's doubles partner, told the *Palm Beach Post*. "Coaching, tournaments, court time. It's too hard. At home, I can't get sponsorships. I have to travel on my own. You think I get $1 from the Russian [tennis] federation? If you're not from Moscow, forget about it. They didn't help me at all."

Lansdorp also coaches Anastasia Myskina, No. 10 in the world and the top-ranked Russian woman. Vera Zvonareva, a smart counterpuncher, upset Venus Williams at the French Open. Yet another top-ten prospect from Russia is highly athletic Nadia Petrova. A surprise semifinalist at Roland Garros, Petrova knocked off 2000 champion Jennifer Capriati in a super high-caliber match there.

Sharapova considers herself "totally Russian" and declares that she'll represent her motherland in the Olympics if asked. Even so, she likes different aspects of both countries. "In Russia, I love the culture and the sightseeing. It's really beautiful, especially where I live," she says. "In America, it's great doing the schoolwork online. That makes it easier to travel. The shopping is better in America. There are no big markets in Russia. Here we just go and get food —everything in the same place— in your car and drive to your garage and just get out. It's a different lifestyle."

Talking with Sharapova, you soon discover there's very little about her unusual life she doesn't like. When I asked her to describe herself, she replies, "Happy, funny, I'm a fighter, and I'm very classy."

What makes Sharapova smile and laugh so much? "The people around me and the people who believe in me," she quickly answers. "They make me happy and make me laugh. All the moments that I can laugh and be happy are the greatest. That's what keeps me going."

One thing that does bother Sharapova is the controversy created by the loud noises—screams, squeals, and shrieks—she emits when she whacks the ball. The umpire in Birmingham asked her to tone it down. A mischievous London tabloid recorded Sharapova's screams at an eardrum-bashing 100 decibels on its infamous grunt-o-meter, far louder than Serena's second-place primal yells of eighty-eight. "I've been doing it since I was four and it's automatic," insists Sharapova. "I can't help it and I can't stop doing it."

Since Sharapova's noisemaking ranges from stentorian to barely audible, depending on the match, Lansdorp doesn't accept her excuse. "After they told her to shut up at Birmingham, she played the next match without too much noise, so she's capable of doing it," says Lansdorp. "I've told her enough times, 'Shut up, it sounds obnoxious.'"

Lansdorp also believes the noise distraction makes her more vulnerable to critics. "You don't want it that extreme because then people start saying, 'Yeah, all she does is scream.' The better you become, the more people find things wrong with you. The jealousy is so enormous in this world. It's sad, but that's the way it is."

Aside from that discordant note, Sharapova is one of tennis' most charming personalities since Chris Evert. "Even when I call her a dumb blonde," says Lansdorp, "she just laughs and says, 'Oh, Robert.' She never gets upset." She doesn't even get annoyed when Lansdorp jokes about her sex symbol image and calls her "the next Kournikova" and says, "Anna, come over here."

Sharapova has a stock answer to the frequent comparisons with Kournikova. "I can't do anything about people making comparisons between us and I don't pay it much attention," she says. Sharapova would much rather people watch her matches, her tennis skill, and will, than her pretty face. Indeed, the intrusive paparazzi forced her to don a wig and glasses as a disguise in the Wimbledon village. Her high-pitched voice takes on a definite firmness when she stresses, "I didn't come to the United States to be a model. So when people tell me that [I'm attractive], I want them to tell me how good a player I am. And not tell me, 'Oh, you looked really good today.'"

Sharapova tries to keep her extraordinary life in perspective. "On the court I'm really tough. But off the court I'm a different person," she says. "I just enjoy the moment and have fun and just do the everyday things a teen does—except practice and stuff. Even though I'm not the average teen and get to travel around the world, I get to spend time with friends and family."

Sharapova also listens to Enya CDs, collects stamps, does fashion drawings, e-mails her friends, and loves shopping. Reading engages her curious mind, and after reading books in the Sherlock Homes and Pippi Longstocking series, she recently enjoyed the latest Harry Potter book, *Harry Potter and the Order of the Phoenix.* "It's fun because I was in England, and it's big there," she says. "I just wanted to be part of the scene."

Last year she appeared on *Teen People's* list of "20 teens who will change the world." That may take a while, of course, but Sharapova compellingly explained her impact: "A great tennis career is something that a fifteen-year-old normally doesn't have. I hope my example helps other teens believe they can accomplish things they never thought possible."

On whether she can someday reach No. 1 on the brutally competitive pro tour, Sharapova exudes her characteristic confidence. "I'm sure I will be because all the hard work will pay off," she says. "God gave me a big talent, and why not use it? If I stay a fighter and use the talent God gave me, I'm sure good things will happen."

---

## FASCINATING FACTS:

- In 2007, the Russian edition of *Forbes* magazine ranked Maria Sharapova No. 1 on its list of the 50 richest celebrities.

- In early 2007 seven-time Grand Slam winner Mats Wilander described world No. 1 Maria Sharapova in *Tennis* magazine (U.S.) as ". . . just a thoughtless pounder of the ball."

- Maria Sharapova, the selector for the 100 male model candidates for the 35 ball boy positions at the 2006 WTA Championships in Madrid, asked them this question: Who won the Wimbledon ladies' singles title in 2004? (Sharapova did.)

- In 2005 Maria Sharapova said she does not have a boyfriend because her father, Yuri, scares off the men.

- Maria Sharapova says is the hardest part about being famous is being constantly surrounded by bodyguards.

# 19

# Tennis Has an A-Rod, Too
# 2002

*Nothing great in the world has been accomplished without passion.*

—Georg Wilhelm Friedrich Hegel

**A**ndy Roddick grimaced and swirled around, waving his arms with the angry agitation of a child told he had to go to bed. Roddick was about to receive serve at match point of his terribly disappointing 6-3, 6-2 Monte Carlo Open loss to fifth-seeded Tommy Haas in April.

Just as a little boy hates bedtime, Roddick despises losing. Without murmuring a word of protest, Roddick's exasperated body language said everything. Monte Carlo spectators spontaneously applauded in appreciation of the almost-beaten but still-furious fighter.

The humbling defeat mirrored the crowd-pleasing American's frustrating 2002 campaign up to that point, after a dazzling breakthrough that had catapulted him to No. 14 last year. Tabbed as the Next Great American Player to help replace the "Fab Four"—Sampras, Agassi, Courier and Chang—Roddick has run into a few potholes on his road to the top, such as second-round losses at the Australian Open (an injury default) and the Nasdaq-100 Open (to Juan Ignacio Chela).

Even so, the ambitious and confident native Nebraskan, who quips that he's "the poor man's A-Rod" (compared to $252 million baseball great Alex Rodriguez), revels in the near-universal prediction of his future stardom. "People have been saying that I'm the one for almost a year now. I'm used to it and I embrace it," Roddick said last year.

Why shouldn't he, considering that:

- In 2001 he beat four current or former No. 1 players—Sampras, Ríos, Moyá, and Kuerten.

- He owns a perfect 7–0 Davis Cup record.
- He plays well on all surfaces and has won three tournaments on clay.
- He has won as many singles titles (five) as a teenager as Sampras and McEnroe and trails only Chang (six) and Agassi (ten) among American teen phenoms, and he doesn't turn twenty until August 30.
- He surpassed the best year-end ATP ranking of a player the year after being crowned junior champion—Ivan Lendl (1979) and Stefan Edberg (1984) achieved No. 20—with his No. 14 ranking.

After a brilliant junior career in which he captured the Australian Open, Eddie Herr and Orange Bowl tournaments in succession, a first, Roddick's life changed dramatically at the 2001 Ericsson Open. Ranked No.119, he overpowered Ríos 6-4, 6-1 and then "played with no fear" as No. 4 Sampras put it, to upset the thirteen-time Grand Slam champion 7-6, 6-3. Afterward, the baby faced, eighteen-year-old kid who admitted he still watches cartoons and is sometimes mistaken for a ballboy, said, "He's probably the greatest player of all time. So I made a statement to myself."

The statement was heard around the world, but Sampras heard it loudest. He felt it, too, when a 136-mph Roddick serve pounded him so hard in the rib cage that Sampras recoiled in fright. Spectators loved his youthful exuberance as much as his rocket serves and bullet forehands. Former world No. 1 Jim Courier enthused, "I haven't been this interested in watching someone play tennis in a long time."

Keeping his breakthrough victory in perspective, Roddick said, "I'm not a hero at all. I play tennis. I'm not the President or anything special. Pete Sampras and Andre Agassi are still my heroes." The impressed Sampras considered Roddick quite special, however, calling his explosive conquerer "the beginning of the new American breed," and adding, "This style [Roddick's] is the future." *Tennis Week* magazine agreed and put America's best prospect in years on its cover above the headline "Finally more hope than hype."

At Key Biscayne, Roddick also thanked his supportive, loving parents. "I'm happiest of all for my mom," he said. "She's been driving me to practice since I was eight years old. With my parents, my dad's the salt and she's the sugar. Dad's the enforcer, and mom is the sweetest lady there ever was." Fortunately, for a tennis world too often sullied by overbearing tennis parents, Jerry and Blanche prefer the background to the limelight. In fact, when a magazine writer turned up at the Roddicks' home in Boca Raton after the Sampras match, his mother baked cookies for the uninvited visitor.

Roddick was only six when a TV match turned him on to tennis. He watched a cramping but courageous, seventeen-year-old Michael Chang shock heavily favored Ivan Lendl at the 1989 French Open. "I went out and played three hours after that," he recalled.

Ironically, an eerily similar match twelve years later against the veteran Chang at Roland Garros turned fickle French fans on to Roddick but also created controversy.

This time Chang found himself on the receiving end against a young, refuse-to-quit fighter who somehow overcame leg cramps that had him writhing in pain to prevail 5-7, 6-3, 6-4, 6-7, 7-5. "Yeah, I thought about that match as we played," said Roddick afterwards. "Michael wouldn't lay down and die, and I wasn't going to either."

Not everyone gave the dramatic performance rave reviews, though. Several players criticized the extroverted Roddick for tearing off his shirt after his victory, and some in the Chang entourage doubted the extent of his cramping. In the next round Roddick retired against Lleyton Hewitt with a pulled thigh muscle after splitting two sets. That also provoked skepticism from his peers because he went to a dance club the same night.

Chalk up most of that to player envy because Roddick's popularity was steadily increasing everywhere else. The media loved his frank, intelligent, and funny answers. Parents liked his politeness that included saying "Please" and "Thank you" to ballkids. Traditionalists appreciated his calling Wimbledon "majestic."

Charity appearances to benefit the Tim & Tom Gullikson Foundation and his prep school—an event he organized himself—and other worthy causes showed he cared about more than just his own game and fame. And gossip didn't hurt either. Although Roddick said he didn't have a girlfriend, he was linked to sixteen-year-old Mandy Moore, Ashley Harkleroad, and rumor had it that he had a date with teen pop star Jessica Simpson.

What next? How about Roddick's being tabbed by *GQ* magazine as "Man of the Moment," by *People* magazine as a "breakthrough performer" in 2001, and by *US Weekly Magazine* and ESPN as one of the "World's 20 Sexiest Athletes." He was also sighted at the Los Angeles Tennis Club, not whacking balls with Sampras, but playing himself on the set of "Sabrina, The Teenage Witch," a popular TV show. Sabrina had to resort to magic to compete against her boyfriend on the court, something Roddick could have used against nemesis Lleyton Hewitt at the 2001 U.S. Open. In a quarterfinal duel that rivaled the Sampras-Agassi classic for scintillating shotmaking, Roddick played evenly with the lightning-fast Aussie and eventual champion until late in the fifth set.

A dubious line-call overrule by umpire Jorge Dias on the first point of the final game infuriated Roddick who shouted, "Are you an absolute moron?" Dias hit Roddick with a verbal warning for the temper tantrum. And soon after the earnest but immature teenager lost his poise, he lost the big match 6-7, 6-3, 6-4, 3-6, 6-4.

"My reaction was the worst I have ever lost it on a tennis court," the hyper-competitive Roddick admitted afterwards. The costly loss taught Roddick a lesson. In recent months Roddick has been seeing a sports psychologist "so I'll have my fire. But I'm going to have it in check."

More than improving his volley, shot selection, or anything else, Roddick's ability to control his boundless passion will determine his tennis destiny. And Roddick knows it.

# 20

# When Tennis Players Rocked

# 2004

*I'm a picker, I'm a grinner,*
*I'm a lover and I'm a sinner . . .*

from *The Joker* by The Steve Miller Band

**B**orgasms. Three hundred shrieking schoolgirls got them when they "attacked" Björn Borg at Wimbledon thirty years ago. They dragged the lean, teenaged Swede down on a road and pinned him on the ground for twenty minutes until police rescued him. Borg later confided he was a little scared, but lying there with frenzied teenyboppers all over him "was fun, too."

The glam rock era of men's tennis had arrived with a seventeen-year-old blond heartthrob who said little and emoted even less. "The Iceman" was joined by a controversial and colorfully nicknamed cast of characters—Nasty, Jimbo, Count Dracula, Junior, and Broadway Vitas—who turned tennis from a niche sport to the chic sport in America and much of Europe.

In fact, whenever he appeared in public, Borg was besieged like a rock star or movie idol. To protect him from autograph hunters, journalists, and rabid fans, he needed a police escort simply to move from the clubhouse to the courts. To the consternation of tennis traditionalists, Borg fanatics even scampered across sacred Wimbledon turf in platform heels to get close to their hero. "I've never known anything like it," said the long-haired lust object. "It's not safe for me to walk around. It was unbelievable."

The following year the secretary of the All England Club, which hosts Wimbledon, wrote to the heads of sixty girls' schools and asked them to keep their girls under control. All sorts of secret entrances and exits, including climbing down from rear windows, were devised at Wimbledon and elsewhere so that Borg could escape the madding crowds. The intrigue created a Garbo-like mystique that only heightened his charisma.

If Borg was the Paul McCartney of tennis, his foil was in-your-face Jimmy Connors, the Mick Jagger. If Borg was a lover—his T-shirt proclaimed, "Never love a tennis player—to him love means nothing"—Connors was a sinner, at least to his critics.

Simultaneously, Connors entertained and disgusted sports fans. How could you not love a guy who fought for every point like it was match point and for every match as if it were a matter of life and death? But how could you like a punk who harangued officials, made obscene gestures at hecklers, taunted opponents, and got his kicks by mimicking masturbation with his racket?

A psychiatrist would have a field day analyzing the complicated and conflicted Connors. He came from the wrong side of the tracks in Belleville, Illinois, and he never forgot it. He was a public parks player, an outsider "from the country club clique in East St. Louis," as he put it. After his father and the family separated early in his life, Connors was raised and taught tennis by his mother, Gloria, and grandmother, "Too-Mom," as he affectionately called her. Connors took some crap from other kids for that, and he responded by bringing brass knuckles to junior tournaments.

Connors got his combativeness from his mother, once an accomplished tournament player herself. "Jimmy was taught to be a tiger on the court," she recalled. "When he was young, if I had a shot I could hit down his throat, I did. And I'd say, 'See, Jimmy, even your mother will do that to you.'" Former champions Pancho Gonzalez and Pancho Segura refined his game in Los Angeles, but not his rough edges (although they lectured him about spitting on court). Those primal instincts would make the odds a little more even for the 5'10," 155-pound middleweight against the game's heavyweights and intimidate or infuriate the rest of his opponents.

Tennis had historically been a gentleman's game until Connors, Ion Þiriac, and Ilie Nastase ushered in its roughneck era. Echoing George Orwell's assessment of sport as "war without the shooting," the twenty-year-old Connors declared, "People don't seem to understand that it's a damn war out there. Maybe my methods aren't socially acceptable to some, but it's what I have to do to survive. I don't go out there to love my enemy. I go out there to squash him."

Squash them he did! In 1974, his wonder year, Connors captured three-quarters of a rare Grand Slam, winning the Australian Open, Wimbledon, and U.S. Open as well as an amazing ninety-nine of 103 matches. The International Tennis Federation (ITF) barred him from entering the French Open, the remaining Slam event, because he had played World Team Tennis (WTT), an unsanctioned league with a radical format and zaniness that appealed to non-traditional fans.

Off the court, too, Connors was a rebel without a pause. He refused to join the groundbreaking Association of Tennis Professionals (ATP) and the World Championship Tennis (WCT) circuit and rarely played Davis Cup. Instead, he was showcased on the much-weaker Independent Players Association (IPA) circuit run by roguish promoter Bill Riordan. Connors's renunciation of the ATP, the men's union, earned him the enmity of fellow players, some of whom scribbled scathing insults about him on locker room walls. Ever embattled, Connors sued ATP executive director Jack Kramer, super-agent Donald Dell, Arthur Ashe, and tour sponsor Commercial Union, was sued by Riordan, and managed to get into a legal dispute with the president of his own fan club. Even his diehard fans could not excuse his snub of the 1977 Wimbledon Centenary ceremonies.

Connors did have one redeeming feature everyone could like—Chris Evert. They became engaged and at the 1974 Wimbledon achieved, at 36-to-1 odds, the "Lovebird Double." Connors would say, "You know that Helen Reddy song, 'You and Me Against the World'? That's Chrissie and me." The two superstars broke up when they realized they were too young, different, and ambitious to make it work. Evert went on to become America's favorite sports heroine.

Whatever his gaucheries, fiery Connors was undeniably the most exciting Open Era player to watch. His animalistic grunts, vicious groundstrokes, screeching footwork (sometimes he wore out a pair of tennis shoes in a single match), fist pumping (he claimed he invented it in tennis), Jimmy Cagney strut, and repartee with spectators made him can't-miss TV watching for the sporting masses. If the famous 1973 "Battle of the Sexes" extravaganza between Billie Jean King and Bobby Riggs ignited the Tennis Boom in America, Connors accelerated it. By the end of 1978, the sixteen highest-rated tennis telecasts on American TV (excluding the BJK-Riggs match) all involved the brash basher. "No top player lasted longer as a major attraction or so thoroughly captured the admiration and sympathy of the public for the same length of time," praised Ashe in his 1993 book, *Days of Grace*.

Not since Frankie Kovacs, the "Clown Prince of Tennis" in the 1940s, had big-time tennis witnessed anything like the buffoonery of Năstase. Kovacs was known as "the greatest player never to win anything" of importance, and the magnificently talented Romanian would surely have achieved more, too, had he kept his roving eyes on the prize.

Although Năstase won the French, Italian and U.S. Opens plus three Slam doubles titles (two with Connors and one with Þiriac), he was a compulsive jokester and provocateur. In a doubles match at Paris, he and sidekick Þiriac were bedeviling Roger Taylor and Onny Parun by incessantly lobbing into the blinding sun so their opponents could only feebly hit the ball back. During a prolonged rally Năstase spotted a gorgeous French girl in the front row, sidled over, and persuaded her to scribble her phone number on his wrist. Just as he returned, Tiriac was blasted in the solar plexus by wicked smash.

"Where the hell you been?" Þiriac demanded to know.

"Talking to the blonde."

"You should have been here to get smash."

"Ion, there will be another smash along in a minute. There might never be another blonde."

There were many more blondes (although Năstase married a beautiful Belgian brunette) and shenanigans galore. The incorrigible Năstase "mooned" a referee, threw his shoe at a baseline judge who had called a footfault on him, and changed his shorts *during* a match. Once he let a stubborn umpire know it was raining too hard to keep playing by standing under an umbrella (he borrowed from a fan) to receive serve.

At a tournament in Louisville, Năstase and doubles partner Ashe were chided for wearing different colored outfits. So the next day naughty Nasty returned painted in blackface, quipping, "Now we are the same color—no problems." Ashe cracked up laughing. Năstase also got away with calling Ashe "Negroni." He had unflattering nicknames for lots of players: Bob Hewitt and other South Africans were "Racist"; Czech Jan Kodes was "Russian"; other East Europeans were "Commie"; and female icon Billie Jean King was reduced to "Bill." Few were offended and most agreed with Ashe that "he's the kind of guy you can't stay mad at very long."

Not everyone found Nasty's antics amusing. One of his most celebrated *tete-a-tetes* incited American Clark Graebner, a tall, well-built Clark Kent look-alike, at Royal Albert Hall in London. Furious at Năstase's baiting the crowd, officials and him, Graebner hopped over the net, jabbed Năstase in the chest and warned him not to try any more dirty tricks. His bluff called, a terrified Năstase walked off the court, saying, "I'm too frightened to continue." Năstase and a forgiving Graebner, who were friends and occasional doubles partners, went drinking afterwards.

Other incidents ended less happily. In a mixed doubles match at Nice, Nasty whacked Frenchwoman Gail Chanfreau in the body with powerful volleys. Enraged, she threw her racket at him. During a Paris tournament final, Nasty provoked intensely competitive Cliff Richey, and they nearly got into a fistfight. Nicki Spear, a mild-mannered Yugoslav, tried to slug Nasty who had cursed him and his female relatives in a Boston doubles match. Nasty's obnoxious behavior in a Rome doubles final caused a near-riot that police were summoned to quell.

What made Năstase tick? In 1976 the popular psychologist Dr. Joyce Brothers speculated about his aberrant behavior in *Tennis* magazine: "With children, temper tantrums are normal. When older people act up, it's usually because they're getting something out of it. Năstase likes attention and because tennis has been considered a gentleman's game, he keeps his opponents so shook up they can't concentrate."

Letters to leading tennis magazines called for the game's governing bodies to crack down hard on the volcanic Romanian. Tired of seeing him pampered, scolded, fined, and reprimanded, journalist Neil Amdur advocated Nastase be banished for a year. That never happened. But the court jester/bad boy of tennis (pick one) did inspire the ATP to create a Code of Conduct with point penalties for various offenses.

It didn't come too soon because the new breed of rowdy tennis fans wanted violence, or at least some dangerous confrontations that threatened it. They got it in spades during the infamous 1979 U.S. Open evening match between antiheroes Năstase and John McEnroe. Fights broke out among dangerously inebriated spectators. They booed, chanted, and angrily threw trash on the court to protest Năstase's disqualification for repeatedly arguing a point penalty and stalling during a seventeen-minute interruption. To prevent total anarchy, the tournament director replaced the umpire and allowed Năstase to play. The inmates, encouraged by Mr. Nastiness, were now running the tennis asylum.

Nãstase had absorbed his manners and morals not from tennis' unspoken code of honor that passed down through generations of players but from the larger-than-life Þiriac, his mentor and Davis Cup partner. Nicknamed "Count Dracula" for his glowering demeanor and hulking (6'2," 210-pound) presence, he more than lived up to his menacing Transylvanian image.

When "The Count" interviewed for a WTT coaching position with the Boston Lobsters, John Korff, the twenty-three-year-old general manager, bet him $100 he couldn't eat a wine glass. No problem. He took two big chomps. After his boss wisely declined a chance to get even, Þiriac challenged, "For five hundred dollars I take care of that ashtray over there."

Þiriac had taken care of business ever since he had to work in a truck factory as a teenager to help support his impoverished family after his father died. An Olympic ice hockey player for Romania, Þiriac once fearlessly stood up to an enraged Czechoslovakian team that approached him with sticks raised, by breaking his stick into two jagged pieces and staring them down. He explained his violent play and the incident with an old Transylvanian proverb: "It is better to have his mother cry than my mother cry." Concussive when he wanted to be, Þiriac was also renowned for brutal headbutts that induced headaches in bars around the world.

A late-starter in tennis, the modestly talented Þiriac best described his awkward game by calling himself "the best player in the world who cannot play tennis." Often a charming man off the court, he could play tennis hardball when necessary, and did at the 1973 Spanish Open. With Þiriac playing doubles with Borg against Dutchman Tom Okker and Nastase, the slightly built Okker several times called Þiriac "a cheater." Fed up, Tiriac swung his racket at Okker's head. Okker probably saved his life by getting his hand up in time.

Gamesmanship, though, was the weapon of choice by Þiriac, who rarely let a smile out from underneath his sinister-looking Fu Manchu moustache. And he never concocted more bedlam than in Bucharest during the infamous 1972 Davis Cup final against the U.S.

Þiriac shamelessly orchestrated a hysterical crowd by stalling, protesting, and encouraging hometown linesmen who cheated for their man so that he eventually beat demoralized Tom Gorman. The same hijinks failed in the decisive match against formidable Stan Smith, and the upright Yanks took the Cup home. No matter. Thousands of admiring Romanian fans, chanting his name, lined the streets, and mobbed Þiriac when he arrived for the post-match banquet.

If Borg played like a machine and Connors like an animal, then the exquisitely gifted McEnroe performed like an artist, caressing the ball on his strings and producing the most sublime shots. Like Mozart, he was a tormented genius. Not surprisingly, Tom Hulce studied McEnroe for his role as the eccentric, half-crazed eighteenth-century composer in his 1984 film *Amadeus*. Compelling and repellent in equal measure because of his irascible personality, McEnroe was the third member of the *troika* who polarized sports fans. You either loved him, or you loved to hate him. Connors called him "That fuckface McEnroe" and confided, "I don't know that I changed all that much. They just found somebody worse," referring to you-know-who. In 1981 Australian Davis Cuppers, disgusted by McEnroe's disgraceful court histrionics, vented their animosity toward him by taking potshots at his picture with whipped cream. The venerable *New York Times* once denounced the misbehaving son of a Wall Street lawyer, as "the worst advertisement for our system of values since Al Capone."

Spectators, fascinated with his dazzling talent, were just as lured by the prospect that "Junior" would explode and lash out at a poor umpire or linesperson. At Wimbledon his vitriolic tirades, such as "You are the pits of the world," caused shocked proper Brits to spill their strawberries and cream. McEnroe's memorable "You cannot be serious!" rant inspired "You cannot be serious!" parties in the UK and was repeated so often that it now appears in *Bartlett's Familiar Quotations*.

Like Connors before him, McEnroe was blessed with the ideal foil in archrival Borg. The contrasts between two superstars could hardly be sharper. The good guy versus the bad guy. The imperturbable, patient introvert against the intense, almost hysterical extrovert. The bastion of Old World values and behavior staving off the Ugly American. The incandescent McEnroe-Borg confrontations were matched by passions aroused in the sporting masses for their favorite.

Their 1980 Wimbledon final pitted the greatest champion of the 1970s going for his fifth straight title against the rising challenger . . . the immovable, unerring baseliner against the marvelous serve and volleyer. In a fluctuating duel filled with electrifying shot-making and excruciatingly tense drama, McEnroe staved off seven championship points but Borg ultimately prevailed 1-6, 7-5, 6-3, 6-7, 8-6. Many rate it the "match of the century," a classic we still remember and savor.

The sex appeal of leading players helped popularize tennis then by making it a world-class male-watching event, just as Anna Kournikova and Maria Sharapova would later quicken the pulses of guys. Besides Borg, the chick magnets included dashing, darkly handsome Mexican Raúl Ramirez, who just happened to marry Miss Universe.

In the days when real men wore real shorts, rugged Argentine Guillermo Vilas scored ten for his muscular legs and sultry Latin looks as well as his sensitive soul, which he expressed by writing poetry, philosophy, and musical lyrics. "Vilas is God in Argentina," said compatriot and world No. 4 José-Luis Clerc. Vilas's heroics ignited a tennis boom in South America. He romanced Princess Caroline of Monaco, among other lovelies, and long remained a most eligible bachelor.

Tall, sloe-eyed Italian champion Adriano Panatta caused mass hysteria when he played big matches at Rome's Foro Italico. Adoring fans chanted *"Ad-riano! Ad-riano!"* and threw coins at his opponents to fluster them. "There are other things in life besides tennis," this indulger in *la dolce vita* once said.

All things considered, the ultimate lady killer was the flamboyant New Yorker with the golden curls, Vitas Gerulaitis. Often, he dramatically arrived at tournaments in one of his Rolls Royces. When he departed, girls chased after him, and screamed "Take me home! Take me home!" Although he worked diligently on his game and captured Australian and Italian Opens, Gerulaitis happily followed Plato's advice that "A man should spend his whole life at play."

"Broadway Vitas" was a grinner, a sinner, a lover, and a nonpareil partier. The popular playboy hobnobbed with luminaries, such as actresses Jennifer O'Neill and Dina Merrill, composer Burt Bacharach, pop artist Andy Warhol, and former Canadian first lady Margaret Trudeau. For his raucous band of Team Tennis fans called the G-Men, he threw parties after his Pittsburgh Triangles won matches, once renting the entire floor of a hotel. At Studio 54, Infinity, Le Club, Xenon, and Les Mouche, his favorite clubs in New York, and the fashionable Jackie O's in Rome, fun-loving Gerulaitis danced with beauties until early in the morning.

High-living Gerulaitis liked to wear the latest St. Laurent, Cardin, Dior, and Gucci attire. He dated Evert and was engaged to actress Janet Jones (who later married hockey legend Wayne Gretzky). "If I did as well on the court as I do off the court, I'd be No. 1 by now," he once quipped.

When Gerulaitis too candidly admitted in a *New York Post* interview that he smoked marijuana and experimented with cocaine, it caused a furor, including a couple of court appearances. But he was also a giver. Through his Vitas Gerulaitis Foundation, he raised money for tennis equipment and tennis clinics for underprivileged New York City kids. In 1994 Gerulaitis died tragically at only 40 from accidental carbon monoxide poisoning in a guest cottage at the Long Island estate of a friend. Nearly 500 mourners, including Borg, Connors, McEnroe, Vilas, Jones, Evert, Mary Carillo, Billie Jean King, and comedian Alan King, attended his funeral Mass and exchanged colorful stories about their longtime friend.

We cared so much about these engaging characters—despite their foibles and frailties—because they gave us so much passion. And no one brought more passion than Connors. After Borg humiliated him in the 1978 Wimbledon final, Jimbo swore revenge. "I'll follow that sonofabitch to the ends of the earth," he vowed. "Every tournament he plays, I'll be waiting. Every time he turns around, he'll see my shadow across his . . . I'm going to dog him because I know that what we do in the next few years is going to be remembered long after we're both six feet underground."

Not exactly the Gettysburg Address, but we got the point. Those really were the good old days of tennis.

---

### FASCINATING FACTS:

- When Bjorn Borg completely loses his temper in a Swedish TV commercial, an understanding John McEnroe consoles him.
- When Romania joined NATO in 2002 and President George W. Bush visited Bucharest for a big reception for him, Bush asked Ilie Nastase: "Who threw the racket farther, Nastase or Jimmy Connors?"

---

This article received 1st Place in the 2004 United States Tennis Writers' Association Writing Contest in the Feature Story division.

PART 3

# Compelling Characters Hold Court

# 21

# Unique Yannick
# 2003

Picture this. On a 1971 goodwill tour to Africa, Arthur Ashe serendipitously discovers a talented eleven-year-old black player in Yaounde, Cameroon. The boy aces him. Impressed, Ashe gives the awestruck kid a fancy racket. He sleeps with it for a year and dreams of future greatness. Ashe recommends him to the French tennis federation, which trains him at its National Tennis School in Nice. Twelve years later the muscular 6'4" man wins the French Open, cries tears of joy, and becomes a national hero.

Yannick Noah's odyssey from obscurity in West Africa to international stardom is a Hollywood story thus far ignored by Tinseltown. This odyssey also plunges sensitive Noah into what he calls the "jungle of pro tennis" and produces culture shock that buffets him to this day. With the same adventurousness that impels him to serve and volley on Roland Garros *terre battue*, Noah's vast appetite for life pushes him in many directions. Fast cars, beautiful women, drugs, charity work, and a blossoming music career distract him from tennis but help him achieve a balance for which desperately searches.

While he never gains the No. 1 ranking and even flees fame in France in mid-career for anonymity in New York City, he has no regrets. He says the most important thing to him is "to make a whole stadium enjoy themselves." Noah continues to entertain people. His hit single, "Saga Africa," has topped the charts in France. In his fifth and most successful album, "Yannick," the soulful singer says "things I always wanted to say." Noah does forty to fifty concerts a year and confides that he loves the "danger" of performing live. In this interview, just before the twentieth anniversary of his memorable Roland Garros triumph, Noah talks about his life, today's celebrated stars, and burning tennis issues with the same passion and conviction that have made him one of the sport's most compelling personalities.

**In 1988 you said, "When there are 10,000 people in the stands, we are all actors. There is the serious one, the one who always screams at the umpire, the one who never says a word, the one who is a clown." Would you please describe the roles played by today's leading actors.**

Venus and Serena represent the ghetto, the black people. They also represent physical tennis, and they bring a totally different level to the women's tour. This physical, athletic game of the new era and the fact there are two sisters at the top level make it very interesting. Kournikova is the pretty one. She adds a lot to the game. So, yes, there is the feminine side to it, the beauty side. For the girls, yes, I can feel the difference in personality. They really try to give more than just winning or losing. But the men are pretty much the same. I don't see much comedy. For drama, I don't really see them as actors. Their only goal is winning or losing. They have no other dimension.

**You once said, "Personally, I have always considered tennis as a combat in an arena between two gladiators who have their rackets and their courage as weapons." Who are the most courageous gladiators today?**

They are the guys playing on Court 8, with 200 people watching, and competing for ATP points and money to pay their hotel bill. These guys are really courageous. To get on Center Court for the semifinal or final, the toughest part is already behind you. The really tough part is for the guys playing on Court 5, 7, and 12 in the qualies. They really need to dig deep. Sure, you need certain qualities to reach No. 10 or 15 in the world, but I really believe it's toughest on the kids who are [ranked] 80, 100 to, like, 300.

**"Nothing great in the world has been accomplished without passion," wrote German philosopher Hegel. Do today's players have the passion that Connors, McEnroe, Gerulaitis, and you displayed?**

I believe they *had* the passion. But after you are on this tour a few months, the Code of Conduct rules kill your passion because you cannot express yourself.

Basically what the rules say is: Play and shut up. So you have a new generation of guys who just learn the game with these new rules. You look at these guys, and they are frustrated. We were lucky not to have that [in our era]. I believe these guys do not lack passion, but it just doesn't show.

**Does Lleyton Hewitt, for example, show passion?**

There is so much anger there. I'd be interested in talking to a psychiatrist about him. There is also something lively about him. But I'm not excited and about to go, "Wow, I'm going to see Hewitt play." I don't want to sound too negative, but after five minutes of seeing him excited, excited, excited, jumping up and down, I'm tired. I want more. Where is Ilie Nastáse? Where are the Adriano Panattas? Yes, Hewitt has life, fire, definitely something. But something crazy is going on.

You can say that anger is part of it, yes, and that rap is good music. But after all this anger is out, you need more.

**You are the last Frenchman to win Roland Garros. The French have fared well in Davis Cup, but why haven't they had more success at the French Open?**

We've definitely had a team spirit for the last fifteen years. The result of that is success in Davis Cup, which is totally different from the Grand Slams, which are obviously more individual. And we don't have a guy among the top four or five seeds, anyway. If we do, then it won't be a problem for him to win a Grand Slam.

Another reason is now a lot of guys are not growing up [playing] on clay. I was probably [in] the last generation growing up on clay because I was staying in the south of France. Therefore, my game was more suited to clay. Now all these guys come from Paris where they spend most of the winter playing indoors and on hard courts.

**Pete Sampras has won seven Wimbledons, five U.S. Opens, two Australians, five ATP Finals, one Italian Open, and two Davis Cup titles. Does all that make Sampras the greatest player of all time?**

In my mind, it's between Sampras, Borg, and Laver. I believe Borg would have won a few more [major titles], if he didn't retire at twenty-six. Laver won two Grand Slams [in 1962 and 1969]. He was an unbelievable player and beautiful to watch. We were lucky to have him. Being a player of the 1980s, I really believe Sampras is the best ever.

**John McEnroe said that in the 1980s cocaine was the popular drug and he experimented with it. In 1991, you said, "But for the good of the sport they [drug users] should be caught and stopped. The ATP should test at every tournament, not just a few like they do at the moment." How prevalent were drugs on the men's tour then, and how prevalent are they now?**

There is a big difference between using drugs to enhance performance or just as a social drug. Cocaine has never helped someone win a match or have a better life. But I also know that plenty of people, especially in America, freely take performance-enhancing drugs and are protected by the system. And nobody says anything about it. I don't believe you can be happy when you have cheated and won. Your conscience won't let you. But now drug cheating is becoming so strong and powerful that some players *are* protected, depending on where they come from.

**What do you mean by "protected"?**

They *are* protected. We *know* for a fact that it's better to come from America than from France. It has nothing to do with the ATP. It has to do with the whole sports system. If you are French, you are tested no matter what sport you play because it's part of our culture. Here, you have the ATP, and if it's not the ATP, it's going to be another organization; I don't know what the Olympic Committee is called in America. But, at the end of the day, everybody is trying to hide, and nobody wants to be responsible. Nobody really tackles this problem and tries to catch violators. Each sport has its own rules. In America, you find over the counter in pharmacies things that are totally forbidden in France and in Europe. Even children can take it here. It's really a different world here.

**In 1996 you admitted that you smoked marijuana during the 1983 French Open. Did that help you win the title?**

Well, I said I smoked marijuana during 1983. But I didn't smoke during the tournament. I never smoke during a tournament — never. I smoked a lot *after* the tournament. It's funny how people made it into such a big deal. It's a recreational drug as opposed to a performance-enhancing drug. If you are just talking about recreational drugs, then you have people tell you how you are supposed to be a role model.

**Aren't famous athletes supposed to be role models?**

I believe the best role models are the father and the mother. If somebody can be influenced by what he sees on TV, then there is a problem with his education. Yeah, I smoked, yeah! If my children are smoking, I hope they will be able to talk to me about it. It's not that I am going to judge them. And I also know the majority of people have tried marijuana. So why would we hide? Hiding is not attacking the problem. And I really believe it *is* a problem for young kids. And the way to deal with it is to talk about it. Let's not just say, "This [sports] star smoked," and that's it. I haven't smoked in ten years.

**You are the last black man to win a Grand Slam singles title. Why is it so difficult for black men to excel at the sport's elite level?**

For two reasons. The first is that most black kids are looking for black role models, and most of their role models are excelling at other sports. So their first priority is to play basketball or football [soccer]. Tennis is probably their third, fourth, or fifth choice. And, obviously, tennis is more expensive than most sports.

**In 1988 Arthur Ashe predicted, "Given the same chance as others have had, blacks would dominate our sport as they have done in other sports." Do you agree?**

If you give a racket and a coach to an inner-city kid who doesn't have much, he's going to do more with it than a kid who has rackets and a court in his backyard. They're not going to take for granted the opportunity. A lot of athletes, including blacks, Hispanic minorities, in Africa, or in Asia, don't have these opportunities. In Paris, we have programs and when you give tennis to poor people, 95 percent of kids are from north Africa. Yes, they *will* ultimately dominate the game if they get the chance. Any sport where they get the chance, blacks dominate, including in France where we've been world champion in soccer with a team that is mostly [composed of] immigrants.

**Ashe added this prophetic comment: "There is a terrific apprehension among some people that blacks will take over the sport . . . It will create problems because their behavior, speech and dress is just a completely different culture." Is there still a terrific apprehension among whites?**

I don't believe so. Also, his time was so far from now. Tennis had been pretty much a white sport with certain upper-class attitudes. Now I see a lot of kids coming from a lower class. Frankly, I don't see how many black guys would change the sport in terms of behavior. That might have been a possibility thirty or forty years ago, but not now.

**Are the outspoken Williams sisters and their controversial father creating exactly the problems Ashe predicted?**

I don't think so. I don't see Venus and Serena and Mr. Williams as the ambassadors of black sport. They are the Williamses. I do not see myself in much of what they say and the way they behave.

**Would you please tell me about Les Enfants de la Terre (Children of the Earth), which you and your mother, Marie-Claire, co-founded.**

We started it eighteen years ago in northern Cameroon. Slowly we became bigger and bigger and wanted to be more socially active. So we started to buy houses and build houses to help orphans and others who don't have parents around and need to regroup and recuperate physically. While they regroup, we take them in our houses. Basically, that's the main objective. We've helped about 3,000 kids so far.

**You are also involved with a project called "Féte le Mur" ("Celebrate the Wall") in collaboration with the French Tennis Federation. What does this project do?**

We provide courts, rackets, and coaches to kids from the inner city. And we open what we call our centers, which are places with at least two courts and a wall. We started that four years ago, and now there are nineteen centers all over France. It's really blossoming very fast. It's working well because the kids are really interested. We're building these courts within the inner city so kids can walk to the courts. It's their courts. Some of the kids built the courts themselves. We have tournaments for them. It's really working.

**Can you produce a champion from those kids?**

I definitely would love to.

**Would you please tell me about the new album you will release soon.**

It's going to be our sixth album. The last one we did was by far the most successful. Now I'm in a totally different world, which is playing at a lot of places. Yes, there are a lot of expectations for this album. I'm really happy with it. Now we are going to see if people like it. The last album looked like me and sounded like me and said things I always wanted to say. So we called it "Yannick." Three years ago I decided this [singing] is where I want to put my soul. We don't know the name of the new album yet. We just finished it. Now we're going to mix it, listen to it, and then we'll have a better idea of the whole spirit of it. It's going to be about giving and sharing.

**You've had a highly successful music career as a singer and songwriter, producing several top-selling albums with your band Urban Tribu. Many tennis players have attempted music careers. What is the connection between tennis and popular music?**

I do not know. A few guys have tried it. John McEnroe, Mats [Wilander], Jim Courier, well-known guys. People assume all players want to be musicians. When we are on the road, to call Mats or John and say, "Let's meet in this room and jam together," was a way to throw the competition aside and just do something together. Since I was a professional athlete playing an individual sport, music gave me an opportunity to share, to find a team spirit, and melt into a group, which I really love. I love being a Davis Cup captain just because I had missed the idea of a group, a community. Tennis is sometimes too individualistic and egotistic. And playing music started to be a fantasy and then it worked. I just feel so privileged that I can experience that.

**Whose music do you most admire?**

Bob Marley, by far. Also Fela Kuti from Nigeria, mostly African people, and another musician called Manu Dibango.

**What are your favorite CDs?**

One CD will be the whole collection of Bob Marley. The others would be "Manu Dibango in Jamaica" and "Fela Black President."

**In 1991 you said, "I don't believe it hurts me to have many affairs. In Africa, where my roots lie, the men have many wives. To put it simply, I love women." Do you still feel that way? And what do you love most about women?**

It's only normal for you to repeat what's in your youth. Yes, for me, coming to America, or in Palm Springs, is like being on another planet. It's very different — the way people behave, the way people are. Even though I respect that, I am not this way. I like people, in general. Yes, I do like women. I'm like anyone else. I like to touch someone in every way possible.

**You once had sex in the locker room just before a match, and you occasionally had a cognac before you played. Did they help you play better?**

About the sex before the match, I was kind of relaxed and got tired by the end of the game. But it was not an important match. As for the cognac and cigarettes before playing, I enjoyed doing that once in a while at the end of my career when I was playing indoors. That *definitely* helped me. It was really fun. I did that in the [players] lounge before the game when everybody was getting all tense and nervous. Some people take life so seriously sometimes. I thought I was just going to take a step back and relax about this whole thing.

**You had lots of fun during your playing days and were something of a Renaissance man. But, in retrospect, did you squander some talent with your less than ambitious training program and lack of single-mindedness?**

Well, probably. I look at all these guys who were in front of me. And there is nothing that I really miss that they have.

**Not their titles?**

Well, what do you do with it? It's another cup. A memory. Everybody has his own choices. People look at me and say, "God, you sacrificed so much. You sacrificed your youth to be a tennis player. You left home, you could have stayed in Africa." Yes, I know what I gave up to achieve what I did. And, yes, I could have done more. But *everybody* can do more.

**What prevented you from doing more?**

There was a point when I really believed it wasn't healthy. When I looked at the guys, like the Ivan Lendls, even though I respected what they were doing, I could not do those things and have this lifestyle. And even today I cannot have this lifestyle. We are just different. The cultures have a lot to do with it. I was not ready *at any cost* to do anything and prepare myself with whatever product or win at any cost just to have a No. 1 in front of my name when people present me. I had a No. 4. So what!

**During your pro career you had to overcome bouts of depression on occasion. Were they caused by the tremendous pressure caused by the high expectations the French public and media burdened you with?**

I was searching for a balance. I had my period of sadness. Most athletes start their soul-searching after their careers. I was doing it while I was playing. When I stopped [my career], it was actually a good time. I went through this period in a very smooth, easy way. When a lot of my friends stopped, it was a shock to them.

I went through some tough, lonely times in my career, and a lot of people thought I couldn't deal with the star system, the pressures of being recognized.

But that was not the case. I was just trying to cope with what other human beings go through. And, yes, coming from Africa, I've had a lot of changes throughout my life to deal with.

**So it's difficult to be an African in the tennis world?**

It's pretty lonely, that's for sure. That's the way I would put it.

**You wore and still wear attire that showed off your superb physique, and in 1992 you created your "Just Say Noah" sportswear collection. What is your opinion of today's baggy shorts that go to the knee and shirts that extend to the elbow?**

You won't find it in my collection. But I have this conversation with my son, who is eighteen, and it just makes me laugh. I remember my parents not understanding why I used to wear these very large pants. I used to be crazy about James Brown and wear these hot pants to school. It's funny because I would not wear what these kids and players are wearing today. It's very ugly. My parents used to think I was wearing some ugly stuff, too.

**In 1991, after losing in the first round at a tournament in Bordeaux, you refused to accept a guarantee, or appearance fee, of $30,000 as a matter of principle. Would you please explain that principle.**

This tournament director invited me to carry his tournament, and I was the number one seed. Even though it was guaranteed money and I did some publicity before the tournament started, I didn't feel comfortable taking this money. I wasn't worth this money, which I felt was a little too much. But sometimes I felt that when I really worked as hard as I could, well, that's OK, if somebody gives me this [appearance] money. But this time I didn't feel good about it. So I didn't take it.

**But why shouldn't all tournament money be distributed as earned prize money?**

That is mostly the case, but in some situations, guarantees help sell a tournament. If the tournament director wants to make money, he basically makes it two months before. He wants a tournament with his top seeds guaranteed, and then he can go chase the sponsors. This is where guarantees originated. It's still going on.

**What are the effects of guarantees paid to players just for showing up?**

Look at the rankings now. The more you play, the better your ranking is. What they want with this Masters Series is to guarantee the big names for certain sponsors. But they don't care in what state [condition] they come. They don't care whether they win or lose. What they guarantee is that Agassi, Hewitt, Safin and Kuerten are going to come to your tournament. The old ranking system [which counted all tournament matches] was better.

*Yannick Noah: "Davis Cup is the most beautiful event in tennis."* Courtesy of the International Tennis Hall of Fame & Museum, Newport, Rhode Island

**You once said, "What I love about Davis Cup is it is not about contracts, schedules, and business. This tradition is much bigger than dollars. What you do in Davis Cup is sacrifice for others . . . that's why Davis Cup is great." In recent years Sampras and Agassi have complained that the Davis Cup format is too demanding and that it should be played every other year. Is there anything you'd change about the Davis Cup?**

No! I wouldn't change anything. Every Davis Cup weekend, you have players playing for their lives, whether it's in Zimbabwe or in Germany or in Korea or in Brazil — all the different [geographical] zones, all the different divisions. Davis Cup is the most beautiful event in tennis. You have two spoiled guys who want to change the whole thing because they are powerful. This is the most selfish thing. I've never heard them talk about all the beautiful qualities of Davis Cup.

**Was France's winning the Davis Cup in 1991 for the first time in fifty-nine years the highlight of your thirty-year tennis career? And what do you remember most about it?**

The joy, looking at all the joy around. Being able to hug my best friends at this particular occasion. Just crying. It's unusual to cry in happiness with your best friends. And I'm glad I experienced that with Guy [Forget] and Henri [Leconte]

and Patrice [Hagelauer], who used to be my coach and who was coach of the team. To be able to share this [experience] was very special because we were already true friends. That made our friendship very special.

**You are one of the few people ever to captain both your country's Davis Cup and Fed Cup teams and the only one ever to win titles in both events. What are the differences between coaching men and women? And which did you enjoy more?**

I didn't see much difference. But obviously there are differences because the people and the personalities are different. But my basic coaching approach and philosophy were the same. I enjoyed coaching the `91 French team more than any team, whether it was in `96 when we won again, or in `97 when we won with the girls. That's because I was coaching my friends, and they had asked me if I would become captain. That came from the heart. To win the Davis Cup was really, really special. It also helped build my confidence to continue after they were gone. So I was really thankful to them.

**In 1997 Jimmy Connors said, "Big money encourages tanking. In my opinion, tanking is going on even with a lot of the top guys today it is quite evident." During your twenty-six years as a pro player and coach, how prevalent has tanking been?**

Well, there are so many degrees to it. Where does tanking really start? When is it that you lose your motivation? Is it when you decide not to practice tennis the week before? Is it when you decide to have a couple of beers two days before the game? Or is it when you psychologically fall and crack and lose the game in front of people? I truly believe we all want to be rich. And when you have all the money you need, it affects your motivation. That's normal. That's human.

**But not for all players.**

You have some people who have this thing with the game or this thing [hidden] in their past lives that make them want to prove something about whether they need this love from the fans or they need this recognition to be part of history. It's really interesting to see some guys say, "I want to be part of tennis history." So the money doesn't matter to them at that point. But this is very unusual. When you get everything you want and you're not hungry, you don't work hard.

**In 2000 Andre Agassi said, "There is too much money in the game nowadays." Then Yevgeny Kafelnikov complained that "the money on the ATP [tour] is ridiculous compared to what other athletes are making." Who is right?**

It's easy to say there is too much money when you are a billionaire. Andre should be the last one to say there is too much money. And, if there is too much money, I never heard of a problem of having too much money. In my world, there is never enough money. So, if Andre has too much money, I can give him thousands of ways to use it for good purposes.

**You once said, "I have never had a problem being black, but the Cameroon Tennis Federation never supported me. The reason, my mother was white." Is it rather ironical that blacks, who have been discriminated against by whites for centuries, sometimes discriminate against blacks?**

Yeah, it's human. In Cameroon, I was already privileged. To play tennis in the first place was unbelievable. So, yes, the federation would not help me because I was the son of a white woman, which equaled being rich, which was not totally untrue.

**In 2001 Nicolas Ayeboua, the executive director of the Confederation of African Tennis, told me, "Yannick Noah is a very charming person, and I know he's doing a lot of wonderful things for humanitarian causes. But he never took any action toward the development of tennis in Africa." Why haven't you helped tennis in Africa where you were raised for your first eleven years?**

First of all, I never had any contact whatsoever with any of the African federations. My participation is helping Cameroon tennis. I'm not going to help Africa. It's not because I come from Cameroon that I need to or I must help African tennis. When I work with inner-city tennis in France, I'm talking about 2,500 disadvantaged kids coming from Africa. Yes, they play tennis, but they could play soccer. I don't have to help tennis in Africa. I can help my brothers, and my brothers are all over the world. As far as tennis in Africa, what I *did* was work in programs in Cameroon.

**What did you do there?**

We have a couple of clubs in Cameroon that are open to children. Personally, I've brought about fifteen guys from Cameroon to France, and they are now coaches or tennis teachers and have families. I am really proud of that. Some of them are my friends. But I am very reluctant to do such spectacular things like going to tournaments and presenting cups [to finalists] in Africa. A lot of people, especially presidents of tennis federations, are there for the limelight and not much for what's really going on in tennis. Obviously, I'm very sensitive to that and very picky about dealing with them.

**Do you believe that sub-Saharan Africa possesses a hotbed of athletic talent just waiting to be found and developed into world-class tennis players and even champions?**

Africa is a hotbed for *anything*. I would not limit the potential of Africans to just sports. It could be computers, chess, and many fields. But there is nothing there. Africa is in a state where everything is needed. In Africa there are priorities these days, and tennis is not a priority. But yes, there is great [tennis] talent there. If you give a kid a racket and some balls, he's going to play all day. He's going to enjoy it. And, yes, he's going to be naturally tough because he's used to living in certain difficulties with not much food, in the heat, or no shoes. He can take the pain at a very young age. Therefore, he can do anything, if he's given the opportunity. It's up to us, or whoever, to give them the opportunity.

**Lots of players hit, or try to hit, a spectacular back-to-the-net, between-the-legs shot today. Did you invent that trick shot which you used at the 1983 U.S. Open?**

No. The one I first saw hitting that was [Victor] Pecci. He used to do that. [Guillermo] Vilas was the second one to do that. And I was the third one. The only shot I invented was the overhead jumping high with my two legs together like Sampras does.

**The slam-dunk overhead.**

Exactly. That is my shot.

**Meeting Ashe as a boy literally changed your life. What do you remember most about Ashe as a person?**

He cared. He cared about people. He cared about humanity. He had this dimension. And he was very literate and articulate. He was a citizen of the world and an activist. Everything that I try to be is because of him. He not only helped me the first day I met him, but he remains a great example for me. And he should be for many athletes now. Whatever the sport, Arthur was up there, by far the best person.

**Voltaire, the great French philosopher, historian, and satirist, said, "Appreciation is a wonderful thing; it makes what is excellent in others belong to us as well." What do you appreciate most?**

I appreciate what I have. I see a lot of people around me who are really trying to get more or something they don't have. I'm happy and comfortable with what I have.

**When you die, would you rather be known as a great tennis player, a talented musician, or some combination of the two?**

I hope people will see me as a decent guy. I tried everything I could playing tennis. I'm enjoying music now. It's more than a hobby, but I'm not putting my heart and soul into it, which was the case when I was playing tennis. I *know* that people will remember me as a tennis player. And that would be right.

# 22

# Jim Courier: From Dade City to Paris to Newport

# 2005

*The secret of success is constancy to purpose.*

—Benjamin Disraeli, prime minister of England, in an 1872 speech

Other players called him "Rock." The reverential nickname captured the virtues and characteristics of the man and the player. Like a massive rock, Jim Courier possessed a steely resolve that could not be budged during competition. Almost as hard and durable as a rock, his physique developed through grueling training sessions and created a Borgian level of stamina that further intimidated foes. Like some rocks, though, rough edges marked—and marred—both his game and his persona.

Driven by a prototypical American ambition to be No. 1, Courier achieved the pinnacle of pro tennis in 1992. His reign proved short, but one cannot gainsay its brilliance. From mid-1991 to 1993 Courier won four Grand Slam titles, two French and two Australian, plus Rome (twice), and Key Biscayne. He also reached three more Slam finals, including the final of every major—something Sampras, Borg, Connors, McEnroe, Becker, and Wilander never accomplished—and helped the U.S. capture two Davis Cups.

The International Tennis Hall of Fame will honor those achievements on July 9 when it inducts Courier at the storied Newport Casino in Rhode Island. His acceptance speech will undoubtedly relate how his work ethic developed from his family and small-town roots in Dade City, Florida, and how his knowledge broadened from international travel to Paris and Tokyo and Melbourne and Sao Paulo and other fascinating destinations.

Courier made tennis history as part of America's "Greatest Generation" with Sampras, Agassi, and Chang. In this highly candid interview, he reflects on his career, warts and all—including his prickly dealings with the media and occasional indifference toward fans—analyzes tennis' burning issues, and talks about his second career as a Champions Tour player, TV commentator, businessman, promoter, and philanthropist. Courier is determined to remain relevant in the tennis world, and together with Agassi and Chang, his off-court beneficence is already creating a "Greatest Generation" of a more important kind.

**You were a Little League baseball standout. How did you get turned on to tennis?**

My great-aunt Emma [Spencer] gave me a racket when I was seven. She coached the women's tennis team at UCLA in the 1960s and had her own tennis club at her home in Sanford, Florida, where I was born. My first experience with organized tennis was through her. She had a club team of juniors that would play against other local clubs in central Florida. I joined her team and was the tenth man on a ten-man team. And at seven, I was playing mostly against twelve- and thirteen-year-old girls. They were beating up on me pretty badly. In any case I liked it. That experience through the summer led me to my first organized tournament in September at the Palmer-Bollettieri Tennis Club in Bradenton.

**The next turning point came at age 11 and involved Harry Hopman, the renowned 1950s-60s Australian Davis Cup captain. What happened?**

I had a friend from the Northeast who was coming down with her mother for a week to train at Harry Hopman's [tennis academy] in Largo. I had never been there and wanted to see what it was all about. And fifty dollars a day was the charge. My mom [Linda] made me cough up the money. So I raked leaves to earn the money to go there for a day. And while I was there, my mom ingeniously engaged Mr. Hopman and told him, "Jim's very eager, he likes to play, and he's doing very well in competition in Florida, but we can't afford to be here. Is there anything you can do?" Mr. Hopman came and took a look at me. And pretty quickly he decided that it would be quite all right if I just showed up on weekends and played the players there at no charge. It was one of the forks in the road that changed my career.

**Then at fourteen you went to the Nick Bollettieri Tennis Academy.**

I got a phone call from Nick and the opportunity to attend his academy because I reached the Orange Bowl fourteen-and-under final. That was the second real fork in the road, the second person out of the kindness of his heart to provide an opportunity for me to get out of the small hometown in Dade City and get into the big leagues.

**What lessons about tennis and life did you learn there?**

One was that there was an incredible depth of global talent. I also realized that plenty of players there struck a nice ball but couldn't win matches. Although my game was a little less orthodox than others, I was a better competitor than most people. And that was a good lesson for me to learn. The overall package of a tennis player was first presented to me there as not only the actual striking of the ball, but also weightlifting and running and fitness and the mental side of the game. I began to approach the game in a more professional manner, even at the age of fourteen.

**In the 1991 book _Hard Courts_, you acknowledged, "There's no question I gave up my childhood to become a tennis player."**

That's a fair statement because I wasn't able to do the typical things that children do. But having said that, what I have been able to live [since then] has far exceeded most typical lives.

**In _Hard Courts_ you also confided, "The first year, every Sunday night when my parents dropped me off, I would go off by myself and cry. But I got through it." Please tell me about those difficult times.**

My recollection is that maybe the first five or six times they dropped me off, it was tough because I hadn't been away from home for an extended period before. The egos were constantly at battle at the academy. Not only from your age-group competition, but also from other kids of different ages and in different places in their tennis lives. The boys were constantly jawing at each other and posturing and hormones [raging] and all that stuff that happens in high school. And it was amplified in a very competitive environment.

**You won four Grand slam titles, finished 1992 ranked No. 1 in the world, reached the final of every Grand Slam tournament—something Sampras, Borg, Connors, McEnroe, Becker, and Wilander never did—and helped the U.S. capture two Davis Cups. Which achievement or achievements are you most proud of?**

You're asking me to pick which kid I prefer in my family. It's hard to pick one over the others. It's a lot to be proud of. The achievement that was the most impactful was the first major [title] that I won at Roland Garros. That's because it changed my life. I went from a very good tennis player to a Grand Slam champion. And those are two very different things.

**After you aced Andre Agassi, your former roommate at Bollettieri's academy, on championship point, to win the French in 1991 for your first major title, you ecstatically threw yourself on your back and covered yourself in red clay.**

Yeah. (Laughter) That was not premeditated. That was very much in the moment. And the surprise of actually achieving that was overwhelming and wonderful at that moment. It was one of those moments that don't last long enough. The moment between hitting the ace and holding the trophy and being back at the hotel goes in a lightning flash.

**Few players in history have enjoyed as brilliant a period as yours from the middle of 1991 to 1993 when you gained the final in seven out of ten Grand Slam tournaments and won four of them—and also had a twenty-five-match winning streak in 1992. What made you so successful, so hard to beat, then?**

Mentally, I was tough and guys knew that. I had an edge because of my [winning] momentum when I stepped on the court because I was very confident and they were fearful. That played a big part, the biggest part. I've always controlled points with my serve and my forehand. I didn't lose matches due to fitness. The fitness was merely a means to an end. It's an intimidation factor, but nobody wins matches on fitness. They lose matches when they lack fitness.

**What was the biggest disappointment in your career?**

It was definitely losing the [1993] French Open final to Sergi Bruguera when I was going for the third title in a row. I was up a service break in the fifth set and then cramped and wasn't physically capable of playing my best tennis. It was a bit ironical because I was known for my fitness. I had some tough matches earlier in the tournament and some weird rain delays, and the stress and strain all added up on my body. I just ran out of gas against a terrific player, no doubt, but a player who had never beaten me before.

**You relished competing in big matches before big crowds. You once said, "I love this game. You can't go to Kmart and buy the feeling you get in front of a packed house." Please tell me about that experience and that feeling.**

When you're a performer, and that's very much what a tennis player is, you compete on the one hand against your opponent, and it's one-on-one combat. But you also take energy from the arena and the public that are witnessing the battle. The bigger the battle, the more energy you draw from the audience, whether they are with you or against you. There's excitement. That's what every performer lives for. And that's what I lived for.

**You were especially popular in Paris because you gave your 1992 victory speech in French and in Melbourne where you did the unusual by diving into the polluted Yarra River after your triumphant finals. Was there a symbiotic relationship between you and the French and the Australians?**

A player who wins a tournament will always be and feel something special in that city. And my doing something out of the ordinary after a major victory got the attention of the public. I didn't do it to get the attention of the public. Both of those acts were personal things I wanted to do for me. But it still connected me on a deeper level to the public in those countries and made me real to them, and not just a robot hitting tennis balls. They saw some personality there. When I jumped into the Yarra, it was to win a bet I made with [my coach] Brad Stine.

**In *Tennis Week* you recently said, "I was a winner, a guy who found a way to win. My game was self-taught in many ways and reflects my personality." How did your self-taught game reflect your personality?**

Because my personality is one that constantly wants to learn. I read a lot. I'm a curious person by nature. But I'm not a studied man as far as traditional education goes. I didn't go to [a university for] higher learning. I graduated high school at sixteen. And my education has come through experience. That's what I mean when I say my game was self-taught in many ways. I've had *many* great tennis teachers from the beginning to the end of my ATP [Tour] career. I've always taken what they've taught me and adapted it for my personality and my game. That's the way I operate in my life. I try and glean nuggets from people, but then I adapt it to my needs.

**Let's talk about your biggest rivals. You boasted a winning record, 7–5, against Andre Agassi, including three huge wins over him at the French Open. Why did you fare so well against Andre?**

In that period when I was playing Andre at the French Open, he wasn't as much a percentage player as he is today. And I was able to frustrate him because I could match him on a power basis from the baseline then. I served better than he did. And I was fitter and more patient. Clay was a better surface for me than Andre. And I was able to take advantage of all of those factors and turn it into some nice victories over there. I was more mature, too. Andre has matured later in his career and has reaped huge benefits from that maturity. But he wasn't as disciplined at that point, while I was extremely disciplined then.

**You also were 6–4 lifetime against Stefan Edberg and 4–2 in Grand Slams, beating him on every surface—in the 1992 and 1993 Australian finals, the 1991 French quarters, and the 1993 Wimbledon semis. Why did you hold the upper hand over him?**

Match-ups are everything in a one-on-one sport. And my game matched up well with Stefan's because he couldn't overpower me with his serve. And as beautifully as he volleys—and he certainly was the best volleyer on tour then—I could still get the ball by him on returns often enough to sneak a break in a set. And I was able to control play from the baseline with my serve and my power. It was just a good match-up for me—no discredit to Stefan because he was a great champion. He gave me the worst beating in a major in my career in the final of the [1991] U.S. Open. After that I didn't lose to him again. I figured something out, and the strategy started working for me.

**You also had some terrific matches against Pete Sampras, whom many experts consider the greatest player of all time. Which match or matches stand out in your memory?**

Two stand out for me. The first one clearly is the Australian Open quarterfinal in '95. (After a spectator shouted, "Do it for your coach, Pete"—a reference to Sampras's seriously ill coach, Tim Gullikson—Sampras broke down in tears.) That match was so emotional and produced a very high level of tennis. Pete ended up coming back and winning in five sets. The second memorable match was the '93 Hong Kong final. Pete beat me 7-6 in the third [set] with a 7-5 tiebreaker. It was a barn burner. I couldn't have played any better, and I don't know that he could have either. And I was so frustrated because I still got clipped by the slimmest of margins. I remember thinking—as opposed to Edberg—that is *not* a good match-up for me. I just threw my ninety-nine-mile-per-hour fastball, and he just hit it out of the ballpark.

**What did that unforgettable Melbourne duel reveal about Sampras?**

Pete was a great champion at that stage in his career. But people had never peered into his soul. People had no clue who Pete Sampras was. And that match in Australia gave them their first look behind the curtain.

**When you play TeamTennis, you will likely face former rivals Boris Becker and Agassi as well as current world No. 3 Andy Roddick. Can you beat Roddick?**

(Laughter) Can I beat Roddick in a set? That depends on what kind of handicap you give me.

**Do you relish the challenge of playing these great players?**

Listen, I appreciate the fact that I'm still able to play tennis at a very high level. I can be competitive at times. But if I were really serious about playing on tour, I'd just go back and play on tour and really test it. What I dislike is when people in the past, who were in my situation—i.e., retired from the regular [ATP] tour— take their shots [at current players] and say, "I could beat these guys, they're a bunch of chumps." Because if you can beat them, [then you should] go out there and play them. I'm not playing those guys because I'm not committed to a day-to-day existence of getting myself in shape again and mentally steeling myself for five-set battles. I'm not sure who I'm going to play in World TeamTennis, but I hope it's someone very good so I can test myself. I love that.

**But you did return to the ATP Tour in April in Houston at the U.S. Clay Court Championships when you played doubles with Agassi. What inspired you to do that?**

Quite simply, Andre and I played an event for charity that my company, InsideOut, put on in Tampa before the Nasdaq-100. We played singles against [James] Blake and [Mardy] Fish, and then we played doubles against those guys. We had such a great time. I told Andre that if you ever want to play dubs, let me know because I had a blast. And sure enough, a couple of weeks later, he called me and said, "Let's play in Houston." Even though I lost in singles, I still had a great time.

**How did you do in doubles?**

We beat Blake and Fish 7-5.

**What is a typical Jim Courier day like?**

If I can get out and hit some balls in the morning—which depends on the business schedule—I like to hit for an hour or an hour and a half, which I'll probably do three times a week. And then I'll be in the offices of InsideOut afterwards down in SoHo for five, six hours, maybe more.

**You created a company called InsideOut Sports & Entertainment (www.insideoutlive.com) last year because you want to remain "relevant" in the game. What is InsideOut?**

My partners [Jon Venison and Tim Stallard] and I provide events for tennis fans. Our Mercedes Classic on May 21 in Fort Lauderdale has four players performing in one evening. It's tennis and entertainment. Our events aim to keep the game moving forward and really bring energy and entertainment more in line with typical entertainment fare like an NBA game or a concert where excitement and energy is high. Tennis is in a competitive environment against all forms of entertainment, and we have to fight not only to keep our audience but to get new audience. That's what we're doing. We have a Champions Tour-type event in November in Houston called Champions Cup Houston featuring eight legends of the game. We have several other projects that I can't disclose until they are finalized.

**In 1998, you told *The Age*, an Australian newspaper, "I used to think you guys [the media] were the anti-Christ. As far as I was concerned, I was the No. 1 player in the world, and you guys were there only to take it off me. And I would only speak to you because I'd be fined if I didn't." You matured as your career moved along, and now, ironically, you are part of the media. Please talk about both changes.**

When I was young, I was so combative in every aspect of my career. A lot of that was immaturity. You have to be a combative person on the court to play high-level tennis. But what I didn't understand—and I wish I had—was that off the court you don't have to be combative and you can be cooperative. Everyone is part of this machine that makes tennis successful. As I matured, I was able to understand my responsibilities better. I regret that I overreacted to a few articles that were not so positive and overlooked all of the positive articles. Immaturity causes you to overreact. As I've matured, I've understood how the game works and breathes and lives.

**In *Tennis Week*, you recently confided, "The thing that I am most upset about is**

that we had arguably the best generation of American [men] players in history, but at the same time, the popularity of the game declined in America . . . Part of that has to be my fault." What caused the popularity of tennis in America to decline in the 1990s? And what were your own errors of commission and omission?

> If I had a broader perspective on my place in tennis, I would have done as much media as possible to keep tennis on the front page [of newspapers and magazines]. I would have been a lot more accessible—even though at that stage I felt like I didn't have room to breathe. I felt like I had very little free time. [But] you have to make time. You have to appreciate the fact that you are in business, and you have to help that business grow. There were autographs I didn't sign. There were times I was tired and didn't want to be bothered at dinner, and I was abrupt with people. I attribute that to immaturity and take full responsibility for all of that. But, if I could do my career again, I wouldn't change the way I played the game. I would change the way I played the game of off-court tennis so I could have helped the popularity of tennis instead of just focusing on preparing for my next tournament. But I wasn't the only culprit.

**Who were the other culprits?**

> I wasn't the one who took the [season-ending] Masters tournaments from Madison Square Garden and put it in Germany for short-term cash. I wasn't the guy who took the TV rights and put them on packages where fewer tennis fans had access to them. Those mistakes were a shame. We lacked the long-term vision.

**Please tell me about your important role in helping organize the January 31 exhibition event in Houston that raised $518,932.50 for the Bush-Clinton Tsunami Relief Fund.**

> That event was the product of a conversation that I had with my InsideOut partners and Jim and Linda McIngvale. Jim asked what tennis is doing for tsunami relief. I said I know tennis is doing fund-raising events in India and Australia but nothing to my knowledge in America. He said, "We should put an event together and do it in Houston now." It was January and Jim wanted to do it by the end of the month.

**What did you do then?**

> I called [John] McEnroe and [Chris] Evert. She saw Roddick that day and got Andy in. Anna Kournikova and Tommy Haas, I'm forgetting some people, but everybody stepped up. The Tennis Channel stepped up big. Virtually everybody we called said, "I'll be there. It's the right thing to do. How can we help?"

**You flew in from Australia, not having slept for twenty hours, and put on a great event, making sure the other players were accommodated.**

I would do it again tomorrow, for sure, because it's such a necessary thing. That tragedy is, I hope, the worst we'll ever see in our lifetimes. I would stand up again and do it again as would all the participants. I shouldn't get any more accolades than anyone else.

**In *Tennis Week*, Chris Evert gave you this accolade: "Jim is a great example of someone getting better in every way after retiring from tennis. He said to me once that it was amazing to him how much nicer he was now than when he was playing." In what ways are you a better person now? And what are the reasons you are a changed man?**

Maturity has done wonders for me. (Laughter) More knowledge and awareness and a little less myopia, which is necessary when you're on tour. But when you leave the tour, you are able to broaden your vision. That's been a real positive for me. I circle back to my curiosity and my willingness to open up. It wasn't there during a large part of my career.

**During your career, you notched several very important and high-pressure Davis Cup triumphs. In fact, you scored the decisive win in five Cup ties, three times succeeding in the ultimate fifth match with the score 2-2: over Jacco Eltingh at Rotterdam in 1994; Russian Marat Safin at Atlanta in 1998; and Britain's Greg Rusedski at Birmingham in 1999. Please tell me what about them, and what they meant to you.**

All three of those are special. I didn't expect the Eltingh match to be live because Sampras was playing the fourth match. We went ahead 2-0 in that tie because Pete and I won the first two singles matches. When I came out to play Eltingh, I felt a little under-prepared mentally, but I steeled myself pretty quickly, put on a hard hat, and went to work. Two of the three matches you're talking about were away. Those matches are very significant because it is you and your team with everyone else against you. I relished the opportunity and stood up to it and really enjoyed it. The Birmingham match was epic. The crowd was immense. The court was lightning fast, perfect for their serve and volleyers. [Tim] Henman and [Greg] Rusedski were ranked a lot higher than I was then, and I still held the linc and knocked off Rusedski when he really needed that match.

**From 1990 to 2005, America won three Davis Cup titles, in 1990, 1992, and 1995 and since 1995 we've reach the Cup final only twice, in 1997 and 2004. Despite having the "Greatest Generation"—Sampras, Agassi, you, and Chang—for part of that period, why haven't we fared better in Davis Cup?**

We didn't fare well in Davis Cup in the '90s because we didn't all play at the same time. That broke my heart. But you can't make people do things they don't want to do. It wasn't a priority for some of us, and that's a real shame. We had the best players, but we couldn't put the best team together at all times. And that's what it takes. Now we have the best players playing, and we've had some success, but we haven't been able to put the ball over the line [into the end zone]. It was great for us to reach the final last year. No one expects us to beat Spain on clay in Spain. But the next time we play Spain—and I hope it will be in a final— that will be in America. Hopefully, the result will be different.

**You were a loyal and successful Davis Cup player, and you served as Davis Cup coach in 2002 and 2003. You have the respect of the players and the USTA. Would you like to serve as Davis Cup captain some day?**

I've stated publicly that when Patrick's [McEnroe] reign ends—and I want to make it clear that I'm not lobbying for his job—and I want Patrick to stay as long as he wants because he's earned that right and done a terrific job as captain. But when Patrick is no longer captain, if I'm in the right place in my life—if I have the time to do it right—I will raise my hand and say I'd like to be considered because I'm very passionate about Davis Cup, and I hope to contribute to it on an ongoing basis.

**In 1999 you asserted, "Tennis unfortunately doesn't encourage any kind of intellectual development. It actually discourages that. The dumber you are on the court, the better you're going to play." What exactly did you mean by that?**

Strategy is essential in tennis. But I also think a clear head is equally essential to be able to execute your shots. There's a balance there. But you'll see players without fear hit shots that a player who is aware of ramifications will not even attempt. That's why a player with a clear head is better off than someone with more intelligence. The trick is to be smart on the court but allow yourself to have no thoughts when you're actually swinging.

**In 1999 you told the *Boston Globe*, "Life is too interesting to limit yourself to tennis." You've always been an avid reader. What are the most interesting books you ever read?**

Life *is* too interesting to stay so narrow. Reading is very necessary and has been one of the joys of my life. I love Cormac McCarthy's *The Border Trilogy*. I highly recommend it. He's a really visual writer, almost a lyricist. He paints a picture of the landscape with a gorgeous vocabulary. That draws me into his novels. For nonfiction I really enjoyed *From Beirut to Jerusalem* by Tom Friedman, the excellent *New York Times* columnist. He's a Middle East expert, and shortly after 9/11 we all wanted to understand on a deeper level the root causes of the conflicts there. Friedman had lived and worked in both Beirut and Jerusalem and wrote the book before 9/11. It's an amazing read. I highly recommend it.

**When Tennis-X.com asked you in late 2004 about the successor to Mark Miles as ATP CEO in 2006, you said, ". . . it's time for a change, we need a visionary, we don't need a politician. We need somebody who can take the game, step outside**

the box and say we're competing against these other sports. How do we raise the profile of tennis? Because we've been lapped—over the last fifteen years we've gotten lapped." Who, in addition to you, would make a topnotch CEO of the ATP? And why?

Tennis needs to look outside of the tennis circle. We need someone who has a vision. We also need someone who is empowered, which is the key, because we have so many different and divided factions that it's difficult to allocate blame or credit. We need someone who understands the marketing angle and has a sophisticated background with experience outside the tennis world. I know Mark had experience. He had a Pepsi background and the Pan-Am Games and all that. But tennis didn't take advantage of its assets in those years.

**What, specifically, is the vision the ATP CEO should have?**

One of our biggest strengths is that we're a global game, but I also firmly believe it's our biggest weakness. Everything in sports is driven by television. And if we don't get our television package lined up, we're going to be in deep trouble. And if we don't change some rules in our game to accommodate television, we'll continue to suffer. The first priority is: How do we make tennis more viable as a product for television? Everything else stems from that. Why is the NFL so successful? It's because Paul Tagliabue, the commissioner, is the only one who controls the television rights for the NFL. It's not the owner of the Bucs or the Giants or the Jets. It's Tagliabue. So when the TV networks discuss how much they're going to pay for the rights, they don't play one team off of the other. They have to talk as one unified voice, which tennis does not have.

**But should pro tennis be televised on the major networks almost every weekend the way golf is?**

We have to walk before we run. While it would be ideal to be on network television on a weekend-to-weekend basis, the best starting point for us is the U.S. Open Series. That is the best model so fans know to go to ESPN or ESPN2 from three to seven PM on a Sunday to see two finals at the men's and women's tournaments. That's imperative. I totally appreciate ESPN and know that they're in virtually every home that matters. But being on network television for those hours is better. I understand the economic model better than most and know that it's not as simple as it appears from the outside.

**Althea Gibson once said, "No matter what accomplishments you make, somebody helps you." Looking back at your illustrious career, whom would you like to credit for helping you? And what specifically did each person do?**

I would start with my parents because they sacrificed more than anybody during my life, let alone my career, to help me and give me the opportunities I've had to succeed. My great-aunt Emma was really the pioneer for our family. Harry

Hopman allowed me to come play for free, and then Nick Bollettieri gave me that same privilege. José Higueras and Brad Stine and trainer Pat Etcheberry formed the core team for the bulk of my career. José taught me how to make my strengths stronger and how to hide my weaknesses. I was a ball striker when I went to José and a tennis player when I worked with him and left him. Brad was the road warrior with me. He was in the trenches day to day and was as much a sports psychologist as a tennis coach because it's an emotional business and you ride a roller-coaster on the tour. So Althea Gibson is definitely right!

## FASCINATING FACTS:

- Jim Courier believes that pro tennis administrators' failure to advertise on television the many players who give their time, money and expertise to charity is a "huge [public relations] oversight."
- In 2002 Andy Roddick said his proudest achievements have been raising money for charity and playing Davis Cup for the U.S.
- Jim Courier called Nicolas Massu's feat of strength and skill at the Athens Olympics—when he played 10 sets in two days to win singles and doubles gold medals—"the most impressive physical performance I've seen in tennis."
- Four-time Grand Slam champion Jim Courier, now a TV analyst, would like to see pro players do television interviews after each set because "people like to see the humanity of their champions."
- Young and compassionate Boris Becker once made his manager, Ion Tiriac, give tennis tickets to the homeless in Hamburg.

# 23

# Martina Hingis: The "Spice Girl" Champion

# 2004

When Martina Hingis, the Open Era's youngest No. 1 player at sixteen, was compared with golf's new superstar, she shot back, "I think I'm even better than Tiger Woods." The Swiss Miss was the leader of the brash and beautiful brat pack—nicknamed "the Spice Girls of Tennis"—featuring black phenoms Venus and Serena Williams and sexy Anna Kournikova. Teen queen Hingis backed up her cockiness with a sensational 1997 when she came within one match of capturing the Grand Slam, losing only in the French Open final.

"Hingis beats you with court savvy and high-percentage tennis. She is the best all-court player I've ever seen," raved Pam Shriver, the former doubles star-turned TV analyst. But the smiling assassin could buck the power trend only until 1999 when she won her last major singles title. Her slight 5'7" frame gradually broke down, and painful foot, knee, and hip injuries prematurely ended her career in early 2003 at age twenty-two.

Never shy about voicing her opinions, Hingis has transitioned smoothly into TV tennis, commentating while also pursuing several business and recreational interests. I caught up with always-engaging Hingis at the 3rd Annual Adidas Tennis Smash, a two-day extravaganza benefiting the Tim & Tom Gullikson Foundation (a charity for brain cancer research and assistance for brain tumour patients and their families), at the Ocean Edge Resort in Brewster, Massachusetts, where she was representing longtime sponsor adidas.

**You appear quite happy. What have you been doing since you retired eighteen months ago?**

I've really enjoyed working as a TV commentator for Channel 7 at the Australian Open and Eurosport at Roland Garros and ESPN at Wimbledon. I've learned a lot because everyone else is so experienced. I've done motivational speaking

179

at schools. I tell them how I had to fight the Williams sisters and how it wasn't easy because of my body stature. I enjoy doing that because it feels good giving something back. I renovated my home in Switzerland. I've been making sponsor appearances around the world for adidas, Yonex, and V-Zug, a laundry washing machine. I've been studying English. I've been horseback riding, and I have a couple horses I've been competing with. And I've been skiing with my boyfriend, Stefan. We met in the Alps at St. Moritz, and that's how I fell in love with skiing again.

**When you look back at your career, what accomplishments are you most proud of?**

There are many. Being on the tour for almost ten years. Of course, my five Grand Slam titles in singles and nine in doubles. Winning my first tournament when nobody expected it. Every one of my titles (forty in singles and thirty-six in doubles) was a unique and special victory. I have many great memories even when I didn't win tournaments—when I played great matches. I was even more proud of beating the Williams sisters back to back [at the 2001 Australian Open] than if I had won that Grand Slam. Those were great matches. Every time we played, it was a real battle.

**You set several "youngest ever" records. Which one means the most to you?**

My career started a little sooner and ended a little sooner. I've always been a little quicker in doing things. I won the French Open junior title at twelve. I was the youngest [in the twentieth century] to win a Grand Slam [sixteen years, four months at the 1997 Australian Open]. I was the youngest to rank No. 1 [at sixteen years, six months]. I can't pick out any one of them. They were all so special.

**In 1994 Martina Navratilova, whom you were named after, warned, "Fourteen is too bloody young to turn pro. Hingis might be No. 1 in two years, but will she last five years?" You lasted eight years, but, in retrospect, was Navratilova somewhat right because serious injuries ended your career prematurely?**

Definitely I would have liked to have played longer. I was surprised my career ended so soon. But I'm not judging other people—what they do. It was great I was given the chance to play at a young age because when you are a woman, it's more difficult to learn, but when you're on the pro tour at fourteen, fifteen, you can still learn. I wasn't devastated when I was losing to my peers 6-0, 6-0 because that's the time when you can learn. And I'm not judging Martina when she's playing on the pro tour when she's forty-seven. (Laughter) I'm really happy that I've already accomplished so much, and now I can start a new life.

**What do you miss most about the pro tour? And least?**

I miss the competition. I miss the challenge. I always look for challenges in my life in different ways. It's a challenge for me to do the TV commentary because

I'm not as good as the other people. But I do have the knowledge from ten years in the professional game as a player. So now I have to learn to express it. I can always get better at that. That's why I love working with the different TV teams, such as Chris Fowler at ESPN. What I miss least is the stress and all the travel and getting ready for the matches, practices. But I still like having a workout and a routine in my day.

**After playing against you in the Hopman Cup, former Wimbledon champion Ivaniševic once said you returned his rocket serve better than anyone. Do you remember that match? And was the service return your best shot?**

I remember that match, yes. (Laughter) And he remembers it. He gave me a great compliment. I think he still remembers my returns today. (Laughter) He will take that memory into his retirement. My return of serve was my best shot along with my backhand.

**Martina Navratilova called Maria Sharapova's Wimbledon triumph "the best thing that could have happened" to women's tennis. Do you agree?**

It was great to see her win because it spices up the whole game. It would also be nice to see Serena win. Both are champions now. I just saw on [ESPN's] SportsCenter for five minutes those two paired against each other [as a new rivalry]. It was nice. It's great that women's tennis has a new face and a new champion.

**You said, "Maria reminds me of me." How?**

She is fearless. That's how you are when you are that young.

**Lindsay Davenport once said, "Professional sports are like that in general. Most of the great players are assholes or bitches." Is that true in tennis?**

That's not a very nice quote, if I may say so. You definitely become very selfish and have a big ego when you are a professional athlete, no matter where you are and what you do. But I would be really surprised if Lindsay said those words. I wouldn't express it that way.

**You received the Family Circle Cup's "Player Who Makes a Difference Award for 2001" for your involvement with international health organizations. Please tell me about your humanitarian work over the years.**

I worked with UNICEF as an ambassador to help reduce poverty around the world. You can help in different ways, and I wanted to help any way I could. I chose the street children in Bogota [Colombia]. That was quite a scene. We needed five trucks filled with soldiers carrying machine guns to protect us. We met victims of poverty, prostitution, and drugs. I also worked with the World Health Organization in Nepal. That was quite emotional, too. The WHO is trying to eradicate polio there. You come from Melbourne and Tokyo and you go to countries like that, and you really acknowledge what a privileged life you have. Other players should do that, too.

**Your nine Grand Slam doubles titles amazingly came with six different partners, three of whom, Mirjana Lucic, Mary Pierce, and Anna Kournikova, didn't experience that much doubles success with any other partners. How did you do it?**

Lucic, Pierce, and Kournikova were players who could hit hard, and I did the rest. I was a much better doubles player than a singles player.

**In Fed Cup competition, you were a terrific 18–2 singles and 8–2 in doubles. How important was it for you to represent Switzerland in the Fed Cup?**

I love the team spirit. I always did well playing for my country. I never lost a match playing at the Hopman Cup either. I was more of a team person. I was such a good doubles player because that requires teamwork. I think you have to have some kind of charisma and character to excel at doubles. It's not easy to play long-term with somebody. You have to get along well. And I think I was an easy person to deal with. And I love to play for somebody else as well.

**During your career, you played and beat several all-time greats. In what order would you rate the five best players you competed against?**

Serena, Venus, Lindsay, Monica, and Jennifer. Serena had tremendous power. She didn't have much feel. But she doesn't need touch when she's serving aces all the time. She also has great [service] returns. Graf wasn't on my list because I didn't play her that much. But maybe I should put her in there somewhere.

**Last year eight Wimbledon singles champions, including John McEnroe, Boris Becker, and Martina Navratilova, were among more than thirty well-known tennis figures who signed an open letter, urging the International Tennis Federation to "consider reducing the width of the head of the racket from its present limit of 12.5 inches to nine inches, perhaps in stages over four or five years." They contend that pro tennis today has become one-dimensional, played mostly from the baseline, because rackets give power and excessive topspin an undue influence over skill. You are a skill player. Where do you stand on this issue?**

Now you don't have that much time to have the finesse and touch and an all-around game. It's all so much power. Boys and girls today are not given the time to practice different styles. I spent five or six hours [a day] when I was a little girl on the court and played a lot of doubles. I wasn't physically worn out when I went to bed. Today it's hard for players to really develop their games and evolve. It's only hit, hit, hit, and they don't think anymore. There is no time to serve and volley anymore. By the time you get to net, the ball is past you. I think the problem is not with the rackets or the ball, but with the people you work with—the coaching.

**In the past ten years, little Switzerland, a mountainous country with four languages, has produced two great champions, you and Roger Federer. Is this a coincidence? Or will Switzerland become like Sweden and keep producing top players?**

I think a country like Switzerland produces individuals. We've done that in other sports. Skiing is a big sport in Switzerland. But you always have good young players in Switzerland because you have the money, the market, and Swiss are strong-willed people. Roger and I are a coincidence.

**Your mother never seemed to get full credit for the great coaching job she did with you. Is she one of the best coaches in the world?**

I think she is the greatest coach in the world, and she was the best coach for me. She knows the game very well. She played [high-level] tournaments herself. And she always knew the answers about how to get me to play better. She always prepared me well for each opponent. She always had strategy. She knew everything about the game. She still moves with the future in mind and gets better and better. She's always willing to learn, which is the most important thing for a coach.

**In 2001, you said, "For me, the greatest feeling is to be the No. 1 player and to know that on a good day you can win against anybody." Is it fair to say that you had a great time with many other things in pro tennis, too?**

Yes, the variety of experiences made the tour very enjoyable. The only time you don't like it is when you're really tired, worn out, and you've done ten interviews and eight TVs. And maybe after a Grand Slam when you're happy to be in your own bed. That's the only time. I think the WTA should market the girls more because they're good at it, and the game needs it.

**You also had a reputation for being friendly and fun in the locker room.**

Yeah, I had a good relationship with most of the players off the court as well. I've never been so streamlined [single-minded] as other players. That was my personality. But you can't have everybody be the same way.

**And did you like the roar of the crowd?**

I liked the attention. Who doesn't? You'd be lying if you said you didn't. (Laughter)

**How do you think you will be remembered in the tennis world?**

It's nice that people still come up to me and say, "We miss your game because you were so different—like smart-thinking and clever and interesting because you didn't have that much power." So I'm so happy about the way people treat me now. I love being remembered this way. And I hope it stays that way.

# 24

# Bryan Brothers: Double Shot of Excitement

# 2004

They chest-bump after winning big points, read each other's minds, and rank No. 1 in the world. What's more, Bob and Mike Bryan, towering identical twins from California, don't just want to rule doubles this decade, they want to save it.

**What does it feel like being the best doubles team in the world?**

MIKE—It feels great. We've dreamed about this our whole lives. It's even more special doing it with your brother. It was a dream come true to win the French Open and the Masters Cup last year. It feels like we're on top of the mountain now, and we want to stay on top as long as possible.

**You said you have six dreams you want to accomplish. What are they? And which ones have you accomplished?**

MIKE—One is to play Davis Cup, and we did that last year. We wanted to win our first Grand Slam [title], we did that. We wanted to be the best brother doubles team of all time, and we passed Tim and Tom Gullikson's ten titles last year. We wanted to finish the year No. 1, and we did that. Now we want to win the Davis Cup for the U.S. and win an Olympic gold medal. So we have two to go.

**What about a career Grand Slam?**

MIKE—We can win a lot more Grand Slam titles. We've been to the final of three of the last four. We can win the French again. We love playing on clay. Wimbledon and the U.S. Open would be awesome to win. We've done well there. I want to win at least five or six Grand Slam titles and maybe even go for Woodbridge's record [seventy-nine career doubles titles]. But we have only one Grand Slam right now, and we're twenty-six years old.

184

**Which matches stand out as the most exciting and important in your career?**

BOB—The most important match was the [2003] French Open final. Winning that first Grand Slam final got the monkey off our back. We had been one of the top teams in the world for the last three years, but you never know if you're going to win a Grand Slam. A lot of good players compete their entire careers and never get it. That final was huge because it also showed [U.S. Davis Cup captain] Pat McEnroe we could play well in big matches and pressure situations. He told us we needed to win a Grand Slam to be on the Davis Cup team. That victory catapulted us to No. 1 in the world and put us on the team.

**You seem to epitomize the joy of doubles. What makes you so exuberant during matches?**

BOB—We're exuberant because we love the game. And we've also been taught to play with enthusiasm. It's still really fun for us to be out on the tour. It's still exciting, and we don't see it as a job.

*The Bryan brothers and their trademark chest bump. courtesy of Wayne Bryan*

**You high-five, chest-butt, encourage each other a lot. You are the most high-energy, animated team on the tour since the colorful Jensen brothers. Did they influence you?**

> BOB—Yes, they did. They were the fourth or fifth biggest draw in tennis in the mid-1990s behind Agassi and Sampras. They made doubles big the way they played it and the way they played to the crowd. People loved to go watch the Jensens play. We saw the way they created excitement, and we wanted to emulate it. We throw in the chest bump. Tennis is not just a sport. It's entertainment. And we like to put on a show for the people. We've looked up to the Jensens and like what they've done for doubles.

**How did opposing teams react to your boisterous behavior early in your pro career? And how do they react now?**

> BOB—We came on the tour as young guys chest-bumping, and most players don't like the rookies when they arrive. They didn't have any respect for us either. We had to prove ourselves. Some people didn't like us and showed that by trying to hit us if they got a high ball. And some guys didn't talk to us in the locker room or practice with us. Now that we're on top of the game, they think we're helping doubles with our antics. They welcome us and like the fact that we're selling out stadiums, and that fans are coming out just to watch us because we're a big name now.

**Mark Knowles and Dan Nestor wanted to kill you in one match. What happened?**

> MIKE—Yeah, they actually did. (Laughter) That was our first year on the tour, and we were playing the RCA Championships [in Indianapolis]. The match was pretty close and it was late at night and the American crowd was really pumping us up. We threw in a few chest bumps, and they didn't like it.

**One team actually spit at you after losing.**

> MIKE—That was in Miami against [Olivier] Delai`tre and [Fabrice] Santoro. I wouldn't like it [either] if young rookies were yahooing or getting super excited. That's just how they felt. They were a little bitter.

**Do American and foreign fans react to you differently?**

> BOB—The American fans get behind us more because we play Davis Cup and they know who we are. We've been on the cover of *TENNIS* magazine in the States. There's a little more buzz about the Bryan brothers in the U.S. than in Europe. But I can see it growing in Europe. The crowds are getting bigger there.

**Having twins is always a great challenge for parents. How do you think your parents handled it?**

> MIKE—Our parents handled it really well. It's easier for parents to have twins if

they want to become athletes because Bob and I always had each other to hit with, and we practiced together every day. They also did a great job because they didn't make us compete against each other at a young age. Our relationship came first. In the finals of junior tournaments one of us would always default to the other. That helped us because neither of us would get overly confident. They made tennis fun for us.

**Was there an intense rivalry on the tennis court when you were growing up? And, if so, how did it end up being channeled into positive doubles cooperation?**

BOB—I don't think there ever was a rivalry between us. Our parents squelched that pretty early by our defaulting and having us work together on the court. We channeled our rivalry positively by pushing each other to improve. For example, if Mike went into the gym, I wouldn't want him to get the edge on me. So I'd go in there and work hard with him. We always pushed each other. If Mike was getting a little better than me, I would work a little harder to try to catch up. If Mike was ranked a little higher, I'd practice a little harder to catch up in the rankings. So we pushed each other and stayed pretty much even throughout our whole careers.

**Your mother, the former Kathy Blake, was a world-class player, and your father, Wayne, is a tireless promoter of the sport, and both are teaching pros. How have they influenced you?**

BOB—They are a good combination. My mom was a pro player, and she basically did all the dirty work when we were growing up. She would be on the court with us for two hours a day. She molded our games the way they are now. My dad owned a tennis club and ran big group clinics. He kept the game really fun for us. He knew how to motivate us. He took us to pro matches and college matches. Watching the greats like Agassi and Sampras really inspired us. On the other hand, my mom probably knew what it took [to reach the top] more than my dad.

**Please tell me about the Bryan Bros Band.**

BOB—We've been playing music as long as we've been playing tennis. My dad was in a band, and he knows how to play all the instruments. He got Mike playing drums at four years old, and he got me playing on the piano. He taught us songs, all the oldies. He does all the singing. And we made a little family band. We play rock and jazz at our club for parties, especially Christmas parties, and at our county street fairs. We've played at a lot of tennis tournaments all over the world.

**It's been said identical twins possess a kind of sixth sense, mental telepathy. Have you two ever experienced this playing tennis?**

BOB—I can't read Mike's mind right now. (Laughter) But we've been together our entire lives. We basically think the same on the court. Knowing my brother and his game so well definitely helps. We don't have to talk a lot. We've been through all these situations [before], and I know where he's going to be and how he's going to react.

**Davis Cup doubles means you are actually a team within a team—the ultimate team experience. Does that give you the ultimate high?**

MIKE—It does give us the ultimate high. The reason we play doubles is because we like sharing victories with our teammates and our family. And Davis Cup is the ultimate team experience. You're playing for your teammates, but you're also playing for your country in the biggest tennis event possible. Definitely after a Davis Cup win we have our biggest highs.

**"This [Davis Cup] is when doubles becomes a big deal. You don't get that elsewhere anymore," pointed out Yannick Noah, former French Davis Cup player and captain. Because your point is so pivotal, do you feel more appreciated and recognized in Davis Cup?**

MIKE—Yeah, definitely. We're half the team. There are four players on the team, and our family takes up half. And they dedicate a whole day, the middle Saturday, only to doubles. Doubles doesn't get any recognition anymore, but it [Davis Cup doubles] is televised on ESPN for two hours on Saturday. It's a huge point. From 1972 to 2003 the country that won the Davis Cup final also won in doubles every time but twice. Everyone values that doubles point, and the U.S. and the fans really support us.

**The Davis Cup schedule is so spaced out from February to December that it loses momentum and excitement. Does it make more sense to have the World Group play all four rounds in one month, say November?**

BOB—For the fans and the American audience and maybe the world audience, that would be better. But that would take a lot of revenue out of the countries. They make a lot of money on those home matches. Davis Cup does lose a lot of steam because we just won a [quarterfinal] tie, and we have to wait three or four months to play the next one.

In the future I would like Davis Cup to be like college tennis where they just play all the matches in a row, like the NCAAs. Maybe three singles and two doubles on one or two days. It might be easier on the players, too.

**You don't hear much about doubles coaches in pro tennis. Would you please tell me what Phil Farmer does for you.**

BOB—Phil makes sure the chemistry between Mike and me is right. He scouts the other doubles teams. He makes sure we have a game plan for every match. He helps us keep our strokes sharp. He also keeps on us about physical fitness. He makes sure our careers are going in the right direction.

**You've said you admire Andre Agassi for his charity work. Would you please tell me about what you do for charity, and why you do it.**

> MIKE—We love to give back to the game. One of the reasons we're playing tennis now is because people like Andre Agassi gave back and signed autographs for us and did clinics for us. So whenever we get an opportunity, we do clinics and sign autographs. During our off time, we do charity events for the Ventura County and Santa Barbara junior tennis associations, for the men's and women's teams at the University of California at Santa Barbara and Cal Poly, and for the Elton John Aids Foundation and Tim & Tom Gullikson Foundation. We also raise money for battered children. It's called Interface.

**Murphy Jensen once broke his brother Luke's ribs when they excitedly chest bumped. You've sucker punched each other. Please tell me about that.**

> MIKE—(Laughter) We definitely have our brawls off the court. We're not going to talk about that. On the court, we've had a couple altercations, but basically the only time we're going to get injured is on a chest bump. If we jump up at the same time, we're going to be OK.

**Isn't it true that Bob punched you in the stomach on the stadium court at Cincinnati in 2001?**

> MIKE—He did, but I don't think many people saw it. He actually gave me a good blow to the ribs.

**Did you go down for the mandatory 8-count?**

> MIKE—I didn't go down. But I couldn't fake that he didn't hit me. He got me good. I've done the same to him a couple times. (Laughter)

**What tricks have you played on people who cannot tell you apart?**

> MIKE—When we were younger, we pulled tricks on people. We switched school classes, and Bob would take a test for me. We don't do tricks too much anymore. We actually look different now. Bob is a little taller and heavier. But when Bob's girlfriend calls, I'll talk to her while he's in the shower, and she won't know. I don't think our parents can tell us apart on the phone either. I'll talk to them and I'll say I'm going to get Bob, and Bob's not there and I'll keep talking. Sometimes girlfriends will come behind us and give us kisses, and they think I'm Bob or he's Mike. So we gladly accept them.

**Believe it or not, you didn't get a single minute of on-air time on U.S. network television last year even though you reached two Grand Slam finals. What would you tell TV sports producers to rectify this injustice?**

> MIKE—That's kind of a shame. They could do a lot for doubles if they give us some airtime and show a few points of our matches. That's bad judgment on

their part because doubles has been suffering a little bit. And the reason is because it's rarely on TV, and doubles doesn't have the [big] names out there. If they want to grow the game, they've got to promote singles *and* doubles, because doubles is a huge part of the sport. A lot of people love doubles and play doubles. When they see doubles, they say it's great tennis, and sometimes they say they like it better than singles. For proof of that, at the Masters Cup in Houston last year, all three of the doubles-only sessions were sold out. Yet we were in the final of the U.S. Open last year, and they didn't put it on TV.

**Now that singles has become quite one-dimensional—mostly hard-hitting baseliners with only seven full-time serve and volleyers in the men's top 100—is the health and welfare of doubles more important than ever?**

BOB—Yeah. You look at doubles and you see all-court players. A lot of those players don't make it [the top 100] in singles anymore just because it's such a physical game and there are so many baseline rallies. Yeah, it's pretty one-dimensional now. Singles matches are all sort of the same. But in doubles you need to have it all. You see every shot in doubles. You see finesse, which you don't see in singles, except for drop shots on clay. You see power. You see so much tactics and strategy. You see serving and volleying, great net duels. You see chemistry between players. You see lobs, everything. So you need doubles more than ever to spice up the game. Tennis has to promote doubles more.

**Are there any doubles players or doubles teams that you idolized before you turned pro? And why?**

BOB—We looked up to a lot of teams and took a lot from them. We watched tapes of the Woodies [Todd Woodbridge and Mark Woodforde]. We idolized the way they played. Bob and I have a lot of power. The Woodies didn't. But they used the angles and timed their poaches so well and devised different strategies. They knew the court so well. They made the right moves at the right times. We're trying to incorporate that now. When we were growing up, we also looked up to Ricky Leach and Jim Pugh. They were the first Davis Cup team we saw in person at La Costa, and we were friends with the Leach family.

**Last year you said you have a great opportunity to leave your mark in doubles. What exactly are your career goals?**

MIKE—We want more doubles on television. The Tennis Channel is going to help. I think we're bringing doubles back. We can feel more popularity in doubles. From that standpoint, we want to leave our mark on doubles. But we also want to be considered one of the greatest doubles teams that ever played the game. To do that, Davis Cup is huge. We have to have an excellent record, like [Ken] Flach and [Robert] Seguso, and win a few Cups for the U.S. We also have to start winning Grand Slams.

**You look so alike that players on the tour call both of you "Twin." How can tennis fans tell you apart?**

MIKE—On the court Bob is lefty and I'm righty. Bob always wears a bead necklace. I have a mole below the ear. So remember, it's Bob beads and Mike mole.

---

## FASCINATING FACTS:

- Bob and Mike Bryan won their first doubles tournament, a 10-and-under event, at age 6.
- When Bob and Mike Bryan celebrated winning a point during a Stanford college match, they bumped chests so hard that the impact cracked Bob's sternum.
- SFX's John Tobias, the client manager of Bob and Mike Bryan, the world's No. 1 doubles team, said in 2006 their off-court income is comparable to "most top 10-15 singles players."
- Identical twin brothers Tim and Tom Gullikson elected not to play doubles together in 1981. "We were too argumentative, too negative with each other," Tom told *World Tennis* magazine. A year later, the ultra-close Americans reunited and became the No. 3–ranked doubles team in the world and repeated that ranking in 1983.
- Vigilant doubles star Bob Bryan says "I always scan the passengers for shady characters" because of the increased threat of terrorism when he flies on airplanes.
- After losing to doubles stars Bob and Mike Bryan in a Minnesota exhibition, Andy Roddick and Mardy Fish paid up on a bet to the Bryans by running naked outside their bus in 10-degree weather.
- Two things that Bob and Mike Bryan, who live together, don't share are girlfriends and toothbrushes.

# 25

# Stefan Edberg: The Gentleman Champion 2004

*The first law of tennis is that every player must be a good sportsman and inherently a gentleman.*

—Bill Tilden

If there ever is a Sportsmanship Hall of Fame, Stefan Edberg should be the first athlete selected. Meanwhile, the International Tennis Hall of Fame will induct highly respected Edberg at its July 11 ceremony in Newport, Rhode Island.

The stylish serve and volleyer twice captured singles titles at Wimbledon and the Australian and United States Opens and boasted season-ending No. 1 rankings in 1990 and 1991. Edberg also sparked Sweden to four Davis Cups. But his most extraordinary achievement and inspiring legacy is winning the Association of Tennis Professionals sportsmanship award for a record five years. In recognition, the ATP renamed it the Stefan Edberg Sportsmanship Award.

In this interview Edberg, thirty-eight, talks about his most thrilling successes and biggest disappointment, how he maintained his moral values and down-to-earth persona despite wealth and fame, his views on the pro game today, and his life since retiring nearly eight years ago.

**When you were a boy growing up in the seaside town of Västervik, did you ever think you would become a tennis champion and some day go into the International Tennis Hall of Fame?**

No, not in my wildest dreams! Tennis was just another sport to try. It wasn't until the end of my junior career that I realized I had a chance to go on the pro tour. [He won the junior Grand Slam in 1983.] When I was young, I was just trying to become a better player and maybe No. 1 in my age group. I didn't think much further than that.

**What was your reaction when you were told you were going into the International Tennis Hall of Fame?**

Obviously I had a feeling it probably would happen at some point. But it's a great honor to be selected and be among a small group of champions who have been selected over the years.

**Tennis stars often become coaches or TV commentators or compete on the senior tour after they retire from the Tour. What have you been doing since retiring in 1996?**

TV commentating is not for me. I don't feel like playing the ATP tour for seniors either. I've tried to live as normal a life as I possibly can and have my kids grow up in a quiet environment. Apart from that, I'm still involved in tennis a little bit. And I do quite a bit of work from home, managing my investments.

**Why did you start a tennis foundation in Sweden?**

Tennis has been so great to me. It's meant a lot to my life and made me what I am today. So I wanted to do something for the young generation coming up to give them a better chance of succeeding in tennis. Instead of writing a check for the Swedish Tennis Federation, I decided to start a foundation at the end of my playing career. I want to run it for the long term and make sure the money is used for the right things. It's not a big foundation, but it does help, and that makes me feel good.

**Specifically, what does your foundation do for young players?**

The foundation is for fourteen- to sixteen-year-old kids. You can earn a scholarship if you perform well during the year. We put quite a bit of money into what we call Davis Cup and Fed Cup schools. They bring the best kids in the country to Bastad to train for a few days. It's more for the elite juniors than a grass-roots program because that's quite an important age in your career when tennis costs a lot of money. We help with travel expenses. The kids have other coaches, but I do visit the two schools and play with them a little bit. They hardly recognize me because I haven't played for seven or eight years. They know the stars of today, but they don't know what happened before. It's usually their moms and dads who recognize me, not the kids.

**You've said tennis is less popular compared to other sports in Sweden today, and it's difficult to get hold of talent. Why is that true? And which kids, age ten to sixteen, have a lot of potential?**

Tennis has lost some interest, but it was at a very high level before so maybe it's gone back to normal now. You have only so much athletic talent in a country of nine million because football [soccer] and ice hockey are so big, and most talented athletes go to those sports. There's still talent in tennis, but not as much as there was ten or fifteen years ago. We have a group of fourteen- and fifteen-year-olds that are quite good. Rasmus Jonasson is the best fifteen-year-old, but there is still a long way to go [to become a world-class player].

**Looking back at your career, what were your three biggest on-court victories?**

Winning the first Wimbledon final over Boris [Becker, in 1988,] is a great memory. The best match I ever played was beating Courier [6-2, 6-4, 6-0] in the '91 U.S. Open final. I had a great day. Also, the 1984 Davis Cup final was huge when we beat America in Gothenburg. Anders Järryd and I beat McEnroe and Fleming to win the final. I don't think they had lost in fourteen or fifteen Davis Cup matches previously.

**You competed against several great champions during your fourteen-year career —McEnroe, Connors, Wilander, Lendl, Becker, Agassi, and Sampras. Who were the best players?**

It's a tough question because they were all at their best at different times. The only thing I can say—and I haven't seen Laver play and other champions before him long ago—is that Pete Sampras stands out as the most complete player of all because he could play well from the back of the court and he could serve and volley. I'd pick Sampras as the best. It's hard to pick the order after that. McEnroe at his best was a great player. So was Lendl and Mats and Becker. I would put them together in a group.

**There is a famous Chinese saying: "May you live in interesting times." What did you find most interesting and exciting about your era?**

It was a great era of tennis. Tennis was building up in the `70s, and a lot of money poured into the sport in 1980 to 1982 when I started. Tennis grew in popularity because of the stars, but also companies put a lot of money into tennis. It was a special era. You had Connors, McEnroe, Lendl, Vilas, and Borg— all the big names that made tennis prosper. Along I came as a youngster to join that great era. They had thrilling rivalries like Connors-Borg, Borg-McEnroe, McEnroe-Lendl. I was lucky to have a close rivalry with Boris. Rivalries have always created great excitement and been important in an individual sport like tennis.

**Which men and women players today do you most like to watch?**

Federer because he has all the weapons and moves well. The Williams sisters have brought lots of attention to the sport of tennis. The women have had lots of personalities in recent years, which is good for tennis. It's always good to watch the top-ranked girls. Henin [Hardenne] plays the best way. She has a one-handed-backhand, which is nice to see. It's quite an unusual shot. And she's a very good athlete.

**During your last U.S. Open in 1996, Andre Agassi said about you, "He only adds to the game. His image and his person are impeccable." Pete Sampras said, "If you're looking for a role model for kids, he's the guy." How did you maintain an unblemished reputation in a high-pressure, high-stakes individual sport filled with controversy?**

It's a good question. I really don't know myself sometimes. (Laughter) I've stuck to a simple strategy: to be myself and not try to act like somebody else. It's quite important—because young kids look up to stars—to show them what's right and wrong. That means being a good citizen and showing respect for other people, whether they are drivers or people working at the tournament. They are part of the big picture so you shouldn't forget about them, too. That's part of the reason. And I'm lucky because I'm quite a calm person. I keep a lot of emotions inside. That sometimes may look good but may not be so good for myself. (Laughter) Because sometimes you have to let your emotions out.

**You won an amazing five ATP Sportsmanship Awards and were so admired for your sportsmanship that the ATP renamed their award the Stefan Edberg Sportsmanship Award. Is that the legacy you are most proud of?**

Yeah, that's quite an achievement. At the same time, maybe it came a little early, so soon after I retired. I have mixed feelings about that. When you think about it, it's really quite honorable to have a sportsmanship award named after you.

**In 1999 Mats Wilander said, "John McEnroe, Ivan Lendl and Jimmy Connors weren't the nicest people in the world, they were the most selfish players, but they were great for the game. Tennis needs players who don't care about pleasing sponsors, who don't care about being nice." Since you are a nice guy, do you agree with Mats?**

In a way, I do. Because you're never going to have a perfect world no matter how hard you try. Having only nice players may have worked thirty, forty years ago, but we live in a different society today. It's almost abnormal to be normal today. If you are normal today, you don't get any attention. You need to be really good or really bad.

**So it's good to have normal people like you and crazy people like McEnroe?**

It creates discussions and attention around the sport. And even bad publicity today is good publicity. It's almost like you need a good guy and a bad guy to create the best concept. But being a bad guy is nothing I recommend. We're all very different. And contrasts and conflicts create a lot of attention.

**Agassi and Laver are the only men players to win all four Grand Slam events during the Open Era. But you came very close when you led Michael Chang two sets to one and had 10 break points in the fourth set and then were twice up a**

**service break in the fifth set of the French Open final. Was losing that exciting final your biggest disappointment?**

Not at the time because I thought I'd have more chances. But as the years went by, I realized that was my great opportunity. It was similar to the great chance McEnroe had against Lendl [in the 1984 French Open final]. With my game I wasn't going to get that many chances in Paris. And I was playing very well that year. If I had played one big point better, that would probably have been enough to win the match. But Chang had God on his side, or whatever you call it. (Laughter) Maybe he was destined to win that year. That was a big, big chance, and it's obviously something I regret today. But, what the heck, you can't win everything.

**Today players change coaches more often than ever. Tony Pickard coached you for nearly your entire pro career. You once said, "Tony is really my friend, not just my coach." Is that why your relationship with Tony was so successful and so long?**

I think so. That's part of the reason. We were well suited together. He became a friend, almost like a father. What he did for me was great, and I'm very thankful.

**You helped Sweden, a country of less than ten million people in a cold climate, win four Davis Cups. Pretty amazing! What were your most memorable Davis Cup matches?**

The first is winning against America in '84, as I said before. Playing against Michael Westphal in the fifth rubber in Germany with all the Germans screaming for him was a great win. I really remember that one. And my first Davis Cup match in Santiago, Chile, where I played Hans Gildemeister, is a match I'll always remember. That was the toughest and wildest crowd I ever played in front of. They were very loud, screaming and using mirrors to blind me. That was the second time we went down there . . . the first time a big earthquake of 8.0 magnitude hit the country.

**You won a gold medal at the 1984 Olympics when tennis was a demonstration sport. Are you pleased with the way tennis is staged at the Olympics?**

Yes and no. In 1984 having tennis in the Olympics was a bit suspect. But at the same time you have to be supportive because the Olympics is a big event. It wasn't until Agassi won it [in 1996] in the U.S. that you got a little pop about winning the Olympics. But I don't think tennis really needs the Olympics. I'm not sure football [soccer] does either. Tennis can stand on its own feet without it. Maybe the tennis format would be better if we had a team competition rather than an individual one. In 1984 I felt it would take twenty years before tennis gets accepted. It's hard to tell how accepted it is now because some players skip the Olympics.

**American TV tennis analyst Mary Carillo in 1991 said, "Stefan is the world's funniest man." Do you have an excellent sense of humor?**

Maybe I have a good sense of humor, but I'm not the kind of guy who will stand in the middle of a group just telling jokes. I'm better communicating one-on-one, so to speak. I probably have a little English humor—dry humor for short versions of stories. I'm never going to become a TV comedian.

**You were one of the most elegant, athletic, and effective serve and volleyers in tennis history. But today there are only seven frequent serve and volleyers in the top 100 and another seven who serve and volley occasionally. What should tennis do so that this entertaining and important style of play does not die?**

That's a good question. If I was playing today, I would not play as aggressively as I did because it's too predictable and the guys return serve far better than previously. With serve and volley, it takes a couple more years to learn about the game. It's riskier, there is less margin for making mistakes. I don't think serving and volleying will die. I just wish there will be more serving and volleying because it's beautiful to watch.

**Arlen Kantarian, chief executive of professional tennis for the United States Tennis Association, says "The sport is best marketed as tough, athletic, and macho. The Williams sisters have done as much as anyone to market the sport as macho. Tennis players are up there with basketball players as the finest athletes in the world. They've got agility, power, and mental toughness." Do you agree with that?**

Not totally. You need to be athletic. But the game itself—the way it's played, the scoring system—is exciting the way it is. You can play badly for 45 minutes, but it's still the last point that wins the match. We don't need to be like other sports. Tennis has always been a gentleman's sport, and that's the way we should keep it. Otherwise, it will be like everything else. They [the ATP] tried to put all these new things into tennis, like playing music at changeovers and making it more hip hop. But in the long run, that's not a good idea.

**Why not?**

Because you go to all these other sports—basketball, football, and ice hockey—and it's loud and they scream and there's popcorn. It's nice to have a sport for people who like it a little more quiet where you sit down and enjoy what's going on out there. You don't need to stand up and scream at everything. You need respect for other people, too. Tennis is very different because you keep quiet when the point is on, and you clap after the point.

**In America some coaches teach junior players to grunt, pump their fist, and yell, "Come on!" What do you think of that?**

It's good to show your emotions to some extent, but you don't have to overdo it.

It's OK at an ice hockey game where it's extremely loud and everyone is into it. At Wimbledon you're out there in the fifth set, and it's as exciting as you can get, and you can hear a pin drop on the floor. That's quite astonishing. That kind of tension is great for tennis. Everybody is holding their breath almost because it's so exciting.

**Fame never seemed to matter much to you, but you once said, "Sports always has been my passion. It has given me a chance to be somebody." Would you please explain that?**

I'm a low-key person. Fame comes with the sport. Tennis has given me a lot. It's given me a career, and I can support my family for the rest of my life. That's the great part of it. I can deal with being famous and recognized. It's kind of nice. It helps you in normal life. At restaurants if you're Mr. Svensson, people don't take notice. But if you're Mr. Edberg, you may get that table you want. In many ways it's quite good to be famous. I think people are nice to you.

**Even though you became a somebody, you never really changed. You once told an Australian newspaper, "As a good Swedish man, I was brought up to believe in household work. Even as a millionaire, I think it is important to take responsibility for my own laundry. It is part of my philosophy . . . never become a *prima donna*." How did you stay so normal in a tennis world which is so abnormal?**

Yeah, it's quite abnormal to stay that normal. It comes down to the way you are brought up, what you believe in. Today I am quite a famous person. But what's important to me today is to bring up my kids in a normal atmosphere. That's part of the reason we live in the country. They go to a public school. We try to have our feet on the ground and have the kids not taking things for granted. Kids look up to you. If you are a good example for your kids, you teach them good manners, what is right and wrong, and respect for other people. They have to do that to get through life.

## FASCINATNG FACTS:

- The national tennis center in Switzerland started a fine system for misbehavior because a young and angry Roger Federer threw his racket and swore so much.
- Goran Ivanisevic, Mario Ancic's inspiration, urged 12-year-old Ancic to "keep on breaking rackets."
- Seal, British Grammy-winning singer, told *Sports Illustrated* that when he hit a volley and Stefan Edberg, his partner, said, "Great volley," it was "not only a tennis fantasy but one of the highlights of my life."

# 26

# Michael Chang: The David Who Slays Goliaths
# 2003

Just as the youthful David, armed with a sling and pebbles, slew the giant Goliath in the Bible legend, Michael Chang created his own legend at the 1989 French Open. At a callow seventeen, the 5'8," 134-pound prodigy overcame world No. 1 Ivan Lendl with guile, skill, and, above all, courage, withstanding painful leg cramps. Chang fought back from two sets down using clever tactics, such as an underhanded trick serve, moonballing, and receiving near the service line to intimidate Lendl into double faulting. Chang then became the youngest Grand Slam champion in history with another stunning five-set win, this time from two sets to one down, over No. 3 Stefan Edberg in the final.

Chang was inspired by David's heroics in the Bible. "I think I was meant to be this size," he confided. "It was the Lord's plan, like David and Goliath. The story fits me." Chang wore his Christian faith on his sleeve—he often credited "the Lord" for his victories—which impressed some and grated on others. But no one can deny that he set a noble example with his good works for worthwhile causes. Of Chinese extraction, Chang will also be remembered for his huge and symbolic role in popularizing tennis in Asia. Of his thirty-four tournament victories, twelve came in the Far East, in seven different Asian cities.

Religion, hard work, and his close-knit Chinese-American family provided the keys to Chang's success. He traveled with his mother, Betty, for his first four years on tour and thereafter with his brother-coach-best friend Carl. Indeed, Michael so insulated himself within the "Chang Gang" that in 1995 Andre Agassi said, "Nobody knows Michael Chang."

The rest of America's "greatest generation"—Pete Sampras, Agassi, and Jim Courier—pulled away from Chang in the early 1990s. Chang longed for another major title (thrice he bowed in Grand Slam finals) and the No. 1 ranking. He never achieved either goal. But Chang, now thirty-one, never stopped trying. As another ultimate competitor, Jimmy Connors, once put it: "With him, no matter the situation, you get your money's worth."

Chang's twelve-tournament farewell tour will culminate at the U.S. Open. I tried to discover more about this self-described "private person" in this probing interview.

**Andre Agassi said, "Not just in tennis but in all of sports, he's as great a competitor as you'll ever see." What do you think of that high praise?**

That's pretty flattering coming from a guy who has done so much in his own career. It's hard to say who the greatest competitor is because I've played some great competitors, including Andre himself. Jimmy Connors was a terrific competitor, for sure, and Becker and Edberg, even though you wouldn't always see it on the outside with Stefan. But it's great to receive that kind of compliment.

**Let's walk down Memory Lane and revisit the tournament that made you famous, the 1989 French Open which you amazingly won at age seventeen. What do you remember most about it?**

The matches with Lendl and Edberg stand out most vividly in my mind, particularly the match with Ivan, who was No. 1 in the world. I lost the first couple of sets against Ivan, fought my way back to win the third set, and then I started cramping at the end of the fourth set. The fifth set was a dogfight. I tried to fight every which way I could to win a point, including moonballing, serving underhanded. Against Stefan in the final, I won the first set pretty easily. He came back and won the second and third sets convincingly. Then he had twelve or thirteen break points in the fourth set and wasn't able to break [serve]. In the fifth set he got up a service break early, but he got tired, and I got that break back and ended up winning. It was an incredible match for me and my family. A lot of incredible things happened that week, not just on the court at Roland Garros but off the court in China with the demonstrations at Tiananmen Square.

**Your *tour de force* in Paris coincided with 50,000 students demonstrating for democracy at Tiananmen Square in Beijing. While you won, hundreds died in a ruthless crackdown, as the Chinese government turned tanks and guns on its own people. How do you look back on that historic connection?**

The crackdown in China in 1989 was a very sad time for the Chinese people. They didn't gain their freedom from their protests in Tiananmen Square, but their demonstrations really opened a lot of other doors for people in other countries. Many of the eastern European countries started to open up, as people fought for freedom and democracy there.

**Amazingly, your mother, Betty, had predicted you would win Roland Garros right before it started. Can you explain how your mother did that?**

(Laughter) Your guess is as good as mine. That was the only time my Mom ever said anything like that and maybe the only time she ever will. It might have been the same type of thing like when my Dad talked to you quite a few years back and predicted we had the opportunity to win the Davis Cup in 1990. It's hard to understand. But maybe they have an intuition the rest of us don't know about.

**Your mother would quote a Chinese saying: "A mother will move many times for the sake of a child." Please tell me about how your parents sacrificed for your career.**

Wow! My parents have given so much to both Carl and me—all the extra money, their time, their effort, and mostly their love. It's really helped us not only become great tennis players but develop as people. We have the comfort of knowing that our parents gave us a tremendous amount of love, regardless of whether we won or lost. When we played junior tournaments, sometimes my mother slept on the floor or even in the bathroom of cheap motels so we would always get the beds. Our parents wanted to get a car for Carl, so they had to take out a second mortgage on our home. My Mom even quit her job to travel with me for the first four years of my career. It was a great sacrifice for her, my Dad and their marriage. They never even had a honeymoon until their twenty-fifth anniversary.

**You've said that the one word that sums up your life is perseverance. In what ways have you persevered the most?**

Sometimes I've persevered through difficult matches. Sometimes I've persevered through difficult circumstances such as injuries. Sometimes early in my career, people tried to discourage me from turning professional and playing on the tour at such a young age [fifteen]. I had to cope with certain things and persevere and know what I believed in.

**After you won your third straight Salem Open in Beijing in 1995, the boisterous crowd thunderously cheered you when you gave your victory speech in Mandarin Chinese. Were you then the most popular and famous athlete in Asia?**

That I don't know. But when I go to China, I definitely get an incredible amount of support there and am greeted with an incredible amount of warmth. And it's definitely a great feeling to visit China and compete there.

**Please tell me about your Stars of the Future program in Hong Kong and your Reebok Challenge across all of Asia.**

We sponsored the Stars of the Future program in collaboration with the Hong Kong Tennis Patrons Association in the mid-1990s. We were able to promote tennis in the inner city there for kids who otherwise wouldn't have had an opportunity to play tennis. Reebok has been kind enough to sponsor events with its Reebok Challenge in China and in other Asian countries. That also benefited kids.

**With this burgeoning tennis interest, do you think Asia will ever produce a Grand Slam men's or women's singles champion?**

For sure! Asians have done so well in other racket sports—badminton, table tennis. I'm living proof that they can do it. Hopefully, they'll get the facilities and the right kind of coaching and be able to achieve that. I believe it's only a matter of time before an Asian wins a major singles title.

**You first visited the People's Republic of China in 1990 and have been back there every year since. You've said China "is a place that people don't really understand." What don't people understand about China?**

In many ways China has changed a lot over the years. It's one of the reasons why I got behind Beijing to get the Olympic bid for 2008. China is one of the most misunderstood countries, and the Olympics will allow the rest of the world to see what China is like. And that's a great thing.

**Specifically, what is China like now?**

China is definitely more open nowadays in many ways. When I first went there, it was very difficult to sign autographs or go out on the town. Now when I go there, I'm able to do pretty much anything I want. They translate everything I talk about. And I can sign as many autographs as I want to. The Chinese people have always been very warm, and that is one of the first things that visitors will recognize there.

**During the 1995 Salem Open you smacked balls against The Great Wall of China for a Reebok TV commercial. I found the symbolism fascinating and ironic because here was a young Chinese-American engaged in a capitalist venture in a Communist country at an ancient wall built to protect China from foreign invaders. Did you also see it that way?**

Well, I can't say I thought about it in that complicated a way. I just felt it was a wonderful opportunity because it was the first time I visited The Great Wall. The day we went there from sunrise to sunset was incredibly fascinating because it was a clear day, and we looked out at the horizon and it looked like The Great Wall was never going to end. We also learned a little about the history of China. It was a spectacular experience. So shooting a Reebok commercial there was a great opportunity to tie in two things that have meant a great deal to me—tennis and the people of China.

**Even though you've lived in America all your life, you once said, "I definitely feel more Chinese than anything else." Would you please explain why.**

I always say that I'm Chinese-American. I'm always Chinese first. In the food that I eat and the way I live my life and the culture, I'm Chinese before anything else.

That's not to say I'm not American because America is such a big melting pot. We have so many different cultures and races. That's one of the great things that makes America what it is today. But I'm definitely more Chinese than anything else.

**You racked up eight wins over Sampras, seven over Agassi, and twelve over Courier in your storied career. Which matches stand out most in your mind against each of your longtime American rivals?**

With Pete, it was the 1996 U.S. Open final [which Sampras won 6-1, 6-4, 7-6]. It was a good opportunity for me to win another Grand Slam, but I came out a little too pumped up. I fell a little bit short. That loss lingered in my mind the most. With Andre, the two most vivid in my memory are when we played in the U.S. Open and Australian Open semifinals in 1996. Those two matches against Andre meant a lot to me. I had lost to Andre at the U.S. Open the previous year, and Carl was very disappointed I lost. I remember telling Carl in the locker room, "There'll be another time when we'll play Andre, and the result is going to be different." So I really looked forward to playing him in '96 with a little more intensity and fight.

Both times, strangely enough, I felt like he didn't really want to grind points with me. At the U.S. Open, Andre had a really tough four-setter against Thomas Muster in the round before. And in Melbourne it was very hot and windy for our match. Those were definitely two of the best matches [winning 6-1, 6-4, 7-6 at Melbourne and 6-3, 6-2, 6-2 at Flushing Meadows] of my career. With Courier it was a first-round match we played in the 1993 World Championships in Germany when I beat Jim 6-4, 6-0. Another memorable match was our U.S. Open quarterfinal in 1995. I had set points in all three sets, and I ended up losing in straight sets [7-6, 7-6, 7-5]. (Laughter)

**At 5'9" and 160 pounds, you are a David slaying Goliaths on the tour, an inspiration for little guys. What advice can you give shorter and smaller players?**

Shorter and smaller players at every level have to understand their capabilities. Generally speaking, you're not going to overpower people to win points and matches. You're not going to serve and volley people off the court. But you need to use your speed and quickness, outthink your opponent, and work the ball around [the court], exploiting weaknesses, and turn defense into offense. That's how smaller players have been successful. Lleyton Hewitt is a great example of that. Attitude also plays an important role. You have to fight like crazy and believe in yourself.

**To combat the Goliaths and their powerful games, you and your brother-coach Carl re-designed your Prince racket, adding an inch in length in 1994. You and Carl also decided, after you reached a career-high No. 2 in 1996, to increase your physical strength and bulk up during a grueling six-week program to try to become No. 1. Why did one move pay off while the other backfired?**

The racket change definitely gave me more power on my serve. I was able to get a few more aces and service winners, and that enabled me to hold serve more easily. It also gave me a little more reach, which helped me get to a few more balls. Because I got stronger and put on about ten pounds, I lost speed and also wasn't as agile and flexible. That hurt me. But since then we changed the training and achieved a balance so speed wasn't an issue anymore. That weight and bulk may help some players, but it didn't work for me.

**You've received several awards for your exemplary character and good works. You were one of five athletes named as Most Caring Athlete by *USA TODAY* weekend in 1995 and received one of seven Asian-American leadership awards in 1997 by *A. Magazine* for being a role model for Asian-American youth. Which award or awards mean the most to you?**

Obviously, awards are great. But what really matters is when you have an opportunity to touch a person's life. That means a lot more. I realize not everyone sees me as a role model. But for some people who do, I want to be a positive influence in their lives, and I hope, represent a Christ-like character.

**In 1995 a week after the Great Hanshin earthquake decimated Kobe and left 5,000 dead and tens of thousands homeless, you contacted the Japan Tennis Association to express your desire to hold a charity event to help survivors. Your humanitarian initiative resulted in an exhibition and charity auction that raised more than $150,000. Please tell me about that.**

I've played in Japan for so many years, and the Japanese people have been so gracious to me. The earthquake in Kobe was a very sad thing. In recent years some tournaments, particularly the French Open, have staged charity events before the tournament. This was a great opportunity to do the same for the people in Kobe. It turned out very well. It was nice to play an exhibition, a doubles match with Kimiko Date, Shuzo Matsuoka, and Ai Sugiyama. We had fun. And we benefited people at the same time.

**Who are your favorite people in the Bible? And what are your favorite passages?**

I enjoy reading about a lot of people. I learned a lot reading about David's life. In certain ways I feel similar to David in the situation with David and Goliath. At the same time I can see where David has failed in his life. But I admit that, of all the people in the Bible, God says this is a man that I love who is after my own heart. That is very, very important. Job is a good example of how to get through some very difficult times. And I love to read some of the psalms, particularly some of the psalms that David had written about. I know that I can come to the Lord whether I'm happy or angry or sad. No matter what emotion I may be feeling, I can express it to the Lord. I can tell Him exactly how I feel without being afraid. That's what I get from reading the psalms. The psalms have been great examples for me and my life.

**You sign autographs "Jesus Loves You! M. Chang." Since some autograph seekers are not Christian, do you have any misgivings about doing that?**

No, I don't. I don't because even if people aren't Christian, I feel they need to know that the Lord loves them. Love never does anyone any harm. So, for the most part, people have appreciated that I have written that [message]. And, obviously, people who share the same faith know where I'm coming from. But love never does its neighbor any harm.

**How do you respond to people who react negatively to your open display or expression of your faith?**

I've had times where people have criticized me for [displaying] my faith. But showing my faith is just about my personal experience and wanting others to be able to share in the love and peace that I have in my heart from knowing the Lord. Never do I try to force people to become Christians or to read the Bible or to know the Lord because that's not what Christianity is all about. I never try to force anything upon anyone.

**You've called yourself "an evangelist with a racket" and have mentioned taking some seminary classes when you retire. Would you like to be ordained at some point?**

I don't know if I necessarily want to become a pastor. But I would love to take some seminary classes to gain a better knowledge of the Bible and God's work. If that will help me understand things better and help me grow stronger in my faith, then I will be able to provide more encouragement and support for other people. And that's a good thing.

**In your autobiography, *Holding Serve*, you wrote how much you look forward to the next chapter of your life. What do you plan to do in the next chapter?**

We have a lot of things to do in our Chang Family Foundation. I will definitely take a much more active role in that. I know I'll still be involved in tennis one way or another. I would love to work with youngsters. I don't see myself as an on-the-road coach. But I would love to be able to have some of the camps we've had, encourage kids in their talent, give them guidance and direction, and tell them what it takes to be successful on the pro tour. It doesn't make sense that Asians can be so good at other racket sports but not necessarily tennis. I believe it's just a matter of time before they succeed in tennis, too.

**What is the mission of the Chang Family Foundation? And how has it changed people's lives?**

Our mission is to touch lives and hearts through local and international programs and events, to bring people to know the Lord, to nurse people who know the

Lord already in their walk. We held our first NeXt Generation Tennis Camp in the summer of 2000 at Industry Hills. It's a Christian outreach camp. In 2001 the second tennis outreach camp was held in Taipei, Taiwan. We've made a lot of impact on lives so far, which has been great. The response we've received from our programs, such as our basketball and volleyball leagues and tennis camps, has been tremendous. We're getting more demand to do more things.

**In 1998 your mother told _Sports Spectrum_ magazine, "In my family, everybody went to college and beyond. Especially to a Chinese family, education is considered a necessity. For Michael to turn pro and not completely finish high school, let alone not go to college, was almost unthinkable." Your family made a difficult decision when you turned pro at 15. How much have you missed not having a college education?**

My situation is unique. When I was growing up, my parents emphasized education much more than athletics. If I didn't do well at school, I wasn't allowed to go to practice or play tennis. My parents realized not everyone can make it as a professional athlete. They wanted to make sure I had an education to fall back on.

So, when I turned pro just before my sixteenth birthday, my parents made sure I had my high school diploma. I graduated from high school after my first semester of tenth grade. So education has always been very, very important. After I turned pro I furthered my education by reading a lot and learning about the different cultures I experienced. I do wonder what college would have been like. I don't plan to attend college full-time, but I would like to take some classes. I want to encourage students to focus on school rather than concentrate on tennis or whatever sport they're playing.

**During your sixteen-year pro career, you played in only six Davis Cup ties and occasionally turned down requests to represent your country in Davis Cup competition. Do you have any regrets about that?**

I do in certain respects. I wish the Davis Cup scheduling had been easier. Pete and Andre share my concerns. We've been hesitant at times to play Davis Cup. The biggest difficulty has been the schedules. We already play a pretty tight [tournament] schedule. And Davis Cup sometimes falls when maybe the Cup surface isn't being played then [on the tour]. I don't know if people realize how much Davis Cup takes out of you. The Davis Cup ties I played in always took me at least two weeks to get back to normal because I was so drained physically and mentally. But I enjoyed playing Davis Cup. I loved the competition. I loved the chance to play for my country. It's an honor for me to say I was part of a winning Davis Cup team in 1990.

**But, specifically, what happened after that high point?**

There were other times when I wanted to play Davis Cup and wasn't asked or invited to play. When we won in 1990, [captain] Tom Gorman had said, "We did so well this year that we're going to stick with the same winning team for next year." So I automatically assumed the following year I would be playing Davis Cup. [But] it didn't work out that way. Before I knew it, the team was already picked. That was disappointing.

**You've met some famous people during your tennis career. Who were the most impressive?**

I've met some great people. It's been an honor to meet Dr. Billy Graham on two occasions. I also met Princess Di twice, which was great, a treat for me. I met George Bush Sr. at the White House in 1989 when he was president. It was fun to be there in the Oval Office. He walked with us out to the tennis court. I had some conversations with Dr. Graham and his right-hand man, Maurice Scobee. Dr. Graham has been a great inspiration for me, and he's a great example of how to live your life. Even now, his health isn't that great, yet he's still making the most of the strength he has and he touches lives and hearts.

**Would you rather be remembered as a great tennis player or as a great Christian?**

I don't know how I'll be remembered. But if given the choice, it's a greater honor for me to be remembered as a great Christian. If people do remember me as a great tennis player, I hope they won't forget that, for me, to be a Christian has always been more important.

## Ten Fascinating Facts about Michael Chang

- In 2001 he was forced to retire from a match for the first time in his career— breaking a 937-match streak—in a second round encounter against Andrew Ilie in Hong Kong with back spasms.

- The largest of the several fresh-water aquariums Michael Chang has set up in his home in Mercer Island, Washington, is 240 gallons and eight-feet-long by two-feet-wide.

- He is the only player of Chinese descent to reach the Top 10.

- In 1987 he became the youngest player at fifteen years, six months to win a main draw match at the U.S. Open.

- In his autobiography, *Holding Serve*, Chang, who has abstained from having sex throughout his life, encourages teens and young adults to wait until marriage to have sex.

- He goes through about ten string jobs a day during clay court tournaments.

- He says that he hasn't hit an underhanded serve in a pro match since doing it against Ivan Lendl at Roland Garros in 1989.

- He estimates he's signed his autograph about 200,000 times in his career.

- In a 1989 *Los Angeles Times* column titled "This Kid Isn't Nasty Enough to

Become a Tennis Champion," distinguished sportswriter Jim Murray wrote, "The way Michael plays it, the world might start liking Americans."

- He once checked into the players' hotel at the Memphis tournament using the alias "Christian Brothers."

---

## FASCINATING FACTS:

- Michael Chang needed six bodyguards when he played events in China and Taiwan because he was besieged by admiring fans.

- Larry Scott, CEO of the WTA Tour, envisions transforming Beijing into "a true tennis capital of the world."

- In 2001 The Chinese Tennis Association told Sports Marketing Consultants President Howard Jaffe that it would void the five-year contract they signed to develop 14-year-old Shuai Peng in the U.S. if Jaffe ever uttered the name of Hu Na, the Chinese player who defected to American in 1982.

- In his 2002 autobiography, *Holding Serve*, Michael Chang, who had abstained from ever having sex, encourages teens and young adults to wait until marriage to have sex.

- In a 1989 *Los Angeles Times* column titled "This Kid Isn't Nasty Enough to Become a Tennis Champion," distinguished sportswriter Jim Murray wrote: "The way Michael plays it, the world might start liking Americans."

- He once checked into the players' hotel at the Memphis tournament using the alias "Christian Brothers."

# 27

# Amélie Mauresmo: Vive La Différence

# 2003

Something you may not know about Amélie Mauresmo: the twenty-four-year-old Frenchwoman once single-handedly fought off three knife-wielding muggers. Her powerfully built 5'9" physique contrasts sharply with her soft and gentle voice. Behind that disarming demeanor, though, is a keen intelligence and strong conviction.

Mauresmo first made international headlines as the surprise Australian Open finalist in 1999, though her breakthrough tournament was all but overshadowed by Martina Hingis's infamous "She is half a man" insult. The openly gay Mauresmo deftly defused the controversy by replying, "She was out of line . . . It is her problem."

Since then No. 6-ranked Mauresmo hasn't reached another Grand Slam final although she's tantalized her many fans with telling victories over all the top stars and believes the best is yet to come.

**You have reached the Australian Open final, three Italian Open finals, and the U.S. Open and Wimbledon semis. What is your best surface? And which Grand Slam do you have the best chance of winning?**

I can play well on all different surfaces. Clay courts have been good to me; grass courts too, hard courts too. The one I would *love* to win is the French Open. I think I have a good chance to win there, and I have a good chance in Australia, too. Venus and Serena have their least success at Roland Garros, so that could help me, too.

**In May 2003 you admitted, "The tension is always with me. . . . It's up to me to control it better." Is your becoming too emotional during losses in those big semifinals and finals the main reason you have not won them?**

No. That was probably true, though, for the quarterfinal of the French Open this year. Against Serena I was way too tense and tight. For the other losses, the reason was just that I played against great players. What gives me more confidence now, especially in the third set of big matches, is that I've improved my technique at the baseline and my physical condition.

**In 2000 when you reached the fourth round at Roland Garros, fans voted you the winner of the Prix Sanex du Public as the nicest, best-liked player at the tournament. Why are you so popular?**

They like, first, the way I play. But they also like the way I am off the court, the way I try to share the emotions with them. On the court I like to express myself. I like to show them that I'm happy to be here and give them some pleasure.

**This year you appeared topless on the cover of *Paris Match*, France's leading magazine, with your arms covering your chest. Why did you do that?**

It was a fun thing to do. I spent a very nice day doing the photo shoot. Not only this picture, we did a lot of pictures. Glamour is another part of women's tennis now. We have a lot of press. And, for me, the main press is in France.

**Did it show the feminine side?**

Sure. It showed the feminine side and how I am. It showed that I have a good body, and that I don't have any [psychological] complexes.

**One of the new slogans of the WTA Tour is "Get in touch with your feminine side." Do you like this slogan and theme?**

Yeah. It's good that the WTA is trying to improve the communication and put the players in new surroundings and images to show their attractiveness. When average people see that, they may say, "OK, we're going to look at tennis players on the court." And then maybe they like tennis, and they become fans.

**The Amélie Mauresmo fanpage on the Internet reports that "It is difficult to have a conversation with Amélie without being interrupted by the familiar jingles of her ever-present mobile phone." Who calls you the most? And what do you usually talk about?**

Yeah, I turned it off now. I talk about things that are probably not interesting at all. It can be anything—personal, tennis, something I read in the newspaper, a movie I watched. Close friends call me. I don't give out my phone number easily.

**You love wine and have a wine cellar at home. Please tell me about that.**

I have about 300 bottles, mostly red wine. The only white wine I have is very sweet, sauternes. It's a part of Bordeaux. The oldest one is 1937, and it's the most expensive one. It would sell for more than $1,000. I'm not going to sell it. I'm going to drink it. (Laughter)

**The fanpage on the Internet also says that you hate journalists who try to "steal" your privacy. How exactly have journalists tried to steal your privacy?**

That was several years ago when they all took my coming out [as a lesbian] as the main thing, the big event of the year. But no, it's not true. I like journalists to respect what I like to talk about and what I don't want to talk about. Respect for privacy is the main thing in life, not just in sports and journalism.

**Behind your soft voice and gentle manner, you have plenty of courage. Please tell me about that incident on the beach when three men attacked you and Sylvie Bourdon and demanded your money and you punched them and they fled.**

See, that's the kind of thing that I *don't* want to talk about. (Laughter) This is a typical example of what journalists do.

**But was what I described accurate?**

I don't want to talk about it. (Laughter)

**Do you have a girlfriend now?**

Yes, her name is Pascual.

**Her last name?**

No, that's enough. (Laughter)

**In May 1999, you said, "By talking to Sylvie, I am stronger on court and off it." Is that also true with Pascual?**

Yeah, when you feel good in your private life, it helps you in your job—especially in tennis. It's so sensitive, so emotional to be on the court that when you don't feel good, you can see it right away on the court.

**When you first came out, your relationship with your family took a turn for the worse. Have your parents and brother become more comfortable with your sexuality since then?**

Yeah. I think it's never easy for parents to accept that because you see something else for your kids. But with time it gets better and better. It's not perfect. But who is perfect with their parents?

**You are the first player on the women's tour since Martina Navratilova to talk publicly about being a lesbian. Aside from Martina Hingis's insulting remark**

*Amelie Mauresmo sits down for an interview with the author.*
Courtesy of Timothy Balestri

**that you were "half a man" several years ago, have you encountered any hostile remarks or discrimination on the pro tour since then?**

Not at all. A lot of people have asked me questions about that, but I haven't felt any difference before and after. I think people are getting more open-minded, which is good.

**When you acknowledged your homosexuality at the 1999 Australian Open, Pam Shriver said, "This will be a good test. If the commercial world embraces her, then it's a different era." Has the commercial world embraced you with product endorsements?**

Yeah, of course. Again, you can see that society is getting better and better in terms of tolerance and being open-minded. I have three or four major endorsements.

**You've said your versatility is "a huge asset" and, as a junior player, you served and volleyed sometimes. At age twenty-four, do you plan to serve and volley again on the pro tour?**

Yeah, [but] doing it every point is not my game. Doing it sometimes and varying it with a lot of other tactics is good. But I will never be the kind of player who serves and volleys every time, the way Martina Navratilova used to do it. The returns are much too good now. When you always serve and volley, they get used to it and return better and better.

The same fanpage says, "Amélie is all action while at the same time admittedly lazy. She detests the rigors of off-court training, much preferring the speed of downhill skiing, go-carts, and horseback riding. Is that true? And if you dislike training, will you ever reach your potential?

> That *was* true, but I've improved so much in this respect. I realized a couple years ago that you cannot reach the highest level without working hard and being very involved in your training. I love doing all those things—downhill skiing, go-carts, and horse riding—but I also know that I need to work very hard on *and* off the court. Now I understand this. I don't train eight hours a day like Magnus Norman, but some days I train five or six hours. I do mostly weight training, the bike and wind sprints, and a little bit of plyometrics.

In the 2001 book *Venus Envy*, Sonya Jeyaseelan said, "You can look at the men's draw and find maybe three players who have had a [dysfunctional] relationship with their father. With the girls you might find three who don't." Is Sonya right? And, if so, what can women's tennis do about it?

> It's true you have more of that [problem] in women's tennis than in men's tennis. But what she said is an exaggeration. It's not true in my case. It seems to the public like it happens a lot because a few serious cases make the headlines. I would say this problem involves only twenty percent of the players.

After you lost to Serena at the 2002 Wimbledon, you were so frustrated that you said you were playing only for the No. 3 spot because Serena and Venus were too good for you. That shocked some people. Do you still feel that way?

> No! I was leaving the court and was frustrated. I just said what came to my mind at that time. Even a few weeks later I didn't feel that way. Since then my goal has been to reach number one.

Is it true that when you were a little girl, Yannick Noah's great 1983 Roland Garros triumph inspired you to take up tennis?

> It's a true story. I was very young, almost four, but I knew that what I could see was great. Then I went into the garden and made the motions of Yannick Noah. I copied him. (Laughter) So maybe that's why I have a one-handed backhand. It was great to meet Yannick in the Fed Cup when he was our captain in 1998. I was still very young. I was nineteen.

What makes Yannick so appealing?

> He's very charismatic. He has a lot of interesting things to say. He's a very extreme person. Everything he does is so extreme, so passionate. I like that. I'm a little bit like him sometimes.

**Please tell me about the tattoo near your left shoulder.**

It's an angel holding the symbol of peace, an olive branch. I'm a peaceful person. I hate war. It is nonsense.

---

## FASCINATING FACTS:

- 2006 Wimbledon champion Amelie Mauresmo prepared for The Championships at the British Embassy, which reportedly has the only grass court in France.

- The message on a T-shirt made by her sponsor that Amelie Mauresmo, a lesbian, donned after beating Justine Henin-Hardenne in the Wimbledon final was "2006 Wimbledon Champion. I am what I am."

- In 2006 Amelie Mauresmo said Martina Hingis's derisive 1999 remark that Mauresmo "is half a man" would never be forgotten "because it hurt so much."

- Martina Hingis recalls the main thing she asked Chris Evert when Evert was her WTA "mentor" after Hingis turned pro was: "How do you handle men?"

- The first question that Amelie Mauresmo, the eventual champion, was asked at her first press conference at the 2006 Australian Open was, "Have you a message for all your gay fans in Australia?"

- Amelie Mauresmo received the International Tennis Writers Association's prestigious Ambassador for Tennis award in 2006 for being "a true humanitarian." Mauresmo is a longtime contributor to the Curie Institute of France (for cancer research) as well as a supporter of the Phil Collins Little Dreams Foundation.

# 28

# Brad Gilbert: Coach of Champions
# 2005

Early in Brad Gilbert's eight-year coaching stint with Andre Agassi, the under-achieving Las Vegan explained the odd couple's attraction: "Brad made a career out of winning matches he was supposed to lose, and I was just the opposite."

They soon became fast friends and mutual admirers. Gilbert helped Agassi believe in himself by learning to think for himself. Agassi helped Gilbert become a kinder, gentler person. Agassi, despite roller-coaster highs and lows, racked up six Grand Slam titles and the No. 1 ranking during their partnership.

When Gilbert put a struggling Andy Roddick's career back on track in 2003—he grabbed the U.S. Open and the No. 1 ranking—Roddick praised him as "the genius of all coaches." Stunningly, Roddick fired him in December 2004 after ranking No. 2 but not winning a major title.

In this interview Gilbert candidly discusses his two famous students, his teachers, the secrets of his coaching success, his new book, *I've Got Your Back*, reigning and rising tour stars, and his loving family.

**Your 1993 book *Winning Ugly* sold 175,000 copies, became a classic, and still ranks in the top three among tennis books at Amazon.com and BN.com. What is your new book, *I've Got Your Back*, about?**

*I've Got Your Back* is totally different from *Winning Ugly*. It tells stories about the two players I've coached, Agassi and Roddick, and gives my ideas and opinions about coaching. A lot of what I learned came from my coach, Tom Chivington, who is an honorable person. Just as you become like your parents through osmosis when you're an adult, I found myself doing a lot of the things Tom did without realizing it.

**In *I've Got Your Back*, you wrote that "I'm pretty darn good at paying attention. And I've had the amazing fortune to have had at least two great teachers in my life to pay attention to." Besides Chivington, who was your other great teacher? And what important lessons did they teach you?**

Without question, Tom Chivington and the first person I coached, Andre Agassi. I felt blessed to be around both of them. I was able to learn a lot from them. That's the key to coaching: you learn a lot from everybody and translate it into your coaching. Andre was very thoughtful, intelligent and very much a student of the game. When I started coaching him, as great as he was, he was still striving to get a lot better. He showed me that whatever level you're at, you can get much better. With Tom at Foothill College, it didn't matter if you were No. 1 on the team or No. 12, because he treated everybody the same—fairly—and gave everyone the opportunity to play and succeed. That's the best feeling a college player can have.

**What is the most important attribute a pro tennis coach should have?**

To be adaptable. To be able to look at a player's game and say, "OK, you can help them go in the direction they have the ability to go in." One big mistake coaches often make is to make them go in the direction *you* think. You don't want to take players A, B, and C and make them all the same. Everyone has different strengths and weaknesses and personalities, and you try to work with that. The reason I got along so well with Andre and Andy is that, like me, they are gregarious guys—talkers good at processing a lot of words. But I should have coached Mary Pierce differently. Mary is a quieter person, and I wish I'd done a better job of reading her in the first place. I may have overwhelmed her with verbal input. I think she tried to adapt to me, but really, I should have tried to adapt to her. I should have listened better.

**Roger Federer was the only man in the top fifty without a traveling coach in 2004, yet he dominated the tour. How necessary is a traveling coach for a world-class player?**

I think coaching helps everybody. Federer, obviously, is an amazing exception. People think he travels by himself. But he has a team of four or five people—an assistant coach, who is Switzerland's assistant Davis Cup coach, a trainer, and his girlfriend, a former tour player. So he gets input from them. Everyone else has a coach because everyone is looking for an edge to get better. Whatever your ranking, it always helps to have somebody give you an opinion about what you're doing out there.

**In the foreword to *I've Got Your Back*, Andy Roddick said you have "very few peers as a scout." When you scout opponents, what areas do you focus on?**

Scouting is my favorite part of the job. Shot selection is a huge part of it. Let's say this particular player always hits his backhand down the line and serves wide, but you watch and determine he is now hitting his backhand crosscourt more often. Or maybe he's serving down the middle more often. Or maybe he's not hitting his forehand as well. There's no guarantee he is going to play the same way from match to match. But I study the match and make notes about what opponents are doing and give that input to my player. Maybe that can make a difference on a big point.

**You promote yourself extensively with your website—www.bradgilbert tennis.com—and call your fans "The BG Nation." What is the purpose of your website?**

The purpose of it is fun. I don't make any money out of it. I did it when I wasn't coaching. So many people were asking what I was doing. My wife, Kim, said, "Let's do a website." We get tons of great feedback. It keeps you grounded to know what people think. I have some hard-core fans. Some people like what I do, and some people don't.

**Five of the world's best teenage players are black. France's Gaël Monfils won three junior Grand Slams in 2004, and compatriot Jo-Wilfried Tsonga was the world No. 2 junior in 2003. Timothy Neilly, seventeen, of Tampa became the first black boys' eighteen singles champion in Orange Bowl history, beating fifteen-year-old Donald Young of Atlanta in the final. Scoville Jenkins, a seventeen-year-old from Atlanta, became the first black U.S. boys' eighteen singles champion at Kalamazoo. Which of these promising youngsters has star potential?**

Unfortunately, I've never seen Timothy Neilly play. Donald Young has worlds of talent. Expectations for him are going to be huge. Scoville is going to be able to fly under the radar better. People are going to expect Young to be like [eighteen-year-old Spanish star Rafael] Nadal, and when he's seventeen or eighteen, already be right there [near the top]. The only thing I'm worried about with Donald is his size. He's only about 5'8" or 5'9". If he gets bigger, that increases his chances [for stardom] a lot because size does matter in tennis for the serve and for reaching on the service return. But you can still play great if you're not big.

**What do you foresee for the two French players?**

Monfils has star potential. He's 6'3" and he moves tremendously well. He also has a booming serve. He's copied Andy Roddick's serve and has exactly the same type of motion. He'll become France's best player. He certainly has the potential to be top five in the world. And I think he'll fulfill it. Jo-Wilfried Tsonga has a fair bit of talent and is a big guy, about 6'4," but he doesn't move as well as Monfils. He has top twenty potential, the same as Scoville Jenkins.

**You were a bronze medalist at the Seoul Olympics. Looking back at your career,**

you said, "Not winning the gold was my biggest disappointment. But playing was the best feeling I ever had in tennis." Please tell me about your Olympic experience and why it means so much to you.

It was my biggest disappointment because all of a sudden I was playing the medal rounds, and I started thinking I can win the gold. I got ahead of myself. I should have been more grounded. If I had just thought one match at a time, I think I could have won the gold. I played a really poor match against my teammate, Tim Mayotte. He rose to the occasion a lot more than I did. But the Olympic experience put things into perspective for me.

**What do you mean by that?**

Sometimes, as a tennis player, you bitch about this and that. I met some incredibly dedicated athletes in Seoul. One wrestler I met was training from three in the morning to nine, and then he worked as an insurance salesman all day, and then he trained some more. So it really put things in perspective for me. And getting the chance to walk in the stadium with all the other American athletes was the highlight of my career.

**What achievements during your playing career are you most proud of?**

Playing the Olympics and the Davis Cup. As a kid, I ball-boyed in the Davis Cup, and then getting the opportunity to play it as an adult was a huge thrill. Also, just playing in the U.S. Open. Those were my goals as a kid. I first watched the U.S. Open on television, so I really wanted to play in it. Being ranked No. 4 and beating [Boris] Becker four times were great but not as important. Obviously, I wanted to win a Slam, but I didn't do that.

**Before coaching Andre Agassi, one of the greatest talents in tennis history, you had never coached before. How did you do it?**

I guess I felt like I could do it. I feel like I know tennis. I knew Andre had tons of talent, and he could get more [results] out of his talent. Obviously playing on the pro tour helps a lot because I was still playing quite a few of the players he was playing. I knew a lot of these players and felt Andre could be winning a lot more. The student sometimes predicates the success of the coach. Andre is an amazingly talented player. Maybe other coaches could have done with Andre what I did.

**You love to talk tennis, and you have made several engaging guest appearances in the broadcast booth. You will be doing tennis commentary for ESPN this year. What kind of commentator will you be? And will commentating replace coaching as your full-time career?**

I'm not sure about either. I did a little bit of commentary last year, but I had to be more guarded because I was still coaching on the tour. Maybe I'll speak out more now because I'm not coaching. If I have something on my mind, I'll let it fly. I'll just be myself.

**And how would you describe yourself?**

I'm frank. I'm a hard worker. I'm the guy who'll drive fifty-five miles per hour in the slow lane, but I'll do it for thirty straight hours.

**In a 2003 interview with *Inside Tennis* magazine, you said that Andre Agassi was a better player than Pete Sampras. Yet Sampras clearly has a superior career record. Why did you say that?**

He [editor Bill Simons] was asking me about my guy. I felt like Andre *was* a better player. But he just didn't win [some of] the big matches. If you looked at the whole tournament, Andre's results up to the final would be better. Pete sometimes would struggle, then all of a sudden Pete has this ability, when he played against Andre, to raise his game higher than he did at any other point during the tournament. Pete could struggle, struggle, struggle, and then play brilliantly. That was an amazing quality.

**In *I've Got Your Back*, you wrote "the huge new trend in the game" at all levels is improving movement for players. How do you suggest tournament players improve their movement?**

By starting at a young age and putting emphasis on movement then. When I was a kid, [coaching] was all about stroke technique and hitting the ball. There wasn't much emphasis on movement, other than when you played points. Whether you're doing drills on movement or working with a movement coach, the more opportunity you give yourself, the better you'll move, and the better your ability will be to compete on the pro level. Excellent movement is the biggest thing that all the top players have in common now.

**How can recreational players improve their movement?**

When you get older, you have to be creative. You can't go out and do "suicides" [sprints] and running up hills and that crazy stuff because you'll break down your body. You have to work on your stretching and overall fitness. Obviously, if you're thirty pounds overweight, you're not going to be moving great. You can do little movement drills. The fitter you get, the better you're going to play tennis at *every* level. When you watch the senior forty-five, fifty, and fifty-five events, the fittest guys usually do the best.

**Part of the subtitle in *Winning* Ugly is the phrase "mental warfare." But in *ACE* magazine you asserted, "Tennis is a physically demanding sport that's not as mental as people think." What did you mean by that?**

Sometimes commentators say there's no difference between the No. 1 and No.

100 [ranked] guy—it's just a mental difference. But there's a lot more difference between Roger Federer and whoever the No. 100 guy is than just the mental difference. They say that because a lot of tennis commentators weren't that good themselves. Federer's skills are incredible, and he's won because of that. A lot of tennis people [erroneously] group tennis and golf together. Tennis is really physically demanding. You have to be in amazing shape, and you have to be a world-class athlete. I use Andre, who I coached for eight years, as an example. He is almost thirty-five. I just talked with him yesterday, and he's constantly working on his serve, his forehand, his backhand. That's what drives him. Andre is still playing because he thinks he can get better. Everyone can get better.

**You played up the "winning ugly" label to describe your game. But you actually moved very well and possessed excellent hand-eye coordination and solid strokes, except for your second serve.**

Believe me, when people said, "Gilbert is no kind of athlete," I always felt they never saw me play basketball, baseball, or football as a kid. I wasn't the prettiest, but I was good at everything. People just thought my tennis game was a little stiff. I didn't have a big Western forehand. I didn't do anything outstandingly good. But, other than my second serve, I didn't do anything poorly. And I did move really well.

**How do you reconcile devotion to your family and coaching since you've been on the road so much throughout your married life? Is your wife almost like a single parent?**

Yeah. (Laughter) That's why I'm going to pick my spots now. I'm not going to rush anything. I'm going to wait for the right [coaching] situation. My wife and children have traveled with me sometimes just so we can be together more. My family is more important to me than anything. And my wife is unbelievable. Without her, I have no career.

**Pro tennis has its ups and downs and tends to become most popular when there are charismatic stars and riveting rivalries. What rule changes do you suggest to keep tennis fired up even during the down periods?**

You need rivalries because they are great for the sport. But I like the way tennis is going. One change I think they should make is to legalize on-court coaching. Whether it's [a coaching visit] once or twice a set, or a coach sitting on the court, that's one rule I'd definitely like to see changed.

# 29

# Inside the Mind of Mats Wilander

# 2002

In the mid- and late-1980s, the biggest weapon in men's tennis was often said to be "Mats Wilander's mind." Tenacious and resourceful, Wilander pulled out classic victories against the likes of Ivan Lendl, Boris Becker, John McEnroe, Stefan Edberg, and Pat Cash. The mild-mannered Swede wound up with seven Grand Slam titles, more than Becker and Edberg, and he did it on three different surfaces—clay, grass and hard courts. Wilander ranked No. 1 when he captured the Australian, French, and U.S. Opens in his career year, 1988. He also sparked his country to three Davis Cup titles and two more Cup finals. In recognition of those achievements, The International Tennis Hall of Fame in scenic Newport, Rhode Island, will enshrine Wilander on July 13.

Just as his game always seemed more than the sum of its parts, Wilander's formidable mind unravels tennis' complexities with perception and precision.

**What was your reaction when told that you would be enshrined in The International Tennis Hall of Fame?**

I was delighted. It's something you don't really think about until it happens to you. But once they call you, it's great. It gives you an amazing sense of accomplishment, for sure.

**What were your emotions watching the 2002 Australian Open men's final in which a fellow Swede, Thomas Johansson, won, while the player you had been coaching, Marat Safin, lost?**

I was rooting for the Swede because Sweden has a great tennis history. Sweden has great tennis clubs so they have great tennis programs. A lot of people play tennis, and it's a really big sport. And the press has been really down on tennis in

Sweden because we can't repeat what we did in the `80s, which is impossible and never going to happen again unless we have another Björn Borg. We have so many good players and always do well in Davis Cup, but nothing has been written about the game. For that reason I was rooting for the Swedish guy. I know Johansson really well, and I know his coach [Magnus Tideman] even better. He used to coach me, too. Another reason is that it's more important for Safin to get to the final and lose than it is to win now.

**Why do you say that?**

He learns a lot more from losing. If he wins, he has the confidence of someone who wins a Grand Slam [title], and he's not going to change his game. Whereas you always have to try to change your game and improve some things. He has a bit of an attitude that "I'm good enough to win Grand Slams, so I'll keep on doing what I'm doing." He isn't as motivated to improve as other players are.

**What should Safin do to become a better player?**

He needs to do what I did: develop a different kind of game. The guys are learning how to play him now. They know he's eventually going to have a breakdown, whether it lasts for one minute or five minutes or half an hour. Unless he changes his game, guys are going to keep him out there forever. Safin used to have the biggest game of any player I've ever seen play when he played well. But he's not as dangerous as he used to be because he's playing smarter so he doesn't hit the ball as hard. If you want to change anything in your game, you have to do it between [ages] nineteen and twenty-two. That's where Safin is now. If he doesn't do it now, he'll always be the same player, a great player, but unfortunately, not another Sampras or Agassi.

**Just when Björn Borg retired, you arrived and shocked everyone by winning the 1982 French Open as a seventeen-year-old kid. You came from the same little country, were about the same size and also had blond hair, had the same two-handed backhand and baseline playing style, and even a similar reserved personality. But when you were asked, "Are you the next Borg?, you replied, "I am not Borg No. 2. I am Wilander No. 1." Please tell me about your attitude then.**

To ask, "Are you the next Borg?" is an immature question. No, of course, I'm not the next Björn Borg. I don't look like him. I don't play like him exactly. Even as a seventeen-year-old, it was very hard not to be rude when I was asked that question by Swedish journalists. How can you be the next Björn Borg? He won five Wimbledons in a row. How can you compare a skinny seventeen-year-old with a Björn Borg who had the greatest record of a tennis player?

**In 1987 you confided, "I live a good life being a top three or top six player, and the price Lendl and Borg paid to become No. 1 is too high for me." Yet, the next year**

**you won three Grand Slam titles and the Lipton Championships. With your attitude, how did you produce the second most-dominant year, after Laver's 1969 Grand Slam year, in Open Era history?**

I got married in 1987 [sic], and I really lost my drive. I was playing great in 1985 until I was about 21, and then `86 and `87 were kind of down years. I wasn't working to improve anymore, sort of stuck like Safin is now. Matt Doyle, who was on the ATP Board together with me, got talking one night. He told me my ball striking and natural talent are at least as good as Lendl's, but I just don't do anything off the court. So we started working really hard, 6-7 hours a day, off the court. That's how it happened. I managed to win the first Slam in Australia. Because I won that final 8-6 in the fifth set against Pat [Cash], it was like, "Whoops, I can do it now. I'm stronger than these guys. They know I'm stronger."

**You once confided: "All my career I had dreamed of being number one. But when I finally achieved it and the initial excitement wore off, I felt nothing. I had no sense of elation or pride. I was world champion but so what? I got more excitement out of cutting the grass than playing tennis." How do you explain that reaction?**

I started really young and was basically a pro when I was fifteen. So that was my ninth year as a pro. I started working hard, as I told you, in `87, and we were aiming to peak in 1990 or even 1991. At that time, I thought twenty-six or twenty-seven was the perfect age for a tennis player. You're a little stronger and smarter, but still young enough to run on the court. But it [the great year] happened immediately, and it happened too fast. If I had won one major and felt like I was improving, I could have kept it going, and then maybe my 1988 year should have come in `90 or `91. So when the U.S. Open was over, I just couldn't see myself trying to improve anymore. And it's definitely not as much fun being on top. After that I let other things in my life, like my wife and my friends, take a bigger role. I had achieved in tennis more than what I had ever expected to achieve. They wonder why Tiger Woods has ice in his veins and more killer instinct than Davis Love. It's because nothing is more important than golf in his life. Once something else takes the place of tennis as the most important thing in your life, you are basically done.

**What do you think the next great rivalry in men's tennis will be?**

Unfortunately, I'm not sure there will be one. Tennis players are so even. So many good players can beat the best players. So many guys out there just go for broke [on their shots] all the time. When they have good days, they'll upset the favorites and kill the rivalries every time. You're not going to get Andy Roddick against Lleyton Hewitt in three out of the next six U.S. Open finals. That's too bad because when you get the same guys playing each other on different surfaces and in different circumstances, it's easier for the fans to follow and it's more interesting.

**SébastienGrosjean recently described professional tennis as "a world out of touch with reality." You've been in pro tennis or observing it for the past twenty years. Is Grosjean right?**

He's right. But that's true in all professional sports today. It's so removed from reality. It's a great life. In tennis, I suppose it's worse because we do travel more than any other athletes. We go back and forth from America to Europe and around the world. At least the golf guys, most of them, stay on one continent. In golf, if you're twenty-five or forty-one, and you suddenly hit the ball fifty yards shorter, you can still shoot the same score. But in tennis, if you don't have the killer instinct, if you're not better than the other guy, you're done! And that doesn't happen in other sports either. They get paid before they even start the season in basketball and other sports. Tennis is a little different and a little rougher mentally than any other sport.

The world revolves around you, for sure, because when you get to a tournament, the press is there, and they're not asking about the world, they're asking about *you*. So if people ask questions about you all the time, you're going to think, "Wow, I *am* that big." It's not healthy.

**During much of the 1980s you traveled everywhere with fellow Swedes, Anders Järryd, Joakim Nyström, and Hans Simonsson on Team SIAB, and were coached by Jon-Anders Sjögren. Now players seems to travel alone or with a parent, coach, physical therapist, psychologist, etc., but not with other players. What do you think of this trend?**

It's a necessity in one way. Andy Roddick is so strong at such a young age. He probably can't handle it and gets hurt all the time. You make enough money these days that it's worth it to be healthy all the time and bring guys [physical therapists] with you. But what these players don't understand — because they've never experienced it — is that you learn so much from your peers. I practiced with Nyström a lot. He gave me so many tips on what I was doing wrong because it was so much easier to tell when you're playing against somebody all the time and you're at the same level. He'd say, "You've got a little less zip on those backhands today than yesterday."

That's why we were so good in Sweden. We traveled together, we practiced together. We talked tennis all the time. We brought up a lot of important points about our games. The coach is not going to pick it up because he's standing next to the player and he can't really see it. So the current trend is a bad thing. There's too much individualism today.

**Would you please tell me about your charity work.**

I've been involved in an Irish charity called GOAL for about sixteen, seventeen years. It provides aid to catastrophic areas of the world. We used to go to Ireland to play an exhibition on grass before Wimbledon — me and Joakim Nystrom against Matt Doyle and Sean Sorenson, from Ireland, for the first two years. And eventually we had almost everyone in the top ten: McEnroe, Cash, Edberg, Tim Mayotte, and all the Swedes. Everyone came and supported the cause. I've done a lot of things for them, and they've done a lot of things for me.

**Please tell me about your other charity work.**

DebrA is the [New York City-based] organization that was formed to fight the skin disease, Epidermolysis Bullosa, that my son has. We're trying to help out as much as we can. We've done tennis and golf tournaments at the Westchester Country Club for the past three Octobers. My son has the mildest form of it, and he doesn't need any help. But once you get involved and you see all the other kids . . . once you start helping, you just can't stop.

That's why the lives of [some of] the people in India are unbearable and horrible, but at the same time, the kids in India have a smile on their faces. Whereas, the kids in the Western world do not always have a smile on their faces. They're pissed off about something. Little things irritate a kid in the modern world compared to Third World kids because they don't have anything to get irritated or angry about. All they care about is getting another plate of food.

There is a bigger chance you'll become a great human being coming from the Third World country than from the modern world, for sure. They're so desperate to survive, whereas we take it for granted.

**Last year Andre Agassi said, "There is too much money in the game nowadays." But Yevgeny Kafelnikov complained that "the money on the ATP [tour] is ridiculous compared to what other athletes are making." Who is right?**

They're *both* right. There is too much money in tennis, but at the same time sports people should be paid more than actors. They do more. They certainly work harder. There's too much money in sports, period. But Kafelnikov is right in a way, too. You play NBA basketball or other pro sports, and you're paid [on average] two to three million dollars a year. In tennis, you're *not* making that much money, unless you're a top 5 player in the world. But Agassi is right as well. There's not only too much money in tennis; there's too much money in sports. That money hurts Kafelnikov because fans watch Yevgeny who doesn't look like he has the drive to become the best player in the world. Why? Because he's won too much money. And money is all he cares about. Actually, Kafelnikov is totally right because we used to have contracts with clothes and shoes and rackets [companies]. And I know there are guys out there close to the top ten, and they don't have endorsement contracts for anything.

**How could tennis be going backwards in this important respect?**

I'm not sure. But so many sports compete with tennis today. Soccer will always appeal to people because it's a simple sport and so old and historical. Tennis is pretty expensive, and it's not what the world is promoting today. The world is not promoting a one-against-one, eye-for-an-eye kind of attitude, and I'm going to kick the shit out of you. That's not how we're trying to get our kids to live their lives. We're trying to get them to live together, be happy and do your own thing. Tennis is the opposite of what we want our kids to be.

**Yannick Noah once said, "When there are 10,000 people in the stands, we are all actors. There is the serious one, the one who always screams at the umpire, the one who never says a word, the one who is a clown." Would you please describe the roles played by today's leading actors.**

If you just keep the intensity in a match, then it's interesting for the crowd to watch a guy who cares. Agassi has a rap that is really weird. He's not a fun player to watch; he's a fun *person* to watch. He's very upbeat. At some point he was the rebel, the clown, the showman, or whatever. What did he ever do? I think it was just the long hair and the clothes and the Nike and Canon marketing. They just marketed him as whatever people think he is today. He's much more down-to-earth and normal than people think he is. Professional athletes today feel they're not as much entertainers as we felt we were. They don't care about the crowd that much. It's very rare to see anyone have any interaction with the crowd these days, except for Lleyton Hewitt and Agassi.

**Roddick seems more extroverted. He likes to connect with the fans and loves to sign autographs after matches. Could Roddick bring back the entertainment aspect?**

Yeah. He could. There are entertainers in a way, but we cared more then, or looked like we cared more. I haven't seen anybody care as much as Jimmy Connors or John McEnroe cared—except Lleyton Hewitt. Roddick is a great player and a great guy, I love his attitude. But being that hyper is not what you want tennis players to be either.

**Why do many players lack intensity?**

How can you have intensity if you're like Pete Sampras and hit twenty aces? The point is all over before it starts. Jimmy Connors is intense because he gets to hit thirty balls every point, and he's fighting, and he can't reach every ball with his two hands, and he's grunting. That's intensity. So you can't blame Pete Sampras for not being intense because how could he be with his game? He makes it all look so easy because he's such a great natural athlete. Sports goes in cycles. You got the big guys, the small guys, the undemonstrative guys, the entertainers. It's going to keep changing all the time.

**In 1986, you told *The New York Times*, "We are not like Americans, we don't have Jimmy Connors's fighting spirit. Everyone has a temper, but in Sweden, no one**

throws a racket or screams. We show more manners and common sense. This is a game, not war." Since Swedes have been hugely successful in the past thirty years, do they have the ideal temperament for tennis?

We have a very good temperament for tennis because of our upbringing. The living standards were very high, and at the same time we were basically not a communist country but close to it. There was very little pressure put on kids to perform in school. School is free, hospital care is free, everyone has a new car and a new TV and VCR. Even the guy who doesn't have a job has the same things. There was very little pressure put on kids to succeed or to fail. So it got to the point where I wasn't afraid of failing. I was just trying as hard as I can. I knew my parents and my club believed in me. We grew up in a very secure environment without it making you lazy or scared of success. That's what Sweden had going for itself back then. Because it wasn't just tennis. It had great athletes in general for a little country. It's amazing.

**In 1999 you said, "John McEnroe, Ivan Lendl, and Jimmy Connors weren't the nicest people in the world, they were the most selfish players, but they were great for the game. Tennis needs players who don't care about pleasing sponsors, who don't care about being nice." Since you are considered a nice guy, why did you say that?**

I do agree with that. That's what's missing now. Andy Roddick is great. But what they really need is basically a guy who is an asshole and who really cares and shows that he cares. And he doesn't give a shit if people like him or not. You need guys that people like as well. But I do believe that's why people are watching the NCAA [college basketball] more than the NBA because the intensity of the players is twice as high. The NCAA "Final Four" is more intense than the NBA Finals.

You can see it in the guy's eyes. If he's intense, that's what you want to watch. That's what you need in tennis because it's a one-on-one sport. It's all mental. You don't have to play better than the [other] guy in tennis, and you can still beat him. If you lose that, then you lose the strength in tennis. Look at Hewitt. It's amazing what he can do being so little, just because he has an attitude, a mentality, that nobody else has.

**Pete Sampras has won a record seven Wimbledons, four U.S. Opens, and two Australians as well as five ATP World Championships, one Italian Open, two Nasdaq-100 Opens, and two Davis Cup titles. Does all that make Sampras the greatest player of all time?**

I don't think so. His record is unquestioned. When he played well, he was easily the best player I've ever seen. You cannot do anything against Pete Sampras when he plays well on hard courts and on grass. But he never did anything on clay. Björn did it all. He did clay, he did grass, he did hard courts. He didn't win the U.S. Open, which is really weird, but he got to four finals. Pete Sampras is a more accomplished player than Borg was technically. But Borg somehow managed to play [well] on all surfaces. And that's why Rod Laver was such a great player.

**So you'd give the edge to either Borg or Laver over Sampras?**

Let's put it this way. Sampras played the best tennis ever and he won thirteen Slams.

Nobody has ever hit the ball like him. And nobody has a chance against him when he plays well on his favorite surfaces. But I don't like the fact that Pete Sampras couldn't play on clay. The greatest player ever is not necessarily the player who has won the most. I would say Björn Borg is the greatest player ever because he won Wimbledon five times in a row. And out of those five times, he won the French Open all of those five years (sic), plus another year. How do you beat that? That's *great*!

**You helped Sweden win three Davis Cup titles, in 1984, `85 and `87; and you played twenty-seven ties in eleven years. What were your best and worst moments?**

My best moments were beating the United States in the final in `84 when you guys came with John and Jimmy. We won on clay in Sweden, which seems like we were cheating, I guess. That was the greatest Davis Cup tie. The lowest was losing to [West] Germany at home in 1988 on clay having Edberg and me. He won Wimbledon that year when I won the other three [Grand Slam titles]. We were No. 1 and No. 2 in the world, and we couldn't beat [West] Germany at home on clay. That's when I thought I was done [as a top player]. I lost to Carl-Uwe Steeb when I was No. 1 in the world. And I just couldn't care less really about that match, even though it was Davis Cup. That is not right to say, but that is the way I felt. I cared, but it was not that important. That's the lowest I've ever felt on a tennis court.

**In a 1990 ESPN "Sports Profile," you said, "The most important things for me, in terms of tennis, is that I want more people to play tennis because I think it's a great sport. And that's the way I want to be remembered. It's that people are going to say, 'I started playing because of Mats, Mats Wilander.'" Did that actually become your greatest legacy?**

I don't know. But that's how you like to be remembered. I don't want to be remembered for anything else. If there is one person out there who started playing tennis because of me, yes, that's how I'd like to be remembered.

**No member of the Swedish media attended the 2002 Australian Open that Thomas Johansson won. Why has Sweden, a once-powerful tennis nation, seemingly lost interest in tennis?**

Are you serious?

**Yes.**

The press corp just lost interest. I can't figure it out. We had such a good run from '75 when Björn started winning to '92 when Stefan stopped winning. It was one amazing achievement after another on all levels, even going to Mikael Pernfors' winning the NCAA [title] two years in a row. I think the press got very spoiled. Sweden is a working-class country, and they were eventually getting sick of these tennis players and all the money they were making. They started caring [only] about soccer and hockey again, which are our two biggest sports by far. Imagine if we were as good in hockey as we are in tennis. Soccer and ice hockey are what is in people's blood in Sweden, not tennis.

**You were once vice president of the ATP Players Council. In your opinion, what have been the ATP Tour's biggest accomplishments and shortcomings in the past thirteen years?**

The biggest accomplishment is that they were able to get the [ATP] Tour going. I was very instrumental in getting the Tour going, not administratively, but just being the top player that supported it. And there was not really anybody else supporting it, which was shocking to me at the time. That's great. The ATP and the players had the vision. The worst part of what the ATP has done in the last thirteen years is the TV deal they made. I was in Hamburg three years ago. I was coaching Wayne Ferreira and got really sick. And I thought this is perfect: I can lie in bed on a Friday and watch four quarterfinals at the German Open. There was Kuerten, Moyá, Roís, Haas. It wasn't on TV! How can the German Open not be on regular TV in Germany? It was on some cable channel that reaches [only] 600,000 people in a country that has eighty million people, and they're tennis-crazy. You see, that's not how you promote the game. You don't promote the players like that. What are they going to do when Agassi and Sampras eventually quit? Because those are the only players who are recognizable.

**The latest ATP idea to save doubles is by replacing the entire deciding set with a super tiebreaker. And Butch Buchholz recently said the super tiebreaker should replace the fifth set in men's singles. What do you think of this rule change proposal?**

Certainly you can never take a fifth set out and only play a tiebreaker. That would be totally out of the question. They're experimenting with it in doubles. But doubles is a great game and should not be changed. The only thing they should change in doubles is that the players should *play* it. They should make guys play doubles. Or you should benefit from being the [composite] No. 1 player in the world in both singles and doubles, an extra five million, or two million [bonus], or whatever it takes. If they can't get the best players to play doubles, who cares if doubles specialists play three [full] sets or a tiebreaker because they're not playing on the show courts anyway.

**In 1998 you criticized tennis leaders for trying to tamper with the rules and traditions of the game, saying, "It's time tennis authorities accepted that the game goes in cycles. It is always changing and that is one of the things about it that appeals. If they want to make all these changes, they are going to spoil its complexity and make it like any other sport. I am not in favor of that." Should the ATP heed your words of wisdom once again?**

> You know, they've tried so many things [reforms] in tennis, and nothing ever works. They tried to have music during the changeovers. That's not what tennis is about. The biggest mistake the ATP is making is that they're trying to appeal to every person in the world. And tennis is not a sport that should be watched by every person. You cannot have 50,000 people watching tennis [in a stadium]. You should take care of your fans.

**Would you please elaborate?**

> Tennis is too complicated, too difficult a sport to attract every person from different walks of life. Golf is much easier to understand. A guy hits a 300-yard drive, which is amazing, or he hits the ball near the hole from 100 yards, or he can chip it in. It's very basic. Tennis is not basic. And if you make it into something "pop," like NHL kind of thing or NBA where there's a lot of things going on, you're going to lose the traditionalists. And tradition is what tennis is about. If you try hard to appeal to everybody, you end up appealing to nobody.

**What about other rule change proposals?**

> The proposal to allow only one serve is horrific. What tennis is about is two serves. If you want to change something to reduce the big server's advantage, you make the service box six inches shorter. Make it a foot shorter. That's all you have to do. Sure, a bigger guy is still going to have a bigger serve. But if you make the service box smaller, it's harder to hit aces and service winners. And that's what the problem is. You just can't take the serve away and have only one serve.

**Why does playing on the senior tour appeal to you?**

> It appeals to me to hang out with my old friends. It appeals to me to play tennis under relaxed circumstances in front of an appreciative crowd. When you play against Leconte or Noah, you can just feel they are so happy to be out there. And they really appreciate that they're being given a chance to still be able to show off their skills. You feel like you want everyone to have such a good time. It makes you feel so good about yourself and about the game. It's a totally different mindset from playing on the ATP Tour.

**Do you think you can take over the No. 1 spot from the aging (forty-three) John McEnroe?**

No, I don't. But it doesn't bother me. The senior circuit is not about being No. 1 in the world. The rankings are not that important. The event is the most important thing. How can you get a [top] ranking when you don't have a chance to play *all* the tournaments? You don't get invited to all of them. At the same time I hate playing against John more than I ever have before.

**Why is that?**

He's a better player now than when he was at his best. He is practicing harder. He never used to practice at all. The worst thing you could ever hope for at a tournament was to be signed up for a warm-up with John McEnroe because he was known for hitting between six and nine minutes, and then he's done, gone. How can you warm up like that? Now he's always the first guy out there on the practice court. He plays a lot, every day pretty much for a couple of hours. He hits the ball better than he ever has. He's got better technique. If he saw his technique now, I swear he would say, "Geez, how did I play like *that* before, when I know how to play like this now?" So he's really tough to beat now.

**Women's tennis has been tremendously successful recently. Is there anything that men's tennis can learn from women's tennis?**

Yeah! Women dress a lot better than men. It would be nice if the men got some of the old-fashioned, tight, good-looking stuff back. The men have great physiques, but with the baggy clothing you can't see it. You should show off your physical strength and muscles. A match between two well-dressed guys makes tennis a lot more interesting because it's one-on-one and basically you're on a stage.

The biggest thing is the rivalries among the top eight ladies. You can sense they don't want to lose to anybody. You can sense they feel that "If I lose to her in this tournament, that means she's got the edge over me, come Paris, come Wimbledon." And you just don't get that feeling when the guys are playing. What the women have going for them is that they really care now. That's why they're so much fun to see.

---

**FASCINATING FACTS:**

- When Mats Wilander coached Marat Safin, he taught the volatile Russian to avoid hitting the fence posts when he threw his rackets at the back fence.

- In 1989 Mats Wilander, who won seven Grand Slam titles but never Wimbledon, contended, "You can't be considered a great player unless you win Wimbledon."

- In 2002 Mats Wilander asserted that tennis needs to be played on "the slowest surface possible."

# 30

# This Woody Keeps on Winning—Knock on Wood

# 2002

*"If you remember only one thing, remember that doubles is a little like marriage: nothing destroys the partnership faster than a lack of communication."*

—Harry Hopman, captain of fifteen championship Australian Davis Cup teams, in his
1975 book, *Lobbing into the Sun*

The Woodies. For a decade those two words signified doubles domination almost as complete as that of Pete Sampras and Steffi Graf in singles.

Todd Woodbridge and Mark Woodforde hail from a nation not only with a long and fervent tennis tradition—Australia boasts the highest percentage of players to total population of any country—but also with a passion for recreational doubles. Not surprisingly, most of the premier doubles teams in history come from this remote warm-weather island nation of only 19 million denizens. Bromwich and Quist, Sedgman and McGregor, Newcombe and Roche, and Emerson with several partners rapaciously racked up doubles crowns during the middle of the last century. The Woodies belong in that doubles pantheon, and some believe at the top of it.

In *Australian Tennis Magazine* two years ago, Tennis Australia president Geoff Pollard acclaimed Woodbridge and Woodforde as "the greatest doubles pairing in the history of the game." Pollard praised them as "national icons" who "re-defined the art of playing doubles."

In an era of get-it-over-quick slugging, The Wondrous Woodies parlayed skill, teamwork, poise and, smarts—1970s Aussie standout Ray Ruffels once called the Woodies "the most clever team I've ever seen"—to capture an Open Era-record eleven Grand Slam titles and an all-time record sixty-one doubles titles.

After Woodforde retired, Woodbridge united with dynamic Swede Jonas Björkman. They've notched Australian and Wimbledon crowns, as Woodbridge continues his doubles assault on the record book.

In this interview Woodbridge, the respected president of the ATP Players Council in 2001–2002, candidly assesses his storied career, fearlessly critiques the ATP Tour's handling of the current doubles crisis, and astutely proposes remedies to revitalize once-glorious doubles.

*Sports Illustrated* **magazine called you "perhaps the greatest doubles player of all time." You rank fourth in Grand Slam men's doubles titles with thirteen, behind John Newcombe, Roy Emerson, and Adrian Quist, but ahead of John Bromwich, Tony Roche, and John McEnroe. How do you rate yourself in this pantheon of doubles champions?**

I am completely honored to be amongst them. Comparisons are very difficult because you can only be the best in the generation you're playing against. I don't have the right to say I'm better than Newcombe or Roche or Quist or any of those guys. As an Australian, to be put in the same category as those champions is good enough for me.

**When I asked John McEnroe a very similar question five years ago, he answered, "There's no one up there who I feel was a better player than I was in doubles."**

(Laughter) That's probably more of an American attitude than an Australian attitude. If I came out with that response in Australia, I'd get my head knocked off by most of the other guys. But, to be honest, I think I could hold my own against all those players. Wimbledon brought out a doubles video this year in which McEnroe said he would have loved to play against the Woodies. I say likewise

*"The Woodies" hoist up the U.S. Open doubles title.* Courtesy of the International Tennis Hall of Fame & Museum, Newport, Rhode Island

because the tennis would have been fantastic, great matches, tight matches. And that's what I've always enjoyed.

**You and fellow Australian Mark Woodforde teamed up from 1990 to 2000 and won six Wimbledon, one French, two Australian, and two U.S. titles, plus Olympic gold and silver medals, an Open Era-record sixty-one doubles titles, and boasted a 14–2 doubles record and one title in Davis Cup. What made you an outstanding team?**

We communicated very well with each other both on and off the court. We knew what we were doing was like a business and we had to be professional. We had our moments when he hacked each other off and would have liked to have gone another way. But we realized we had something that was too good. The next point was we almost always found a way to win a match. That's what all champions in singles and doubles do. If we had lost once or twice to teams, we rarely lost a third time. Tactically, I think we were fantastic. Thirdly, we played great in big matches, better than at any other time in the tournament. (In 1993 Woodbridge broke John McEnroe's 1979–80 record of nineteen doubles titles without losing in a final, winning twenty-one in a row.)

**Despite a six-year age spread and differing personalities, you and Mark got along well on and off the court. What are the keys to getting along well with your doubles partner at any level?**

It's one word—communication. Anytime Mark and I held something in and didn't let each other know how we felt, we never played well together. Then one guy was always a little annoyed and didn't let it flow. When we had our worst year in 1999, it looked like we were on the way out. I sat down with Mark and said, "I don't think we should play anymore if we were going to keep playing like this." He looked at me in shock. Then I said, "But I'm willing to work at it, and let's set some new goals." And that was when [in 2000] we ended up winning a French and Wimbledon, the Davis Cup, and finishing [our partnership] with an Olympics silver medal in Sydney. That was probably our most memorable year. And it happened because we laid our cards on the table and said, "This is the way it is. What are we going to do about it?"

**What accomplishments or records are you most proud of?**

I have a lot, obviously. (Laughter) One achievement that is fulfilling to me is that I've been able to win another couple majors [titles] with a different partner. Because it meant I was able to adapt. Winning Wimbledon this year with Jonas was a big thrill. Mark and I felt like that was our property, and it was, I guess. But to do it again there with a new partner was my individual best as a doubles player. I'm also really proud of winning five Wimbledon in a row with Mark. It's the biggest, most prestigious tournament on our calendar. To win it five in a row and nearly six—in the sixth final we lost 10-8 in the fifth—was our greatest achievement.

**Jonas Björkman and you have successfully paired up for the past two years, winning the 2001 Australian and 2002 Wimbledon and five other titles. How does Jonas compare to Mark as a partner?**

They are totally different. Mark was unbelievably consistent, a superb volleyer, and had terrific second shots. Jonas is more athletic around the net. He intercepts better. Jonas has a more one-hit serve return than Mark had, but Mark had a return with something in mind for a second shot. The reason I chose to play with Jonas is that I didn't like playing against him. He put a lot of pressure on me, and I'd rather have him on my side of the net. And I felt our games could blend well together to win majors. We're not as consistent as Mark and I were. But when we have our best days, we may even be a bit better because we are a bit more explosive.

**Two-handed backhands, semi-Western forehands, and the sharp decrease in serve and volleyers have dramatically changed the way singles is played in the past generation. How has doubles changed since you played it as a kid back in the 1980s when you captured a record seven Grand Slam junior doubles titles?**

There is less finesse now than there was then. Because of the points you just made, guys tend to just pound the ball. They don't try to work the ball and get the ball low and set up the net man and use as many lobs and create openings on the court. That has to do with the way technique has changed. They have better coaching and they play better than they did in the `70s and `80s, so they're able to do more right off the bat with the [service] return. There's not as much thinking about where to place a ball to set a point up. Now players try more to finish a point with one shot.

**That being the case, is doubles played at a higher level today than before?**

In the early and mid-`90s, there were better matches than at the start of this century. Fitzgerald-Jarryd and Eltingh-Haarhuis were superb teams and would have done well in any era. The mid-`90s, especially, had a lot of very good teams.

**When Pete Sampras thrashed you 6-2, 6-1, 7-6 in the 1997 Wimbledon semis, you said, "Sampras is human, but not by much." Would you please tell me what it is like playing Sampras?**

You're playing someone that you know if you hit your best shot, it's coming back better. That's what it's like. What made him the greatest player was his second serve. He would miss his first serve, but he knew he could [still] go for a free point because he had the best second serve in the world. On grass, it was so difficult to beat the guy because he would just bide his time and chip returns and then come over them, and he'd find a way to break you. And he knew he'd never lose his serve. That was the hardest part about playing Pete on any surface, but particularly on grass. That's why he has the record he has.

**In your opinion, is Sampras the greatest player of all time?**

He's the greatest player I've ever played against. In that Wimbledon, I played fantastic tennis. I made the semis. And I still played reasonably well in that semifinal. I was only one of two people to break Sampras's serve in the whole tournament, out of something like 96 service games. That year was probably the best he ever played. In the final he killed [Cédric] Pioline easier than he beat me.

**You like and admire current world No. 1 Lleyton Hewitt. This year you said, "I don't know of any player who doesn't wish he had some of Lleyton's mongrel." What exactly did you mean by that?**

He gives 110 percent every time he walks on the court. That what Connors did. That's what Lleyton fights like. And he does not give you any free points. It wears people down. And now it wears them down *even before* they play the first point. Because they wonder if they can stay with him in that department. Like last week when he won [the Tennis Masters Cup] in Shanghai. He wasn't physically at his best, but he manages to win. He finds a way to grind the guy, to wear him down. His mental strength is phenomenal. His desire to win is the "mongrel" part I was talking about. He can't bear to lose.

**For twenty-four of the past twenty-five years, the winner of the Davis Cup final has also won the pivotal doubles match. That being the case, is it not in the best national interest of tennis federations around the world to promote doubles and develop topnotch doubles teams?**

Absolutely. Unfortunately, the ITF cut out the opportunity to use regular doubles teams [in Davis Cup] and create doubles teams by adding the rule allowing substitution for singles matches. In the last year [2000] the Woodies played together, I could not play Davis Cup because we had Rafter, Philippoussis, and Hewitt for substitution singles. They all played the right court, and we had Mark [Woodforde] who was a left-court player in doubles. So Australia had the best doubles team in the world, and it wasn't able to use it in Davis Cup. If the Davis Cup opted to allow five team members—and now teams always have a reserve sitting on the bench anyway—nations could concentrate on working on a doubles team for Davis Cup and have singles players as well. Then the Davis Cup would be the best competition in the world. By disallowing some of the best doubles players now, the competition isn't doing itself justice.

**After winning a Davis Cup doubles match with André Sáagainst Canada, Gustavo Kuerten said, "I always have fun playing doubles. Everything happens so fast—**

**you have to be really quick." Do you think other singles stars would have fun, too, if they played doubles more often?**

Yes, I do. And they would become better players as well. Jonas and I played Guga and Cédric Pioline in Paris in the last [doubles] tournament of the year, and we lost to them. Guga always returns serve from ten feet behind the baseline in singles and struggles against the likes of Rusedski and other good serve and volleyers because he goes back, back, back into the fence. Against us it was noticeable that he was returning from the baseline and working on his returns. And that can only benefit him the next time he plays Max Mirnyi and Wayne Arthurs and all the guys who give him trouble. His volleying and anticipation around the net will also improve because of the net duels in doubles. There is no better place to sharpen your singles game than in doubles. If you go out and practice three hours a day after you've lost in singles, there's no pressure on you. But in doubles there are break points for and against you, second serves, linesmen, all kinds of situations. There's still pressure.

**The movement to reduce power in pro tennis during the past decade has obscured and, ironically, even contributed to a true crisis: the near extinction of the serve and volleyer in singles. How did this crisis happen?**

Cries of too much power and too few rallies, especially from uneducated segments of the tennis media, have persuaded tennis leaders to slow the game down considerably. That change could damage the game more than anything else has in the past 100 years. It happened because balls have changed significantly in size, pressure, and thickness of the cover. The surfaces have also been altered. When Wimbledon changes the blend of grass to provide a surface that bounces higher and slower, we know we have trouble. When you consider that for the first time in history, not one serve and volley point was played in the [2002] Wimbledon men's final, you realize how quickly this change has happened and how disastrous it is. These changes have all but taken away the serve-and-volley aspect of the game, and thus tennis has lost much of its beauty, skill, and athleticism. That loss is as terrible for tennis as it would be if all of a sudden the forward pass was abandoned in American pro football.

**How can tennis leaders reverse this destructive trend?**

There are two ways to alter this slide. Officials need to realize that the game *must* have variation. Clay courts, hard courts, and grass courts — slow, medium, and fast surfaces—create an attractive diversity of playing styles. By slowing up the balls and courts, they have all but killed the serve-and-volley player. It has become impossible to serve and volley and approach the net on anything less than a perfect shot when the surface gives the opponent a ball that sits up and says hit me every time. Second, coaches must make their junior players play more doubles. Doubles is the avenue to learn about volleying and the net. When you consider that the USTA doesn't play a doubles event along with the singles at their national junior championships, it is little wonder after McEnroe, hardly any Americans, with the exception of Sampras, have played the net well.

**Talking about pro tennis players today, 1950s champion and Tennis Hall of Famer Tony Trabert commented, "They're the least accessible athletes that I know of. You can't get to them. They spend very little time talking to the press. That hurts them, hurts the game, because you don't get to know them as well." Is Trabert right?**

I agree with that, for sure. There obviously has to be some sort of limit, but honestly, most of the great players are quite young, for instance, Lleyton Hewitt. Most other sports have more mature athletes in age, and they are able to handle these situations. Tennis doesn't. Tennis is a multi-national sport. You cannot control cultures and the way people are brought up. I also lay some blame on the agents because it's an agent's job to educate players to perform at their best, to help them with their schedules, to teach them to invest their money. The agents are their guardians. Nearly every top junior has signed with a management company at eighteen or nineteen. I don't think agents are educating young players about what will happen to them if they become great players.

**Carol Seheult, a clinical and sports psychologist who works with elite athletes and their partners, asserts, "It takes a special kind of woman to be the wife of a top-class tennis player, especially these days. It's a horrible life, and not glamorous at all. You are constantly living out of a suitcase, packing and unpacking, with no privacy. Your life is ruled by the demands of sponsors, coaches, and fitness trainers. It is far from easy." You've been married to Natasha for nearly eight years. Is the life of a tennis wife really horrible?**

(Laughter) She'd probably say yes. It has its moments—incredible highs and incredible lows. And, let me tell you, it takes a special person to be able to cope with it. Because one day you win a match, and you think you're the best in the world, and the next day you lose, and you think you're the pits. And she has to deal with those roller-coaster emotions. My wife is a sports psychologist, a friend, a partner, a lover. She has had to deal every role that has been thrown at her. It is not easy to deal with a professional athlete. We made a pact when we were very young and agreed we were doing this for a goal that we've now reached. We have two beautiful children [Zara Rose and Beau Andrew] and a lovely house and a lifestyle we like. That was the goal we shared, and she had to give up what were her goals. That's the kind of partner you need to find. I got lucky and was able to. [But] I wouldn't recommend being a tennis wife as a glamorous lifestyle, I'll put it that way.

**So you give Natasha high marks for handling it.**

Oh, absolutely. Natasha has traveled with me most of my career and has been there for the highs and lows. I've had lots of highs and a lot of lows. My wife has been outstanding. And we have fantastic memories and gained a lot out of what we've done together. I wouldn't change the way we've done it. It would be interesting to ask her whether she would. (Laughter) I'm pretty sure she agrees with me.

**You achieved a career Grand Slam in mixed doubles, capturing six Grand Slam titles with four different partners—Liz Smylic, Arantxa Sánchez Vicario, Helena Suková and Rennae Stubbs. Whom did you enjoy playing with most?**

I enjoyed playing with Arantxa a lot because she had a great attitude. She was a fantastically positive person. That was important because I got down on myself a lot. Mixed [doubles] is the most difficult game I've ever played. (Laughter) In the pro ranks it doesn't matter how well the guy plays. If the girl plays really well, then you win. If she doesn't play really well, then it's tough for you to win. It's very frustrating.

**Who was your best partner?**

Helena Suková—when she was playing at her best. She had bad days, though. She was a lot taller than I was, she had a great serve and a good volley, and she lobbed unbelievably well. On her day, she was the best.

**Were you, one of history's greatest men's doubles players, ever outplayed by your mixed doubles partner?**

Sometimes, yeah! I wouldn't say I was outplayed for a whole match. In the [1994] Wimbledon final with Suková, she kept us in the match until I started to play well, and in the third set I played great, and we finished it off. I'll say that I've been outplayed by girls for a set. They can play.

**Who are the best doubles teams that you faced during your 14-year pro career?**

The best was [John] Fitzgerald and [Anders] Järryd. Mark and I played them in our youth as a partnership. They were fantastic. Järryd was a great returner, and Fitzy put so much pressure on you when he was at the net. They combined well together. They were probably the best team in the early 1990s. Then came [Jacco] Eltingh and [Paul] Haarhuis. We had epic battles with them at Wimbledon and the U.S. Open. At the Olympics we had an epic 16-14 in the third-set match against them in the semis.

**You have been president of the ATP Player Council in 2001–2002. What is your position on ATP policies toward doubles in recent years?**

Our goal is to get the Tour back to one whole, where you play both singles and doubles. The new rules are intended to deter nineteen- and twenty-year-old players who are struggling in singles from thinking they can do OK and make a living out of doubles. I call it the "tanking the career singles syndrome" which is trying to be a doubles-only player. We have twenty doubles-only players on the circuit from Australia, and the majority of them are under twenty-six. The reforms in place are going to stop that.

**In 2003 doubles draws with twenty-four teams will be reduced to sixteen teams, and draws with thirty-two and twenty-eight teams will be reduced to twenty-four. Would you agree that all reductions of doubles draws are bad to some degree?**

Sure. I would much prefer that we didn't have any reductions at all. Some indoor tournaments have too few courts for the amount of time that matches take. But when you have outdoor tournaments that generally have more courts, I don't understand why tournaments need *less* matches. This is one of the arguments tournament directors make: they don't need as many doubles matches. I don't understand why.

**In 2003 only half of the doubles spots in twenty-four-team draws will be reserved for players with legitimate doubles records and rankings. Isn't it unfair to have the thirteenth through twenty-fourth best available doubles teams potentially replaced by singles players?**

I don't disagree with that. I can't give you an adequate answer except that in trying to negotiate to keep the doubles game alive and not resort to super tiebreakers replacing the third set and not take away any more prize money, that was the point they got to. If I entered with Lleyton Hewitt, we would take a singles spot, which means another doubles team is getting in. In the case of two singles guys, they will take a singles spot. The policy that came about at the Moscow meetings was a little bit of damage control for doubles. If we didn't have all this stuff, it would be fantastic, but we had to do something.

**In 2003 Tennis Masters Series tournaments are reducing the allocation of doubles prize money from 22 percent to 17 percent of the total. Is that sharp reduction acceptable because the Tour is hurting financially?**

Well, that's what had to happen. What the doubles prize money has gone to now is the same split that the Tour had before the ATP Tour began in 1990—17 percent for doubles.

**If that's the case, then it was wrong then, too.**

Yes, it definitely was. I think doubles prize money increased then because total prize money went up and they decided to put a little more into the doubles purse as well. I learned this recently, and it surprised me.

**What about the ATP's decision to abolish doubles qualifying events?**

I totally disagree with that. It's appalling that you don't give people that opportunity. I look at it as young players getting an opportunity to qualify, people trying to break in and get better. You're not allowing them to do that, and that's something I'm dead against. The U.S. Open is one tournament that can get away with that. It has no men's or women's or mixed doubles qualifying.

**Since the U.S. Open gives out only 10 percent of its $160 million gross income in prize money—which is extremely low for tennis tournaments and other sporting events—isn't awarding prize money for those three qualifying events quite reasonable and affordable?**

That [sixteen million prize money] figure includes singles qualifying prize money. To add another $500,000 prize money for those three qualifying events would be peanuts out of the $160 million. Can you imagine the USGA not having any sectionals and regionals qualifying to get into the U.S. Open championships?

**Starting at the 2003 event in Houston, the season-ending Tennis Masters Cup will feature the top eight singles players and doubles teams for the first time since 1985. What is your reaction to that policy change?**

It's great! Highlighting singles and doubles together is much better. Obviously doubles is not the star event, but it's going to be showcased as the lead-off event before the singles. We discussed this with some players who competed in the '80s at Madison Square Garden, and they felt it was a really great event where all the doubles guys felt they were part of the whole tour. It created a very positive atmosphere. The season-ending doubles championships in Hartford and Indonesia just weren't successful. We have to get doubles back to where it used to be. All the tennis fans, the real tennis fans, love doubles. The people that play it, the people who buy the tickets for the first few days of the tournament before the corporate people eat them [the tickets] up. We have to keep doubles so they can enjoy that part of the game as well.

**In *Tennis Week*, Michael Mewshaw wrote, "A personal confession: I don't play doubles, and I don't especially enjoy seeing it. But even if I did, it strikes me as specious to argue that people will pay to watch what they play. Most Americans who play basketball on a recreational basis after their school years stick to a half court game with two or three players per team. Yet I don't notice anybody calling for the NBA to repackage its game. Nor do I notice anyone profitably marketing the downsized product." What do you think of non-player Mewshaw's analogy and reasoning?**

It sounds like an uninformed, uneducated opinion from someone who has never played doubles. Doubles has been an integral part of tennis from the very beginning. It's part of the history of the sport. And it's not a pick-up game like Mewshaw is mentioning in basketball. To say people don't like to watch doubles is quite silly. The truth is the opposite of what he claims. The fact that people play doubles makes them more knowledgeable and enthusiastic about watching doubles because they appreciate the skills and athleticism that go into it.

**Luke Jensen, the 1993 French Open doubles champion with his brother Murphy, in *The New York Times*, argued, "The day of the doubles specialist is gone. You have to streamline. You have to get rid of people who do not sell tickets. The Woodies are rare, and so are the Jensen brothers." Is the money bottom line really the only bottom line for doubles?**

I don't believe it is, totally. Sure, it's got to be an issue for some tournaments. I call doubles "the insurance package of the tournament." I can't tell you how many night sessions where the Woodies played to back up a weak singles match and gave the fans a lot of pleasure. People wouldn't buy tickets to those things if they didn't have an extra bit to watch sometimes. In Madrid in October Jiří Novák forfeited the singles final, and fortunately doubles was showcased there with a best-of-five-set match between Bhupathi-Paes and Knowles-Nestor, two Grand Slam champion teams. And they played to a packed house.

**But even if there isn't a weak singles match, doesn't doubles provide plenty of entertainment of its own?**

Yeah, I believe people do want to come and watch doubles. It's a welcome addition to the tournament. Doubles may not sell tickets directly, but it certainly adds to the value of an event. And thus it's important to have it.

**What other constructive solutions do you suggest for the doubles crisis?**

We've tried to get tournaments to play the doubles finals before the singles final. But directors counter that they need the doubles match afterwards in case something goes wrong in singles. Our hands get tied, whenever we give them something new to consider, because they say, "I've got live TV at 2, and I'd like to put doubles on in case I've got nothing to put on. We need a back-up." But we've started doubles at noon on a couple of occasions and had a good final. We started with not so many spectators and finished with a great crowd. That's like the warmup event for the singles final. It's like going to a concert and having a guy play before Bruce Springsteen, or whoever else you go to watch. That happens all the time, and it gets people in the mood for the main act. That's the perfect thing for doubles.

**How about a doubles final on Saturday?**

Sure. Saturday night, or any time on Saturday, would be great. Perhaps between the two singles semis. These are all scheduling issues that we've tried to get done. And tournaments reject them on the basis that they need us—as backups. That's the weird part of these discussions in recent years.

**Would it help to reduce the court changeover time in doubles from ninety to forty-five seconds to speed up matches and reduce "dead time"?**

Sure it would. Let's face it. I don't get tired playing doubles. Maybe in a five-set, four-hour match with pressure and nerves you do. That rule change would be good because you keep the match moving, you keep it fast and exciting. And that, in itself, will make it more attractive to watch in person and on TV.

**What about identical outfits for both players on a doubles team and players' names on the back of their shirts?**

I think so. I played a Davis Cup match in September against India, and the Indian team had their names on their backs. Leander Paes had "Leander" on the back, and the other players had their names. I didn't know three of the other guys, and by that [identification] I did. So if the spectators come across a player again, they'll know that guy and his name will stick in their heads. They'll know, for example, what [doubles standout] Kevin Ullyett looks like. That's a good idea.

**Do you have other constructive proposals?**

I believe doubles has not been marketed well. The Masters Series tournaments had daily glossy 6-, 7-, 8-page draw sheets that go into their tournament magazine that they sell. There is *never* a doubles article in that daily supplement. There are never profiles on Bjorkman, Woodbridge, Knowles, Nestor, etc. The ATP staff don't go out and market the job on site properly. People say, "I've never heard of [doubles star] Mark Knowles from the Bahamas." Well, why isn't Mark Knowles in the magazine for people to read about? Every player in the draw should have something, at least a short profile, written about him in the magazine prior to his playing. And then once the tournament starts, something should be written about the top four doubles teams and other teams that win, whether it's their results or where they're from, or anything interesting writers come up with. Instead, there is a picture of a guy stringing a racket in the stringing room and some other ridiculous stuff. If you want people to know about players, you've got to do a better job of publicizing them. And a lot of this comes down to the tournament staff and not only the ATP people.

**Mark Woodforde said his most memorable doubles match was the 1999 Davis Cup final against France in front of raucous spectators in Nice. You were down 6-1, 5-2 but rallied to win that match, and the next day Australia won the Davis Cup. Was that also your most memorable doubles match?**

That was the most defining match for us because it allowed us the next year to win the French Open, a tournament we had never won. We had always struggled on clay, mentally more than with our game. We tried so hard to win the French that it became nearly impossible. After coming back from a set and 5-2 down and then set points for two sets to love, we roared back to win comfortably. That gave us the belief on clay and let us relax going into Roland Garros.

**What then was your most memorable doubles match?**

When we beat Pete Sampras and Todd Martin in Washington in the semis of the Davis Cup in '97. That was the most memorable because at that stage of our career, Mark and I were under this cloud of "Well, they've won a lot, but they haven't really beaten the best." At that time Pete was No. 1 in the world and Todd was in the top ten. We were playing in the States before a vocal crowd and were down a set and a [service] break, and we turned it around and won. I felt from that day on we could say to anybody, "We are one of the best because we've beaten the best individuals." Sampras and Martin didn't have that good a doubles record, but that win gave us the pleasure of going back to people and saying, "I told you so."

---

**FASCINATING FACTS:**

- Todd Woodbridge confided to *Inside Sport* magazine in Australia that "It wasn't until I was 28 that I thought I was doing OK."
- In 2001 William Hill bookmakers no longer accepted bets on streakers at Wimbledon because some of those people who placed bets then ended up streaking.
- Before winning a doubles gold medal at the Atlanta Olympics, Todd Woodbridge was arrested because of an inadvertent altercation with an officious security guard.
- In 2002 Australia was the nation with the highest percent (9.5) of its people playing tennis.
- "All's fair in love and war and doubles," says 1980s doubles superstar Pam Shriver on her propensity for hitting doubles opponents who "ticked me off" by standing on the center service line when their partners returned her serve.

# 31

# A Pioneer and Promoter Who Shaped Open Tennis
## 1999

Only one character on our sport's swirling stage has been called "Tennis' Renaissance Man," "the most controversial figure in the game," *and* "the conscience of the tennis world." While not the most famous figure in the game, sixty-one-year-old New Yorker Gene Scott is undoubtedly the most eclectic. Scott's massive resume begins with his privileged, well-to-do background—his grandfather, Dr. Eugene C. Sullivan, headed a small group of scientists at the Corning Glass Works who invented Pyrex—and education at prep schools, Yale, and the University of Virginia Law School.

Scott soon made his mark as a Wall Street lawyer and outstanding amateur player, peaking with a No. 11 world ranking in 1965. When tennis entered its revolutionary Open Era in 1968, Scott plunged skillfully and zestfully into this brave new world of bountiful opportunity and challenge.

"I was like a kid in a candy store," recalls Scott, who became involved in virtually every area of the burgeoning sport. He promoted more than 150 men's and women's pro tournaments, including the prestigious Nabisco Masters and, since 1990, the Kremlin Cup; wrote and produced three award-winning documentary films on the U.S. Open; represented world-class players; did TV tennis commentary; co-founded the National Junior Tennis League; had tennis bylines in *The New York Times*, *Sports Illustrated* and *Esquire*; and authored *Björn Borg: My Life and My Game* (which hit No. 5 on the *London Times* best-seller list), *Tennis: Game of Motion,* and the just-published *OPEN!*.

Scott also was a consultant for companies looking to get involved with tennis; owned a tennis retail outlet; and served on the executive board and as a director-at-large of the USTA, as president of the Eastern Tennis Association and the U.S. International Lawn Tennis Club, and as vice president of the International Tennis Hall of Fame.

A rarity in that he seemingly is not motivated by power, fame, or money, Scott treasures the varied experiences these ventures—or rather adventures—have brought him. His motto is: "People either stretch themselves to reach their full potential, or they will make a pact with the status quo."

These diverse, talent-stretching experiences have broadened Scott's perspective immeasurably. "I think I'm better off than most people in the business," he once told *TENNIS* magazine. "I see the game from many different vantage points." His "Vantage Point" publisher's column, in fact, has provoked thought, and occasionally anger, for the past 25 years in *Tennis Week*, the highly regarded magazine he founded for the serious tennis fan.

In this wide-ranging interview, the inimitable Scott expounds on the great events and issues of tennis with a profundity and passion that reveals why he is a leading tennis authority as well as an invaluable mover and shaker.

**You were unbelievably prescient when you played with a metal racket at the 1967 U.S. Championships, and as a young lawyer and part-time tournament player, surprisingly reached the semifinals. What was your thinking back then?**

There were three things. I had a little bit of tennis elbow, so I was willing to risk anything. Second, I had not had a stellar record at Forest Hills previously, so the risk was not that great. Third, I had always been pretty experimental. It didn't really bother me what racket I played with. I could have played with a broom, and the results would have been more or less the same, not great, not bad. Three of us, Billie Jean King, Clark Graebner, and I, used the Wilson T2000, and it created a lot of buzz. Billie Jean won the tournament that year, and she could have played with a pogo stick and won. She was the best. So it really didn't say anything about the racket. But Clark got to the final. About me, you could say that when I was an alleged full-time player, I never got past the round of sixteen. And all of a sudden, I'm a part-time player, and I reach the semis. So people said: It can't be him, it must be the racket.

**What were your other experiments?**

My next experiment was with the Head "snowshoe" racket. I was the only person Head thought was lunatic and experimental enough to try the racket. I was a weekend player again. There was no pro game to speak of. They thought I'd be the only bridge to the recreational player—a guy who was good enough to do OK, but someone who was willing to take a risk and try something new. Arthur Ashe and I were pretty good pals, and he tried it and liked it. And Head dropped me [as an endorser] like a hot potato. They didn't think [initially] that someone as good as Arthur, someone on the main tour, would try it. It kept on going. The next racket Head put out was the "Red Head," and I was also the first person ever to use that, and I won the national thirty-five clay and grass court championships with that. They thought, well, it'll just be for senior players, and then [world top tenner] Bob Lutz started playing with it. I was having great fun with all these products.

**In retrospect, you were quite a pioneer in the evolution of racket technology.**

It was an easy place to be a pioneer. Very few people were experimenting, and that's still pretty much true. Pete Sampras is not going to try a brand new racket because he's played with one type since he was twelve years old. He's not apt to jeopardize $3 million a year on tour, $4 million a year off court, to try something new. There weren't the financial risks at stake when I played. So it was pretty easy to keep current with the new products.

**You played in, won, and even promoted tournaments on the famous and beloved Eastern grass court circuit. Its almost-total death—aside from the Hall of Fame event in Newport, Rhode Island—and the paving over of American tennis into hardcourts are twin tragedies of the Open Era, in my opinion. Do you agree?**

In 1974 I wrote an obituary for grass in *Tennis Week*, and it will appear in my new book [*OPEN!*], and I say exactly the same thing. It's too bad that the way decisions are made in our sport is whimsical. Not a lot of science and research goes into some unbelievably important decisions. For example, the USTA had very little deliberation before deciding to switch from grass to clay for the 1975 U.S. Open. I don't think it was a bad choice at the time because three majors [Grand Slam tournaments] were played on grass then. But no research was done as to the consequences. The only reason grass was taken out is that Forest Hills' grass, with a very sandy base, was the worst of all the grass court majors. Finally, the USTA couldn't take the criticism any longer. Grass should have maintained a small but stylish pocket on the tournament calendar. One of the reasons is that Wimbledon is in jeopardy. In 1989 Wimbledon, because of the ranking system, did not have twelve of the top twenty-five men players. But it also was equally absurd in the Open Era for grass to occupy three of the four majors.

**As it turned out, clay didn't last long as the surface at the U.S. Open.**

The same thing happened in 1977 when they went from Har-Tru [clay] at Forest Hills to Deco Turf II at Flushing Meadows. That decision came about when Slew Hester went around to the top American players and said, "OK, we're not doing so well, other than Jimmy Connors, on Har-Tru. What surface do you want?" And everyone of them—Ashe, Smith, Connors—said hardcourts. No research was done on that decision, and that was appallingly bad judgment. Because the minute that happened, every major college that had clay and Kalamazoo [the National Junior Championships] that had clay, switched to hardcourts. That's not good for Joe Average Tennis Player.

**As a TV tennis analyst along with Rosie Casals, you played a prominent role in**

the famous "Battle of the Sexes" extravaganza between women's libber Billie Jean King and male chauvinist Bobby Riggs. How did that one bizarre but important match help change tennis, the sports world and even America?

It changed America in two ways. First, it changed in that an awful lot of people were brought into the game. That match was beamed into an incredible number of living rooms whose occupants had no interest in tennis heretofore. Second, as a sociological phenomenon, it was one of many forces for change toward equality of the sexes. Bobby Riggs was spouting very comically right until the end that the woman's place is in the kitchen and the bedroom, not in the boardroom. It was not enough that Billie Jean King just played that match. Her victory proved women were OK, that not only could women compete with men in some ways on the athletic field, but they could win. It gave an awful lot of women bragging rights when people would say they should be seen and not heard, as far as their opinions or their performances. I had a lot of fun working with [commentator] Howard Cosell. I was naturally in Bobby's corner. [Rosie Casals was the female analyst.] I picked him to win. I got the score [6-4, 6-3, 6-3] right. I just predicted the wrong winner.

**The Open Era has proved a bonanza for tennis in many ways, but not necessarily for the Davis Cup, which celebrated its centennial in 1999. You eagerly and proudly played Davis Cup for your country. Why don't some top players, like Sampras, Chang, and Philippoussis, care much about Davis Cup today?**

No, I never turned down a Davis Cup assignment, but I never was asked a whole lot. Maybe if I had been ranked No. 1, I would have been a little more picky. Actually, none of the major American players is perfect in that department. Even McEnroe has turned down Davis Cup assignments. For Ham Richardson, the Rhodes Scholar, and Dick Savitt, the Wimbledon champion, and some other terrific players, Davis Cup wasn't always in their interest for one reason or another, and they loved playing Davis Cup. Some other issues and priorities came up. The golden rule is that it's not nice or smart to be judgmental about why Sampras and these guys don't play. They think differently from a lot of the older generation. It's profession-driven, whereas thirty or forty years ago, there was no profession. The player's attitude then was: I'm going to play. It's a lark. I love representing my country. And there's more excitement and fun in Davis Cup than any other tournament, except maybe the Grand Slams.

**What constructive ideas do you have to maintain the glorious Davis Cup tradition?**

If you want all the great players to participate every year, you have to listen to them. No one has ever spent four hours with Sampras and said, "OK, we know Davis Cup is not high on your agenda, while winning the Grand Slam tournaments and being No. 1 are most important." Believe me, Sampras would change his mind if Davis Cup counted in the [world] rankings. It's a sin that Davis Cup and Fed Cup don't count in the rankings. The governing fathers should look in the mirror and see that they are the ones to blame. The fact that Davis Cup is not part of the tournament commitment [in the new ATP ranking plan for 2000] is asinine. All you have to do is listen to these players to learn this. Another idea is that tennis could play the entire Davis Cup over a two-year period, and Sampras would only play two rounds a year. Or we could reduce the World Group from sixteen to eight countries so we play three rounds a year.

**Back in 1970 when the Virginia Slims circuit was founded, Arthur Ashe predicted that a women's tour "won't draw flies." In six of the last seven Grand Slam singles finals, the women have outdrawn the men in American TV ratings. Becker, McEnroe, Lendl, and John Lloyd, among others, even say they'd rather watch women's tennis now. How do you account for this sea change?**

Arthur was a great American and a great world citizen, but he was very often wrong in his judgments. One of the beautiful things about Arthur was he kept on admitting that he was wrong and moving on and getting better in his judgments. Obviously, he was wrong about women's tennis. While it's true the women's TV ratings are better here, that's not true in any country in Europe. They still don't even want to televise women's tennis there, even with the apparent resurgence. The reason for women's increasing popularity is that you can actually watch tennis strategy unfold, and it's not just crashing and bashing balls. There is definitely an audience, though, for crashing balls back and forth because that's the real world. Having Sampras and Agassi smack balls back and forth in the [1999] Wimbledon final was very macho. In 90 percent of the world, people want to see the men's game even in its reduced, viewer-friendly character.

**What else makes women players so appealing?**

The women's game is in an incredible position to drive off into the marketing sunset. They've got incredible sex appeal, they're all athletic, they look great. Also, their fitness quotient is growing, even though there are some exceptions. Women do have to respond tactically to what their opponents are doing, whereas the men are reacting, rather than responding. There is a thought process in women's tennis and it's beautiful. The dynamism and articulateness of their personalities is another strength. And this is one area where tennis—men and women—has a big edge over other sports. If you listen to the hockey players, or even the golfers, they don't have any edge to what they're saying. The hockey players may be great athletes, but their quotes are somewhat uninteresting, and they are uninteresting interviews.

**Many tennis lovers believe *Tennis Week*, which you founded in 1974, is the most authoritative tennis publication in the world. It clearly offers the most**

**comprehensive coverage of tennis politics. Why did you create *Tennis Week* then?**

In the beginning of Open Tennis, we were like kids in a candy store. Opportunity abounded. Almost everything you did, no one else was doing it. In the first four or five years of Open Tennis, I was making a movie a year for CBS, I wrote a book every year for three years, I ran six or seven tournaments a year, I represented athletes, I owned an enormous racket store and had a teaching academy. None of these were great businesses, but they were all pilot programs. We were just throwing these projects up against the wall to see which ones would stick. One of those we thought would stick was *Tennis Week*. The [major American] magazines then were monthlies, *World Tennis* and *TENNIS*. Since international tennis then was played every week, we thought we ought to do something that reports on it every week. We thought that even if the magazine lost $50,000 or $60,000 a year, it would be a great advertising vehicle for the projects we were producing. That was the advertising purpose.

**What about the editorial purpose?**

We found how magazines were normally launched—they did a big reader survey and asked what the readers wanted. We did one and found that the readers wanted to have stories on resorts, equipment, and instruction. So I said, "Wait a minute. I don't want to do that at all." I wanted to find an audience who knows with what to play, where to play, and how to play. That's the audience I went after. I wanted to talk about not that McEnroe won Wimbledon, but *why* he won Wimbledon and what it's like in the trenches.

**Has *Tennis Week* fulfilled all your goals and dreams?**

Never will one fulfill all of one's dreams and goals. The reason I do *Tennis Week* is that we get an unbelievable amount of psychic income from positive response. However small our audience is—and we think there are maybe 400,000 readers out there—basically we get an incredible amount of positive feedback. Without that, I would have stopped this thing twenty years ago. Our readership cares about these issues, and they're incredibly grateful there is a publication that satisfies their appetite.

**In your heyday you were a serve and volleyer. There will always be arguments about which playing styles are more athletic to play and more entertaining to watch. But many former world-class players, coaches, and fans criticize pro tennis today for presenting too much power, too little finesse and strategy, and too-short points. Are the critics right?**

One of the really hopeful things about tennis—as far as people criticizing it for being too fast—is that the athlete has an incredible ability to adapt. We've seen hundreds of examples of this. In one of Chang's matches against Edberg, there were 18 service breaks when Edberg won. When Agassi won the U.S. Open and

Wimbledon, he showed that "if you serve something up to me 1,000 miles an hour, I'm going to knock it down your teeth." We've seen over and over again that our players specifically and our game generally adapted. And I think we're going through that craziness now. One of the healthy things about the evolution is Björn Borg and Ilie Năstase and Jimmy Connors changed the grass court game before my very eyes. We used to have a regular ritual on grass when you practiced. You always had someone at the net. You never had two people in the backcourt, practicing rallying, because you didn't think it could be done. You thought you had to get to the net and not let the ball bounce. The bounce was so erratic that you didn't want to hinge the outcome of the match on these crazy bounces. Connors, Borg, Năstase, and even Vilas, when he won the Masters on grass in Australia, convinced the world you can rally from the backcourt on grass. So there was a sense of adaptation, and there is one now. But it may not be going fast enough for people's appetites.

**What can and should we do to solve this power crisis?**

First, there is absolutely no problem with 99.9 percent of tennis. Everyone is having a good time in recreational tennis. All the new products make playing

*"Tennis's Renaissance Man,"*
*Gene Scott.* From the
Fernberger Collection at the
International Tennis Hall of
Fame & Museum, Newport,
Rhode Island

tennis easier, and even the ninety-year-old players can hit the ball with pretty good pace. They have much more fun than they did with the wood racket where, when they hit the ball off-center, it would dribble near their feet. And no one has even suggested the game is [getting] too fast for the women on any surface. Maybe in five years it will be, but right now it's great. The same goes for all the juniors. For all these groups, there's no power crisis. We just have a tiny group of 300 or 400 men professionals who hit the ball too hard. And even with the men, there's no problem at the French [Open]. That is the best tennis of all. The solution is very easy. You change the surface. At the U.S. Open it is really easy to slow down the surface. You talk to the people who put the surface in, and you find out there's never been any discussion about how fast the surface should be. The people in charge are very nice. But David Meehan, the technical guy at the U.S. Tennis Center, shouldn't be in charge of that. That ought to be a policy decision of the U.S. Open Committee, where the Chairman of the Board of the USTA, after speaking with the board and the research people, comes out with a conclusion about what's best for the game. That's never been done. It would be easy to improve the product at Wimbledon, too. With all the wear and tear, they could make the grass a little bit longer and thicker around the baseline. They could start tinkering with the balls, too, like changing the pressure and adding more felt. It's interesting that if you talk to four scientists, they'll disagree on whether you add pressure, add weight, or do the opposite to slow the ball down. Even the experts don't know.

**You were making major moves up the USTA hierarchy and were seemingly headed toward the presidency. What ended your progress?**

I was what they call a director-at-large. The process by which I was elected was something of a miracle. I was probably the most surprised of all because I thought I was probably too controversial an article to have in the chicken coop. I had a heck of a good time in the two years I was there. While I was disappointed and had hurt feelings for about three weeks after not being re-appointed, it was probably the right thing. While I think they do need more tennis experts on the board, the message I was giving was probably not so popular all the time. It was pretty hard for a volunteer board to be comfortable with me sitting there and taking shots at them inside the room. It's one thing if they read my criticism in a publication, and they can discard it and say, "Well, there he goes again." But if I'm in the room they sort of have to deal with me.

**If you were USTA president, what specific decisions would you make to advance American tennis?**

The question is: What would your crusade be because you only have two years as president to do something? What is your giant thought? Slew Hester had it when he changed [the U.S. Open] from Forest Hills to Flushing Meadows. That was a big deal. The one issue that has been totally ignored and one I would crusade for and spend every dollar of the $174 million USTA budget I could on is the Schools Program [now called USA School Tennis]. It would be a home run, in theory, because everyone loves kids and everyone loves education. It's the real grassroots project. The USTA says its Schools Program touches five million kids a year—a figure based on 23,000 high schools and roughly 200 kids in each high school. The numbers are somewhat cosmetic, but there are real numbers there somewhere. You could achieve them if the Schools Program had a major strategy.

**What strategy do you recommend for the Schools Program?**

You want tennis to be part of the curriculum. You don't want to send a very nice but low-level administrator to a secondary school think-tank session because that person is going to get handled and ambushed. They're not going to get anywhere. To make some significant changes in the Schools Program, you'd have to have some major support from major political leaders. David Dinkins [former New York City mayor], a board member of the USTA, could really help here if he uses his influence and tries to get to the school boards and says, "We would like to have tennis be as vital a part of the curriculum as recess." There was a model in California. Some very bright tennis enthusiast got an edict passed, saying that any new high school that was built, starting from 1970, had to build tennis courts on the premises.

**American men stars go in cycles. We had the Connors, Gerulaitis, Tanner, Gottfried, Solomon, and Dibbs era in the 1970s and the Sampras, Agassi, Courier, and Chang era in the 1990s. Now we have no potential stars on the horizon. Is it too soon to panic? How can the U.S. produce more stars?**

All we have to do is look around us and see how the stars are being produced. For years America, along with Australia, had the only program where we had an incredibly big volunteer base and a base of tournaments for people to compete in non-stop. That was our program, plus we have the greatest teaching pros on earth. Australia changed the formula a little bit. They hand-picked some unbelievably great athletes, took them out of high school and put them on the circuit—the Rosewall, Hoad theory. After that European countries—like Sweden, Germany, Spain, and Czechoslovakia—started to emulate what Australia was doing. So you didn't have to have enormous player pools. For example, what Cuba does in other sports, and what Russia did with the Olympics. You had sports schools and you found ways to identify the best athletes and directed them into the sports that needed them. If the goal is to produce champions, the USTA doesn't have a poor program; it doesn't have *any* program. There is no such thing as a Stars Program. It's not a program. It's a jumble.

**After becoming ATP executive director in 1987, Hamilton Jordan, former White House chief of staff under President Jimmy Carter, commented, "After talking to**

**the players in the last twenty-four hours, I've decided that this is more politics than the politics I've been in." Why has tennis historically had so much political conflict and wrangling that it amazed even a veteran political operative like Jordan?**

Most of the other sports had a single governing body, whether it be the PGA or the NFL or NHL or baseball. They all were under one roof, while tennis had a whole community of roofs. The cynical answer to the question "Why doesn't tennis have a commissioner?" is that not all the entities in tennis would agree to be bound by just one commissioner. That's because they've spent years developing and creating their little province, and they're not going to give it up unless someone assures them they're going to be as least as well off. The contrary argument is that [with a commissioner] the overall pie would grow to such great proportions that your piece would become bigger than the small pie whole that you had. Obviously, people there don't believe that's true. One of the nice things about having these hundreds of fragmented interests is that you get rewarded for your own efforts. It's not diluted by someone else. You can take the credit or the blame. The one other difference between tennis and every other sport is that no other sport has an international connection, an international circuit like tennis has. There's no such thing as an international soccer or golf or basketball circuit. And every country has a different language, currency, and political situation. Tennis is trying to go through and make peace with all that. So, to think one leader would be accepted by 200 tennis nations around the world is preposterous. The bad side [now] is the chaos. But the good side is tennis has an extraordinary amount of checks and balances. You don't have one entity taking over the game and being so arrogant that they'd never listen to [proposals for] potential changes. A commissioner isn't a panacea anyway. Supposedly the greatest marketing paradigm on earth is the NBA. They have a commissioner and only one group of players in America—and they aren't playing!

**Throughout the past 125 years, tennis has experienced boom and bust periods in different eras and different countries. As we approach the millennium, what makes you optimistic and what makes you pessimistic about tennis' success and popularity?**

The stuff making tennis popular is so obvious, but we do such a bad job of marketing its positives. For example, take its cross-gender assets. The mixed doubles at the U.S. Open and Wimbledon is part of these and other major tournaments. There's no such thing as a mixed doubles Stanley Cup or mixed doubles Masters or Super Bowl or any of the major professional sports events. There's no such thing anywhere else as mixed *anything*. And there is no such thing as a historic base for father-son and mother-daughter [competitions] in any other sport besides tennis. We have men and women playing together as part of the fabric of our sport, but also our kids can play with us. It's an unbelievable advantage. Tennis is the most family-friendly sport there is. For example, contrast it with golf. How friendly would it be if I told my wife and two kids on Saturday mornings, "So long, dears, I'm leaving at seven in the morning, and I'll see you at seven in the evening"—because at [ages] two and four they can't play golf, and my wife would have to look after the kids. That's unbelievably disagreeable. In tennis, you can have the kids hang around the courts with you, instead of leaving them most of the day. The other great advantage is that you can play tennis forever. I played three team sports at college, and it was impossible to invite twelve hockey players into my living room and play shinny after I got out of college. I played soccer and you can't invite twenty-two people over and play on my lawn. The logistics of team sports after you get out of school are impossible. And in tennis you need only one other person. And you can do it until you're ninety. The USTA just created a ninety-and-over championships. But we don't do a very good job of saying how great tennis is.

**What makes you pessimistic about tennis' future?**

Tennis, by and large, is not a very good spectator sport. Maybe 10 percent of the 127 matches in the singles draw at the U.S. Open are worth watching, as far as getting really competitive, close, dramatic, where the contrast in styles is evident. That is because doing things by rote and monotony is encouraged in tennis, while genius and variety are most often punished. Stan Smith usually beats Ilie Năstase. Smith is mechanical; he's got good ambition and concentration, he's strong, athletic, but he's not an improviser. And yet he's going to beat the improviser because tennis usually rewards the steadfast, rather than the artist. So that's too bad. On the other hand *if* you're lucky enough to be at one of those 10 percent of the matches that are real barnburners, *then* you've got the best of all sports as far as drama. You know a finish line is coming, and all of the action and risk-taking is about to climax and then there's no way out for either athlete. That is incredibly powerful. But watching people rally back and forth is not why tennis was invented. It was built for players, not for spectators.

**As writers we are told to keep our objectivity and not play favorites. But since you've played many roles, besides being a writer, in the tennis world, I would like to ask who your favorite players have been in the past fifty years.**

I've always liked the artists like Santana. They were the most fun. Santana was this incredible athlete and the man who invented the topspin lob off the backhand. I loved guys who created on the court. Năstase was the same thing. I like the eccentric players. Whitney Reed was definitely one of my favorites. He was ranked No. 1 in the U.S. in the early 1960s. He never won a major championship. He was totally unorthodox, he had a great sense of humor, he looked crazy, and he acted crazy. Rafael Osuna proved that you could just be incredibly fast and be a good competitor and win the U.S. Championships. What's happened today, starting with Becker—and I think it's terrific—is that the guys are very physical about the game, where they throw themselves all over the court. Becker was the first guy to really do that, and it was effective and courageous and very dramatic.

**Who were your favorite women players?**

Billie Jean King, because she was the same way, an improviser. She was reckless and threw herself around the court, as much as a woman could. I just loved her athleticism. My generation was just filled with these exquisitely natural lady players. Maria Bueno and Evonne Goolagong were like royalty playing. They had a somewhat cavalier look to their game, like they weren't really trying, and yet they were so gifted they could produce great stuff from any place on the court. I really like what Chris Evert did in the latter stages of her career. She adapted and hit the ball harder and came to net occasionally. I really like smart players like Seles and Hingis. Seles modernized the game by standing on the baseline and taking the ball so early. Hingis plays such great percentage tennis, just like Bobby Riggs, Jack Kramer, and Neale Fraser. In the old days you would have said Seles and Hingis had killer instinct. Today you'd say they're unbelievably tough competitors and very smart.

---

**FASCINATING FACTS:**

- Inside an attaché case that President George H.W. Bush once inadvertently left at a tennis tournament were the keys to America's nuclear arsenal.

- Billie Jean King, after whom the USTA National Tennis Center was named, said the event she enjoyed the most as a player was "Mixed doubles—then women's doubles and then singles because it was lonely out there [alone]."

- Bill Getzen and the others who played doubles with the late Gerald R. Ford in 1976 at the Field Club in Sarasota, Florida, were stunned when the president of the United States brought his own can of tennis balls.

- Andy Roddick, in a second-grade report about top tennis players, described Brad Gilbert, his future coach, as: "Brad Gilbert, No. 6 in the world. But he's the biggest pusher on the tour."

# 32

# Jelena Jankovic: The Serb with Verve

# 2007

**W**ho else but irrepressible Jelena Jankovic would proclaim, as Julius Caesar did after a great military victory, "I came, I saw, I conquered" when she won the ASB Classic in Auckland to start the 2007 season? It was a mere Tier IV tournament title, but her flair for the dramatic reminded tennis fans and opponents of her prowess and her progress.

Like Caesar, the twenty-two-year-old Serb has overcome adversity to prevail. Ten years ago Jankovic was separated from her family to attend an elite tennis academy in Florida; she had no English but was determined to become a champion. When she was fourteen, the country she was living in, the U.S., led NATO forces that for seventy-eight days bombed the city, Belgrade, where her family was living.

"I would watch on CNN," she told *The Telegraph* (UK). "They bombed buildings I knew . . . My brother was in an apartment next to one of the targets, and the whole building started shaking . . . It was a difficult situation—I always felt scared."

Both ordeals matured and strengthened Jankovic. Early in 2006 she endured yet another severe test. A demoralizing ten-match losing streak made her consider quitting the sport she loved. Not only did she not quit, but she rebounded to reach the 2006 U.S. Open semis. This year she shot up to a career-high No. 3, by winning four tournaments and reaching two more finals plus the French Open semifinals.

Jankovic, along with equally charming compatriots Ana Ivanovic, the surprise Wimbledon finalist, and No. 3-ranked Novak Ðjokovic, have suddenly turned Serbia into a tennis power. "The Serbs are not only great players, they all seem so bright and intelligent," Mary Carillo told the *San Francisco Chronicle*. "Their tennis is interesting because they are interesting. They're dramatic, well-spoken, and they have a good concept of the sport."

In this frank, insightful, and sometimes funny interview, Jankovic talks about her unique past and her aspirations on and off the courts.

**You recently told TennisReporters.net: "I'm Jelena. I have my own personality, image, and am who I am. Sometimes I think, 'Why am I not a regular girl who lives a normal life?'" How would you describe your personality, and why aren't you a regular girl?**

> I'm quite outgoing. I like to have fun. I like to laugh a lot and smile, especially on the court. I have a bubbly personality. I'm not a regular girl because I'm different from the girls my age who live a normal life because I travel around the world, and I don't spend much time at home. I'm doing something that I love and that I'm very passionate about. I'm living my dream, traveling the world, and doing the job I love. And I just want to make the most of it.

**After Jamie Murray and you won the Wimbledon mixed doubles final, you revealed that your playful exchanges were because "I needed to motivate him. So I kept saying things like, 'Good return now, many kisses.'" Was this only clever motivation? Or are you and Jamie becoming doubles partners off the court, too?**

> (Laughter) No. I had a lot of fun playing with Jamie at Wimbledon. He is a great guy. He has a great sense of humor. I really enjoyed playing with him. We had so much fun on the court, which is the most important thing, especially when you are playing mixed doubles. As far as off the court, I think we are just friends. We have only been together for one or two weeks at Wimbledon. I've only known Jamie for very little time. And I cannot say more.

**When you were twelve and thirteen-years-old at the Nick Bollettieri Tennis Academy, you used to make money by winning bets. Please tell me about that.**

> Yes, I remember that. I was a young girl, and from an early age I liked to compete. I didn't like to spend so many hours practicing. I always loved to play matches and games. When I was twelve years old, I remember that I would bet against the other kids, and I would come back home with twenty dollars in my pocket. My mother would ask, "Where did you get this from? What did you do?" My mother didn't believe what I was doing. Then I would buy candies, donuts. (Laughter) It was fun. When I played against boys older and stronger physically than me, I would have more of a chance because they would get scared because money was involved. It was a fun way of playing with a little bit of pressure. It taught me how to deal with pressure when you play matches, especially in big tournaments. It was good for me to get ready when I was young so I knew how it feels on the big stage.

**At the 2006 U.S. Open you were sensational in beating No. 10 Vaidišová, No. 7 Kuznetsova, and No. 5 Dementieva to reach the semis. Then you played one of your most important and dramatic matches against Justine Henin. You led 6-4, 4-2 and had a game point for 5-2 before losing 4-6, 6-4, 6-0. What happened? And what did you learn from that experience?**

Yeah, it was a very good learning experience for me. It was my first Grand Slam semifinal, and I was a little bit overwhelmed by the whole situation. I was very excited and thought in my head that I was in the final. But I missed a big opportunity. I was discussing [a disputed decision] with a chair umpire. That was when they had just introduced the Hawk-Eye [electronic line-calling technology], and the referees were not calling many balls. I was a little bit confused then. I reacted badly at that moment and completely lost my concentration, and my focus was gone for the rest of the match. I let my opportunity slip away. I let Justine come back into the match, and I just lost it. I thought I was completely the better player the whole time. I was dominating throughout the match, but I just lost my poise. I made a huge mistake that time. I was down mentally because I got a bad call. But I learned a lot from it, and I don't want to make the same mistake again. I need to stay positive out there, forget about what happened, and just focus on the next point.

**You have said you are a really emotional person, but you hate that characteristic about yourself. Please explain what you mean.**

I know that it's not good being a cold person without having any emotions. But I would prefer sometimes when I play my matches and when I win these tournaments and when I enjoy the whole atmosphere, I get very excited and happy and have butterflies in my stomach. I don't know how to explain it, but I wish I were a little bit calmer. Also, when things don't go so well, I cry very easily. I have these emotions because I am quite sensitive. I cried after Andre Agassi lost his last match [at the 2006 U.S. Open]. I was in the locker room watching, and tears started pouring from my eyes. I tried to cover it from the other girls. I was the one hiding with a towel on my head. That's how I am. And I cannot change it.

**After you beat Venus Williams 6-4, 4-6, 6-1 at the French Open in June, you called the ten people, including your mother, Snezana, in the friends' box, "My clowns." Why did you call them that?**

No, no, I didn't mean it in that [negative] way. They were doing a kind of move in the friends' box. It was a lot of fun. I love having great people in my box, people who are very supportive of me and believe in me. Especially when I'm playing tough matches, it means a lot to me. I appreciate that support very much. Usually it's a great atmosphere and the people in the box enjoy themselves. I was playing a big match against one of the toughest opponents, but they seemed so relaxed. They were cheering and smiling and laughing. And they actually helped me stay relaxed on the court. I didn't feel that pressure and intensity. But I didn't mean it like they were [actually] clowns. All I meant was that they were enjoying themselves, and they were a little different from the rest of the crowd.

**Now you are ranked a career-high No. 3. But during the first part of 2006 you**

**suffered through a demoralizing ten-match losing streak and admitted that you were "about ready to quit" the pro tour. What happened then at Rome to turn your career around?**

It was a very tough period for me. Nobody likes to lose and when you lose ten matches in a row, it was very tough to deal with. But sometimes some things are meant to happen in order for you to become a better player and to change some things in your life. This is what happened to me. I learned how it was to be down and when things were not going my way, when you are losing so many matches, when you are not satisfied with what you are doing. But everything turned around in May. I made the quarterfinals [at Rome], and since then my results gradually got better and better. I felt more motivated and decided to work harder. I was determined. I felt I could come back again. I never felt I had to prove anything to anybody—except to myself. I just started to believe in myself again and become the best I can be. My family has also played an important role in my tennis. They are always supporting me and always telling me to believe in myself. Recently my mother has traveled to a lot of the tournaments with me, and she has been a very positive influence. All of this added together is why I have made such a huge improvement after I dropped down to No. 39 or 40 in the world, and now I am No. 3. I'm on the rise and having a lot of fun and enjoying my game and enjoying life.

**Ana Ivanovic, your compatriot, says you are mentally stronger this year. Is that partly because you are physically stronger and fitter?**

Yeah, it has a lot to do with it because when you work hard a lot on and off the court, especially in the off-season, when you spend many hours on the tennis court and also in the gym, you know that you are physically very fit. When you play tough, three-set matches, you are confident you can do it. You know that you are better than your opponent, you are fitter. You can hang in there, so you feel more confident. I was practicing with the top guys in hot weather in Colombia at the end of last year, and that helped a lot. It was one of my best preparations in my whole career. I started to do so well [in 2007] because I practiced and trained so hard. All this hard work is really paying off.

**All-time great Monica Seles is not only your heroine. She is also your mentor. Please tell me about both.**

She used to be my mentor. That was when I was young, eighteen, nineteen years old. But now I am twenty-two. I really admire Monica. She is a great person and a legend in the sport. I can learn a lot from her because she has been through everything that I am going through now in my career. But I think when I was growing up, I never really had an idol. I never really wanted to model my game after anyone else or copy their behavior or the way they dress or anything else. I always wanted to be myself and play my own game. But I liked Monica's fighting spirit, the way she played, and everything else about her.

### How and when did you get started in tennis?

I started late at nine and a half, and I never thought I would become a professional tennis player. I just played it for fun, and at the same time I had piano lessons and tennis lessons. That's what I did after I came back from school in the afternoon. I started playing on the red clay courts at Club Red Star in Belgrade. Tennis was more fun than the piano. It was difficult to travel around the country then because of the shortage of gas. So I had to drop one activity. So my parents asked me what I would like to do. I had to choose one, and I chose tennis. I think I made the right decision. (Laughter)

### What was life like for you as a twelve-year-old in a dormitory at Bollettieri's academy without your family and unable to speak English?

It was difficult, especially in the beginning when I couldn't speak English. I came there alone without my family. I really missed them, and sometimes I would cry. I was surrounded by kids from all over the world. I was very shy, and it was difficult for a young girl to come to a different environment not knowing anyone and not knowing the language. But as time went on, I started to learn English. I went to school and I spoke French, and that was the language I used to get around. But I matured a lot faster because of that experience. I learned to do everything by myself. I didn't have any help from anybody else. I learned to be very disciplined and organized.

### Amazingly, you always received A grades. How did you do it?

Yeah, I did that, actually. Wherever I went to school, I went to Serbian school, a diplomatic school, where I learned French, then I went to an American school, and I always had As. I always liked to do the best. I was never satisfied to get a B. I always wanted to do things right.

### Nick Bollettieri criticized you for not mentioning in your Personal Bio in the WTA Tour media guide that you trained for several years at his tennis academy. Which coaches deserve the credit for helping you succeed?

My god, that is a difficult question because not only one coach deserves all the credit. I have had many people who have helped me with my game, and Nick is, of course, one of them. I spent many years there at his academy, and I really appreciate his help and what he has taught me. It was a great experience at the academy. I learned a lot. And I really appreciate everything he has done for me. But other people also put in work and helped me improve my game and helped me get where I am now. Ricardo Sanchez has been helping me on and off between tournaments, and by the end of the year, I hope he will be my full-time coach. He also deserves a lot of credit because he has done a great job. Richard

Brooks was my sparring partner, and he is not working with me anymore.

**After you beat No. 3 Mauresmo 7-5, 6-0 in the Sydney quarters in January, you said, "I have no fear. I feel I can beat anybody." In fact, you have beaten every top ten player, plus Venus Williams, at least once—except for Justine Henin. Five times you have lost to her in three sets. What do you have to do better to beat her?**

Yes, you're right. I've beaten all the top ten players except Justine. She is obviously the better player. She has beaten me so many times. I've lost to her a few times in very close matches, 6-4 in the third [set]. A few things, a few points here and there make a huge difference. I need to learn from my mistakes and keep working hard. She motivates me to keep improving my game in order to beat her. She's, of course, the No. 1 player in the world.

**Richard Brooks told *The Times* (UK), "I believe she will be the No. 1 player in the world, otherwise I would not want to work with her." Do you believe you will become No. 1 in the world?**

Yes, of course, I believe I can be No. 1 in the world. At the moment I am No. 3 player in the world. If I didn't believe that, I wouldn't be playing this sport. I always wanted to be the best. That's why I play. This is what motivates me. These are my goals. If you don't set goals for what you want to achieve, then there is no point. It's useless.

**After you beat Nicole Vaidišová 6-3, 7-5 to advance to the 2007 French Open semis, you said, "Me and my serve. It's just unbelievable. I am now four or three in the world with this serve. Can you imagine if I had a bigger serve, what I would do with these girls?" What is wrong with your serve? And what are you doing to improve it?**

Oh, my god! (Laughter) When I hear some of my quotes that I said before, they are so funny. My serve is an area where I really need some improvement, and I am working hard to keep improving it. But some things don't happen overnight. It takes time. I need more power and accuracy on my first serve. I need a better second serve as well to feel more comfortable. A big kick serve for my second serve would be nice, but not many girls have a big kick serve. Then I can feel more confident on my first serve because I can go for a lot more [power].

**Your parents are economists, and you are highly unusual in that you are in your second year at Megatrend University in Belgrade. What courses are you taking? And how do you manage to combine college with being a professional athlete who is traveling most of the year?**

Education has always been very important to me. I'm trying to do the best I can. I study economics, business, media, and management. I bring books with me to the tournaments and wherever I travel. And I try to prepare for my exams as well as possible. And when I am well prepared and ready, I make an appointment at home in Belgrade and take my exams. I don't do correspondence; I just study on airplanes and on the road. I've been a little behind lately because I've been playing a lot and been very busy with my schedule and everything. But my ambition is to finish my university studies. It's very important to be ready for life after tennis.

**Billie Jean King said, "The media has been so good to me and allowed my thoughts and feelings to be heard . . . Every athlete has to remember that without the media, they are nothing, because the media tells everyone what we feel and think." Do you agree with Billie Jean?**

Yeah, I think she's right. Without the media, people, of course, would not know how you feel. You cannot express your feelings, you cannot tell what happened, and everything else about yourself. But I also think the media can sometimes make up stories that aren't true. They can also create a different image of you that is false. So the media can do good and bad things.

**"People have to understand that all that we have in tennis here came from mud, from nothing," said Janko Tipsarevic ranked No. 48, on why Serbia has three top five players. "No one invested one dollar or one Euro into any one of our players . . . the only people who we can say thanks to today are our families." Do you agree with Janko?**

Yes, that's completely true. We never received any help from our federation because their financial status is not the best. You cannot compare Serbia to the federations, for example, in England or America or countries like that. We had to do everything ourselves, and thanks to our parents, or some other people, such as our managers or others who invested in us, we made it.

**How do you explain the fact that Serbia, a country of only 9.4 million people with very few indoor tennis courts and not much of a tennis tradition now has three players in the top four?**

It's a huge achievement for such a small country like us. It is not something that happens every day. Before it was a huge success for us when I broke the top 100, the top fifty, because when we were growing up, we didn't have anyone to look up to. We didn't have a tradition in tennis, like you said. Now having three players in the top four, it's amazing. I'm very proud of it, and I hope we can continue this success, because who knows after we retire in five or ten years, if there will be another Jelena or another Ana or another Novák who will come after us.

**Serbia has never won the Fed Cup or even reached the final. But with you ranked No. 3 and Ana Ivanovic, the Wimbledon finalist, ranked No. 4, what do you think your chances are in coming years?**

I helped my team almost get into the World Group in April. I played fifteen sets in four days, and I won all seven of my matches. We finally made it into the playoffs to play for the World Group. But then we played against Slovakia this year after Wimbledon, and unfortunately we lost (4-1). I won my singles match, but I got injured so I couldn't continue in the competition. My teammates unfortunately lost, so now we have to go back to the Europe/Africa Group where we came from. We can't actually win the Fed Cup in 2008. Maybe we could in 2009, if we get back into the World Group next year. It's very difficult because Ana and I have never played together. I have played for my country for so many (six) years, but I cannot do it without another [top] player who can help. Ana can help for sure, if she plays.

**"The Serbs are not only great players, they all seem so bright and intelligent," TV analyst Mary Carillo told the *San Francisco Chronicle*. "Their tennis is interesting because they are interesting. They're dramatic, well-spoken, and they have a good concept of the sport." Is there anything you would like to add to that about Novák, Ana, and yourself?**

That's basically the best way you can describe us. Ana, Novak and I are the future of tennis. We are all young with a lot of potential. We are all very charismatic, and I think that is very important in the sport to get the crowd involved so people enjoy watching the sport. It's a lot of fun. And you can attract a lot more fans that way.

**You and your success are inspiring many young Serbs to take up tennis. But you are also an inspiration to a Japanese girl who is a fan of yours. Would you please tell me about her.**

This happened in Japan last year. A fourteen-year-old girl who was sick with leukemia wrote a letter to me and drew a cartoon. She said how much she admired me as a tennis player. When I think about it, because I am a pro tennis player, I can inspire people who are suffering in their lives and really dealing with tough times. That means a lot to me. She said that my breaking a sweat on the court motivated her to help fight her cancer. She sees me fighting on the court, and she says that she can fight and stay strong and get through this. So, if I can help somebody just by playing the game and just being who I am, it's a huge thing.

**FASCINATING FACT:**
- Serbia's world number three tennis player Jelena Jankovic was on Dec. 16, 2007 appointed a national ambassador of the United Nations Children's Fund. Jankovic is the second Serbian tennis star to have volunteered to help promote the rights of children and collect funds for UNICEF after Ana Ivanovic, the world's fourth-ranked player, became an ambassador in September.

# Index

Knowles, Mark, 121, 123; flap with Bryans, 186; rebuts doubles reforms, 40
Kodes, Jan, 64, 148
Kohde-Kilsch, Claudia, 65
Korff, John, 149
Kournikova, Anna, 37, 95, 182; charity event, 174; No. 1 in endorsements, 137; role model, 111; spat with Hingis, 107
Kovacs, Frank, 66, 147
Krajicek, Richard, 14, 69
Kramer, Jack, 3, 256; on decline of serving and volleying, 66; on P. Gonzalez's fierceness, 11; praises Budge, 10; Quist on, 13; sued by Connors, 108
Krishnan, Ramanathan, 125
Kuerten, Gustavo, 237; enjoys doubles, 236; French Open long shot, 9
Kuznetsova, Svetlana, 34, 84, 99, 110, 113; can't get sponsorships, 139; kick serves, 80; on Sharapova, 107; superb genes, 112; Kypreos, Nick, 47

Lacoste, Rene, 10–11; on Tilden's fascination, 12
Laney, Al, 3
Langrishe, May, 96
Lansdorp, Robert, 113; Sharapova's shotmaking, 138; teaching style of, 67
Lapentti, Nicolas, 70
Larsen, Art, 109
Laver, Rod, 3, 6–7, 14, 64; 1962 and 1969 Grand Slams, 4; debate about his record, 10; J. McEnroe on, 12; let racket do talking, 129–130; on serving and volleying, 67
Lawford, Herbert: chop shot, 68
Leach, Ricky, 190
Leconte, Henri, 163, 230
Lemeieux, Mario, 115
Lendl, Ivan, 4, 8, 56, 65, 249; calls Skoff "biggest jerk," 107; inspired Sampras, 85; memorable match against Chang, 249; Noah on, 161; Sampras on, 13;
Lenglen, Suzanne, 96; beats Wills in 1926 classic, 19; fused athleticism with eroticism, 91; near-perfect record, 15
Lenin, Vladimir, 110
Leonard, Sugar Ray, 76
Levering, Julia A., 99
Lieberman, Nancy: conditioning program for Navratilova, 18
Lillee, Dennis, 115
Lindsay, Crawford, 69
Llodra, Michael, 64
Lloyd, John, 249
Loehr, Dr. James E., 52
Lopez, Feliciano, 64

Lott, George: praises Wills, 18
Louis, Joe, 3
Love, Davis, 223
Lucas, John: picks greatest athletes, 49
Lucic, Mirjana, 182

MacTavish, Catherine, 98
Mallory, Anna Margarethe "Molla" Bjurstedt, 19, 91–92
Mandlikova, Hana, 124
Mantilla, Felix, 108
Maradona, Diego, 3
Marble, Alice: first female serve-volley champion, 21; helped Gibson, 93; inspired King, 85; played like a man, 92
Margot, of Hainaut: women's sports pioneer, 89
Marino, Dan, 3
Marley, Bob, 160
Martin, Todd, 244
Massu, Nicolas: feats at Olympics, 178
Mathieu, Paul-Henri, 116
Mauresmo, Amelie: interview with 209–214; on on-court coaching, 33
Mayotte, Tim, 218
Mays, Willie, 3, 115
McCartney, Paul, 146
McEnroe, John, 3, 8–9, 52, 63, 65; athletic greatness of, 49; cocaine use, 157; compares Henin to Federer, 22; famous 1980 Wimbledon final, 43; feud with Connors, 101–102; improved technique, 231; infamous match vs. Nastase, 148; petitioned ITF about rackets, 69; polarized fans, 149; prefers women's tennis, 249; rivalry with Borg, 150; superb Davis Cup record, 6; on Laver's greatness, 12; on Young, 86
McGregor, Ken, 127
McIngvale, Jim, 174
McIngvale, Linda, 174
McMillan, Frew: on promoting doubles, 78
McNamee, Paul, 62; advocates super tiebreaker, 55
Meehan, David, 252
Melkin, Andrew: TV prediction, 86
Merrill, Dina, 157
Mewshaw, Michael, 241
Mikaelian, Marie-Gaianeh, 137
Miles, Mark, 176–177
Mirnyi, Max, 41, 64, 70, 77
Mirza, Sania, 95; most searched-for personality, 100
Molik, Alicia, 64, 75; kick serves, 80
Monfils, Gael: Gilbert's evaluation, 217
Montana, Joe, 3, 95
Moody, Helen Wills. *See* Wills, Helen
Moore, Elizabeth, 90
Moran, "Gorgeous Gussie": panties cause furor, 97
Morozova, Olga, 65, 112; praises Dementieva, 113

Mottram, Joy, 50
Mottram, Tony, 50
Moya, Carlos, 77, 104, 142
Mozart, 149
Murray, Andy, 35; on Agassi's finale, 136; victimized by Player Challenges, 27
Murray, Jamie, 258
Murray, Jim: praises Chang, 207
Myers, A. Wallis, 7
Myskin, Andrei, 112
Myskina, Anastasia, 76, 99, 107, 110, 113, 139

Na, Hu, 207
Nadal, Rafael, 13, 41, 74; muscular physique, 84; sleeveless shirt, 77
Nalbandian, David, 136
Nastase, Ilie, 64, 97, 251; artist, 255; on Borg's genius, 12; roughneck era, 146; shenanigans of, 147–148
Navratilova, Martina, 65; advocates ITF legislation on racket size, 69; calls doubles reforms "ridiculous"; defects to U.S., 98; discovers Sharapova, 138; evaluation of career record, 17; on feuding stars, 103; high praise for Graf, 16; on inter-generational comparisons, 15; perfect Fed Cup record, 52; revolutionized training methods, 18; serendipitous tennis marriage, 120; splits with Shriver, 124; tennis academy, 84; ultimate serve and volleyer, 68; warning about young Hingis, 180
Neer, Phil, 96; lost to Helen Wills, 18
Neilly, Timothy, 217
Nelson, Byron, 52
Nestor, Daniel, 123; flap with Bryans, 186
Newcombe, Angie, 126
Newcombe, John, 949, 64, 78, 123; feud with Cash, 105; lauds Court, 20; on mateship, 128; on mixed doubles, 126; opposes No-Ad, 44; praises doubles, 46; roughhousing with Roche, 131
Nicholes, Stan, 20
Nicklaus, Jack, 3, 52; overweight during prime, 48; tennis lover, 50
Nicolas II, Tsar, 110
Noah, Marie-Claire, 159
Noah, Yannick, 230; importance of doubles, 188; inspired Mauresmo, 213; interview with, 155–166
Norman, Magnus, 72, 103
Novotna, Jana, 33; dumped by Hingis, 124
Nureyev, Rudolf, 21
Nystrom, Joakim, 224

Oakes, Bill: on ATP doubles reforms, 39–40
O'Connor, Ian: celebrates Sampras, 119
O'Neill, Jennifer, 151

Okker, Tom, 64, 149
Oliff, John, 7
Orwell, George, 146
Osterloh, Lilia, 80
Osuna, Rafael, 255
Owens, Jesse, 117

Paes, Leander, 120, 243; on doubles harmony, 125; on leadership, 122
Palfrey, Sarah: on strategy, 32
Palmer, Arnold, 115
Palmer, Jared, 59
Panatta, Adriano, *la dolce vita*, 150
Parun, Onny, 6, 147
Pasarell, Charlie, 39; analyzes tennis vs. golf, 51
Patton, Chris: 300-pound golfer, 48
Pecci, Victor: trick shot, 166
Peer, Shahar, 85
Pele, 3, 117
Peng, Shuai, 207
Pernfors, Mikael, 229
Perry, Fred, 4, 8, 11; 34–4 Davis Cup record, 6; career Grand Slam, 7
Petkovski, Suzi, 60–62
Petrova, Nadia, 34, 84, 111, 113
Philippoussis, Mark, 64, 71, 77, 105
Pickard, Tony, 196; on decline in serving and volleying, 67
Pierce, Jim, 113
Pierce, Mary, 182; admission by Gilbert: 216
Pioline, Cedric, 65, 236–237
Piperno, Enrico, 125
Plato, 150
Pless, Kristian, 117
Pollard, Geoff: lauds "Woodies," 232; supports super tiebreakers in mixed doubles, 60
Portas, Albert, 117
Potanen, Andreyev, 114
Preobrazhenskaya, Larissa, 112
Pugh, Jim, 190

Querrey, Sam, 83, 85
Quist, Adrian: on Kramer's air of aggression, 13
Qureshi, Aisam ul-Haq, 126

Rafter, Patrick, 14, 68–69; on Davis Cup, 6
Rai, Aishwarya, 100
Ramirez, Raul, 150
Raymond, Lisa, 64, 75; America's tennis decline, 84–85 on; evolution of power tennis, 71–72; quiet foil, 122; on Wimbledon grass, 70
Reddy, Helen, 147
Reed, Whitney, 255
Rehnquist, Chief Justice William H., 46
Reyes, Gil, 50; Agassi's trainer-confidante, 133–135

# About the Author

Throughout his ventures and adventures, observers have described Paul Fein as "having a passion for tennis" and "breathing tennis."

At the age of eleven, Fein discovered the joy of tennis at the Bliss Road courts in Longmeadow and the Forest Park courts in Springfield, Massachusetts. He learned from Bill Talbert, Barry MacKay, Ashley Cooper, and other former international champions who played exhibitions and gave clinics at Forest Park. Fein observed savvy New England stars, such as Henri Salaun, Ned Weld, Larry Lewis, and Bobby Freedman, compete at the annual Pioneer Valley Men's Championships there. He was further inspired by double Grand Slammer Rod Laver, a fellow lefty, who hit sensational shots during pro tournaments at the Longwood Cricket Club near Boston.

During the early years, Fein also ball-boyed, called lines, and umpired at tournaments. He played varsity tennis and squash at Williston Academy and Cornell University, where he was coached by astute, former U.S. top-fiver and Davis Cupper Eddie Moylan. He peaked as a top ten-ranked singles and top five doubles New England men's open tournament player and represented New England in the Church Cup and Corish Cup.

A longtime student of the game, Fein then contributed his expertise and enthusiasm to help advance tennis at different levels. He founded and directed the Springfield Satellite Tournament (one of the world's first five satellite events and commended by *World Tennis* magazine), which attracted international fields. Fein also has been a USPTA teaching pro (Pro-1 rating), a college tennis referee, NELTA tournament consultant, and NEPTA ranking committee chairperson.

Fein is the author of *Tennis Confidential: Today's Greatest Players, Matches, and Controversies* and *You Can Quote Me on That: Greatest Tennis Quips, Insights, and Zingers*. Fein's articles have appeared in tennis, sports, and general interest publications in the United States and twenty-five foreign countries. He has received more than twenty writing awards, including five 1st Place awards in the annual United States Tennis Writers' Association writing contest and three *Tennis Week* awards.

Locally, Fein worked as a tennis analyst for Continental Cablevision, teaching pro for the Chicopee Parks and Recreation Department, and varsity tennis coach at The MacDuffie School. He also served as president of the Springfield Tennis Club and Springfield Tennis Council. He lives in Agawam, Massachusetts.